DECOLONIZATION AND THE COLD WAR

New Approaches to International History

Series Editor: Thomas Zeiler, Professor of American Diplomatic and U.S. Economic History, University of Colorado at Boulder

New Approaches to International History covers international history during the twentieth and twenty-first centuries and across the globe. The series incorporates new developments in the field, such as the cultural turn and transnationalism, as well as the classical high politics of state-centric policymaking and diplomatic relations. Written with upper-level undergraduate and postgraduate students in mind, texts in the series provide an accessible overview of international diplomatic and transnational issues, events and actors.

Forthcoming:

Cold War Summits, Chris Tudda

The Environment and International History, Scott Kaufman

Latin American Nationalism, James F. Siekmeier

The History of United States Cultural Diplomacy, Michael L. Krenn

The United Nations in International History, Amy Sayward

The Modern Olympics, Nicholas E. Sarantakes

The International LGBT Movement, Laura Belmonte

International Co-operation in the Early 20th Century, Daniel Gorman

International Development, Corinna Unger

Public Opinion and 20th Century Diplomacy, Daniel Hucker

Reconstructing the Postwar World, Francine McKenzie

The United States and Latin America in the Contemporary World, Stephen G. Rabe

Women and Gender in International History, Karen Garner

DECOLONIZATION AND THE COLD WAR

NEGOTIATING INDEPENDENCE

Edited by Leslie James and Elisabeth Leake

Bloomsbury Academic
An imprint of Bloomsbury Publishing Plc

B L O O M S B U R Y
LONDON · NEW DELHI · NEW YORK · SYDNEY

Bloomsbury Academic

An imprint of Bloomsbury Publishing Plc

50 Bedford Square	1385 Broadway
London	New York
WC1B 3DP	NY 10018
UK	USA

www.bloomsbury.com

BLOOMSBURY and the Diana logo are trademarks of Bloomsbury Publishing Plc

First published 2015

British Library Cataloguing-in-Publication Data
A catalogue record for this book is available from the British Library.

ISBN: HB: 978-1-4725-7120-5
PB: 978-1-4725-7119-9
ePDF: 978-1-4725-7122-9
ePub: 978-1-4725-7121-2

Library of Congress Cataloging-in-Publication Data
A catalog record for this book is available from the Library of Congress.

Typeset by Integra Software Services Pvt. Ltd.
Printed and bound in Great Britain

CONTENTS

Series Editor Preface   vii
Notes on Contributors   viii
Foreword
    Odd Arne Westad   xi
Acknowledgements   xiv
Maps   xv

Introduction
    Leslie James and Elisabeth Leake   1

Part I Developing the Nation: Economics, Modernity and the 'State Project'   19

1   'Fantastic Quantities of Food Grains': Cold War Visions and Agrarian
    Fantasies in Independent India
    Benjamin Siegel   21
2   'The Life and Death of Our Republic': Modernization, Agricultural
    Development and the Peasantry in the Mekong Delta in the Long 1970s
    Simon Toner   43
3   Export Processing Zones, Special Economic Zones and the Long March
    of Capitalist Development Policies During the Cold War
    Patrick Neveling   63

Part II Intellectual Assertions in the Anti-Colonial Era   85

4   Class Struggle and Self-Determination at *Political Affairs*: An Intellectual
    History of Communist Anti-Colonialism in the United States, 1945–1960
    John Munro   87
5   'A Unique Little Country': Lebanese Exceptionalism, Pro-Americanism
    and the Meanings of Independence in the Writings of Charles Malik,
    c. 1946–1962
    Andrew Arsan   107

Part III Contesting Heritage and Identification   123

6   The Malayan Communist Party and the Malayan Chinese Association:
    Internationalism and Nationalism in Chinese Overseas Political
    Participation, c. 1920–1960
    Anna Belogurova   125

Contents

7 Negotiating Russian Imperial Aryanism: Soviet Oriental Studies in the Cold War
   Hanna Jansen   145

8 Grounding Ideologies: Archaeology, Decolonization and the Cold War in Egypt
   William Carruthers   167

Part IV (Re)conceiving Sovereignty and Statehood   183

9 A 'Commonwealth Moment' in South Asian Decolonization
   Daniel Haines   185

10 Sovereignty in the Congo Crisis
   Ryan M. Irwin   203

11 Malcolm X in France, 1964–1965: Anti-Imperialism and the Politics of Travel Control in the Cold War Era
   Moshik Temkin   219

12 From Foreign Concessions to Special Economic Zones: Decolonization and Foreign Investment in Twentieth-Century Asia
   Christopher Miller   239

Part V Defending the State: Intelligence and Violence   255

13 Archives, Intelligence and Secrecy: The Cold War and the End of the British Empire
   Caroline Elkins   257

14 Tinker, Tailor, Soldier, Subversive: India, Pakistan and the Politics of Cold War Intelligence
   Paul M. McGarr   285

Index   303

SERIES EDITOR PREFACE

New Approaches to International History takes the entire world as its stage for exploring the history of diplomacy, broadly conceived theoretically and thematically, and writ large across the span of the globe, during the twentieth century. This series goes beyond the single goal of explaining encounters in the world. Our aspiration is that these books provide both an introduction for researchers new to a topic, and supplemental and essential reading in classrooms. Thus, *New Approaches* serves a dual purpose that is unique from other large-scale treatments of international history: it applies to scholarly agendas and pedagogy. In addition, it does so against the backdrop of a century of enormous change, conflict and progress that informed global history but also continues to reflect on our own times.

The series offers the old and new diplomatic history to address a range of topics that shaped the twentieth century. Engaging in international history (including but not especially focusing on global or world history), these books will appeal to a range of scholars and teachers situated in the humanities and social sciences, including those in history, international relations, cultural studies, politics and economics. We have in mind scholars, both novice and veteran, who require an entrée into a topic, trend or technique that can benefit their own research or education into a new field of study by crossing boundaries in a variety of ways.

By its broad and inclusive coverage, *New Approaches to International History* is also unique because it makes accessible to students current research, methodology and themes. Incorporating cutting-edge scholarship that reflects trends in international history, as well as addressing the classical high politics of state-centric policymaking and diplomatic relations, these books are designed to bring alive the myriad of approaches for digestion by advanced undergraduate and graduate students. In preparation for the *New Approaches* series, Bloomsbury surveyed courses and faculty around the world to gauge interest and reveal core themes of relevance for their classroom use. The polling yielded a host of topics, from war and peace to the environment; from empire to economic integration; and from migration to nuclear arms. The effort proved that there is a much-needed place for studies that connect scholars and students alike to international history, and books that are especially relevant to the teaching missions of faculty around the world.

We hope readers find this series to be appealing, challenging and thought-provoking. Whether the history is viewed through older or newer lenses, *New Approaches to International History* allows students to peer into the twentieth century's complex relations among nations, people and events to draw their own conclusions about the tumultuous, interconnected past.

NOTES ON CONTRIBUTORS

Andrew Arsan is University Lecturer in Modern Middle Eastern History in the Faculty of History, University of Cambridge, and a Fellow of St John's College, Cambridge. He has previously held positions at Birkbeck, University of London, and Princeton. His first monograph, *Interlopers of Empire: The Lebanese Diaspora in Colonial French West Africa*, appeared in 2014 with Hurst and Oxford University Press.

Anna Belogurova is a visiting assistant professor of modern Chinese history at Brown University. Her research focuses on Chinese communism in Southeast Asia. She has co-authored a book with K.M. Tertitski, *Taiwanskoye kommunisticheskoye dvizheniye i Komintern, 1924–1932* [Taiwanese Communist Movement and the Comintern, 1924–1932], and has published in *Modern Asian Studies* and the *Oxford Handbook of the History of Communism*.

William Carruthers is a Max Weber postdoctoral fellow in the Department of History and Civilization at the European University Institute, Florence. He researches the histories of Egyptology and archaeology in relation to the constitution of modern Egypt and post-Second World War political categories. He is also the editor of *Histories of Egyptology: Interdisciplinary Measures* (Routledge, 2014).

Caroline Elkins is Professor of History and African and African American Studies at Harvard University. Her work focuses on British colonial violence in the twentieth century, post-conflict reconciliation processes and the intersections between history, archives and the law. Her publications include *Imperial Reckoning: The Untold Story of Britain's Gulag in Kenya* (New York: Henry Holt, 2005); *Settler Colonialism in the Twentieth Century: Projects, Practices, Legacies* (co-edited with Susan Pedersen, New York: Routledge, 2005); and 'Alchemy of Evidence: Mau Mau, the British Empire, and the High Court of Justice', *Journal of Imperial and Commonwealth History*, 39, 5(2011), 731–748.

Daniel Haines is Lecturer in the History of Environment and Landscape at the University of Bristol. He was previously a British Academy Postdoctoral Fellow in the History Department at Royal Holloway, University of London. He researches South Asian environmental and political history, with focuses on water politics, development and modernity. His current project is a study of the circumstances, causes and consequences of the 1960 Indus Waters Treaty. His publications include *Building the Empire, Building the Nation: Development, Legitimacy, and Hydro-Politics in Sind, 1919–1969* (Oxford University Press, 2013) and articles in *Geopolitics*, *Modern Asian Studies* and *Water History*.

Ryan Irwin is an assistant professor of history at the University at Albany-SUNY. His work focuses on the intersections of decolonization and globalization, with particular interests in US global power and international institutions. He is the author of *Gordian Knot: Apartheid and the Unmaking of the Liberal World Order* (Oxford University Press, 2012). He was previously associate director of International Security Studies at Yale University.

Leslie James is a Leverhulme Early Career Fellow at the University of Birmingham. Her work focuses on the political and intellectual history of anti-imperialism in Britain and its empire and of decolonization in Africa and the Caribbean. She has previously taught at the University of Cambridge, Goldsmith's College and the London School of Economics and Political Science. Her publications include *George Padmore and Decolonization from Below* (Palgrave, 2015) and a forthcoming article in the *Journal of Imperial and Commonwealth History*.

Hanna Jansen is a historian in the Department of Eastern European Studies at the University of Amsterdam. Her research interests include the global connections of Soviet and Eurasian social and cultural history, the formation of Islamic and Muslim identities in a context of decolonization and the exchange of ideas across Cold War political and ideological divides. She is currently completing her PhD dissertation on the politicization of Soviet academic Oriental Studies during the Cold War, focusing in particular on the cultural history of the Tajik Soviet Socialist Republic and on the development of Soviet Islamology.

Elisabeth Leake is a Leverhulme Early Career Fellow at Royal Holloway, University of London. Her work focuses on the political history of South Asia and the global Cold War. Other interests include issues of sovereignty and border-formation in postcolonial South Asia and the decolonizing world and the influence of political Islam on identity- and political-formation along the Afghan-Pakistan border. She has published in *Modern Asian Studies* and the *International History Review*.

Paul M. McGarr is Lecturer in American Foreign Policy at the University of Nottingham. He specializes in the history of diplomatic and political history relations among the United States, Great Britain and South Asia. He is the author of *The Cold War in South Asia: Britain, the United States and the Indian Subcontinent, 1945–1965* (Cambridge University Press, 2013), and has published articles in *Diplomatic History*, the *International History Review*, the *Journal of Imperial and Commonwealth History* and *Modern Asian Studies*.

Christopher Miller is a PhD candidate in the History Department at Yale University. His dissertation examines the lessons that the Soviet Union learnt from China's economic reforms during the 1980s and compares the two countries' economic and political trajectories. He has also worked as a visiting researcher at the Carnegie Moscow Center and at the New Economic School in Moscow.

John Munro is an assistant professor in the history department at Saint Mary's University in Halifax, Canada, where he teaches classes on United States and international history. His articles include 'Roots of "Whiteness"', which was published in *Labour (Le Travail)*, 'Empire and intersectionality: notes on the production of knowledge about US imperialism' in the *Globality Studies Journal*, and 'Interwoven colonial histories: indigenous agency and academic historiography in North America' in the *Canadian Review of American Studies*.

Patrick Neveling is a researcher in the Department of Cultural Anthropology and Sociology, University of Utrecht, and an associate at the Historical Institute, University of Bern. He works in social anthropology, global history and critical political economy and engages with global capitalism since 1800. His first book, *Manifestationen der Globalisierung: Kapital, Staat und Arbeit in Mauritius, 1825-2005*, is forthcoming in the series, *Industrielle Welt* (Böhlau). His chapter for this volume was written during a fellowship at the Institute for European Global Studies, University of Basel.

Benjamin Siegel is an assistant professor of history at Boston University. Trained as a historian of South Asia, his book project – 'Independent India of Plenty: Food and Nation-Building in Modern India' – explores the interactions of food, culture and politics in India's nationalist movement and its first several decades of independence. His other projects include a second book on the politics of expertise in modern India, articles on invasive species, land reform and food adulteration, and a short intellectual history of poverty in India.

Moshik Temkin is an Associate Professor of History at Harvard University's Kennedy School of Government. A specialist in American international history, with an emphasis on twentieth-century transatlantic politics, he is the author of *The Sacco-Vanzetti Affair: America on Trial* (Yale University Press, 2009).

Simon Toner is a PhD candidate in the International History Department at the London School of Economics and the International History Stonex PhD Scholar at LSE IDEAS. His working dissertation title is 'Modernization and Development in South Vietnam, 1968–1975'.

Odd Arne Westad is Professor of International History and director of LSE IDEAS at the London School of Economics and Political Science. He has written extensively on the histories of China and the global Cold War. His most recent book is *Restless Empire: China and the World since 1750* (Basic Books, 2012). His book *The Global Cold War* (Cambridge University Press, 2005) received the Bancroft Prize.

FOREWORD
Odd Arne Westad

One of the big questions for historians of the twentieth century is the relationship between Cold War conflict and decolonization. It is mainly a question of links and effects. For instance, did the perceived Cold War needs of the United States advance the anti-colonial cause? Some historians – my great predecessor at LSE, D. C. Watt, among them – seem to think so.[1] It was hard, they argue, for the United States to stand for global freedom against communist tyranny while being seen as upholding foreign rule abroad. Also, colonial wars produced radicalization and chaos, just the kind of element in which Soviet subversion would thrive. Some go even further: the American Revolution was the world's first successful anti-colonial war, they would argue. Sympathy with the colony would be in the lifeblood of the American Republic.[2]

Given US support for France and Portugal during their colonial wars in the twentieth century, it is hard to give much credence to this argument for the Cold War as a whole, even if it may have played some role in the 1940s. On numerous occasions US presidents proved that they were more than willing to prop up colonizers in the name of Western Cold War solidarity: for Washington, when push came to shove, Europe always mattered more than Africa. Some of this topsy-turvy solidarity may be explained in racial (or at least civilizational) terms: US elites felt more akin to European leaders than to African or Asian regimes during the Cold War. But western Europe and North America were also more mutually dependent: their economies mattered much more to each other than did any other region, except (perhaps) Japan.

So much for the United States: its role for the decolonization process was ambiguous (at best) and detrimental (at worst). What then about the Soviet Union? The relationship between communism and anti-colonialism is a long and complex one: Marxism and other forms of radical socialism inspired both movements, and the Communist International (the Comintern) played a key role in organizing anti-colonial resistance in the 1920s and the 1930s.[3] But the Soviet Union as a state had a more troubled relationship with the opposition against colonial rule. Like the United States, its own priorities for long lay mainly in Europe. And when the Soviets started to get more involved in Asia and Africa, their assistance was linked to didactic attempts at getting adherents for their own development model. Soviet help for liberation movements undoubtedly mattered, for the Viet Minh in Vietnam, the FLN in Algeria, the MPLA in Angola or the South African ANC. But, overall, it is hard to argue that the Soviet Union played a key role in the decolonization process, as inspiration or as provider of practical assistance.

Overall, this probably means that the key links and effects ought to be sought in Europe and in the colonized world itself. For Europe, there are two big fields of inquiry that remain largely unexplored. One is how various forms of European integration influenced the decolonization process. Integration, in this sense, of course means defence and security integration as much as economic integration, if the Cold War era is seen as a whole. Part of the pattern here was a western Europe, including Britain, turning away from empire in order to face the threat from the Soviet Union and its allies (including the western European communist parties). The other is the changing discourse on colonialism within western Europe itself. There is a gradual development here, along a rather crooked path. In the 1940s and the 1950s, the emphasis of European reformers, whether they were social-democrat or Christian-democrat (or, for that matter, Labour or Tory in Britain), was on finding non-communist forms of development that linked technology with comprehensive state intervention and the integration of production and markets. Decolonization did not sit comfortably with these perspectives and was added almost as an afterthought. In France, most strikingly (and much because of the links with North Africa), decolonization as a full-fledged concept came only after a host of various integrationist plans along the *Eurafrique* model had been tried out.[4] Then, in the 1960s and the 1970s, large groups among the younger generations turned against colonialism and prioritized, in a positive sense, links with the postcolonial states or even with anti-colonial liberation movements. But this change seems linked as much to criticism of the development plans of their own countries as to any deeper concern with the fate of the Global South.

The other part of the Cold War/decolonization puzzle may be found within the colonized countries and in the postcolonial states themselves. I have explored this perspective elsewhere, and will not elaborate on it here.[5] The key is that the Cold War, both as warfare and as ideological struggle, took hold in parts of Asia and Africa (and, in a slightly different form, in Latin America) and played a significant part in determining the future development of states and societies. The main aspect of this effect was undoubtedly in the realm of development and concepts of the future. As several contributors to this volume show, the battles for the content of postcolonial states were intimately linked to the Cold War conflict, both before and after formal decolonization had taken place.

One of the strengths of this volume is that its editors and authors are not out to (re-) create hierarchies of significance and meaning. Their point is not to prioritize one aspect of global developments over others. The Cold War and decolonization both had causes and effects that were independent of each other, even though the two processes were roughly parallel in time. For the purposes of this volume, it is especially important to stress that there were many sources for decolonization that were not (at least in any meaningful sense) connected to the Cold War as a superpower phenomenon. We need to explore links and broader explanations where they exist. But we also need to be open for particularities and trends that move well beyond any framework that earlier historiographies have established.

Notes

1 Watt, Donald Cameron (1984), *Succeeding John Bull: America in Britain's Place, 1900–1975: A Study of the Anglo-American Relationship and World Politics in the Context of British and American Foreign-Policy-Making in the Twentieth Century*. Cambridge: Cambridge University Press.

2 Kagan, Robert (2006), *Dangerous Nation*. New York: Knopf.

3 Petersson, Fredrik (2014), 'Hub of the anti-imperialist movement: The League against Imperialism and Berlin, 1927–1933', *Interventions*, 16(1), 49–71.

4 Imlay, Talbot C. (2013), 'International socialism and decolonization during the 1950s: Competing rights and the postcolonial order', *The American Historical Review*, 118(4), 1105–1132.

5 Westad, Odd Arne (2005), *The Global Cold War: Third World Interventions and the Making of Our Times*. Cambridge: Cambridge University Press.

ACKNOWLEDGEMENTS

This book emerged from a shared interest and a fortuitous encounter. Knowing of our mutual curiosity about the Cold War and decolonization, Arne Westad introduced us, suggesting we co-organize a conference on these themes. This resulted in 'Negotiating Independence', held at Trinity College, University of Cambridge, in May 2013. The volume at hand sprung from the conference, its proceedings and the lively discussion the papers engendered. The Economic History Society, Royal Historical Society, LSE IDEAS Centre for Diplomacy and Strategy, Cambridge's Centre of South Asian Studies and University of Cambridge Smuts and Trevelyan Funds provided generous financial support for this conference and its afterlife.

The intellectual curiosity and commitment of all the contributors to this volume have been the foundation for this book. We are grateful for our authors' hard work and attention, which have allowed the quality of each chapter to stand on its own. Arne Westad graciously spoke on the closing roundtable of the conference and agreed to turn his comments into this volume's foreword. Lien-Hang Nguyen, Martin Thomas, Susan Pennybacker, Philip Murphy, Andrew Preston and Piers Ludlow helped us in the earliest stages of shifting from conference to book. Martin and Andrew, as well as Chris Bayly, also generously offered comments on the introduction. Claire Lipscomb has been a patient editor, and we are grateful for her sincere attentiveness to the production of the volume.

MAPS

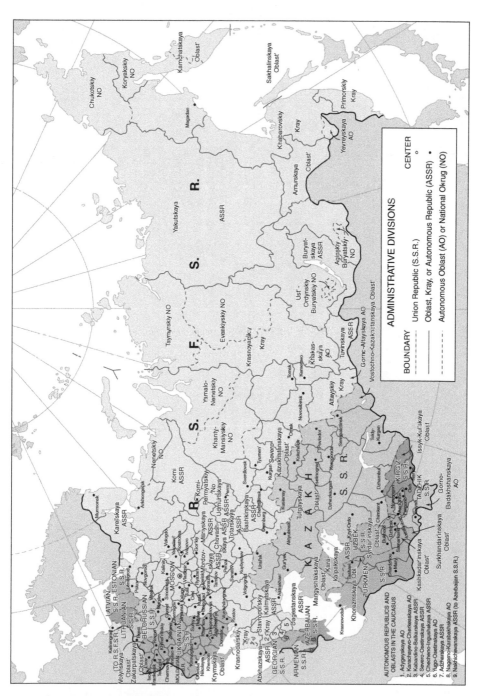

Union of Soviet Socialist Republics

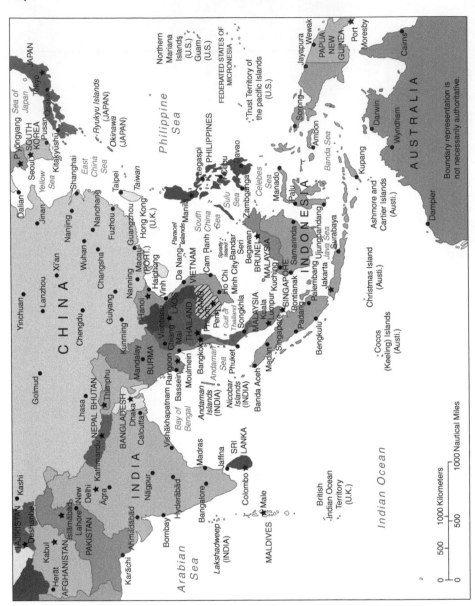

South and Southeast Asia

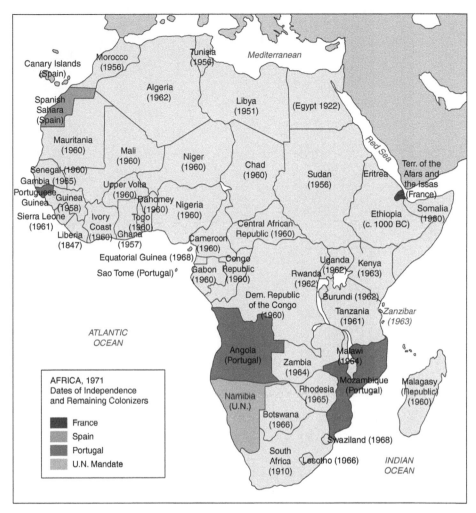

Africa in 1971

INTRODUCTION
Leslie James and Elisabeth Leake

Close to midnight on 14 August 1947, Jawaharlal Nehru, one of India's leading nationalists and anti-colonial resisters, rose to speak to India's Constituent Assembly. In what would famously become known as his 'Tryst with Destiny' speech, Nehru told assembly members, 'A moment comes, which comes but rarely in history, when we step out from the old to the new, when an age ends, and when the soul of a nation, long suppressed, finds utterance.'[1] Mere minutes later, India – and neighbouring Pakistan, which had also been fashioned from colonial South Asia – officially became independent of British colonial rule. For India, decolonization had replaced the fantasy of freedom with its reality.

But was Nehru correct in declaring India's decolonization the end of an era and its nationhood a new age? Certainly, many have seen India's post-independence as such, particularly with Nehru, as Prime Minister, securing the creation of a secular democracy and championing a foreign policy of non-alignment – an alternative to Cold War binaries. But in reality, how independent was postcolonial India? Vestiges of British colonial rule remained, and despite bold claims to non-alignment, Nehru and his government could not wholly divorce themselves from the Cold War when the Soviet Union and the United States offered the best sources of food and economic aid to a starving, developing nation.

The story of India, as of many other countries in the decolonizing world during the twentieth century, has been one of independent statehood and development. These narratives are not wholly inward-looking, but they frequently obscure the complexity of the world in which they emerged: a world not only facing a new phase of self-determination and nation-building, but also one shaped by a global Cold War. As this volume demonstrates, decolonization frequently coincided and merged with, or contradicted and undermined, the Soviet Union's and the United States' fight for global ideological, and frequently political, dominance. The claims of anti-colonial leaders to be entirely independent, including Nehru, as several of the chapters in this volume demonstrate, need some reconsideration.

As the period after India and Pakistan's negotiated self-government indicates, independence from colonial rule was more than a contractual negotiation. Decolonization involved many actors: officials and administrators from former colonizing powers such as Great Britain and France; nationalist leaders of newly independent states; and frequently, at times overtly and at others covertly, representatives from the era's superpowers. All of these agents negotiated an uncertain terrain in which political systems, cultural practices, social traditions, the organization of labour, economies and identities were challenged and reworked. Powerful and marginalized groups alike tried to read the historical moment. What has become increasingly clear is that decolonization did not occur in a vacuum, nor did the other historical phenomena of the twentieth century, the Cold War. Over the last two decades, scholars have increasingly been drawn to the intersections of these two historical ages, recognizing that a Cold War extending far beyond its diplomatic confines moulded social, cultural and economic, as well as political, practices around the world.

Thus, the advent of decolonization shares more than a chronological partnership with the Cold War. While the general economic, political, social and ideological connections between decolonization and the Cold War have been acknowledged, this volume engages with a more detailed, recent interrogation of the junctions of these two phenomena. The ideological battle between communism and capitalism encompassed not only political systems of power but also contentious ideas about states' social structures and economies: both decolonization and the Cold War were also imaginative projects. This volume addresses the role of differing ideas about political, economic and social organization for individuals involved in the bid for independence. Drawing together the latest research from young scholars and established academics leading the way in this new approach to the twentieth century, this volume recognizes a common history of the Cold War and decolonization, viewing them not as isolated, parallel phenomena, but crucially as a broader moment of intertwined, if sometimes paradoxical, local and global change.

Interpreting decolonization and the Cold War

To begin, what do 'decolonization' and the 'Cold War' actually mean? Scholars have provided various definitions and interpretations of each. European imperial structures arguably began to inch in the direction of decolonization shortly after the First World War, as the British Empire's white dominions, such as Canada, Australia, New Zealand and South Africa, embraced political autonomy within a commonwealth system. But non-white imperial subjects had longer to wait. The decolonization of India, Pakistan and neighbouring Burma and Ceylon proved somewhat anomalous: British leaders had not expected them to reach independence so immediately, but they quickly recognized they could not afford to keep them.[2] Only Indonesia and the Philippines also succeeded in gaining independence by the end of the 1940s. But while Britain's Labour Government proved willing to relinquish South Asia, at least officially, neither they nor their French, Dutch or Portuguese counterparts were ready to surrender their overseas holdings in the aftermath of the Second World War. Even in Indonesia, nationalist leaders declared their independence in 1945, but were denied by the Dutch until 1949, following a prolonged war.[3] As Anthony Hopkins has convincingly demonstrated, imperial leaders actually worked to consolidate their overseas power during the early 1950s, only reluctantly accepting changing realities midway through the decade. By this stage, anti-colonial resistance in the colonies, domestic financial and political strains and international pressure led to the independence of countries across Asia, Africa and the Caribbean, including Indochina (Vietnam, Laos, Cambodia) (1954), the Sudan (1956),

Ghana (1957), Malaya (1957), Algeria (1962), Jamaica (1962), Trinidad and Tobago (1962) and Kenya (1963).[4]

But what did decolonization entail? In some cases, as with India, Pakistan or Ghana, independence was negotiated: nationalist leaders and colonial administrators agreed on the nature of the colonial withdrawal, the new countries' political leadership, national borders, divisions of resources and other matters. Other colonies faced a far more fraught transfer of power. Brutal, violent conflicts such as the First Indochina War, the Malayan Emergency, the Algerian war for independence and the Mau Mau rebellion in Kenya marked these countries' struggle for full autonomy.[5] In between these extremes remained numerous other colonies-turned-nations, which experienced varying forms of conflict and compromise. The scars of colonialism remained, even in those countries that achieved independence peacefully. Violence could take many forms beyond the physical: the psychological scars of wars fought for independence; the experience of imprisonment by dozens of anti-colonial resisters; fears of state intelligence systems; forced colonial identities along the lines of caste, tribe, race or religion; economic exploitation; the list is endless.[6]

Thus, decolonization did not just end with the transfer of political power from colonizer to colonized. It was a process of political, social, economic and cultural transformation.[7] The nationalist governments that negotiated independence frequently did not remain in power (as demonstrated tragically by Patrice Lumumba in the Congo, who was assassinated less than a year after coming to power). For those who remained, and those who rose to power, ensuring the well-being of their new nations' citizens created additional obstacles. Newly independent governments needed not only to feed their countries, but also to provide jobs, revenue, education and health services. In these realms, circumstances were not necessarily divorced from the imperial past. While numerous political leaders experimented with economic modernization models, they and their administrations frequently were guided by colonial-era advisers who had stayed on after independence, or who had returned under the guises of the United Nations and other international organizations.[8] Under such circumstances, where new nations were independent but not self-sufficient, problems invariably arose. For leaders and other members of society, defining a country's political sovereignty and cultural identity proved difficult: what were colonial vestiges, and what belonged to the new nation? These questions were equally fraught in those countries that had not been officially colonized but still suffered from informal imperial pressures. From China to Egypt to Cuba, national leaders had to develop local resources and differentiate themselves from past foreign influence.

The global Cold War complicated resolution of these issues within newly decolonized states. The Cold War was an ideological battle: a clash between capitalism and communism, as well as their respective political, economic, social and cultural manifestations. Nevertheless, perhaps more than decolonization, the scope of the Cold War remains highly contested. Cold War studies has proliferated in the last several decades, particularly after the fall of the Berlin wall, and much like imperial historiography, it has undergone a 'cultural turn'. Beyond its political and diplomatic trajectories in the Soviet Union, the United States and Europe, scholars have addressed its far broader influences: its impact on economic development, education practices, social policies, civil rights, cultures of protest and popular engagement, to name but a few.[9]

Crucially, scholars increasingly have recognized that the 'long peace', as John Lewis Gaddis has described the Cold War – with particular reference to events in Europe and Soviet-American diplomacy – proved to be far 'hotter' in the rest of the world.[10] Historians have highlighted the global dynamics of the Cold War, particularly in light of the Korean War, Sino-Soviet relations and Maoism, the failed American war in Vietnam and US–Soviet wrangling over Cuba.[11] Beyond these battlefields, scholars have delineated broader understandings of the global Cold War that encompass almost the entire world. From the Bandung conference and the rise of the non-aligned movement; to competing Soviet and US models of development and projects of modernization; to the parsing out of economic aid; to its influence on family life and daily rituals, this 'other Cold War', as anthropologist Heonik Kwon provocatively describes it – based partly on his earlier ethnographic research on war memory in Vietnam – influenced all spheres of life.[12]

This, then, is the point at which the 'Cold War' becomes blurred. Scholars have defined and redefined the Cold War in numerous ways, ranging from the specific – the minutiae of geopolitical and diplomatic conflict between the United States and the Soviet Union – to the broad – a general period, usually post-1945, vaguely defined by competing US and Soviet worldviews. Duncan Bell and Joel Isaac's edited volume, *Uncertain Empire*, provides a particularly apt entry to this question of characterization.[13] They first assert, quite rightly, that the Cold War should not be seen simply as a range of dates that denote an era, a 'neutralizing historical marker' like the interwar years, that is devoid of specific features and characteristics. In their volume, Anders Stephenson provocatively, if very limitedly, argues that the Cold War was a predominantly American project, focused on the legitimization of US globalism at home and abroad.[14] Other contributors, such as Odd Arne Westad, rightly dispute both this US-centric focus and Stephenson's periodization of the Cold War as a post-1945 phenomenon; Westad notes that for those who lived through the Cold War, no matter their locale, the idea of the Cold War mattered, not least for the Soviet Union, China and the so-called 'Third World'.[15] Other contributors further dispute Westad's arguments, highlighting the incredibly contested nature of the Cold War.

Westad's ambitious book, *The Global Cold War*, further indicates the difficulties and controversies accompanying study of the Cold War in the decolonizing world. In *The Global Cold War*, Westad provides a sweeping history of Cold War conflict across the 'Third World', expansively covering both geography and chronology, from competing US and Soviet Cold War claims to carry the flag of 'European modernity' to the ways this competition played out in Asia, Africa and Latin America.[16] There is little doubt that Westad's text is a seminal achievement; however, for this volume, reviews of *The Global Cold War* are equally revealing. In the *Journal of American History*, H.W. Brands concludes, 'What Westad is up against is the chief challenge to practitioners of international history in general.... [T]he more ground they cover the less thoroughly they plow each patch.'[17] Ian Roxborough, while lauding the project, argues that 'We need some way to parse out exactly what kinds of impacts the Cold War had on Third World societies and to separate these from processes that were occurring quite independently of the Cold War.'[18]

This volume attempts to respond to some of these critiques, joining a growing body of literature that not only recognizes the intertwined nature of events in the 'global South' and the Cold War, but also addresses the intersections in a variety of ways.[19] Given the critiques by Brands and Roxborough, among others, scholars' frequent decisions to approach the Cold War and decolonization through edited volumes are unsurprising. Such publications allow various specialists to enter into a broader dialogue while addressing specific, common themes. These volumes cover an impressive array of subjects, from diplomacy between newly independent states and the United States and the Soviet Union; to the search for non-alignment and neutral unity within the decolonizing world; to the impact of race and ethnicity on US Cold War policy towards the decolonizing world; to the influence of techno-politics on superpower-decolonizing world relations; to the rise in political activism in the United States and abroad.[20] Other authors have tackled these subjects in their own books. Moving beyond histories of international diplomacy and foreign relations, they recognize the importance of international institutions as a place of mediation between anti-colonial and Western leaders; the widespread use of cultural and economic diplomacy; collaboration between transnational anti-colonial resistance movements; the violence that frequently accompanied processes of decolonization and was exacerbated by Cold War tensions; and the influence of both phenomena on discourses about gender, generational differences and social structures in newly emergent nation states.[21]

This volume is located neither fully in the decolonizing world, nor in the realm of the superpowers.[22] Our work has been driven by several primary beliefs. First, we consider the Cold War as a global ideological struggle between communism and capitalism, even if its practical manifestations frequently obscured this divide. As C.L.R. James, the Caribbean intellectual whose political life spanned the interwar wave of anti-communism through to the end of the British Empire, declared, 'All political power presents itself to the world within a certain framework of ideas.'[23] Certainly for many anti-colonial leaders, the United States and the Soviet Union offered competing models of economic and social development that were based on their respective ideological frameworks. This was undoubtedly evident in the interwar years: as the Comintern encouraged the establishment of global-minded communist-nationalist parties in various colonies, communism was established as an ideological and organizational alternative to Western modes of political and social development. Nevertheless, the experience of local communist organizations differed from the international diplomatic struggle between 'Communism' and 'Capitalism'. These tensions were only exacerbated once decolonization became a negotiated, sometimes violent, process, and the geopolitics that accompanied ideological competition became increasingly obvious. Ideological conviction frequently gave way to political pragmatism in the decolonizing world, when leaders and civilians alike sought stability and success; however, the revolutionary fervour that drove new nations to look either to the United States or to the Soviet Union for aid cannot be overlooked.

Second, while we have necessarily had to limit this volume's scope, we recognize that processes of decolonization have occurred across the globe and in various eras. Beginning with independence movements and the emergence of new states across the Americas in the late eighteenth and early nineteenth centuries, to the dissolution of the Ottoman and Tsarist Russian empires during and after the First World War, decolonization has been ongoing. In the mid-twentieth century, some independent states formally emerged from colonies in the Pacific, Asia, Africa and the Caribbean, while others tried to escape informal imperial pressures in the Middle East and Latin America, whether from recognized European empires or from the more controversial US empire. This volume focuses predominantly on regions where European empires relinquished their power in the mid-twentieth century.

Finally, balancing the narrative of history 'from below' and 'from above' is a crucially important but fundamentally difficult task. The 'subaltern' turn, first in imperial and decolonization historiography and subsequently in Cold War studies, has provided a much-needed counterweight to elite discourses and diplomatic histories. The Cold War has been 'de-centred', and the experiences of non-elite and local groups reconsidered. This has led to an argument that 'the master discourse of the Cold War was always contested and never fully dominant'.[24] Many people asserted their capacity to live outside these agendas, while others found their own understanding and lived realities of the 'global Cold War'. As several chapters in this volume attest, the ways in which citizens or institutions perceived decolonization or the Cold War sometimes clashed with government intentions and perspectives. Nevertheless, the subaltern perspective cannot be studied in isolation: high-level decision-making invariably moulded subaltern responses, and vice versa. As Brenda Gayle Plummer has most recently argued, ignoring the role of dominant elite groups can result in missed information, a misconstrued representation of the realities of rank and order and a 'misunderstanding' of dominant groups' relationships 'to ideology, policy, and those they ruled'.[25] This volume recognizes the authority employed equally by leaders and civilians in countries emerging from decolonization as well as metropolitan centres.

Something old, something new

Given this welcome expansion of the temporal and theoretical boundaries of the Cold War and imperial decline, there is a danger of a tautology. If the Cold War was an ideological battle that fundamentally drove the foreign policy of the world's superpowers (and consequently rippled through and ruptured politics, social structures and cultural practices around the world); if empires (and their subsequent destruction) encompassed not only colonizing local land and government, but also metropolitan and colonial religious practices, gender relations, social hierarchies and psyches; and if this occurred in an age before the end of the Second World War and after the fall of the

Soviet Union, then is there anything that existed outside these powerful schema? How do they influence – or not influence – everyone and everything? The Cold War and decolonization only retain their analytic value through a careful rendering of the key themes and forces that existed as part of their respective logics and agendas.

This volume intentionally takes the form of case studies, since there was not one lived experience of decolonization and its Cold War influences. This should not lead to the conclusion that 'anything goes' but, rather, to increased sensitivity to the specificities of geography and time, and consequently a more substantive understanding of global continuities. This volume extends several key threads of analysis, building on a body of literature that has both expanded the scope of decolonization and the Cold War, and honed its analytical framework.

First, as we have already alluded to, the relationship both superpowers themselves had with empire requires greater integration into a narrative that intertwines decolonization and the Cold War. While both superpowers in the Cold War conflict were ideological anti-imperialists, each also negotiated complicated past and present projects of empire. On the US side, scholarship now recognizes the ways in which black American activists connected their civil rights struggles to anti-colonial resistance not only in Africa but also in the Caribbean and Asia.[26] Formal and informal imperial projects in the Philippines, Central America, Cuba and Haiti during the early twentieth century also meant that the United States had to confront its own tortuous position towards empire.[27] In 1952, the United Nations also recognized that the US government had 'decolonized' Puerto Rico. On the Soviet side, with the end of the Russian Civil War in 1922, the Bolsheviks inherited and slowly worked to incorporate the former Tsarist empire into the fold of a Union of Soviet Socialist Republics. This project, which has been analysed by historians and ethnographers in greater detail over the last two decades, assumed a narrative that attracted some anti-colonial activists to look to the Soviet Union as a model of decolonization.[28] The Cold War and decolonization were not external to the affairs of the US and USSR: they played out in the domestic, as well as the foreign, sphere. Thus our thinking about the motivations of each superpower, as well as the ways that formerly colonized people approached the United States and Soviet Union, acquires a slightly altered perspective.

The 'Cold War' and 'Decolonization' as capitalized, titular events often feel like totalizing forces. But this disregards the crucial importance of human agency. One way to address this is to pay close attention to the independent movement of groups and individuals, whether the superpowers, former imperial powers, political parties, nationalist leaders or leading intellectuals. We can also reconsider the composition of these groups, as Andrew Arsan's chapter does in this volume, although it is important to retain an understanding of how access to power frequently preserved certain types of group cohesion and hierarchies. This also requires an approach that does not view either decolonization or the Cold War as static and fully known events. As we have already discussed, both the Cold War and decolonization came to signify not only events but also an idea. Thus when we ask questions about how the Cold War and decolonization impacted the making of history, we should always understand that those who lived through these times constantly struggled to accept, reinterpret and apply or extend the meanings that an ideological clash between communism, capitalism and the dismantling of empire entailed.

One of the most contested issues that the end of colonial rule prompted was the substance of sovereignty and self-determination. It is commonly assumed that the Cold War limited options for postcolonial states to chart their own paths of development, including the kinds of political and economic systems that they could construct. Yet despite recent excellent studies of the 'alternative visions' initiated by decolonization through events like the Bandung conference and its accompanying ideas and meetings, we must learn more about the wealth of visions and opportunities perceived to be generated by the end of empire.[29] Daniel Haines's chapter in this volume addresses this crucial mid-twentieth-century moment when political configurations were flexible, and the nation state not inevitable. Haines takes a theoretical stab at one such political alternative, the British Commonwealth, which he approaches as 'an alternative configuration of international relations' that developed simultaneously to the bipolar order of US and USSR Cold War alliances. Ryan Irwin's chapter then zeroes in on the ambiguous meaning of sovereignty for postcolonial states. He takes as his focus the secession of Katanga from the Republic of Congo shortly after independence, one of the most extensively researched events in recent years. He asks how this predicament, which marked a critical intersection between decolonization and the Cold War, challenged the most fundamental question of decolonization: what is sovereignty? Rather than debating the roles and motivations of the numerous players in the Congo's 'crisis' and its importance for the United Nations and international relations, Irwin reflects on the ideological and theoretical implications of Katanga's secession. By flagrantly challenging Lumumba's electoral victory and his assertion of Congolese unity, Katanga's secessionist demands challenged African leaders and international activists and diplomats to reconsider what exactly freedom and self-determination meant. As Irwin pointedly asks, 'was it possible for an African leader to demand freedom *from* postcolonial nationalists?'[30]

Finally, while periodization of both the Cold War and decolonization has expanded and contracted in scholarly debates over the last two and a half decades, those who are now interested in bringing these two phenomena together argue that doing so provides an additional temporal layer to this period. That is, the periodizations of the Cold War and the end of European colonial rule have not merely changed: by keeping the history of both these phenomena in mind, they provide a variant analytical framework. Christopher Lee has argued that the Cold War 'offers an alternative framework' by 'questioning differences and continuities of power'. He approaches the Cold War as a global event, including it within the twentieth-century epochal time frame of 'colonial' and 'postcolonial'. (Another major time frame would be, for instance, 'pre-war' and 'post-war'.)[31] Furthermore, by drawing both the superpowers carefully into a frame of empire and decolonization that respects the different histories of imperialism for both these countries as well as Europe, it is possible to draw the periodization of both decolonization and the Cold War backward, to 1917 most explicitly.[32] Our volume focuses on the key period of European decolonization – the 'moment' that began in

1947 and culminated in the mid-1960s. However, some of our chapters date back to the interwar years, and others project forward, considering the implications for their narratives as far as the 1980s. In this way, this volume recognizes the continuities and disjunctures in attitudes of anti-communism and anti-capitalism, anti-colonialism and anti-racism and nationalism and internationalism, which propelled decolonization in a Cold War context.

Volume organization

This volume suggests several crucial areas for scrutinizing the Cold War and decolonization without claiming an exhaustive framework. First, it highlights some of the latest threads of analysis that can help inform our understanding of the links between decolonization and the Cold War; second, it emphasizes new approaches to this history. Some of this means asking new questions, but it also entails approaching key issues from alternate vantage points. This volume is by no means a complete study of either decolonization or the Cold War, or their many intersections. The included chapters do not necessarily present one neat reading, but rather in some cases introduce arguments that suggest diverging interpretations. We have intentionally presented a set of chapters from authors with diverse approaches and interpretations.

The volume opens with a section that explores an increasingly popular thread of analysis: the ideas of modernity, development and economics as Cold War and postcolonial projects. If we need to explore the tensions of the Cold War and decolonization, one way of doing this is to consider how the ideological project of the Cold War and postcolonial nation-building played out materially. The ways in which Cold War and decolonization projects made *objects* out of *subjects*, the way *people* were turned into *projects* are essential to understanding these two phenomena. How and to what extent these transformations occurred can actually help answer key questions about power and influence, and reveal much about what the phenomena of the Cold War and decolonization actually were.

The volume begins with a chapter by Benjamin Siegel on competing Soviet and US food aid to Nehruvian India. Siegel recognizes that the fundamental question of providing food for India's population brought forth questions about the formation of the new state's economy and systems of governance. The quest for food thus becomes a key marker for better understanding the contestations over ideological orientation and international relationships. The centrality of food production and agricultural modernization is further recognized by Simon Toner in his chapter on rice production in war-torn Vietnam. Toner's chapter takes one of the most direct outgrowths of Cold War competition in the postcolonial world – modernization theory – and analyses its application in both non-communist South Vietnam and communist North Vietnam. Toner's chapter emphasizes American and Vietnamese officials' faith in technology and in modernizing projects as initiatives that could mould and direct populations, even in the midst of a protracted and devastating war; he reminds us that even in 'hot zones', the

Cold War not only encompassed the frenzy of battle, but daily devotion to planting crops and feeding nations.

Patrick Neveling subsequently broadens our scope on modernization and development. He begins with the creation of the world's first export processing zone in one of the key spaces of contestation for US empire and its own official decolonization, Puerto Rico. He then turns his eye to the capitalist search for new markets and supply routes for consumer goods, ultimately broadening the scope of global economic history. This allows Neveling to contribute provocative arguments to one of the key debates about Cold War causation: namely, he undermines the rush to read the end of the Cold War as the demise of the Soviet Union and the centrality of the failed economic policies of the Soviet system in the Cold War.

In the second section, key themes such as US empire and modernity remain, although our analysis turns to the era's intellectual history, particularly focusing on approaches to Cold War ideology, both at home and abroad. John Munro takes as his subject a seemingly obscure and inconsequential publication, a political cultural magazine published by the US Communist Party, in order to rethink one of the major questions in US Cold War history: the supposed silencing of the left in the first decade after 1945. He addresses ongoing critiques of US empire that were tied to African American struggles for racial equality and independence as well as US expansionism abroad. He thereby highlights that McCarthyism did not quash ideological resistance within the post-war United States. Importantly, too, for our consideration of periodization and of reading the Cold War and decolonization together, Munro reminds us that 'decolonization has its own periodization longer than and autonomous from that of the Cold War'. Andrew Arsan's chapter then moves to a reconsideration of the ideological predominance of US liberalism. He provides an analysis of the intellectual journey of the Lebanese diplomat, Charles Malik. In doing so, Arsan emphasizes that as much as decolonization and the Cold War were frequently reactive, frenetic and tense, intellectuals continued to reflect upon the potential political routes in the early Cold War and the implications of ideology for new and emerging states. By complicating Malik's supposedly staunch support for the United States, Arsan further reveals how intellectuals from former colonies harnessed the language of the Cold War while not necessarily viewing 'the West' as a monolith.

The third section interrogates emerging forms of identity that fought for supremacy in an era of increasingly complicated allegiances. Anna Belogurova's chapter focuses on the sometimes competing, sometimes cooperative, identities harnessed by the interwar Malayan National Communist Party and its political successor during the era of decolonization, the Malayan Chinese Association. Despite ideological divergences, leaders in both parties varyingly drew on communist, nationalist, Malayan and Chinese identities to resist British colonial rule. Belogurova's chapter highlights the expanding temporal boundaries of decolonization and geographical and ideological parameters of the Cold War by taking up several crucial questions that were fundamental to both decolonization and the Cold War: how should anti-colonial nationalists establish 'national' parties in multi-ethnic colonial territory, where countries did not yet exist? How did Soviet-aligned communist parties balance the dictates of Soviet policy, which shifted with the international geopolitical situation, and the specificities of their own communal dynamics? Hanna Jansen takes this story of multiple, sometimes conflicting, identities into the Soviet heartland. Jansen focuses on Bobodzhan Gafurovich Gafurov, a leading Party official and scholar in Tajikistan, whose work on Tajik identity reflected various historical interpretations of Russian decolonization, depending on Soviet policy changes. Scholarship by Gafurov and other leading Soviet 'Orientalists' was further used to expand Soviet relations with the decolonizing world as a means of creating a common narrative of Asian identity-formation.

William Carruthers tackles identity and identification from a different perspective – literally from the ground up. In his study of Egypt's archaeological representations and attempts by US practitioners to continue to mould Egyptian sites, Carruthers provocatively shows how Egypt balanced a range of alignments and identities. Looking at Egyptian archaeology reveals that 'non-alignment' was neither simply a question of being 'inside' or 'outside' the power-bloc system, nor even of creating separate alignments of postcolonial solidarity. Moreover, Carruthers's chapter illustrates how citizens and institutions could view decolonization and the Cold War in conflict with government perspectives and intentions, complicating the idea of a single national identity: who speaks for the nation? Cultural sites perhaps provided the space where an independent past could be asserted and manipulated into a present that straddled multiple alignments.

The fourth section further reflects on the construction of the nation and national identity, although focusing on ideas of sovereignty and state control that move beyond longer-standing narratives of diplomacy and duplicity. Moshik Temkin expands on themes introduced by Haines and Irwin, by analysing the deportation of Malcolm X from France in 1964. His chapter shows that Malcolm X's specific articulation of anti-imperialist and racial politics – a politics that ignored the distinction of borders and drew together the struggles of black people in Africa, the United States and, crucially in this instance, Europe – posed a threat to French sovereignty at a crucial moment in its imperial retreat. Malcolm X's transnational activities prompted France to exercise the best means it had at its disposal to pacify those who engaged in unwelcome international political activity: border control. Temkin's and Irwin's chapters, taken in conjunction, display the numerous discourses on independence and sovereignty that emerged as a result of decolonization and perceived US imperialism, particularly as provoked by events in the Congo.

Christopher Miller considers the quest for political sovereignty through an economic lens. Miller takes up the People's Republic of China's and Taiwan's different roads to, but ultimate acceptance of, special zones for foreign trade. His chapter is a reminder that because European imperialism in the nineteenth and twentieth centuries came under a number of guises, our analysis of decolonization and the Cold War must be similarly nuanced. Decolonization in these places differed from other states, where colonial rule transitioned into political independence after either protracted negotiations and/or violent resistance. Yet precisely because of these less-formal variants of rule, concern with imperial-minded foreign dominance was highly relevant at a time when states sought economic self-reliance but were increasingly under pressure from world markets.

China's experience of European empire in the nineteenth and early twentieth centuries was always one of informal imperialism, frequently of an economic nature, that did not conform to formal political rule and complete loss of sovereignty. Export processing zones and special economic zones threatened something similar during the later twentieth century. As Miller argues, 'one of the main ideological debates about how to interact with the global economy focused on political outcomes rather than economic ones.'

The final section considers the matter of defence. Political security was of grave importance to a number of actors: not just representatives of the United States and Soviet Union, but equally for new national leaders and European colonial officials who clung to the vestiges of imperial rule. Paul McGarr and Caroline Elkins address these concerns in light of decolonization in the British Empire. Elkins encourages us to reconsider the ties between Britain and empire; drawing on the recently released Hanslope Disclosure, she highlights the links between intelligence and torture methods used by the British during the Second World War, and colonial officials' later counterinsurgency tactics against nationalists demanding their independence. In McGarr's chapter, we have the classic Cold War theme of spies and intrigue told from another angle: the co-option of Western intelligence by postcolonial states, such as newly independent India and Pakistan, as a means of countering perceived foreign and domestic threats. McGarr considers whether intelligence liaison relationships forged between the former colonizer and colonized can account, in some measure, for the obsession with conspiracy, intrigue and subversion embedded in the socio-political fabric of the contemporary decolonized world.

In sum, this volume reconsiders the influence wielded by both political statesmen and everyday citizens as they sought to construct their societies in specific ways. The rhetoric and ideas of both the Cold War and decolonization infiltrated the anxieties and actions of the twentieth century. This was true as much for the large superpowers as it was for small emerging states, and this produced particular social, political and economic dynamics generative of the era. Taken as a whole, this volume not only reflects on the intersections of the Cold War and decolonization, but also reconsiders the meaning and breadth of each phenomenon. This volume has made one foray into untangling the twentieth century, pointing out specific ways that ideology, race, political strategy and economic planning influenced elite and non-elite actors. Nevertheless, we have had trade-offs along the way: the world that is presented often takes the form of a rather heteronormative, male-dominated story, and certain empires like the British or French are more visible than others like the Dutch or Portuguese. Perhaps most tantalisingly, this volume's chapters highlight that how scholars define 'empire', 'imperialism' and 'decolonization' plays a fundamental role in the conclusions they draw. The fact that a conclusive definition of 'decolonization' still eludes us should urge collaboration between those from different ideological, regional, linguistic, thematic or methodological perspectives. If nothing else, we hope that this volume points to the many new directions in which study of the Cold War and decolonization can and will move.

Notes

1   Gopal, S. (1985), *Selected Works of Jawaharlal Nehru*. Vol. 3. New Delhi: Jawaharlal Nehru Memorial Fund, 135.

2   See Moore, R.J. (1983), *Escape from Empire: The Attlee Government and the Indian Problem*. Oxford: Clarendon Press; Tomlinson, B.R. (1979), *The Political Economy of the Raj, 1914–1947: The Economics of Decolonization*. London: Macmillan.

3   See Wild, Colin and Carey, Peter (1988), *Born in Fire: The Indonesia Struggle for Independence, an Anthology*. Ohio: Ohio University Press; Bayly, Christopher and Harper, Tim (2008), *Forgotten Wars: The End of Britain's Asian Empire*. London: Penguin.

4   Hopkins, Anthony (2008), 'Rethinking decolonization', *Past and Present*, 200(1), 211–247. The literature on decolonization is extensive. For a useful recent summary of British decolonization historiography, see Davis, Richard (2013), 'Perspectives on the end of the British Empire: The historiographical debate', *Cercles*, 28, 1–23. For a comparison of French and British decolonization, see Thomas, Martin and Thompson, Andrew (2014), 'Empire and globalisation: From "high imperialism" to decolonisation', *International History Review*, 36(1), 142–170. For a comparative perspective on British, French, Dutch and Portuguese decolonization, see Thomas, Martin, Moore, Bob and Butler, L.J. (2010 edn.), *Crises of Empire: Decolonization and Europe's Imperial States, 1918–1975*. London: Bloomsbury Academic. Other recent useful comparative overviews of decolonization include Duara, Prasenjit (ed.) (2004), *Decolonization: Perspectives from Now and Then*. London: Routledge; and Dulffer, Jost and Frey, Marc (eds.) (2011), *Elites and Decolonization in the Twentieth Century*. Basingstoke: Palgrave Macmillan.

5   See Lawrence, Mark Atwood and Logevall, Fredrik (eds.) (2007), *The First Vietnam War: Colonial Conflict and Cold War Crisis*. Cambridge, MA: Harvard University Press; Harper, T.N. (1998), *The End of Empire and the Making of Malaya*. Cambridge: Cambridge University Press; Elkins, Caroline (2005), *Britain's Gulag: The Brutal End of Empire in Kenya*. London: Jonathan Cape; Connelly, Matthew (2002), *A Diplomatic Revolution: Algeria's Fight for Independence and the Origins of the Post-Cold War Era*. Oxford: Oxford University Press.

6   Bayly and Harper (2008); Thomas, Martin (2012), *Violence and Colonial Order: Police, Workers and Protest in the European Colonial Empires, 1918–1940*. Cambridge: Cambridge University Press; Berman, Bruce, Eyoh, Dickson and Kymlicka, Will (eds.) (2004), *Ethnicity and Democracy in Africa*. Athens: Ohio University Press; Fanon, Frantz (1967), *Black Skin, White Masks*. New York: Grove; Khan, Yasmin (2007), *The Great Partition: The Making of India and Pakistan*. New Haven: Yale University Press; McHale, Shawn Frederick (2004), *Print and Power: Confucianism, Communism, and Buddhism in the Making of Modern Vietnam*. Honolulu: University of Hawai'i Press.

7   In particular, the 'cultural turn' leading to new imperial histories, which have extended far beyond more long-standing consideration of the political and diplomatic histories of empire, has been crucial to the approach to decolonization. For the beginning of the 'cultural turn' in imperial history, see Mackenzie, John M. (1984), *Propaganda and Empire: The Manipulation of British Public Opinion, 1880–1960*. Manchester: Manchester University Press; Mackenzie, John M. (1986), *Imperialism and Popular Culture*. Manchester: Manchester University Press. For thinking on imperialism and the 'postcolonial', see Stoler, Ann Laura (ed.) (2013), *Imperial Debris: On Ruins and Ruination*. Durham, NC: Duke University Press; Chakrabarty, Dipesh (2000), *Provincializing Europe: Postcolonial Thought and Historical Difference*. Princeton: Princeton University Press; Chatterjee, Partha (1986), *Nationalist Thought and the Colonial World: A Derivative Discourse?* Minneapolis:

University of Minnesota Press; Chatterjee, Partha (1993), *The Nation and Its Fragments: Colonial and Postcolonial Histories*. Princeton: Princeton University Press; Chatterjee, Partha (2011), *Lineages of Political Society: Studies in Postcolonial Democracy*. New York: Columbia University Press; Kennedy, Dane (1996), 'Imperial history and postcolonial theory', *The Journal of Imperial and Commonwealth History*, 24(3), 345–363; Pratt, Mary Louise (1991), 'Arts of the contact zone', *Profession*, 91, 33–40. For relations between the metropole and colony, see, for example, Hall, Catherine (ed.) (2000), *Cultures of Empire: Colonisers in Britain and the Empire of the Nineteenth and Twentieth Centuries: A Reader*. Manchester: Manchester University Press; Hall, Catherine and McClelland, Keith (eds.) (2010), *Race, Nation and Empire: Making Histories, 1750 to the Present*. Manchester: Manchester University Press; Webster, Wendy (2005), *Englishness and Empire, 1939–1965*. Oxford: Oxford University Press; Aldrich, Richard and Ward, Stuart (2010), 'Ends of empire: decolonizing the nation in British and French historiography', in Stefan Berger and Chris Lorenz (eds.) (2010), *Nationalising the Past: Historians as Nation Builders in Modern Europe*. Basingstoke: Palgrave Macmillan, 259–281. On gender, see Levine, Philippa (2004), *Gender and Empire*. New York: Oxford University Press; Levine, Philippa (2010), 'Gendering decolonisation', in *Histoire@Politique: Politique, culture, societe*, 11, <http://www.histoire-politique.fr/> [accessed 28 February 2014].

8   For the United Nations and European empires, see Mazower, Mark (2009), *No Enchanted Palace: The End of Empire and the Ideological Origins of the United Nations*. Princeton: Princeton University Press.

9   See Borgwardt, Elizabeth (2005), *A New Deal for the World: America's Vision for Human Rights*. Cambridge, MA: Belknap Press; Dudziak, Mary L. (2000), *Cold War Civil Rights: Race and the Image of American Democracy*. Princeton: Princeton University Press; Friedberg, Aaron L. (2000), *In the Shadow of the Garrison State: America's Anti-Statism and Its Cold War Grand Strategy*. Princeton: Princeton University Press; Hixson, Walter L. (1997), *Parting the Curtain: Propaganda, Culture, and the Cold War, 1945–1961*. Basingstoke: Macmillan; Suri, Jeremi (2003), *Power and Protest: Global Revolution and the Rise of Detente*. Cambridge, MA: Harvard University Press. For a number of books in this field, see the University of Massachusetts Press' series *Culture, Politics, and the Cold War*, e.g. Dean, Robert D. (2003), *Imperial Brotherhood: Gender and the Making of Cold War Foreign Policy*. Amherst: University of Massachusetts Press.

10 The diplomatic history of the Cold War, particularly in the United States, has extensive roots, arising from various political perspectives. Beyond Gaddis, John Lewis (1987), *The Long Peace: Inquiries into the History of the Cold War*. New York: Oxford University Press, see Williams, William Appleman (1972), *The Tragedy of American Diplomacy*. New York: Dell Publishing Co.; LaFeber, Walter (2005 edn.), *America, Russia, and the Cold War 1945–2000*. Boston: McGraw-Hill. For the Soviet side, see Zubok, Vladislav M. (2007), *A Failed Empire: The Soviet Union in the Cold War from Stalin to Gorbachev*. Chapel Hill, NC: University of North Carolina Press.

11 See Lüthi, Lorenz M. (2008), *The Sino-Soviet Split: Cold War in the Communist World*. Princeton: Princeton University Press; Radchenko, Sergey (2009), *Two Suns in the Heavens: The Sino-Soviet Struggle for Supremacy, 1962–1967*. Stanford: Stanford University Press; Bradley, Mark Philip and Young, Marilyn B. (eds.) (2008), *Making Sense of the Vietnam Wars: Local, National, and Transnational Perspectives*. New York: Oxford University Press; Nguyen, Lien-Hang (2012), *Hanoi's War: An International History of the War for Peace in Vietnam*. Chapel Hill, NC: University of North Carolina Press; Guerra, Lillian (2012), *Visions of Power: Revolution, Redemption and Resistance in Cuba, 1959–1971*. Chapel Hill, NC: University of North Carolina Press. On the Korean War, see the work being done as part of the

international research project, 'Beyond the Korean War', <http://beyondthekoreanwar.com/> [accessed 7 March 2014].

12 Kwon, Heonik (2010), *The Other Cold War*. New York: Columbia University Press.

13 Isaac, Joel and Bell, Duncan (eds.) (2012), *Uncertain Empire: American History and the Idea of the Cold War*. Oxford: Oxford University Press.

14 Stephanson, Anders (2012), 'Cold War degree zero', in Isaac and Bell (2012), 19–50.

15 Westad, Odd Arne (2012), 'Exploring the histories of the Cold War: A pluralist approach', in Isaac and Bell (2012), 51–60.

16 Westad, Odd Arne (2005), *The Global Cold War: Third World Interventions and the Making of Our Times*. Cambridge: Cambridge University Press, 4.

17 Brands, H.W. (2006), 'Review: *The Global Cold War: Third World Interventions and the Making of Our Times* by Odd Arne Westad', *The Journal of American History*, 93(3), 930–931, p. 931.

18 Roxborough, Ian (2007), 'Review: *The Global Cold War: Third World Interventions and the Making of Our Times* by Odd Arne Westad', *The American Historical Review*, 112(3), 806–808, p. 808.

19 For a summary, see Bradley, Mark Philip (2010), 'Decolonization, the global South, and the Cold War, 1919-1962', in Melvyn P. Leffler and Odd Arne Westad (eds.) (2010), *The Cambridge History of the Cold War*. Vol. 1. Cambridge: Cambridge University Press, 464–485. For an analysis of the confluence of imperial and Cold War logic, with their more recent contemporary resonances in the 'war on terror', see Drayton, Richard (2005), 'Anglo-American "liberal" imperialism, British Guiana, 1953–64, and the world since September 11', in Wm. Roger Louis (ed.) (2005), *Yet More Adventures with Britannia: Personalities, Politics and Culture in Britain*. London: I.B. Tauris, 321–342.

20 See Grandin, Greg and Joseph, Gilbert M. (eds.) (2010), *A Century of Revolution: Insurgent and Counterinsurgency Violence during Latin America's Long Cold War*. Durham, NC: Duke University Press; Hecht, Gabrielle (ed.) (2011), *Entangled Geographies: Empire and Technopolitics in the Global Cold War*. Cambridge, MA: MIT Press; Joseph, Gilbert M. and Spenser, Daniela (eds.) (2008), *In from the Cold: Latin America's New Encounter with the Cold War*. Durham, NC: Duke University Press; Lee, Christopher J. (ed.) (2010), *Making a World after Empire: The Bandung Moment and its Political Afterlives*. Athens: Ohio University Press; McMahon, Robert J. (ed.) (2013), *The Cold War in the Third World*. New York: Oxford University Press; Mooney, Jadwiga E. Pieper and Lanza, Fabio (eds.) (2013), *De-centering Cold War History: Local and Global Change*. London: Routledge; Muehlenbeck, Philip E. (ed.) (2012), *Race, Ethnicity, and the Cold War: A Global Perspective*. Nashville: Vanderbilt University Press; Goscha, Chris and Ostermann, Christian (eds.) (2009), *Connecting Histories: Decolonization and the Cold War in South East Asia, 1945-1962*. Stanford: Stanford University Press.

21 For studies that emphasize 'alternative' diplomacies, transnational institutions and networks, see Von Eschen, Penny (2006), *Satchmo Blows Up the World: Jazz Ambassadors Play the Cold War*. Cambridge, MA: Harvard University Press; Rotter, Andrew Jon (2000), *Comrades at Odds: The United States and India, 1947-1964*. Ithaca: Cornell University Press; Horne, Gerald (2007), *Cold War in a Hot Zone: The United States Confronts Labor and Independence Struggles in the British West Indies*. Philadelphia: Temple University Press; Plummer, Brenda Gayle (2012), *In Search of Power: African Americans in the Era of Decolonization, 1956-1974*. Cambridge: Cambridge University Press; Prashad, Vijay (2007), *The Darker Nations: A People's History of the Third World*. New York: New Press; Chamberlin, Paul Thomas (2012), *The Global Offensive: The United States, the Palestine Liberation Organization, and*

the Making of the Post-Cold War Order. New York: Oxford University Press. For economic diplomacy, race and empire, see Parker, Jason C. (2008), *Brother's Keeper: The United States, Race, and Empire in the British Caribbean, 1937-1962.* Oxford: Oxford University Press. For an important critical appraisal of the relationship between the Cold War, liberation movements and violence, see Connelly, Matthew (2000), 'Taking off the Cold War lens: visions of North-South conflict during the Algerian War for Independence', *The American Historical Review,* 105(3), 739-769; also Furedi, Frank (1994), *Colonial Wars and the Politics of Third World Nationalism.* London: I.B. Tauris; and Gleijeses, Piero (2002), *Conflicting Missions: Havana, Washington, and Africa, 1959-1976.* Chapel Hill, NC: University of North Carolina Press. Other academic disciplines increasingly address the intersections of the Cold War and decolonization as well; see, for example, Klein, Christina (2003), *Cold War Orientalism: Asia in the Middlebrow Imagination, 1945-1961.* Berkeley: University of California Press; and Kwon (2010).

22 We recognize the additional importance of interactions between the Soviet bloc and the decolonizing world, even if this volume touches on the issue only peripherally. For more on the so-called 'Second World-Third World' relationship, see Engerman, David C. (2011), 'The Second World's Third World', *Kritika: Explorations in Russian and Eurasian History,* 12(1), 183-211.

23 James, C.L.R. (1977), *Nkrumah and the Ghana Revolution.* London: Allison Busby, 27.

24 Mooney and Lonza (2013), 2.

25 Plummer (2012), 12.

26 See Plummer (2012); Von Eschen, Penny M. (1997), *Race against Empire: Black Americans and Anticolonialism, 1937-1957.* Ithaca: Cornell University Press; Horne, Gerald (2008), *The End of Empires: African Americans and India.* Philadelphia: Temple University Press; Pennybacker, Susan (2009), *From Scottsboro to Munich: Race and Political Culture in 1930s Britain.* Princeton: Princeton University Press; Slate, Nico (2012), *Colored Cosmopolitanism: The Shared Struggle for Freedom in the United States and India.* Cambridge, MA: Harvard University Press. For a reading of African American intellectuals' engagement with both US empire and Soviet decolonization, see Baldwin, Kate (2002), *Beyond the Color Line and the Iron Curtain: Reading Encounters Between Black and Red, 1922-1963.* Durham, NC: Duke University Press.

27 See Mann, Michael (2012 edn.), *The Sources of Social Power: Globalization.* Vol. 4. Cambridge: Cambridge University Press, 86-128; Kramer, Paul A. (2006), *The Blood of Government: Race, Empire, the United States, and the Philippines.* Chapel Hill, NC: University of North Carolina Press. Histories of US empire have a longer trajectory, from Williams, William Appleman (1969), *The Roots of the Modern American Empire: A Study of the Growth and Shaping of Social Consciousness in a Marketplace Society.* New York: Vintage Books; to LaFeber, Walter (1963), *The New Empire: An Interpretation of American Expansion 1860-1898.* New York: Cornell University Press; and Stoler, Ann Laura (ed.) (2006), *Haunted by Empire: Geographies of Intimacy in North American History.* Durham, NC: Duke University Press.

28 For an example of postcolonial activists who were attracted to the Soviet model of decolonization, see Lee, Christopher J., 'Tricontinentalism in question: the Cold War politics of Alex La Guma and the African National Congress', in Lee (2010), 266-288. For work on Soviet decolonization, see, for example, Suny, R. Grigor and Martin, Tony (eds.) (2001), *A State of Nations: Empire and Nation-Making in the Age of Lenin and Stalin.* Oxford: Oxford University Press; Hirsch, Francine (2005), *Empire of Nations: Ethnographic Knowledge and the Making of the Soviet Union.* Ithaca: Cornell University Press; Martin, Terry (2001),

The Affirmative Action Empire: Nations and Nationalism in the Soviet Union, 1923–1939. Ithaca: Cornell University Press; and Dawisha, Karen and Parrott, Bruce (eds.) (1997), *The End of Empire? The Transformation of the USSR in Comparative Perspective.* Armonk, NY: M.E. Sharpe.

29 See Lee (2010).

30 For a recent analysis that fuses questions of sovereignty, decolonization and early Cold War socialism with the question of minority 'rights', see Imlay, Talbot C. (2013), 'International socialism and decolonization during the 1950s: Competing rights and the postcolonial order', *American Historical Review*, 118(4), 1105–1132.

31 Lee, Christopher J. (2011), 'Decolonization of a special type: Rethinking Cold War history in Southern Africa', *Kronos*, (37), 6–11, p. 9.

32 Greg Grandin has made a compelling case for moving the Cold War in Latin America even further back to the Mexican Revolution (Grandin et al., 2010), Kwon (2010) and Mooney and Lonza (2013) also persuasively argue against seeing 1989 as a distinct end to the Cold War due to its lingering cultural and institutional influences.

PART I
DEVELOPING THE NATION: ECONOMICS, MODERNITY AND THE 'STATE PROJECT'

This part questions the influence wielded by both political statesmen and everyday citizens, as they sought to construct their societies, both newly independent and already established, in specific ways. It emphasizes that this was true as much for the large superpowers as it was for small emerging states, and this era produced a particular kind of development dynamic. It also emphasizes planning and state projects that drew on international networks and ideas; ways in which some borrowed ideas or asserted new systems; and how projects regarding food, trade and manufacturing were not just about material development but also about assertions of power.

CHAPTER 1
'FANTASTIC QUANTITIES OF FOOD GRAINS': COLD WAR VISIONS AND AGRARIAN FANTASIES IN INDEPENDENT INDIA

Benjamin Siegel

On 20 June 1951, Ivan Semënovich Trikov, first mate of the Soviet freighter *Krasnodar*, came to the ship's deck to speak, via radio, with the Odessa correspondent of *Izvestiia*, the Soviet Union's paper of record. The creaky tanker had returned from three weeks in the Port of Bombay, where it had unloaded 7,000 tons of wheat, in a first effort to combat the near-famine conditions evident in India since the closing months of the previous year. Throughout the *Krasnodar*'s mooring, the ship had been surrounded by food ships from five countries, unloading nearly 90,000 tons in total.[1] Bombay's municipal government had called up all of its reserve labour force to meet the ships and take the cargo into the city and onwards to India's dwindling grain stores.

With pride, Trikov announced that the ship's mission, of 'delivering grain to the starving population, has been honourably fulfilled'. News of the Soviet assistance, Trikov had heard in Bombay, had spread faster across India than wire services could report. Indians sitting resignedly next to funeral pyres were roused by news of the Soviet grain, summing up their strength to live, instead. It was clear that 'the working people of India understand full well who brought their country to starvation. One frequently hears curses there against the Anglo–American imperialists and their flunkeys', alongside praise for 'the leader, best friend and teacher of working people the world over – Comrade Stalin'.[2]

The *Krasnodar*'s captain was a veteran of assistance programmes to India, having come in 1947 on a ship named *Vtoraia Piatiletka* ('the Second Five-Year Plan'). In Bombay, he had trumpeted the readiness of every Soviet Republic to contribute to India. 'We are not worried what it costs us to [ship] the food grains', he announced. 'Our chief concern is how soon we can get them to India.'[3] The crew of the *Krasnodar* had been fêted by Bombay's Progressive Group at a reception attended by the Regional Food Commissioner, Soviet Russian diplomats and socialists from around Bombay, including the renowned writer Mulk Raj Anand.

Yet however well Trikov's report played among *Izvestiia*'s readers, it fared less well in India. News of the first mate's account soon arrived back in Bombay, where a *Times of India* reporter dismissed it as a 'not unimpressive example of how facts may be suitably "coloured"', and scoffed at the notion that Indians were 'transformed' upon hearing word of Soviet agricultural largesse.[4] The correspondent seemed to intuit what later experience would show: that the Cold War battle over aid to India was as much a battle of ideas and narratives as it was one of grains and geopolitics.

Many incisive narratives of the Cold War in South Asia begin from the shared assertion that India was a central battleground in the same, with economic assistance to industry and agriculture serving as vital instruments for coaxing India out of its famed stance of non-alignment. In many accounts, food aid is held as central to Soviet and American strategy alike: shipments of grains to meet Indian shortages are cast, alongside gifts of industrial machinery and various military, diplomatic and economic inducements, as weapons in the battle for India's affection and alliance.[5]

Yet by reducing Cold War contestations to their diplomatic and economic terms, these accounts risk neglecting the complex, competing visions of national development extended to the new, decolonizing countries of Asia and Africa.[6] These competing visions animated dramatic political and intellectual contestations in India, where a newly independent nation debated what course its national development should follow. As the Gandhian vision of a village India quickly receded at the moment of independence, India's leadership and its citizens disagreed mightily as to what models of industrialization, agricultural growth and economic development the nation would follow.

These competing visions are perhaps nowhere more apparent than in India's efforts to feed a hungry nation in the decades following independence. Attaining freedom in the wake of the devastating Bengal Famine of 1943, India found itself contending with continued shortages that bound it to imports and aid and threatened to undermine the legitimacy of its independent leadership. India's efforts to feed itself, therefore, concretized urgent questions about the shape of national development.[7] The American consul in Madras wrote in 1950 that 'foreign policy is an abstract issue, remote to the vast bulk of Indians; it is the giving or withholding of food he eats that will determine whether the average Indian will view the US with good will or bitterness'.[8] Yet food stood in for much more than foreign policy: for Indian citizens of all backgrounds, the food problem distilled competing visions of national development, and the rival models that East and West proffered as examples.

Examining Cold War visions of agricultural development and food aid in India complicates the notion of a simple, quantifiable 'competition' between East and West, played out in aid shipments and on Indian steel plants, dams and industrial farms. Inasmuch as such competition existed, it was short and one-sided, with the Soviet Union mounting an offence for only a few short years in the mid-1950s, powered by a brief moment of economic vigour.[9] American aid dwarfed that offered by the Soviet Union, and American experts outmanoeuvred their Soviet counterparts in agriculture as in other fields.[10]

The more evocative competition might best be seen as comprising several phases, beginning with Indian nationalists' and planners' embrace of the Soviet Union as a model for national development in the years before independence. That vision transformed into a brief moment of real competition over aid to India against the backdrop of shortages in the 1950s, before it became clear that the USSR had far less to offer than the United States. In the latter half of that decade, left-wing bureaucrats looked to the cooperative and collective farms of the Soviet Union and China as promising models for India's agrarian reform, before the objections of landlords, capitalists and conservative thinkers thwarted their adoption in India. And as the 1960s progressed and India's national leadership fragmented, the allure of socialist development receded even further into the distance.

An examination of these contestations and transformations in India illuminates a Cold War battleground on the terrain of ideas as much as material aid. Similarly, unpacking the distinct 'instruments and idioms' of national development in Cold War South Asia allows for new insight into the ways in which decolonizing nations were influenced not so much by assistance as by the exchange of developmentalist thinking across national borders and Iron Curtains.[11]

The Soviet Union in the Indian imagination, c. 1920–1950

Indian nationalists' romance with the Soviet Union predated the nation's independence by at least two decades.[12] For Indian planners throughout the 1920s and the 1930s, the Soviet Union represented a potent, alternative inspiration for India's industrial modernization – what Francine Frankel has cast as 'a more congenial model of modernity'.[13] Jawaharlal Nehru himself had his first exchange with doctrinaire Marxists in February 1927, when, in the wake of the Brussels Conference of Oppressed Nationalities, the young Indian National Congress leader proceeded to Moscow for a brief, four-day visit. In the wake of these encounters, Nehru recounted, 'I turned inevitably with good will towards communism, for, whatever its faults, it was at least not hypocritical and not imperialistic. [These features] attracted me, as also the tremendous changes taking place in Russia.'[14]

The Indian National Congress' first National Planning Committee in 1938 looked frequently to the Soviet Union as an example of a planned economy and social system. Among the Soviet leadership itself, there was a faint reciprocation of this warmth, largely in the form of official platitudes echoing Lenin's thought on the 'backward and oppressed nations'. 'We shall exert every effort', Lenin had written in 1916, a year before publishing his *Imperialism: The Highest Stage of Capitalism*,

> to foster association and merger with the Mongolians, Persians, Indians, Egyptians. We believe it is our duty and in our interest to do this, for otherwise socialism in Europe will not be secure. [We] will help them pass to the use of machinery, to the lightening of labour, to democracy, to socialism.[15]

Six years later, M.N. Roy attended the Congress of the Toilers of the Far East in Moscow and Petrograd as India's representative-in-exile.[16]

Among Indian planners, the Soviet infatuation cut across political divisions. Nationalists on the left, like the Ghadar Party revolutionary, Pandurang Khankhoje, celebrated the Soviet Union's putative agricultural success: before planting the seeds of the Green Revolution in Mexico and India, Khankhoje met famously with Lenin in 1921 to discuss the caloric needs of Indian and Russian labourers.[17] In the 1930s, bureaucrats like Mokshagundam Vishveshwariah pushed for a 'planned economy', seeing in the Soviet

Union and its five-year plans an eminently borrowable model for national development and reconstruction.[18] The Communist Party of India and affiliated groups like the All-India Kisan Sabha extolled the seeming ability of the Soviet Union to provide food for all of its citizens – drawing a stark contrast with the British Government's inability to do so during the recent Bengal Famine.[19] 'India', an Indian planner wrote on the eve of independence,

> is marching in this [global] procession of planners, whose leader is redoubtable Russia, wearing its flag of successful Soviet planning from ignorance to education, from superstition to science, from poverty and penury to prosperity and plenty, from disease, dirt and doubt to health, cleanliness, and a great new godliness, the faith in a new future for the great masses of mankind.[20]

India's first official exchanges with Soviet planners began even before independence: in 1946, Nehru welcomed representatives from the Soviet Asian Republics to Delhi for the Asian Relations Conference, lauding the countries that had 'advanced so rapidly in our generation and which have so many lessons to teach us'.[21] Later that year, as Indian nationalists in the Congress and the Muslim League joined an interim government to prepare for the transition to freedom, the Indian Science Congress welcomed four delegates from the Soviet Academy of Sciences to Delhi.[22] Already, representatives of the incipient nation were looking to the Soviet Union as a benefactor on the food front. Nehru dispatched V.K. Krishna Menon – later India's ambassador to the USSR – to meet with V. M. Molotov, the Soviet Commissar of Foreign Affairs, in Paris, in an unsuccessful bid to garner gifts of food. 'If we do not send you food', a sympathetic Molotov was reported to have said, against the backdrop of widespread scarcity in the Soviet Union, 'it is only because we cannot'.[23] The Soviet's reticence did little to dampen Indian politicians' ardour: in the debates over the nature of the Indian constitution, Soviet Russia served as a critical example of how a state might guarantee the economic rights of its citizens. The author of a Hindi primer on India's food problem took note of the Soviet Union's Five-Year Plans and its collective farming, said to be bringing forth great quantities of grain from the earth.[24] This enthusiasm echoed in the Constituent Assembly debates, where one delegate declared that the state 'must provide the means of livelihood for every one. Russia has addressed itself to this problem and has concerned itself with the growing of food and the feeding of every citizen of the country by nationalising the means of production'.[25]

When Soviet planners and academics regarded India in this same period, they saw the ultimate example of the ruin wrought by colonial rule and economic expropriation. A month after Indian independence, the Soviet Academy of Sciences heard a report on India's wrecked agrarian economy and the potential for socialist reform.[26] By 1949, the Soviet journal, *Voprosy Istorii* [*Questions of History*], urged 'Soviet historians of the Orient' to 'show that British domination has brought India not culture and civilisation, but poverty, famine, epidemics and a shocking death rate'.[27] And even as the Soviet Union's own economic assistance to India remained restrained, save for a small wheat deal in

1949 providing 200,000 tons of wheat in exchange for jute and tea, Soviet spokesmen and journalists lambasted American food aid as a means of conducting surveillance on Indian political activities, operating through the Red Cross and missionary groups 'under the pretext of "aid" to the starving people'.[28] For its part, the US Embassy in India trumpeted its own successes in increasing agricultural production at home through books, pamphlets and an information service, which competed with the efforts of the Telegraph Agency of the Soviet Union and other Soviet news agencies.[29]

In the years prior to 1950, Soviet and Indian thinkers engaged with each others' nations primarily in the realm of the imagination. Concrete exchanges suggesting the USSR as a model for planning to Indians were infrequent; India still represented an example of imperial underdevelopment yoked to capitalist benefactors. These exchanges would grow more substantive as independent India weathered its first major food crisis in 1951.

'Fantastic quantities of food grains': Soviet promises and American aid in a competitive decade

India's nationalist leaders had promised that independence would be accompanied by a solution to India's perennial food problem. Yet by late 1950, the nation was careening towards famine again, rendering India an important site of Cold War posturing. Floods, droughts and earthquakes had hampered production to the tune of a six million-ton food deficit, and Nehru's promise of self-sufficiency by 1951 was a hollow memory.[30] India's Food and Agriculture Minister, K.M. Munshi, was an American backer in a socialist-leaning cabinet, and in November, he reached out secretly to Ambassador Loy Henderson to suggest that, even though Nehru would object to a major appeal, the Prime Minister would be aggressively challenged by those who recognized America as the only real source of food aid.[31] In a December meeting with American Secretary of State Dean Acheson, Indian Ambassador Vijayalakshmi Pandit formally put forward India's request for two million tons of food. But she demurred when the Americans suggested that a strategic alliance and an end to India's support for China in the Korean conflict would be in order.[32]

Throughout the first months of 1951, Nehru publicly lamented the need for imports but contended that there would be no 'bartering of freedom for food', and declared that India would not accept aid 'with strings attached'.[33] And as American food aid bills snaked their way through Congress and Republican senators pressed India for the trade of strategic minerals in exchange for aid, Indian leftists saw proof that their allies were indeed in the East. The Marathi daily *Navabharat* contended that American reticence would 'aggravate the starvation of Indian people and reveal the sham character of American democracy', while the Gujarati-language *Hindustan* reported on the rich irony of 'a country with huge surpluses [burning] food grains while millions are struggling for one full meal'. Castigating 'American farmer-barons', the communist weekly *Atom* lauded the Chinese and Soviet farmers who were said to be fighting to be the first to send aid.[34] Henderson reported with anxiety on the 'fantastic quantities of food grains' being promised by Chinese and Soviet representatives, the latter of whom were assuring no cap on the amount of wheat they would offer.[35]

The UK High Commissioner in Delhi noted that the American delay in signing the food bill had 'greatly aggravated' the resentment felt by Indians towards the United States. 'It will long be remembered here', he wrote, 'that the United States Congress spun out discussion of ... unacceptable conditions of the loan for weeks, while the need became more and more urgent and the opportunity finally passed'.[36]

The India Emergency Food Aid Act of 1951 was enacted in the middle of June, dispatching two million tons of food grain from the United States to India. It marked the end of a diplomatic and legislative process that had dragged on for close to half a year. As the American grain made its way across the ocean, Radio Moscow continued to broadcast daily reports on the food shipments, lambasting the American delay as 'five and a half months of noisy propaganda and hubbub ... revealing US imperialism in all its savagery'.[37] Yet over the summer, with American grain finally reaching India, the Indian government put an end to the fixing of Soviet propaganda posters on cars traveling through the country carrying bushels of Soviet grain.[38] As grain distribution continued into the fall, American agents worked to ensure that Indians knew the source of their food, producing an emblem for trucks and grain bags bearing the American and the Indian flags together on a shield, with the slogan 'Strength from America to the free world' in Hindi and other languages.[39]

Throughout the summer, as they watched their grain shipments dwarfed by the arrival of American surpluses, Soviet journalists and experts continued to tour India and report on the nation's exploitation by the West. Beyond the report of the *Krasnodar*'s crew, the Soviet press published a long series of reports on Indian food shortages, frequently exaggerating the scope of the shortages and their political impact. Not infrequently, Soviet correspondents seemingly fabricated the details of food protests and riots, as in a *Pravda* report in April alleging widespread food demonstrations across Assam.[40] Reports like these drew connections between India's hunger and the machinations of the West. A representative of the Soviet Academy of Agricultural Sciences toured India in the summer of 1951. The famine conditions now evident, he reported, owed their origins to outsiders 'who for centuries have exploited and robbed India, preserved and cultivated the feudal institutions advantageous to them'. Was it therefore shocking, the agronomist wrote, 'that starvation is the theme that has recently figured constantly In Indian newspapers?'[41]

In the wake of the events of 1951, both the United States and the Soviet Union sought to capitalize on their famine relief efforts, in spite of the disproportionate quantitative advantage the former enjoyed. The delay in American aid and the quick recurrence of famine conditions made for diminished returns on public opinion. By November, one of the *Hindu's* more influential correspondents warned the UK High Commissioner in Delhi that the West would need to make a major gesture towards India on the food front if it wished to enjoy any lasting influence. He suggested that an American-administered permanent food-relief bank might serve that purpose well.[42] The Commissioner agreed with the sentiment: a failure to help India solve its food problem, he felt, would lead to a 'hostile India [under] communist control', undermining 'the whole of our politico–strategic position'.[43] In the United States, President Harry S. Truman trumpeted the 1951 assistance bill in his State of the Union address, lauding the 'work Americans are doing in India to help the Indian farmers themselves raise more grain', particularly that of technical advisors under the Point Four Program.[44] In India, however, there was widespread sentiment that American aid amounted to little but fetters. For the average Indian, *Amrita Bazar Patrika* asserted in August, 'words such as Colombo aid, US technical aid, US economic aid, have begun to be tyrannous and oppressive, seeing that there are less substance in them than words.'[45]

Soviet representatives, in the early years of the 1950s, worked to consolidate their propaganda gains. The *Pravda* report on the Indian elections of 1951–1952 declared that 'the elections have aroused the Indian people'. The countless placards in India's villages declaring that 'a vote for the Congress Party is a vote for hunger' heralded, to this correspondent, the imminent triumph of the Communist Party of India.[46] Alongside these reports came allegations that the 'Yankees [descending upon India in droves] were using "technical aid" as a pretext for subterfuge', proclaiming that Norris E. Dodd, the American chief of the Food and Agriculture Organization, was using that office as cover for espionage.[47] The Soviet press reported that the continuing American food aid was provoking 'great indignation in India', consisting of 'rotten wheat, unfit for consumption' and contingent only upon the continued export of strategic minerals.[48]

Russians could hear on Moscow radio a report from Bihar on the enduring food crisis there.[49] 'The torments of hell depicted by Dante', *Pravda*'s correspondent reported, 'seem pale in comparison with the horrors one meets here at every step'. Workers had left their homes to search for food, the state's railroad stations were clogged with emaciated people and starving Indians ate tree bark to stave off hunger. Bihar's plight was worsened, so the Soviets claimed, by those who were 'getting rich on famine'. These included Ashutosh Bhattacharia, a man alleged to control the whole of the black market in grains and who had become 'a millionaire on the Bengal famine', and the 'trans-Atlantic imperialists' who had only agreed to deliver grain in exchange for 'sterilisation' and 'castration' of Indian citizens.

Yet the desire of Indian administrators to centralize the distribution of aid meant that the Soviet Union struggled to send even modest amounts of food aid. In August 1952, an effort by the All Unions Central Council of Trade Unions of Soviet Russia to send food grains 'from the working people of Soviet Russia' to famine districts in Andhra Pradesh met with a new wave of Indian resistance.[50] The proposed gift – 10,000 tons of wheat, 5,000 tons of rice, alongside cash and condensed milk – had been arranged directly between the General Secretary of the United Famine Relief Committee of Andhra Region and V. Kuznetsov, Chairman of the Central Council of Trade Unions of the USSR. Yet in early September, New Delhi insisted that relief 'be kept apart [from] political controversies', and that all aid go through either the government or groups like the Indian Red Cross Society. The Central Council's Secretary gave his assent, but published an objection in the Soviet journal published from New Delhi, *Soviet Land*.[51]

The Soviet propaganda efforts seemed at times to be countered entirely through the efforts of Chester Bowles, the United States' outspoken ambassador to India from 1951 to 1953 (and once again from 1963 to 1969), who saw the risk of India 'going red' in every trip to a village. In a 1953 visit to the 'hunger areas' of Hyderabad and Madras, Bowles grew

> alarmed at the seriousness of the crop failures and the dissatisfaction that was evident among the people. [People] were not starving, but thousands were dying because of undernourishment. Land reform had been ineffective or nonexistent and Communist strength seemed to be growing.

Nehru, informed by Bowles of this hunger area, returned from an exploratory trip to the region reporting that the presence of the Prime Minister had staved off communist influence.[52] In another visit to Tanjore district, Bowles listened to a young villager angrily reject the Ambassador's claim of a Soviet menace. 'I am not concerned about this faraway Stalin against whom you warn of', Bowles recalled the villager saying. 'We have our own Stalin here in this village – the man who owns the lands we till. First tell us how to get out of his grip.'[53] Statements like these, and the pervasive placards bearing slogans like 'Land to the Tiller' and 'Five Acres for Me and Mine', suggested to Bowles that it was on the terrain of land and agriculture that the battle for India's hearts and minds would be fought.[54] And indeed, for the remainder of the decade, the debate over India's agrarian reconstruction would emerge as the nation's most pressing political conflict, looking to experiences in the East and the West for cues.

'Hotels Where We Will Be Given Our Meals': Visions of cooperation, fears of collectivization

The 'fantastic quantities of food grains' promised by the Soviet Union did not materialize in the early years of the 1950s. Grains did, however, arrive in India under the auspices of the United States Agricultural Trade Development and Assistance Act agreements with India in 1956. More popularly known as PL480, these shipments were billed as an effort to secure foreign currency resources for development, although by many later interpretations, it was equally useful to US policymakers as a means of disposing agricultural surplus.[55] Yet even as American aid dwarfed that of the Soviet Union, the USSR nonetheless continued to fuel the imagination of Indian planners, even if the particulars of its economic and social landscape remained opaque, and China would soon supplant the USSR as an example.

India's First Five-Year Plan, published in 1951, took inspiration in name and form from its Soviet antecedent, and its particulars outlined plans for 'the improvement of agriculture [through the] experience gained by Soviet Planning'.[56] The year after its publication, the Urdu writer, S. Mahmuduzzafar, spent six months in the Soviet Union in 1952, reporting back in India that 'the Russian *moujhik*, the Asiatic peasant, the nomadic herdsmen have all vanished in the course of a generation, and a prosperous farmer with an outlook and standard of life approaching modern city folk has taken their place.[57] The Indian statistician, P.C. Mahalanobis, travelled to the Soviet Union in 1954 to seek inspiration for India's planning efforts. In 1956 Mahalanobis steered the drafting of India's Second Five-Year Plan, ensuring that this iteration owed even more to the Soviet Union than the First Plan. Yet it was not only India's intellectuals who saw in Soviet experience a model for successful agricultural development. One Hindi daily called the Congress government to task for its inability to act upon the popular cry for industrialized agriculture, wondering why India could not do the same as Soviet Russia, 'creating massive farms, and planting more crops than ever before. [Russia] gave machines to the common farmer, and united them through power of law, creating farms the size of two, or even four villages'.[58]

It was that latter vision which would prove to be most influential on Indian planners. One of the largest challenges facing the new state – and one that bore directly upon the nation's food problem – was that of determining an appropriate plan for agrarian reform. Since the 1920s and the rise of *kisan* (peasant) movements across India, Indian nationalists had promised an end to the hereditary landlordism of the *zamindari* and *jagirdari* systems, and beginning in 1951, had begun to enact legislation to abolish it. Yet even as this process advanced fitfully, the question arose of how agricultural land should be best utilized, as planners balanced the potential productivity of large-scale agriculture against the greater social equity promised by the distribution of land into small plots.

Nehru had considered the question in the 1940s, concluding that 'cooperatives are the one and only way for agriculture in India. There is no other way'.[59] Yet Nehru's vision was not uncontested: as early as 1954, groups like the Calcutta Employers' Association warned against the planned agrarian economy of the USSR, seeing in it a poor model for India's own. The Association argued that the seizing of land in the USSR, as well as state directives dictating the particulars of ploughing, sowing and harvesting, 'have undermined that traditional pride of ownership of land which is so important a factor in agricultural economy'.[60]

Nonetheless, the vision of cooperative, large-scale agriculture along Soviet lines gained traction among many left-wing Indian planners throughout the decade, assisted by outreach from the Soviet Union under the direction of Nikita Khrushchev.[61] In late 1954, a delegation from India's Ministry of Food and Agriculture accepted an invitation from the Soviet Union to visit a number of collective farms in Russia, Poland and Czechoslovakia. The Ministry's economic advisers, statisticians and agricultural experts returned to India admitting that 'there are such strong prejudices either for or against Soviet Russia that it is not an easy matter to make an unbiased assessment of men and things in that country'.[62] They were impressed by the USSR's 'great determination to lift agriculture from the old ruts', although they remained unconvinced that collective farms and industrialized agriculture had much applicability to the small plots held by Indian farmers.[63] Building on this visit, a second agricultural delegation, led by Panjabrao Deshmukh, returned to the Soviet Union two years later.

As the age of superpower competition heated up, Soviet largesse fuelled a series of agreements with India on the agricultural front. In 1954, the USSR offered India a gift of three Soviet tractors, before opening a Bombay showroom for Soviet tractors and agricultural equipment near the Mahalakshmi racecourse.[64] India and the Soviet Union announced the joint establishment of a steel plant in Bhilai in February 1955, and followed up six months later with an experimental, Soviet-style farm to be formed in Rajasthan. The Suratgarh Farm was built and planted expeditiously throughout the late summer: Soviet agronomists and farmers came to supervise the planting of wheat, barley, lentils and mustard; gifted sixty-six tractors; and built a power station, a telephone exchange and four train stations before sending a follow-up delegation the following spring to survey the use of the Soviet machinery.[65]

This mid-decade flurry of tractor diplomacy paved the way for Khrushchev and Bulganin's tour of India in November 1955, a sequel to Nehru's visit to the USSR that July. Khrushchev spoke frequently in India of the Soviet Union's eagerness to serve as a model for and a benefactor to the modernization of Indian agriculture. 'Without advance in agriculture', Khrushchev contended in Delhi,

the plan for industrial development cannot be fulfilled. [It] is interesting to watch an elephant at work.... But tractors, automobiles and locomotive engines are stronger and more obedient to man. We have learned this by our own experience; we have no elephants but we used to work with oxen and horses, and when we replaced them by machines things improved a good deal.[66]

Speaking a day later in Punjab, the Soviet Premier promised new assistance to Indian agriculture and programmes to train Indians in the Soviet Union. 'I want to tell the people of India', Khrushchev proclaimed, 'that we are their friends and we are willing to share with them even our last piece of bread'.[67] (The Indians, too, were willing to share with the Russians, describing Bulganin and his party as 'the most hearty-eating VIPs ever to have stayed at Rashtrapati Bhavan'.)[68]

Returning to the Soviet Union, Khrushchev and Bulganin both delivered their reports on the Indian trip to the Supreme Soviet.[69] Bulganin detailed India's agricultural problems at great length, and highlighted the ripe possibilities for Soviet-style agricultural modernization. India's state-owned farms, such as Suratgarh, were 'small, but well-organised establishments which, in our opinion, are unquestionably fulfilling their positive role as experimental farms'. Meanwhile, Soviet histories of India traced a long and continuous tradition of providing agricultural assistance to India from the nineteenth century onwards, while the Soviet press office in Delhi published accounts of Soviet agriculture in their broadsheet, *Soviet Land*, and seductively illustrated publications explaining *How the Agrarian Problem Has Been Solved in the USSR*.[70] One American report suggested that, after the consolidation of Chinese communism, the Soviet leadership 'has shifted its attention increasingly to India', noting the role of Mahalanobis in formulating India's Five-Year Plans and his frequent meetings with 'Soviet planning experts brought to India as consultants'.[71]

As the decade progressed, however, Indian planners began looking elsewhere in the Communist Bloc for agricultural inspiration. As early as 1954, Indians had begun to hear rumours of success in the East, learning that agricultural land in China was being reorganized into collective and cooperative farms, with encouraging results.[72] The Indian Trade Union Delegation returned from China in 1955 with reports of 60,000 bustling producers' cooperatives, and the celebrated Chinese social scientist Chen Han Seng told the Planning Commission late that same year that Chinese cultivators were anticipating a 35 to 40 per cent increase in agricultural production over the next five years. On the other hand, proponents of free trade and peasants' rights saw China as a warning, not a model: one concerned writer, contending that China's efforts were only stepping stones en route to collectivization on Russian lines, declared that 'the rice we import from Red China is stained with the blood of the Chinese peasants'. He dedicated his manifesto to India's peasants, 'with a prayer that they should escape the doom which parasitic and self-righteous bookworms and politicians of the cities plan for them'.[73]

Those bookworms and politicians, however, continued to look across the Himalayas with enthusiasm. In 1956, as the Planning Commission pushed India's state governments to increase the pace of their agricultural cooperation efforts, two separate missions were launched to survey Chinese developments in greater depth, touring producers' cooperatives and cooperative farms before returning to suggest that India plan for thousands of cooperative farms along Chinese lines.[74] 'Surely', Nehru affirmed, 'it should not be beyond our powers to do something that China can do'. The confidence was not universal. 'As in all democratic countries', one Congress planner warned in the wake of the Chinese tours, presaging a future showdown,

> the [Indian] peasant is a firm believer in his [proprietary] right. Hence any attempt at collectivization on the [Chinese or Russian] model, which does away with the individual peasant's economic autonomy, is bound to meet the peasant's emotional resistance from the very start.[75]

A Congress politician, writing in 1956, agreed with the dissenters of the Chinese missions, contending that in India, 'the question of mechanised farming to save labour hardly arises. As a matter of fact, collectivisation in Russia for the first two years brought near famine conditions'.[76]

These warnings were prescient. As word of the Congress' plans spread, it stoked the fears of landed interests and peasants alike. In one Uttar Pradesh village, a group of poor farmers lamented the impact that forced cooperation or collectivization would have on their lands and livelihood. 'We all know', one farmer proclaimed, 'now that *chakbandi* [consolidation] has been done, the next step will be to take away our lands. *Russibundi* [Russian-style rule] will come here'. Another added, sarcastically, that in the village, 'We hear the government will take away our lands and make hotels for us where we will be given our meals'.[77]

The anxieties of these villagers hinted at political contestations in Delhi, as the divergent visions of bureaucrats within the Congress and outside of it moved closer to open conflict. And it hinted at another cleavage between modernizing planners, who found convivial examples in the Soviet Union and China, and the realm of popular politics, where these models were unnerving ones. The push towards agricultural cooperatives in a Soviet or Chinese vein had begun to galvanize conservative thinkers, who saw in these plans an assault on private property, family farms, capitalist agriculture and Indian 'tradition' itself. The loudest opposition came from the conservative thinkers who met at the Bombay Forum for Free Enterprise, among them the former socialist mayor of Bombay M.R. Masani, peasant leader N.G. Ranga and the veteran Congressman C. Rajagopalachari. Towards the end of 1958, the Forum invited Japan's ambassador to India to speak on the progress of land reforms in Japan, in hopes of finding a more agreeable model than those offered by China or the Soviet Union.[78]

In what would later be recalled as one of the most significant strategic missteps of Nehru's Prime Ministership, the Congress Working Committee met at Nagpur on 6 January 1959 to endorse a 'Resolution on Agrarian Organizational Pattern'. Beyond calling for the expedition of land reforms and the introduction of new ceilings on land holdings, the Resolution affirmed that India's 'future agrarian pattern should be that of cooperative joint farming, in which the land will be pooled for joint cultivation, the farmers continuing to retain their property rights, and getting a share from the net produce in proportion to their land'.[79] The resolution galvanized conservatives, who over the year would organize themselves into a new opposition party, Swatantra, which 'self-consciously set out to exploit the alleged menace of collectivization of agriculture, while at the same time relating this specific issue to a broader pattern of "statism" which it felt prevailed'.[80]

Visions of the failures of the Soviet Union and China, real and imagined, fuelled opposition to Nagpur. Conservative think tanks contended that these models had little use in India: a position paper written at the Institute of Political & Social Studies in Calcutta contended that the only examples of functioning cooperative farms overseas existed in Israel and Mexico, and that Indian planners' infatuation with the Soviet and Chinese models was a fantasy.[81] In February, M.R. Masani lambasted the Congress' 'adventures in the field of agrarian legislation' and their Eastern Bloc inspirations, vowing 'unrelenting opposition to the proposals for joint farming in place of the traditional Indian method of peasant family farming'. If the Soviet Union and China had served as inspiration to Nehru and his allies on the left, they were presented as warnings by Masani and others, as they capitalized on the sentiments of anxious peasants and threatened landholders alike. 'Collective farming of the Soviet-China model', Masani declared in the Lok Sabha, had no place in India. If Nagpur went forward, he alleged in a debate with Finance Minister Morarji Desai and the veteran communist leader S.A. Dange, 'the same conditions will recur here as happened in Russia. You will have chaos, you will have a catastrophic drop in food production, and you cannot let the country starve'.[82]

Throughout the spring of 1959, the Swatantra Party and others continued to agitate against the adoption of a Soviet or Chinese model in India, arguing, as Masani did, that collective farming had actualized little agricultural gain, and that it was a system 'erected on the backs of the groaning peasantry of Russia and China'.[83] These sentiments in India were amplified by events across the Himalayas: as news of China's suppression of the Tibetan revolt in March and April arrived in India, and the Dalai Lama sought refuge there, Indians of diverse political orientations grew wary of the Chinese example. 'After Tibet', the Planning Commission's land reforms director would later recall, 'everything Chinese became taboo. Even those persons who still believed cooperative farming was the best sort of organization dared not say it'.[84]

Nehru and his allies began to beat a retreat from the Nagpur Resolution, adopting a watered-down substitute bill in May. By the end of the year, a young Congress politician from Madras reviewed some of the year's events at a small seminar held in Ooty.[85] C. Subramaniam had been frequently identified as a likely food minister, and his scepticism of the Soviet and Chinese vision was apparent. 'It has been demonstrated', he said, reviewing the reasons why these models would fail in India,

> that the vast majority of our people are unable to see any difference between these 'joint farming co-operatives' and the collective farms of Soviet Russia. They do not believe that 'Collective Farms' can work without the compulsions of a totalitarian State.

Five years later, as Food Minister, Subramaniam would work to establish an inputs-based, market-driven agricultural system that owed its shape to the United States and Japan, not to Russia or China.

Early in 1958, a delegation of members from the Supreme Soviet, including a large number of agricultural experts, had arrived in India. Making the 'usual round of hydro–electric projects [and] agricultural farms in the Terai', their Indian host, the former ambassador to the USSR 'was obviously bored stiff', and Indian MPs were unimpressed by the 'over-obvious propaganda in which the Russian visitors indulged'.[86] The year before Nagpur, it was apparent that Indian planners were looking elsewhere for inspiration, particularly in the realm of agriculture.[87] Yet neither did the Chinese model then in vogue offer a fundamentally more persuasive vision of agricultural transformation. The events of 1959 and the overstep of Nehru and his allies indicated the clear limits of planners' Cold War visions, which foundered on conservative resistance, popular scepticism and dissent within the governing party itself.

'Let us compete': Inputs and ideologies in 1960s India

By the end of the decade, it was clear that the Soviet Union's ability to 'compete' for India's ideological allegiance had been markedly diminished, and Eastern Bloc models more broadly had crashed against the resistance of factions in India growing more assertive, particularly as Nehru's personal influence had waned.[88] Meanwhile, American initiatives in Indian agriculture had begun to find warmer reception in India as the 1950s progressed.[89] Under the auspices of the United States Technical Cooperation Program and related agencies, Indo-American agricultural teams had undertaken extensive joint projects throughout the decade, from community development schemes to the establishment of a network of agricultural universities.[90] (The United States Information Service had worked to extend the model of American agriculture in less traditional ways, sponsoring a bazaar calendar, which showed Nehru admiring one of President Eisenhower's black Angus show cows.[91]) The Americans had also supported the creation of an Indian Farmers' Forum – the Bharat Krishak Samaj (BKS) – which sought to create profit-driven farmers who would become 'better purchaser[s] in an expanded industrial system, and thus contribute substantially to the development of the nation as a whole'.[92]

It was the BKS' efforts, in 1959, that demonstrated just how far behind the Soviet Union had fallen. In August, twenty BKS farmers were sent to the United States to study American agricultural techniques and farmers' role in the nation's politics and economics. Returning to India, the group reported that in 'the best fed [country] in the world', farmers' ability to produce 'is the best in terms of moral and humanitarian considerations'.[93] An effort to set this claim in international perspective led the BKS to plan a World Agriculture Fair to be held in Delhi. The Fair opened in December as a joint project between the BKS and the Indian government, with proceeds designated for the government's 'Freedom from Hunger Fund'. The Indian Postal Service brought out a commemorative fifteen-paise stamp for the occasion: on it, a farmer driving two bulls sits under a sheaf of wheat and maize, with a projection of Asia and India glowing in its centre.[94]

Over the next several months, millions of Indian citizens and foreign visitors attended the fair's many pavilions, and in particular, the three big-ticket exhibitions of the United States, China and the Soviet Union. Attendance at the first exhibition, however, dwarfed that of the second two. *The New York Times* made the Cold War politics of the fair plain, calling it 'a typical example of the competition between the Communist and non-Communist worlds in its Indian manifestation'.[95] China – in the throes of its own major famine – saw its pavilion's guestbooks defaced with the slogan 'Chinese go home'.[96] At the American exhibition, visiting Indian citizens were asked, rhetorically, 'Can one farmer feed 23 people?' before being shown how, with borehole pumps, motorized tractors and better wheat strains, such feats were indeed possible. Four American pillars, the exhibit proclaimed, were at the heart of the United States' agricultural success: food, family, friendship and freedom.

President Dwight D. Eisenhower visited the World Agriculture Fair in December, becoming the first sitting president to visit India. Declaring his intent to become a farmer once his 'present form of occupation comes to a close', Eisenhower vowed that 'in no way whatsoever is the American exhibit an attempt to portray our agriculture as superior to any other'.[97] Yet it was clear that 'Amriki Mela', the American pavilion, was designed to do just that, capitalizing upon the ascendant strength of a model of capitalist agriculture whose appeal had grown in the wake of Nagpur. After opening the fair alongside President Rajendra Prasad and Prime Minister Nehru, Eisenhower went to the American pavilion to inaugurate it, watching proudly as Prasad proclaimed that the fair would allow Indian farmers to make comparative assessments of other nations' agricultural progress.[98]

Sino-Indian relations had soured in the wake of the Dalai Lama's escape to India, and the nations would soon be at war; the Soviet Union and China were also on the verge of a precipitous split. The Chinese presence was minimal at the fair, and the cursory attention that the Soviet leadership gave to it suggested that they were aware that their influence was on the wane. Two months after Eisenhower, Khrushchev returned to India en route from Indonesia to attend the Fair.[99] Where Eisenhower had charmed his Indian hosts, Khrushchev grumbled through the pavilions and exhibition halls. 'Reticent and thoughtful', observed one reporter, 'the Soviet leader asked few questions, volunteered fewer opinions, and the quips, for which he is known the world over, were absent'.[100] At the Soviet pavilion, Khrushchev took milk from prize-winning Russian cows before leaving the Fair behind for a whirlwind second tour of India.[101] Khrushchev's quick visit was a far cry from the 1955 tour, a testament to the diminishing influence that the Soviet Union could claim on India's agricultural future and the nation's envisioning of the same.

Khrushchev's visit presaged the last throes of Eastern Bloc influence on the Indian agricultural landscape. In July 1960, India's new Minister of Agriculture, P.S. Deshmukh, toured the Soviet Union alongside several state ministers, studying 'the working of Soviet farms, reclamation of virgin lands, cattle-breeding farms and orchards, consumers' cooperatives and agricultural exhibitions'.[102] Soviet radio proudly asserted that Deshmukh had proclaimed that the Soviet Union was 'the best model for the transformation of Indian agriculture'.[103] Yet the events of the year prior and shifting geopolitics belied this claim: several months after leaving Delhi, President Eisenhower signed the largest-ever foodgrains agreement under PL 480. 'The food that we make available under our special programs', Eisenhower noted at the White House, 'will be reflected in India's accelerated progress tomorrow'.[104] Increasingly, that progress would be linked to American models and programmes. The deepening of American assistance provoked worries among Indians, yet this worry was couched in concerns over the weakening of incentives to farmers rather than over Cold War paradigms of 'aid with strings attached'.

More importantly, however, it was clear that the broader mechanisms of agricultural transformation in India were shifting: Soviet aid, always piddling, had shrunk to almost nothing, and the Chinese and Soviet models of collective farming had become politically unpalatable. Subramaniam, as the Food Minister appointed by the new Prime Minister Lal Bahadur Shastri after Nehru's death, was working to implement market incentives and import new food technologies – strategies radically different from those pursued by his predecessors.

In 1963, Chester Bowles returned to India for his second stint as US Ambassador. Speaking at Delhi University shortly after his return, Bowles mused over the Soviet failure in agriculture and the lessons it offered to India. 'Even in the most rigid police state', Bowles said,

> slogans have their limitations, as the Soviet Union has been learning by hard experience. After working for forty years to organize its national agriculture on a mass basis, the small kitchen gardens which Soviet farmers can really call their

own still produce much more efficiently than the rigidly organized state farms where adequate personal incentives are lacking.[105]

In the wake of Nagpur, India's political landscape had begun to shift, and models from the East no longer stood as useful exemplars for Indian agriculture. Proof, perhaps, was in the warm approval that Bowles received from Ashok Mehta. As Chairman of a Foodgrains Enquiry Committee in 1957, Mehta had extolled the virtues of cooperative farming and state trading in foodgrains, even as he excoriated the Soviet experiment and argued instead for a democratic socialism adapted to Indian experience and sentiments. Mehta, as Chairman of India's Planning Commission from 1963 to 1969, agreed with Bowles that technological expedients alone offered a solution to India's food problem:

Mr. Bowles attaches the highest importance to agricultural development now on its way in India. He watches with fostering care the many changes in the rural scene…. Small farm steads operating with modern techniques such as high–yielding seeds, irrigation, and use of fertiliser offer the best prospect for not only optimum agricultural production, but for sturdy and progressive husbandry. [Around] agriculture can and should grow a whole network of small and large industries providing varied opportunities to the people and multi–stream sources of income and work to the rural people.[106]

Mehta wrote these words as India was ushering in radical agricultural transformation. Even as politicking in India's states undermined its authority, the new Food Corporation of India, established with the help of American planners, was emerging as a major player in the stabilization of Indian prices. High-yielding seeds and fertilizers from the United States were taking root throughout the country in land irrigated by new wells. In the wake of Nagpur, the Soviet and Chinese models of agrarian modernity had become non-starters in India. A decade prior, India had indeed been a Cold War battleground – though one contested in the realm of ideologies and imagination of planners, politicians and citizens as much as through the aid extended by the West and the East. At that moment, Nikita Khrushchev had posed a famous challenge to the United States at the beginning of his Indian tour. 'Perhaps', he had asked, 'you would like to compete with us in establishing friendship with the Indians? Let us compete'. A decade later, on the agricultural front, at least, scant notion of competition seemed to remain.

Notes

1 'Soviet food ship arrives', *Times of India*, 1 June 1951.
2 'Gratitude of Indian people', *Izvestiia*, 20 June 1951, in Current Digest of the Russian Press (CDRP) 25: 3.
3 'Russia's desire to help India', *Times of India*, 2 June 1951.
4 'A Soviet food story', *Times of India*, 20 July 1951.

5 Three incisive studies of India's Cold War politics are Boquérat, Gilles (2003), *No Strings Attached?: India's Policies, and Foreign Aid 1947–1966*. New Delhi: Manohar; McMahon, Robert (1994), *The Cold War on the Periphery: the United States, India, and Pakistan*. New York: Columbia University Press; and Merrill, Dennis (1990), *Bread and the Ballot: the United States and India's Economic Development, 1947–1963*. Chapel Hill: University of North Carolina Press. Two excellent recent studies unpack the ideological transformations influencing the Indo–Soviet relationship: Engerman, David (2013), 'Learning from the East: Soviet experts and India in the era of competitive coexistence', *Comparative Studies of South Asia, Africa and the Middle East*, 33(2), 227–238; and Mastny, Vojtech (2010), 'The Soviet Union's partnership with India', *Journal of Cold War Studies*, 12(3), 50–90. On 'food as a weapon', see Paarlberg, Robert (1982), 'Food as an instrument of foreign policy', *Proceedings of the Academy of Political Science*, 34(3), 25–39; and Rothschild, Emma (1976), 'Food Politics', *Foreign Affairs*, 54(2), 285–307.

6 An excellent investigation of Soviet visions overseas is Westad, Odd Arne (2005), *The Global Cold War: Third World Interventions and the Making of Our Times*. Cambridge: Cambridge University Press, 39–73.

7 This point is developed more fully in Siegel, Benjamin (2014), 'Independent India of plenty: Food, hunger, and nation-building in modern India', unpublished PhD dissertation, Harvard University.

8 Rossow Jr., R., Telegram #148, 9 February 1950, 'India Comm. Food 1950 April 1951', Box 42, UD 237, RG 469, US National Archives II, College Park (NARA).

9 Two technical studies of Soviet technology transfer and aid to India are Mehrotra, Santosh K. (1990), *India and the Soviet Union: Trade and Technology Transfer*. Cambridge: Cambridge University Press; and Datar, Asha Laxman (1972), *India's Economic Relations with the USSR and Eastern Europe, 1953 to 1969*. Cambridge: Cambridge University Press.

10 David Engerman notes that

> while the level of its economic aid paled before American largesse … the enthusiasm for planning and rapid industrialization resonated deeply with Third World nationalist movements then coming to power in India and elsewhere …. The superpowers' battle for the hearts and minds of the Third World, in other words, was rarely contested on the same ground. And when it was, in the 1960s, it was ground much more easily won by the Americans than by the Soviets. (Engerman, 2013, 235)

On American experts in India, see Rosen, George (1985), *Western Economists and Eastern Societies: Agents of Change in South Asia, 1950–1970*. Baltimore: Johns Hopkins University Press; on Soviet scholars, see Remnek, Richard B. (1975), *Soviet Scholars and Soviet Foreign Policy: A Case Study in Soviet Policy towards India*. Durham: Carolina Academic Press. See also Sackley, Nicole (2013), 'Village models: Etawah, India, and the making and remaking of development in the early Cold War', *Diplomatic History*, (37)4, 1–30.

11 See Bose, Sugata (1997), 'Instruments and idioms of colonial and national development', in Frederick Cooper and Randall Packard (eds.) (1997), *International Development and the Social Sciences*. Berkeley: University of California Press, 45–63.

12 For an early Russian account of emerging planning in India and its Soviet influences, see Shirokov, G.K. and Reysner, L.I., 'Predystoriya Planirovaniya v Indii', *Voprosy istorii*, August 1968, 49–62.

13 Frankel, Francine (1971), *India's Green Revolution, Economic Gains and Political Costs*. Princeton: Princeton University Press, 13. See also Zachariah, Benjamin (2005), *Developing India: An Intellectual and Social History, c. 1930–50*, New Delhi: Oxford University Press.

14 Nehru, Jawaharlal (1941), *Toward Freedom: The Autobiography of Jawaharlal Nehru*. New York: The John Day Company, 126.

15 Lenin, Vladimir I. (1964) *Collected Works*. Moscow: Foreign Languages Publishing House, 67.

16 (1922), First *Congress of the Toilers of the Far East*, Petrograd: Communist International. On Roy, see Manjapra, Kris (2010), *M.N. Roy: Marxism and Colonial Cosmopolitanism*. London: Routledge.

17 Sawhney, Savitri (2008), *I Shall Never Ask for Pardon*. New Delhi: Penguin Books, 217–221.

18 Visvesvaraya, Mokshagundam (1934), *Planned Economy for India*. Bangalore City: Bangalore Press.

19 Namboodiripad, E.M.S. (1943), *With the Ploughshare and the Sickle: Kisan Sabha in the Campaign for More Food*. Bombay: People's Publishing House.

20 Vaswani, K.N. (1946), *Planning for a New India*. Lahore: Dewan's Publications, 19.

21 Nehru, Jawaharlal, 'Asia redux', in Ramachandra Guha (ed.) (2012), *Makers of Modern India*. Penguin: New Delhi, 340–347.

22 Bhatt, G.D. (1989), *Indo–Soviet Relations and Indian Public Opinion*. Delhi: Pacifier Publications, 8.

23 Naik, J.A. (1995), *Russia's Policy towards India: From Stalin to Yeltsin*. New Delhi: M.D. Publications, 27–28. On the Soviet Union's wartime food shortages, see Moskoff, William (1990), *The Bread of Affliction: The Food Supply in the USSR during World War II*. Cambridge: Cambridge University Press; on food supply after the war, see Zubkova, Elena (1998), *Russia after the War: Hopes, Illusions, and Disappointments, 1945–1957* (trans. Hugh Ragsdale). Armonk, N.Y.: M.E. Sharpe. Indians noted with hope the 500,000 tons of wheat that the Soviet Union had sent to France, though little came of their entreaties to representatives in London. 'Russia Has Food to Spare: Indian Mission Visit Suggested', *Hindustan Times*, 31 May 1946. Meanwhile, India was working to ship Burmese rice through Russia, see 'Import of Burmese Rice through Russia', Food–Rationing–RT–1032/7/1946. National Archives of India, New Delhi.

24 Jain, Jagdishchandra (1947), *Hamari roti ki samasya [Our Food Problem]*. Bombay: National Information and Publications Limited, 40.

25 M.A. Ayyangar, Constituent Assembly of India Debates, 9 November 1948.

26 'Soviet Academy of Sciences' session on the history of India', *Voprosy istorii*, October 1947.

27 'Urgent tasks of Soviet historians of the Orient', *Voprosy istorii*, April 1949, in CDRP 36(1).

28 'American Intrigues in Southeast [Sic] Asia', *Pravda*, 24 December 1950, in CDRP 49(2).

29 (1950), Amerika *ke Sakti Strota*. Washington: US Information Service. See also 'Details of material distributed by Foreign Information Services', in (1954), *Report of the Press Commission*. Vol. 3. New Delhi: Manager, Government of India Press, 377–380. On America's modernizing mission, see Ekbladh, David (2010), *The Great American Mission: Modernization and the Construction of an American World Order*. Princeton: Princeton University Press; and Adas, Michael (2006), *Dominance by Design: Technological Imperatives and America's Civilizing Mission*. Cambridge, MA: Belknap Press.

30 For an extensive analysis of the domestic and international politics of the 1951 shortages, see Siegel (2014).

31 Henderson, L., Telegram #1338, 28 November 1950, 'India Comm. Food 1950 April 1951', Box 42, UD 237, RG 469, NARA.

32 'Secretary's press conference; India's food problem', 16 January 1951, 'Food, General Correspondence, 1951', Box 14, 54D341, RG 59, NARA.

33 '"No bartering away of freedom for food": Mr. Nehru reiterates India's policy', *Times of India*, 7 April 1951.

34 Childs, Telegram #399, 31 January 1951, 'India Comm. Food 1950 April 1951', Box 42, UD 237, RG 469, NARA.

35 Henderson, L., Telegram #2654, 2 April 1951, 'India Comm. Food 1950 April 1951', Box 42, UD 237, RG 469, NARA.

36 Nye, Archibald, Letter to Secretary of State for Commonwealth Relations, 17 May 1951, DO 133/71, UK National Archives (TNA).

37 'Russian grain for India', *Economist*, 16 June 1951.

38 Steere, L., telegram to Secretary of State, 5 October 1951, 'Emblem', Box 1, UD 1234, RG 469, NARA.

39 'This grain comes from America' 1951, 'Emblem', Box 1, UD 1234, RG 469, NARA.

40 Murti, B.S.N. (1953), *Nehru's Foreign Policy*. New Delhi: Beacon Information and Publications, 35.

41 Dunin, M., 'Travel notes: Afghanistan, Pakistan, India', *Literaturnaya gazeta*, 7 August 1951, in CDRP 32(3).

42 Roberts, F.K., minute sheet, 18 November 1950, DO 133/71, TNA.

43 Nye, Archibald, Letter to Secretary of State for Commonwealth Relations, 30 January 1952, DO 133/72, TNA.

44 Truman, Harry S., 'Annual Message to the Congress on the State of the Union', 9 January 1952, online at Gerhard Peters and John T. Woolley's *American Presidency Project*. <http://www.presidency.ucsb.edu/ws/?pid=14418> [accessed 3 March 2014].

45 Boquérat (2003), 142.

46 Borzenko, S., 'On elections in India', *Pravda*, 22 February 1952, in CDRP 8(4).

47 Borzenko, S., 'Americans in India', *Pravda*, 29 March 1952, in CDRP 13(4).

48 Yakovlev, Y., 'USA sends India rotten, worthless wheat', *Pravda*, 13 September 1952, in *CDRP* 37(4). At least one part of this report was accurate: The export of strategic minerals was in reality a condition of American aid, and a source of conflict between Indian and American officials.

49 Borzenko, S., 'Who is getting rich on famine in India?', *Pravda*, 12 October 1952, in CDRP 41(3).

50 'Soviet gesture', *Times of India*, 30 August 1952.

51 Bhatia, V. (1989), *Jawaharlal Nehru: A Study in Indo–Soviet Relations*. New Delhi: Panchsheel Publishers, 51–53.

52 Bowles, Chester (1954), *Ambassador's Report*. New York: Harper, 109.

53 Bowles (1954), 173.

54 Bowles (1954), 171–174.

55 See Phillips, Sarah (forthcoming), *The Price of Plenty: From Farm to Food Politics in Postwar America*. Oxford: Oxford University Press. A contemporary view is Rao, R.P. (1964), *The Helping Hand*. New Delhi: Eurasia Publishing House. The best critical assessment of PL 480 remains Shenoy, B.R. (1974), *PL 480 Aid and India's Food Problem*. New Delhi: Affiliated East-West Press. A more concise survey is Hatti, N. (1977), 'Impact of assistance under P.L. 480 on

Indian economy 1956–1970', *Economy and History* 10(1), 23–40. See also Gupta, S.C. (1965), *Freedom from Foreign Food: Pernicious Effects of PL 480*. Delhi: Blitz National Forum; and Rath, N. and Patvardhan, V.S. (1967), *Impact of Assistance under P.L. 480 on Indian Economy*. Poona: Gokhale Institute of Politics and Economics.

56 Murti (1953), 128.

57 Mahmuduzzafar, S., 'The Soviet Scene: III – On the Land', *Times of India*, 27 May 1953.

58 'Let's get farming', *Aaj* (Benares), 4 February 1951.

59 Myrdal, Gunnar (1968), *Asian Drama*. New York: Pantheon, 1347.

60 (1954), *Soviet Planning: A Comparative Study of the Nature of Economic Planning*. Calcutta: Employers' Association (affiliated to the Indian Chamber of Commerce).

61 On Khrushchev's outreach to India, see Naik (1995), 61–120; and Fursenko, A.A and Naftali, T.J. (2006), *Khrushchev's Cold War: The Inside Story of an American Adversary*. New York: Norton.

62 Ministry of Food and Agriculture, Government of India (1956), *Report of the Indian Agricultural Team to U.S.S.R., Poland and Czechoslovakia, September–October, 1954*, New Delhi, 2.

63 Ministry of Food and Agriculture, Government of India (1956), 159–161.

64 'Soviet tractors for India', *Times of India*, 16 June 1954; 'Soviet showroom for Bombay', *Times of India*, 30 December 1954.

65 'Mechanised farm', *Times of India*, 5 December 1956; 'Soviet farmers' delegation: study tour ends', *Times of India*, 28 November 1956.

66 Khrushchev, Nikita (1954), 'Speech at Delhi State Boy Scout Rally, November 21, 1955', *International Affairs*, 1(2), 175–176.

67 'Soviet friendship for India is genuine', *Times of India*, 23 November 1955.

68 'Soviet guests want to eat in "Thalis"', *Times of India*, 27 November 1955.

69 Bulganin, Nikolai and Khrushchev, Nikita (1956), *Report to the Supreme Soviet on the trip to India, Burma and Afghanistan*. New York: New Century Publishers.

70 Solovyev, Oleg Federovch (1958), *Iz istorii russko-indiiskitch sviazei*. Moscow: Ildatelstvo; Kolpakov, D. (1958), *How the Agrarian Problem Has Been Solved in the U.S.S.R.*, Efimov, G. (ed.). New Delhi: Information Dept. of the USSR.

71 Overstreet, Gene (1958), 'Soviet and Communist Policy in India', *The Journal of Politics*, 20(1), 193.

72 Frankel, Francine (2005), *India's Political Economy, 1947–2004: The Gradual Revolution*. New Delhi: Oxford University Press, 139–142.

73 Goel, Ram Sita (1953), *China Is Red With Peasants' Blood*. Calcutta: Society for Defence of Freedom, 83.

74 See (1956), *Report of the Indian Delegation to China on Agricultural Planning and Techniques*. New Delhi Ministry of Food and Agriculture, Government of India (1957), *Report of the Indian Delegation to China on Agrarian Cooperatives*. New Delhi: Planning Commission, Government of India.

75 Guha, Sunil (1957), *India's Food Problem*. New Delhi: Indian National Congress, 36.

76 Chandra, Jag Parvesh (1956), *India's Socialistic Pattern of Society*. Delhi: Metropolitan Book Co., 153–154.

77 Nair, Kusum (1961), *Blossoms in the Dust: The Human Element in Indian Development*. London: G. Duckworth, 75.

78 Rajagopalachari, C., 'Text of speech on "Land reforms in Japan" delivered by His Excellency Dr. Shiroshi Nasu, Japanese ambassador in India', December 1958, C. Rajagopalachari, VI to XI Insts., Speeches and Writings by Others, 20, Nehru Memorial Museum and Library, New Delhi.

79 Frankel (2005), 161–165. Contemporary accounts are given in (1959), *Co-Operative Farming: The Great Debate between Jawaharlal Nehru, C Rajagopalachari, Jayprakash Narayan, K.M. Munshi, M.R. Masani, N.G. Ranga, Shirman Narayan, Frank Moraes, and Others*. Bombay: Democratic Research Service.

80 Erdman, Howard L. (1967), *The Swatantra Party and Indian Conservatism*. Cambridge: Cambridge University Press, 62.

81 Puri, Balraj (1959), *Cooperative Farming – A Critique*. Calcutta: Institute of Political & Social Studies, 17.

82 Masani, M.R. (1959), *Dangers of the Co–operative Farming*. Nidubrolu, Andhra Pradesh: Peasant Protest Committee.

83 Masani (1959).

84 Frankel (2005), 167–168.

85 Subramaniam, C. (1959), 'Land and food: problems of implementation of Congress Party policy', in *Ooty Seminar: Papers Discussed*. New Delhi: All India Congress Committee, 129.

86 Dobbs, J.A., 'Visit of Soviet delegation to India', 14 March 1958, FO 371/135946, TNA.

87 A 1959 joint Anglo–US report suggested, with some satisfaction, that 'Soviet economic aid to India has not generated any sympathy for Communists among the Indian people'. See 'Impact of Soviet aid on India', *Times of India*, 25 November 1959.

88 See Frankel (2005), chapters 5, 6 and 7.

89 'The Indo–American program: A brief resume (1952–1958)', Contracts: Indo–American Team 1955–58, Box 3, P446, RG 286, NARA.

90 A superlative account of these Community Development projects is Immerwahr, Daniel (2011), 'Quests for community: The United States, community development, and the world, 1935–1965', unpublished PhD dissertation, University of California, Berkeley, 54–90.

91 Calendar 1958, Box 111, P46, RG 306, NARA.

92 Wilson, G. (1956), *A National Farmers' Organisation in India*. New Delhi: Farmers' Forum, 10.

93 (1959), 'Farewell to farm leaders going to U.S.A.', *Krishak Samachar* 3(10), 1.

94 The United States Information Service produced a short film on the US pavilion: *From This Land* (1960). In it, an Indian peasant, 'Ram Lal', resists adopting new agricultural techniques until visiting the American exhibition.

95 'Old and new mix at fair in India', *New York Times*, 12 December 1959.

96 'Handsome U.S. hit in India', *Life*, 25 January 1960.

97 Eisenhower, Dwight D. (1959), 'Remarks at the Opening of the World Agriculture Fair, New Delhi', online by Gerhard Peters and John T. Woolley, *The American Presidency Project*. <http://www.presidency.ucsb.edu/ws/?pid=11618> [accessed 1 March 2014].

98 'Mr. Eisenhower calls for war on hunger: 4-point theme given at Delhi fair', *Times of India*, 12 December 1959.

99 Khrushchev, Nikita (2004), *Memoirs of Nikita Khrushchev*. University Park: Pennsylvania State University, 743.

100 'Interest in projects: Soviet leader at agriculture fair', *Times of India*, 12 February 1960.

101 For a more detailed account, see 'Mr. N.S. Khrushchev's visit', in V. Choudhary (ed.) (1995), *Dr. Rajendra Prasad: Correspondence and Select Documents: Presidency Period – The Last Phase*. New Delhi: Allied Publishers Ltd., 381–391.

102 'Visit to Russia: Ministers to study farm development', *Times of India*, 25 July 1960.

103 'Indian agricultural delegation', United States Foreign Broadcast Information Service Daily Reports, 31 July 1960.

104 Eisenhower, Dwight D. (1958), *Public Papers of the Presidents of the United States, Dwight D. Eisenhower: Containing the Public Messages, Speeches, and Statements of the President, 20 January 1953 to 20 January 1961*. Washington: US Government Printing Office, 136.

105 Bowles, Chester (1969), *A View from New Delhi: Selected Speeches and Writings*. New Haven: Yale University Press, 13.

106 Bowles (1969), 3–4.

Key texts

Boquérat, Gilles. (2003). *No Strings Attached?: India's Policies and Foreign Aid 1947–1966*. New Delhi: Manohar.

Engerman, David. (2013). 'Learning from the East: Soviet experts and India in the era of competitive coexistence'. *Comparative Studies of South Asia, Africa and the Middle East*, 33(2), 227–238.

Frankel, Francine. (2005). *India's Political Economy, 1947–2004: The Gradual Revolution*. New Delhi: Oxford University Press.

McMahon, Robert. (1994). *The Cold War on the Periphery: The United States, India, and Pakistan*. New York: Columbia University Press.

Merrill, Dennis. (1990). *Bread and the Ballot: The United States and India's Economic Development, 1947–1963*. Chapel Hill: University of North Carolina Press.

Naik, J.A. (1995). *Russia's Policy towards India: From Stalin to Yeltsin*. New Delhi: M.D. Publications.

Westad, Odd Arne. (2005). *The Global Cold War: Third World Interventions and the Making of Our Times*. Cambridge: Cambridge University Press.

CHAPTER 2
'THE LIFE AND DEATH OF OUR REPUBLIC': MODERNIZATION, AGRICULTURAL DEVELOPMENT AND THE PEASANTRY IN THE MEKONG DELTA IN THE LONG 1970s
Simon Toner

For leaders of newly independent states after 1945, the superpowers offered the most obvious and attractive models of development.[1] While the Soviet Union provided postcolonial elites with a model for agricultural collectivization and central planning, in the early Cold War period, American social scientists feared that the United States did not offer a clear blueprint for postcolonial leaders seeking to mould their societies in the American image. As the focus of the Cold War shifted in the 1950s and the 1960s from Europe to the new nation states in Asia and Africa, these social scientists sought to develop a theoretical framework that would help American policymakers as well as Third World elites understand and guide postcolonial development.[2] Although scholars have noted the earlier antecedents of modernization theory, its formulation as a social science theory and its focus on the postcolonial nation state were direct responses to decolonization and the Cold War.[3]

As Nils Gilman has highlighted, modernization theorists viewed postcolonial societies narrowly. These were all 'traditional': economically unsophisticated, fearful of change and passive towards nature. Modern society, sociologist Edward Shils elucidated, meant an economy based on 'rational technology', education, urbanization and industrialization. All of this required planning; modernization required technocrats, statisticians and engineers. States had to intervene in the economy, control the rate of savings and investment and build factories, roads and irrigation systems.[4] Modernization was thus an elite experiment, as urban technocrats devised social engineering projects and imposed them on supposedly malleable peasant societies.

Modernization theorists argued that American technical assistance programmes could guide peasant societies away from rebellion by making peasant farmers aware that change was possible. In a report submitted to the US Senate in 1960, the Massachusetts Institute of Technology's Centre for International Studies – the institution most closely associated with modernization theory – suggested that agricultural modernization would require 'radical changes' not only in farmers' knowledge, 'but in their values, their perception of alternatives and their motivation.'[5] Walt Rostow, perhaps the most famous proponent of modernization theory, argued that 'a requirement for take-off is … a class of farmers willing and able to respond to the possibilities opened up for them' by new techniques and agricultural arrangements.[6] The modernizing state was responsible for creating these possibilities. Once the psychology of the peasant farmer had changed, higher agricultural production would create a surplus that could be invested in new industrial enterprises. Farmers would become a market for new industries, as consumer products spread beyond the city.

Modernization theory did not go uncontested. In the 1950s, advocates of community-development projects favoured small-scale, grass-roots development that took account of local conditions and needs.[7] But by the 1960s, modernization theory was the dominant development discourse in the United States. Michael Latham has argued that modernization theory did not have an exclusive determinative effect on development policy on the ground but became the ideology guiding US relations with the postcolonial world during the Kennedy administration because it resonated with older strands of American thought and provided a lens through which US policymakers could view the postcolonial world.[8] Therefore, modernization-as-policy did not always directly reflect modernization theory.

Particularly in its more authoritarian forms, modernization theory was the American manifestation of what James Scott has termed 'high modernism', the uncritical mid-century faith shared by many political elites and technocrats that a centralizing state could master nature and comprehensively plan 'human settlement and production'. However, as Scott notes, high modernist faith existed across the political spectrum.[9] While postcolonial elites might have shared US modernization theorists' faith in science, technology and planning, US theorists and policymakers frequently found these elites did not follow their prescriptions to the letter. For new leaders, development was much more about charting the quickest route from 'underdevelopment' to modernity than it was a means of showing ideological commitment in the Cold War. Theorists and policymakers believed that economic convergence with the American model would lead to cultural convergence but found that modernizing nations often built on their cultural and local particularities.[10]

An examination of state-led agricultural development in Vietnam's Mekong Delta in the long 1970s demonstrates the difficulty that postcolonial states had in implementing modernization projects. Both the non-communist Republic of (South) Vietnam (1955–1975) and the communist Socialist Republic of Vietnam (SRV) (1976–) had a high modernist vision for agricultural development, if not always the means to carry it out. Both states pursued specific agricultural modernization projects that envisioned the state guiding a malleable peasantry to serve its economic interests. While several factors account for the failure of each states' policies, throughout the period, peasant responses to state projects proved one of the major obstacles to success. Peasant behaviour frequently did not correspond with the state's vision and often indirectly undermined it.

From 1967 until the fall of Saigon in 1975, the South Vietnamese government (GVN) promoted the widespread cultivation of high-yielding rice varieties (HYVs). These efforts focused primarily on the Mekong Delta, the country's agricultural heartland. In reasoning that was strikingly similar to American 'developmentalist' thought, government planners believed that Green Revolution technology could transform subsistence peasant farmers into commercial agriculturalists. HYVs had the potential to end South Vietnam's dependency on imported food and even raised the prospect of exports. At the same time, GVN officials hoped that wealthy farmers would turn their backs on the National Liberation Front (NLF), joining the ranks of government supporters. While these programmes led to a greater commercialization of agriculture and increased prosperity in the countryside, the GVN could not turn this to its economic advantage. Instead, farmers responded to the market in ways the state could not anticipate or control.

Inspired by the Soviet and Chinese models of development, after 1975 the reunified Vietnamese state under the leadership of the Communist Party in Hanoi tried to extend agricultural collectivization, which had begun in the north in 1958, into southern Vietnam. That effort failed in large part because of GVN and NLF policies and the social and economic dislocation of wartime prior to 1975, which helped shape a 'class of independent tillers' in the delta who, after 1975, would become the fiercest opponents of collectivization.[11] The response of these farmers was an important factor compelling the state to reassess its development vision. The challenges that confronted the two Vietnamese states demonstrate the difficulties of postcolonial development in a heavily contested theatre of the Cold War.

Development or destruction? Agricultural modernization before the Tet Offensive

Rural development was a crucial aspect of the Vietnam wars, particularly in the southern Mekong Delta. During the war against the French, the Viet Minh, a communist-led nationalist movement, assassinated landlords, reduced rents and redistributed land. This secured widespread support among the peasantry.[12] Under the provisions of the Geneva Agreement in 1954, Vietnam was divided along the seventeenth parallel into military regroupment areas, which would reunite under one government following planned elections in 1956.[13] Viet Minh cadres were obliged to regroup to the north, although many remained behind in the remnants of the French colonial state in the south. By 1955, Ngo Dinh Diem had manoeuvred his way to the presidency of the Republic of Vietnam south of the seventeenth parallel and an alliance with the United States.

Some historians portray Diem as a tradition-bound conservative and American puppet.[14] An emerging view in the historiography argues that Diem had a unique vision for rural development that combined elements of high modernism with his personal interpretation of community development. Through a series of programmes, such as land development, Agrovilles and Strategic Hamlets, Diem sought increased agricultural output, political loyalty to the Saigon regime and strategic advantage against the communists.[15] However, the regime's exacting and coercive demands on peasants' labour, its refusal to hold the 1956 elections and its indiscriminate crackdown on suspected communists led to 'profound resentment'.[16] By 1957, dozens of armed units had responded to this repression and began to operate against GVN forces. Fearing Diem's consolidation of power and under pressure from the remaining southern Viet Minh cadres, Hanoi moved towards a more combative stance, culminating in the formation of the NLF in December 1960. One scholar describes this as 'a northern response to genuine peasant uprisings'.[17] By early 1961, the GVN had lost large areas of the countryside and controlled less than half of South Vietnam's population.[18]

As the war in the countryside intensified and the United States began to deploy troops in 1965 to shore up the South Vietnamese regime, the agricultural economy was devastated. Forces sprayed herbicides, bombed hamlets and established free-fire zones. These actions sought to deny the NLF forces access to the peasantry, who the NLF relied on for their taxation, food and recruitment base.[19] South Vietnamese and American officials managed to reconcile this massive destruction with the notion that agricultural modernization in GVN areas could win peasants to the side of the government and help build a viable state.[20] Yet for all Lyndon Johnson's talk of exporting the Great Society to the Third World, South Vietnam went from being the world's third largest exporter of rice in 1963 to depending heavily on imported rice.[21] The GVN subsidized rice to ensure some urban stability, but this proved a disincentive to rural production. In a memo to Johnson in June 1966, Robert Komer, Washington's pacification chief in Vietnam, wrote that despite eleven years' effort, 'we've accomplished so little in agriculture'.[22] In this context, peasant farmers rather than the weak South Vietnamese state acted as the agents of agricultural innovation. Responding to the damaged agricultural infrastructure, these peasants adapted boat motors into pumps to manage water levels in rice paddies.[23]

Scholars have argued that the 1968 Tet Offensive marked 'the death knell' of modernization theory, as after that point the United States abandoned any hope of building a viable nation in the south.[24] Yet, as Brad Simpson argues, the late 1960s and the 1970s saw a shift away from large infrastructural projects towards authoritarian regimes' use of population control and Green Revolution technologies. The central tenets of 'modernization theory-*cum* policy' continued to inform these efforts.[25] Certainly, South Vietnam's experience with modernization did not fit the theorists' vision. War, rather than agricultural change, had induced urbanization. The economy was based heavily on serving the American war machine, while American aid targeted inflation, privileging urban dwellers and short-term stability over rural producers and long-term development. Yet none of this stopped GVN planners from drawing on the tenets of modernization. Indeed, government economists sometimes explicitly employed Rostow's rhetoric of 'economic take-off' (*nen kinh te co the cat khoi mat dat*).[26] For many planners in Saigon, state-led modernization projects continued to offer the most promising formula for economic growth and counter-revolutionary nation-building. However, in the context of the economic and social dislocation noted above, modernization followed a distinctly Vietnamese pattern.

The Green Revolution comes to South Vietnam

Hanoi did not achieve its maximum goal of a 'general offensive, general uprising' during the Tet Offensive, but its impact on the American war effort forced the Johnson and later Nixon administrations to reconfigure the US commitment to Vietnam. By mid-1969, Richard Nixon settled on the strategy of 'Vietnamization', turning the war over to the South Vietnamese as American troops withdrew and, paradoxically, escalating the war beyond South Vietnam's borders into Cambodia and Laos. Nixon's National Security Adviser, Henry Kissinger, also began secret negotiations with Hanoi. With little room for manoeuvre, South Vietnamese President Nguyen Van Thieu complied with this strategy. In return, Nixon promised Thieu four years of increased military aid and another four of economic aid in Nixon's second term.[27]

Vietnamization came at a time of renewed energy and confidence on the Saigon side. In June 1969, Thieu announced that 'general mobilization and the rapid progress in pacification and rural development' had made Vietnamization feasible.[28] Thieu's confidence reflected the NLF's devastating losses in 1968 and Saigon's recovery of many rural areas in late 1968 and early 1969. But this was a precarious security balance at best. In order for Vietnamization to work in the long run, Thieu said, 'South Vietnam must become stronger politically, militarily, and economically.'[29] Rural pacification and agricultural development in Mekong Delta became the twin pillars of this effort. The sixteen provinces of the Delta and Long An accounted for South Vietnam's surplus rice-producing area, and 75 per cent of the country's total rice production. The rest of the country was deficient in rice supplies, relying on the delta or imports to meet demand.

As South Vietnamese agricultural production declined in the mid-1960s, scientists at the Ford Foundation-funded International Rice Research Institute (IRRI) in the Philippines were cross-breeding rice to create high-yield varieties. Traditional rice varieties produced lower yields, and their longer stems meant that even if they responded well to fertilizer, they would become top-heavy and fall over, or 'lodge'. Moreover, traditional rice varieties could only produce one crop a year. IR8, the first strain of 'miracle rice' developed in 1965 and released the following year, matured in 125 days, responded well to fertilizer and did not lodge, thanks to its shorter stem.[30] It could produce yields two to three times higher than the two-ton average of varieties common to Southeast Asia, and in optimum conditions a farmer could grow two or even three crops a year.

In addition to miracle rice's ability to produce higher yields, it appealed to modernizers because it could act as a social solvent, transforming the work habits and psychology of the peasant farmer – and in turn the entire agricultural economy. As Cullather argues, IRRI's work proceeded from the notion that peasants were not yet rational economic actors, but Green Revolution technology could make them so.[31] Because IR8 required higher applications of chemical fertilizer and pesticides, farmers would have to make potentially risky investments in return for higher yields and higher profits. As one American adviser put it, the new rice would 'require substantial alteration of centuries old-farming habits and methods'.[32] In other words, it was precisely the kind of technology modernizers had sought to pull the economically isolated peasant into an agricultural-industrial complex.

Much like American developmental thinkers and policymakers, GVN planners identified poverty as the cause of rebellion; the peasantry's support for the NLF, they believed, resulted from violent coercion and economic privation. Increases in rural wealth, these officials hoped, would undermine the NLF. As Minister of Economy Pham Kim Ngoc put it, Saigon must give 'the rural people … a stake in the prosperity or they will destroy it, with guns or with votes'.[33] Miracle rice was particularly promising in this respect, since it had the potential to break the peasants' bonds with the NLF by creating economic incentives that would encourage farmers to act in individual rather than communal interest.[34] These economic incentives also encouraged farmers to produce larger surpluses, which could feed South Vietnam's deficit areas and perhaps even generate exports. In this sense, the commercialization of agriculture would serve the interests of the fragile state. Although this alone would not resolve Saigon's economic and political woes, it would demonstrate some measure of economic viability to American and international audiences, as well as to Hanoi. The goal, a Ministry of Land Reform and Agriculture (MLRA) document noted, was not only to win the war but also to develop the country 'through a social revolution beginning in the countryside'.[35]

Saigon's development projects focused on incremental wealth increases in contrast to the NLF's redistributive policies.[36] The miracle rice project proceeded from much the same point of view largely by default. Early strains of miracle rice required specific cultivating conditions including level land and access to a manageable freshwater supply. Such conditions were far more prevalent in the central part of the delta than in the rest of the country. Farmers could, and many did, grow miracle rice on suboptimal land, but they almost certainly could not double-crop or produce as high yields. The MLRA encouraged those peasants without adequate land to modernize within the limits possible. But the focus, director of cabinet in the MLRA Tran Quang Minh noted, was to create a 'sizeable corps' of 'progressive farmers'.[37] USAID framed the issue in similar terms, noting in 1969 that South Vietnam could once again export rice 'even if only 30% of small farmers in Vietnam would engage in modern cultural practices'.[38] These were what the NLF termed 'middle' and 'rich peasants', those with sufficient access to land, inputs and credit to benefit from the Green Revolution. The GVN sought to harness these farmers' productive capacity. Thus, the miracle rice programme further aggravated social stratification in the countryside.

In January 1968, following small-scale experiments with miracle rice – now renamed 'Than Nong' (TN) rice after the Vietnamese god of agriculture – the MLRA launched the Accelerated Rice Production Program.[39] Minister Ton That Trinh announced that the goal was to plant 44,000 hectares of new varieties that year and to attain rice self-sufficiency within four years.[40] This was an ambitious goal for a war-torn country heavily dependent on imported food. But it indicated the GVN's hopes for the new technology as a tool for counter-revolutionary economic development. To get the programme started, the GVN and USAID distributed miracle rice kits and launched a 'supervised credit' programme through which farmers received financial and technical assistance to grow miracle rice in return for a pledge to follow the correct cultivation practices.[41] Provincial agricultural services established demonstration plots along well-travelled roads to ensure that passing farmers saw them. Advisers were encouraged to host field days to show local farmers and officials the plots' success.[42] The belief of senior MLRA officials that provincial agricultural cadre could guide the process of agricultural development proved as misplaced as their assumption that the peasantry existed along a tradition–modernity axis. Provincial officials, American and South Vietnamese, found themselves struggling to control events, while peasant farmers proved once again the agents of innovation, as the seeds proliferated beyond GVN-controlled programmes.[43] By 1969, USAID estimated that at least 70,000 farmers had independently adopted TN rice.[44] While the new rice reached some NLF areas, the need for fertilizer, credit and security dictated that most of these farmers were in GVN areas. The proliferation of the new rice was good news for agricultural output, but it became clear almost immediately that tracking the number of plots and volume of rice would be 'practically impossible'.[45]

The GVN also launched the Accelerated Rice Production Programme at an inauspicious time, just a month before the Tet Offensive. This meant that civilian advisers followed American and South Vietnamese military forces as they pulled back to defend towns and cities. Dikes and paddies were further damaged, and marketing links between the delta and Saigon were disrupted for weeks.[46] By April 1968, however, joint GVN-USAID surveys of the provinces suggested that damage was not as bad as originally suspected, and the year's rice production goals might still be met.[47] Average yields for the second harvest in the autumn of 1968 were more than double those of indigenous varieties.[48] Despite the tremendous destruction in the countryside in 1968, rice shipments from the delta to Saigon were slightly higher than 1967.[49] Interviews with farmers in GVN-controlled areas suggest they were genuinely enthusiastic about the new rice varieties, and many associated their introduction with the government.[50] Eager after the results of the 1968 effort, the MLRA set a target of planting 200,000 hectares of TN rice for the following year, and Minister Trinh declared that 'Vietnam will probably return to her position [as] a rice exporting country in the near future'.[51]

TN rice also became more closely associated with rural pacification.[52] Beginning on 1 November 1968, US and Army of the Republic of Vietnam (ARVN) forces launched the Accelerated Pacification Campaign (APC), taking advantage of the NLF's Tet Offensive losses and the resultant power vacuum in rural areas. The GVN established rural security posts in villages' central hamlets along roads and canals and regained control of many NLF areas in the Mekong Delta. Outlying hamlets were bombed and shelled, forcing the population in previously revolutionary areas to relocate around GVN posts.[53] The spread of TN rice closely followed military operations, but only those with land close to GVN posts could benefit from government agricultural programmes. Many peasants found themselves far from their fields, which had become free-fire zones.[54]

While there was certainly a contradiction between development and security, increased government control in the delta from 1969 to 1971 opened up space for development projects in a way not seen since the early 1960s. Although the GVN acknowledged that less than 50 per cent of the country's arable land was under cultivation, 1969 was the first year in which the declining rice production trend was reversed, and the following year the MLRA claimed to have exceeded its target of 500,000 hectares of TN rice.[55] Both American and GVN officials repeatedly suggested that self-sufficiency and exports were just around the corner.[56] Even the reconfiguration of the global rice trade could not dampen such enthusiasm: with so many rice-producing nations approaching self-sufficiency, thanks to miracle rice, export potential by 1969 lay in aromatic and luxury strains.[57] Cao Van Than, the new Minister of Agriculture, wrote that the ministry's targets for 1970–1971 were to increase TN cultivation to meet domestic needs, with the goal of exporting 300,000 tonnes of non-TN varieties.[58] This was hopelessly optimistic, as the economic incentives of South Vietnam's Green Revolution led most farmers to cultivate TN rice for the market. Against this improbable backdrop Saigon launched two projects: the Land-to-the-Tiller programme in 1970 and a Five-Year National Agricultural Development Plan in 1971. The perceived success and continued faith the regime placed in TN rice as a tool for reshaping rural society in its battle against Hanoi was central to these programmes.

The Land-to-the-Tiller (LTTT) programme sought to eliminate tenancy by expropriating land, compensating landlords and redistributing land free of charge to tenant farmers. It was, as one historian notes, 'a massive attempt at social engineering' in that it sought to sway the loyalties of the peasantry towards the government.[59] Several scholars argue that political results of the LTTT were ambiguous. Only the flight of landlords to the cities made the programme politically feasible, while the depopulation of the countryside and military mobilization created a shortage of labour and a surplus of land. The programme may have undermined support for the revolution by granting farmers permanent title to their land, but this support did not necessarily shift to the GVN. Peasants frequently had chosen their loyalties based on the NLF's earlier land reform programmes or were increasingly motivated simply by self-interest and a desire to survive.[60]

Saigon planners hoped that new owners would invest in their land and increase production.[61] Thieu told farmers that once they became owners, they must defend their land against the communists and 'increase production to help the country soon attain self-sufficiency'.[62] However, the economic impact of the programme depended greatly on geography. In the coastal lowlands north of the delta, where the war continued unabated, higher population pressure and less available land meant that the LTTT only affected 5 per cent of the area, with most farmers remaining on marginal plots.[63] Even in some parts of the delta itself, low-yield floating rice was the norm, and the LTTT's three-hectare redistribution rate was far too low for these farmers to engage in commercial agriculture.[64] In contrast, studies indicated that where the GVN had redistributed land in some areas of the delta, farmers had dramatically increased their marketable surplus.[65] The LTTT may therefore have formalized a situation in which some farmers had sufficient arable land to engage in commercial agriculture, while others did not. Many of these better-off farmers would most strongly oppose collectivization after 1975.

As GVN planners framed it, the government was successfully guiding rural modernization. The authors of the Five-Year Rural Economic Development Plan wrote that government efforts in the promotion of miracle rice had reversed agricultural decline and created the potential for agricultural diversification. The authors wrote that 'a majority of our rural people are no longer as conservative as before' having 'understood and accepted new farming techniques'.[66] The plan's goals were self-sufficiency in food production in the first phase (1971–1972) and agricultural exports in the second (1973–1975). These exports would raise foreign exchange and encourage investment in light industries that would process agricultural products for global markets.[67] This was remarkably ambitious and even unrealistic for a state that was still at war and had merely achieved a precarious security situation in some parts of the country. Indeed, one National Assemblyman argued that the GVN was wishing for 'a prosperity that could only be had in one's imagination'.[68]

Saigon's optimism was not entirely baseless. The country had made advances in agricultural production. The GVN estimated that rice output increased by almost 50 per cent from 1968–1969 to 1971–1972.[69] Markets were bustling, and consumer goods such as Honda motorbikes flooded the countryside. Even reasonably partial observers were impressed. 'Rural prosperity' in the delta 'is a fact of life', the UK embassy noted in early 1970, 'and the IR8 programme is an undoubted success'.[70] By 1973, 1.1 million hectares of land had been distributed to some 800,000 farming families under the provisions of the LTTT. USAID research indicated that the new landowners were more likely to make risky investments, adopt new agricultural techniques and purchase consumer goods.[71] As the modernizers had predicted, a stratum of middle and rich peasant farmers in the delta had seized on a new agricultural technology and turned to commercial agriculture. However, the consequences of rural change were not what the modernizers anticipated. For several reasons, these developments did not redound to the GVN's economic advantage.

MLRA officials placed their faith in TN rice for its increased production; however, accelerating production proved less problematic than processing, storing and especially marketing surplus grain. Even as production increased and security improved, rice shipments to Saigon repeatedly failed to meet GVN planners' estimates. Even in the improved security environment of 1970–1971, the delta's waterways remained insecure, and roads and highways were inadequate to handle increased volumes of grain. In addition, a small number of merchants dominated all aspects of the rice economy. For all of the GVN's pretensions of guidance, control and planning, lack of competition meant that these merchants could control the market and manipulate prices.[72] They could reap handsome profits without delivering more rice to Saigon.

The GVN, on the other hand, had inaccurate or conflicting data on production, consumption and demography, inhibiting the rationalization of imports or creation of market incentives for farmers to sell and merchants to deliver to Saigon. Particularly revealing was that the MLRA – responsible for increasing production – and the Ministry of Economy – responsible for scheduling imports – disagreed on rice production levels.[73] GVN agricultural officials at the provincial level, frustrated with the lack of ministry coordination, argued that farmers would respond to incentives if marketing prospects were good.[74] Certainly, GVN officials tried to assert control by intervening in the rice market, reducing subsidies on imported rice or guaranteeing prices.[75] The GVN also tried to maintain security stocks to prevent market disturbances. But in a volatile economy, merchants and consumers speculated on these. Ngoc, in particular, tried to rationalize the rice market, pushing – with US backing – for the elimination of the heavier subsidies on rice in the northern provinces. This encouraged false demand, speculation and a black market in which government and military officials were implicated.[76] Thus, such measures had limited impact.

The trouble with turning peasant farmers into 'rational economic actors' in this unstable, inflationary economy was that 'rationality' encouraged speculative behaviour. An early indication of farmers engaging in such speculative behaviour came in 1969. Despite a bumper crop and increased security, farmers decided to hold on to their stocks as prices steadily rose and eventually doubled during the year. As a result, Saigon had to schedule emergency imports.[77] In 1970, as rice prices fell and hog prices rose, USAID estimated that farmers diverted large volumes of rice to feed livestock. To shore up prices and ensure deliveries to Saigon in 1970, the GVN had to increase its share of the market greatly.[78] In June 1970, Ngoc wrote that rice shipments from the delta to Saigon were far below previous projections, and the GVN would have to sign agreements with the United States for additional imports.[79] USAID hinted at peasant speculation again the following year when it noted that farmers in Long An were 'aggressively developing greater on-farm storage facilities', which would allow them to store rice until prices rose.[80] In early 1971, USAID estimated that there was enough surplus rice in the delta to meet 97 per cent of national needs. However, government rice procurement that year fell well below GVN targets.[81] In order to become self-sufficient in a meaningful way, and given the negligible private rice trade between the delta and the north of the country, the GVN had to procure rice from the delta and ship it to the provinces north of Saigon. When procurement targets went unmet, the GVN had to request further rice imports from the United States. The peasantry, it seems, was responsive to the market. But increased security in the delta, land reform and the financial incentives created by the Green Revolution did not benefit the state economically. Rather, it seems to have increased the economic leverage of wealthier farmers vis-à-vis the state.

In March 1972, the North Vietnamese army and PLAF launched a military offensive throughout the south, shattering the precarious security situation in the delta. Although US airpower stalled the offensive by October, Hanoi had inserted a huge number of North Vietnamese troops into South Vietnam, and the NLF once again made inroads into the countryside. The years 1969–1971 offered an opportunity for the GVN to take advantage of an improved rural security situation to increase the economic viability of the state. Yet while a stratum of commercial farmers emerged and rice production increased, the GVN could not meaningfully benefit from this, and rice imports continued. After 1972, the opportunities for such economic development were severely circumscribed by escalating violence in the delta.

Every grain a bullet: The rice war

In January 1973, the United States and North Vietnam signed the Paris Agreements leading to the withdrawal of American troops and a ceasefire that recognized NLF control of some parts of South Vietnam: Nixon and Kissinger had compelled Thieu to accept a 'leopard-spot' ceasefire that left pockets of South Vietnamese territory under the official administrative and military control of the NLF's Provisional Revolutionary Government (PRG). The peace agreements thus did not end the war, and particularly in the delta, violence and land-grabbing continued. By late summer, a 'rice war' had developed, with both sides struggling for crop control.

In August 1973, the GVN National Intelligence Coordinating Committee reported that in an effort to 'undermine the national economy', communists were paying high prices for unripe rice in the delta.[82] The GVN Social and Economic Council noted that with the communists using rice as a 'weapon', changes in the superpowers' policies and likely problems with further food imports, rice had become 'the life and death of our Vietnam Republic'. To increase production and stabilize the market, the 'only solution is government intervention, guidance, and support to implement the procurement, storage, processing system'. Efforts to promote production that were not coupled with these measures would only benefit the enemy and 'dishonest merchants'.[83] In August, in response to Thieu's request for information on food policies in North Vietnam, the Commissioner for National Central Intelligence noted that although North Vietnam was stepping up its production of IR8 – which the North had 'stolen' from the South – the country would be far short of 1973 rice requirements. It was reported that the North would have to reduce rations, increase productivity and import food from China and the Soviet Union, and still Hanoi would not have enough to feed its 400,000 troops in the South. As such, 'the communists planned to move large amounts of money to buy rice, wheat, and staples' in South Vietnam. Saigon was evidently unaware of the considerable cuts in Chinese and Soviet aid, which made Hanoi's food supply in the South even more tenuous.[84]

As the rice war developed in the summer and autumn of 1973, the GVN launched an economic blockade of PRG territory and enforced strict rice policies. With so many enemy troops in South Vietnam, Thieu believed rice had acquired military, rather than economic, significance. He ordered his forces to 'consider every grain of rice as a bullet'.[85] The formation of the National Food Administration (NFA) in December marked a more interventionist GVN strategy as it acquired a 50 per cent share in the rice market and exercised greater control on rice distribution.[86] Strict blockade measures included prohibitions on movement of rice between villages, restrictions on rice-milling, storage of rice in homes and sale to anyone but GVN-authorized buyers.[87] Addressing GVN employees on 28 December 1973, Thieu said that the blockade played an important role in delaying a communist offensive, and must be maintained 'to the fullest extent possible'.[88]

Thieu hoped that the blockade would atrophy the shadow PRG state within South Vietnam, but in fact it served to choke the rice market and exacerbate a recession that had begun as American forces withdrew. With communists paying high prices for rice in the delta and the rising price of inputs, the low price offered by the NFA proved unattractive to many farmers.[89] Meanwhile, cuts in American economic aid and the spike in prices brought on by the 1973 oil crisis had a devastating impact on South Vietnamese agriculture. Fertilizer and rice prices soared, while fuel and spare parts were increasingly rare.[90] Rice shortages in large parts of the country in 1974 and 1975 led to urban protest, and growing non-communist opposition to Thieu linked these shortages to government corruption.[91]

Thieu's plan to use rice as a lever in the war thus faltered and failed. After the discovery of oil off the coast of South Vietnam in October 1974, and as Hanoi launched its final offensive two months later, an increasingly desperate GVN vested its hope in oil, rather than rice, as the new saviour of the republic. Prime Minister Khiem argued that the GVN strategy should be to 'buy time' until oil could be exported, 'probably in 1976'.[92] As the regime crumbled, the GVN rice procurement and distribution system failed. At one point in March 1975, government rice stocks at the critical port of Qui Nhon – one of only three major ports in central South Vietnam – were entirely depleted.[93] When Saigon fell on 30 April, the GVN had proved incapable of feeding its population, let alone mobilizing agriculture as the saviour of the republic.

Socializing the South

For party leaders in Hanoi, the twin goals of the revolution were national liberation and social transformation.[94] After liberating the south in April 1975, they focused on land reform and the collectivization of agriculture. Collectivization would follow the same pattern it had in the north, first with landholdings redistributed, then farmers organized into work exchange or production teams, followed by low-rank cooperatives and finally high-rank cooperatives. Each step would see a higher concentration of ownership of the means of production in the hands of the cooperative. Thousands of advisers were dispatched from the North to organize production teams.[95] In the Mekong Delta, however, the effort did not proceed far beyond the first stage of land redistribution. Ironically, IRRI rice became part of this effort. To compel larger landowners to share their land with the land-poor, the state required farmers to adopt high-yield varieties. The labour requirements of these varieties meant that larger landowners could not manage all their farmland and had to lend some to others.[96] By 1983, IRRI varieties accounted for more than 65 per cent of rice in the delta.[97] Despite these efforts, the experiment in the delta did not last long. Peasant responses once again undermined the state's modernizing vision and efforts at food procurement.

In many respects, collectivization in the delta after 1975 failed because of the socio-economic transformation brought about by GVN and NLF policies as well as the economic and social dislocation of the war prior to 1975. Opposition to collectivization had been muted in North Vietnam in part because the state was able to mobilize patriotic sentiment during the American war. While northern collectivization came on the heels of land reform, in the south the state attempted to implement collectivization as much as two decades after the Viet Minh and NLF had redistributed to tenant farmers. NLF and GVN land reform as well as the GVN's agricultural development policies created a class of upper middle and middle peasants who jealously guarded their privileges after 1975.[98] The availability of labour-saving devices that had flooded the Mekong Delta prior to 1975 also made labour-intensive collectivization less appealing than it had been to peasants in the north in the late 1950s. Peasants in the delta slaughtered or sold livestock, uprooted orchards and destroyed crops rather than seeing them collectivized, while some lay down in front of tractors ploughing collectivized land. State food procurement decreased dramatically, leading to severe shortages by the end of the decade. Thus while GVN policies between 1968 and 1974 had not translated into political or economic advantage for the GVN, the commercialization of agriculture and land reform, as well as NLF reforms, did lead to socio-economic changes in the delta that one scholar argues 'immunized' the delta from collectivization.[99] War with Cambodia and China in the late 1970s also complicated Hanoi's efforts to repopulate the countryside and exacerbated the crisis.[100]

By 1986 only 6 per cent of farm households in the delta were organized in production teams or low-rank cooperatives, compared with 90 per cent along the central coast. The failure of collectivization was not simply the result of resistance in the south. In the north, local arrangements between farm households and cooperative managers outside the cooperative system had proved more productive since the 1960s. As state grain procurement declined in the late 1970s, compounded by the failure of collectivization in the Mekong Delta, officials began paying more attention to these local experiments.[101] Directive 100 in January 1981 was the state's response to events already under way at the local level. It allowed cooperatives to contract land to individual households. The household produced a quota for the cooperative, selling anything in excess of the quota to the cooperative at a higher price or on the free market.[102] At the same time as this early turn to the market, 'cautious reappraisals' appeared in official publications that presented GVN agricultural policies as having partially succeeded in modernizing the delta.[103] Although Directive 100 did not represent the end of collectivization in Vietnam, it was the first step towards dismantling it. There were additional steps to consolidate cooperatives in the early 1980s. It was not until the 1986 Doi Moi reforms and particularly Resolution 10 in April 1988 that collective labour requirements were abolished and households allowed to negotiate prices with the state.

Conclusion

The GVN harboured high modernist pretensions of centralization and planning but was simply too weak and under too great a threat to observe, guide and control the complicated reality of the agricultural economy. At the same time, Saigon's desire for political control in the cities and competition with the revolution for resources in the countryside conflicted with agricultural development. In spite of the failure of these projects, they helped shape the rural society that Hanoi inherited in the delta in 1975.

The socialist regime faced many of the same difficulties as the GVN after 1975. These included attempts to increase food production in the countryside in a time of war, now with Cambodia and China, as well as difficulties procuring the agricultural surplus of the delta's rich and middle peasants.

Regardless of the failures of the South Vietnamese effort in agriculture after the Tet Offensive, this chapter shows that the GVN was an activist, developmental regime with a vision for the future. Although this vision was contested and sometimes did not conform to reality, this is a picture that is all too often absent from the historiography of the war. This chapter further complicates the historiography by suggesting that modernization did not suddenly disappear in 1968. South Vietnam's agricultural development and land reform programmes after Tet suggest that state-led modernization remained the dominant development paradigm for the regime and for American officials charged with these projects in South Vietnam.

Perhaps most pertinent to a discussion of decolonization and the Cold War, agricultural development in the Mekong Delta in the long 1970s demonstrates the faith that postcolonial states placed in technology and new forms of social organization. That a state as fragile as South Vietnam in the late 1960s believed that new agricultural technology could solve its economic woes demonstrates the lure of modernization schemes for Third World elites. That party leaders in Hanoi believed that it could socialize southern Vietnam after 1975, even as evidence of northern cooperatives' poor performance mounted, is indicative of their faith in the Marxist-Leninist model of economic and social organization. Both cases demonstrate the difficulty that postcolonial states had in employing science and technology to reshape their societies to serve the ideological interests of the state.

Notes

1 Westad, Odd Arne (2005), *The Global Cold War: Third World Interventions and the Making of Our Times*. Cambridge: Cambridge University Press, 397–398.

2 Gilman, Nils (2003), 'Modernization theory, the highest stage of American intellectual history', in Engerman, David C. et al. (eds.), *Staging Growth: Modernization, Development, and the Global Cold War*. Amherst: University of Massachusetts Press, 49.

3 Adas, Michael (2003), 'Modernization theory and the American revival of the scientific and technological standards of achievement and human worth', in Engerman et al. (2003), 25–46; Berger, Mark T. (2003), 'Decolonisation, modernisation and nation-building: political development theory and the appeal of communism in Southeast Asia' *Journal of Southeast Asian Studies*, 34(3).

4 Gilman, Nils (2007), *Mandarins of the Future: Modernization Theory in Cold War America*. Baltimore: Johns Hopkins University Press, 1–5.

5 Center for International Studies (1960), *Economic, Social and Political Change in the Underdeveloped Countries and Its Implications for United States Policy: A Study Prepared at the Request of the Committee on Foreign Relations, United States Senate*. Cambridge: Massachusetts Institute of Technology, 102.

6 Rostow, W.W. (1960), *The Stages of Economic Growth: A Non-Communist Manifesto*. New York: Cambridge University Press, 50–51, 140–142.

7 Cullather, Nick (2010), *The Hungry World: America's Cold War Battle Against Poverty in Asia*. Cambridge: Harvard University Press, 77–85; Miller, Edward G. (2013), *Misalliance: Ngo Dinh Diem, the United States, and the Fate of South Vietnam*. Cambridge: Harvard University Press, 64–84.

8 Latham, Michael E. (2000), *Modernization as Ideology: American Social Science and 'Nation-Building' in the Kennedy Era*. Chapel Hill: University of North Carolina Press.

9 Scott, James C. (1998), *Seeing Like A State: How Certain Schemes to Improve the Human Condition Have Failed*. New Haven: Yale University Press, 4–5.

10 On this point see the essays in Part III of Engerman et al. (2003).

11 Elliott, David W.P. (2003), *The Vietnamese War: Revolution and Social Change in the Mekong Delta, 1930–1975*. Armonk, N.Y.: M.E. Sharpe, 1242.

12 Race, Jeffrey (1972), *War Comes to Long An: Revolutionary Conflict in a Vietnamese Province*. Berkeley: University of California Press, 39–40.

13 Miller (2013), 97.

14 Herring, George C. (2002), *America's Longest War: The United States and Vietnam, 1950–1975*, 58–60.

15 Catton, Phillip E. (2002), *Diem's Final Failure: Prelude to America's War in Vietnam*. Lawrence: Kansas University Press; Miller (2013).

16 Miller (2013), 187.

17 Nguyen, Lien-Hang T. (2012), *Hanoi's War: An International History of the War for Peace in Vietnam*. Chapel Hill: University of North Carolina Press, 52.

18 Miller (2013), 222.

19 Brigham, Robert K. (2011), 'Vietnamese society at war', in Anderson, David L. (ed.) (2011), *The Columbia History of the Vietnam War*. New York: Columbia University Press, 323–324.

20 Fisher, Christopher T. (2006), 'The illusion of progress: CORDS and the crisis of modernization in South Vietnam, 1965–1968', *Pacific Historical Review*, 75(1), 32–36.

21 Dacy, Douglas C. (1986), *Foreign Aid, War, and Economic Development*. Cambridge: Cambridge University Press, 82.

22 Memorandum from the President's Special Assistant (Komer) to President Johnson, 14 June 1966, in Office of the Historian (1998), *Foreign Relations of the United States (FRUS), 1964–68*, vol. 4, Vietnam 1966, no. 155.

23 Biggs, D. (2012), 'Small machines in the garden: Everyday technology and revolution in the Mekong Delta', *Modern Asian Studies*, 46(1), 52.

24 Fisher (2006), 50; Berger (2003), 444.

25 Simpson, Brad (2009), 'Indonesia's "accelerated modernization" and the global discourse of development, 1960–1975', *Diplomatic History*, 33(3), 479; Simpson, Brad (2010), 'One, two, three, many modernizations', *Reviews in American History*, 40(1), 162.

26 'Modelling and backup method for the Five-Year Plan (mo thuc dai tuong va phuong phap du phong cho ke hoach ngu nien)', undated (folder title suggests between 2 June 1970 and 10 July 1971), folder 2720, *Phong Phu Tong Thong De Nhi Cong Hoa* (Office of the President of the Second Republic), National Archives II, Ho Chi Minh City (PPTTDNCH*)*.

27 Nguyen (2012), 140–141.

28 Duc, Nguyen Phu (2005), *The Viet-Nam Peace Negotiations: Saigon's Side of the Story*. Christiansburg, Va.: Dalley Book Service, 219.

29 Memorandum of Conversation, 30 July 1969, Office of the Historian (2006), *FRUS, 1969–76*, vol. 6, Vietnam, January 1969–July 1970, p. 322.

30 Lang, James (1996), *Feeding a Hungry Planet: Rice, Research & Development in Asia and Latin America*. Chapel Hill: University of North Carolina Press, 132.

31 Cullather, Nick (2004), 'Miracles of modernization: The Green Revolution and the apotheosis of technology', *Diplomatic History*, 28(2), 241.

32 'The Development of Commercial Agriculture in Vietnam', November 1967, Program- Agr-1-3-1970, Box 15, MACV HQ CORDS, MR4/New File Dev Div, Agr Br, RG 472 (MR4/AgrBr/RG472), US National Archives II, College Park (NARA).

33 Ngoc, Pham Kim (1969), *Economic independence for Vietnam*. Saigon: Vietnam Council on Foreign Relations, 7.

34 Cullather (2004), 250.

35 'Agricultural Development Activities '70', undated, folder 2558, PPTTDNCH.

36 Race, Jeffrey (1970), 'How they won', *Asian Survey*, 10(8), 645. The ministry's name underwent changes in this period. For consistency it will be referred to as the MLRA throughout.

37 'Agricultural Development in Viet Nam', undated, item no. 2390101002, Texas Tech University Vietnam Virtual Archive (TTUVVA).

38 'The Proposed Rural Banking System in Vietnam', 22 August 1969, Production Support- 1971, Box 24, MR4/AgrBr/RG472, NARA.

39 For these initial experiments see Cullather (2004), 249–250.

40 'Implementation of the Nationwide Rice Increase Programme During 1968', 19 January 1968, IR-8 Rice Program- 1968, Box 6, MR4/AgrBr/RG472, NARA.

41 Viet-Nam Bulletin, 'Miracle Rice Comes To Vietnam', November 1969, Item No.: 16530101011, TTUVVA; 'Than Nong "Rice Kit" Project for Vietnam', 7 February 1968, IR-8 Rice Program- 1968, Box 6, MR4/AgrBr/RG472, NARA.

42 'Important Principles in Carrying Out an Effective Demonstrations *(sic)*', 27 October 1970, Rice Production 1970, Box 17, MR4/AgrBr/RG472, NARA.

43 Biggs, David (2009), 'Americans in An Giang: Nation-building and the particularities of place in the Mekong Delta, 1966–1973', *Journal of Vietnamese Studies*, 4(3), 156–159.

44 Combs, Arthur (1998), 'Rural economic development as a nation building strategy in South Vietnam, 1968–1972', unpublished PhD dissertation, London School of Economics, 133–134; Cullather (2004), 253.

45 Harry Lieberman to Louis Koffman, 30 May 1968, IR8 Program 1968, Box 6, MR4/AgrBr/RG472, NARA.

46 Pike, Douglas (ed.) (1990), *The Bunker Papers: Reports to the President from Vietnam, 1967–1973*. 3 vols. Berkeley: University of California Institute of East Asia Studies, 405.

47 'Post Tet Rice Hectarage Capability 3 March 1968', 22 March 1968, IR8 Program 1968, Box 6, MR4/AgrBr/RG472, NARA; 'Vietnam's Accelerated Rice Production Program', 6 May 1968, IR8 Program 1968, Box 6, MR4/AgrBr/RG472, NARA.

48 'Agricultural Production Memo', 30 October 1968, Agriculture Advisory File 1968, Box 6, MR4/AgrBr/RG472, NARA.

49 Pike (1990), 651.

50 'Excerpted Comments from TN8 Farmers in the Provinces', 31 October 1968, Agriculture Advisory File 1968, Box 6, MR4/AgrBr/RG472, NARA.

51 'Speech Delivered by the Minister for Land Reform and Agriculture on Dedication of the National Rice Production Training Center at Hiep Hoa', 15 November 1968, IR-8 Rice Program, 1968, Box 6, MR4/AgrBr/RG472, NARA.

52 Colby, William E. (1989), *Lost Victory: A Firsthand Account of America's Sixteen Year Involvement in Vietnam*. Chicago: Contemporary Books, 266.

53 Elliott (2003), 1119–1156.

54 Elliott (2003), 1270–1271.

55 (1972), *Vietnamese Agriculture: A Progress Report*. Washington: Vietnamese Embassy, 73; 'Agricultural Development Activities '70', undated, folder 2558, PPTTDNCH.

56 'Agricultural development in Viet Nam', TTUVVA.

57 'Agricultural production memo: Improved rice varieties and production programs in Pakistan- Laos- Thailand- Indonesia and the Philippines', 21 August 1968, Agriculture Advisory File 1968, Box 6, MR4/AgrBr/RG472, NARA.

58 'Report to the Prime Minister Regarding Project Activities 1970–71', 18 September 1969, Folder 2698, PPTTDNCH.

59 Elliott (2003), 1235.

60 Elliott (2003), 1235–1239; Bergerud, Eric M. (1991), *The Dynamics of Defeat: The Vietnam War in Hau Nghia Province*. Boulder: Westview Press, 298–299.

61 (1971), *Five-year rural economic development plan: Agriculture, Fisheries, Forestry and Animal Husbandry*. Saigon: Ministry of Land Reform and Agriculture and Fishery Development, 14.

62 (1972), 34.

63 Muller, William C., 'The Land-to-the-Tiller Program: The Operational Phase', USAID, April 1973, 3, <http://pdf.usaid.gov/pdf_docs/pnabq699.pdf> [accessed 27 February 2014].

64 For a description of the delta's 'hydraulic environment' see Biggs, David (2010). *Quagmire: Nation-Building and Nature in the Mekong Delta*. Seattle: University of Washington Press, 14–19.

65 Callison, Charles Stuart, 'Economic, social, and political effects of land-to-the-tiller program in South Vietnam: A progress report', June 1973, 10. <http://pdf.usaid.gov/pdf_docs/pnaaa218.pdf> [accessed 27 February 2014].

66 (1971), 6–10.

67 (1971), 29.

68 'Statement of Representative Vo Long Trieu about the "The Rice Project" in the "Five Year Rural Economic Development Plan" ', folder 2892, PPTTDNCH.

69 'Report on the Rice Situation', 5 September 1973, Agriculture, Forestry, and Fisheries Committee, Social and Economic Council, folder 3035, PPTTDNCH.

70 'Economic Development', 17 February 1970, FCO 15/1361, UK National Archives, Kew (TNA).

71 'Land Reform- United States Economic Assistance to Viet Nam, 1954–1975: Viet Nam Terminal Report', Agency for International Development, 31 December 1975. <http://pdf.usaid.gov/pdf_docs/pnabh885.pdf> [accessed 27 February 2014].

72 'Economic and engineering study: Grain storage and marketing system, Vietnam', USAID, March 1970, 128–133. <http://pdf.usaid.gov/pdf_docs/pnadx694.pdf> [accessed 27 February 2014].

73 'Report on the Rice Situation'.

74 'National Agricultural Development Planning Conference, October 5–8, 1970', Planning and Programming, Agricultural Production Memo, 1970, Box 15, MR4/AgrBr/RG472, NARA.

75 'Communique regarding rice procurement 1969–70 season', folder 2519, PPTTDNCH.

76 'Making the Rice Market Healthy', 27 June 1970, Folder 2518, PPTTDNCH; Pike (1990), 797–798.

77 Pike (1990), 762.

78 Logan, William J.C. 'Rice Marketing and Situation Report: Vietnam', USAID, January 1971. <http://pdf.usaid.gov/pdf_docs/pnabs393.pdf> [accessed 27 February 2014].

79 'Making the Rice Market Healthy'.

80 Logan, 'Rice Marketing'.

81 Logan, 'Rice Marketing'; 'Report to the Prime Minister regarding the 1972 rice policy', folder 2845, PPTTDNCH.

82 'Communists Popularizing General Notice and Buying Green Paddy to Monopolize the Market', 16 August 1973, Folder 3038, PPTTDNCH.

83 'Report on the Rice Situation'.

84 'Rice Problems and Food Distribution Policy in the North in 1973', 21 August 1973, Folder 3038, PPTTDNCH.

85 Schulzinger, Robert D. (1997), *A Time for War: The United States and Vietnam, 1941–1975.* Oxford: Oxford University Press, 312.

86 Tsujii, Hiroshi (1977), 'Rice economy and rice policy in South Vietnam up to 1974: An economic and statistical analysis', *South East Asian Studies*, 15(3), 277.

87 Long, Ngo Vinh (2006), 'The socialization of South Vietnam' in Westad, Odd Arne and Quinn-Judge, Sophie (eds.), *The Third Indochina War: Conflict between China, Vietnam, and Cambodia, 1972–1979.* London: Routledge, 130.

88 'Saigon Weekly Summary: 18–31 December 1973', FCO 15/1809, UKNA.

89 'Saigon Weekly Summary: 18–31 December 1973', FCO 15/1809, UKNA.

90 'Saigon Weekly Summary: 18–31 December 1973', FCO 15/1809, UKNA.

91 Long (2006), 131–132.

92 'Prime Minister believe [sic] no political solution with communists, US Embassy, 6 January 1975', item no. 2302409011, TTUVVA.

93 Nguyen Van Hao to Minister of Trade and Supply, March 1975, Folder 3308, PPTTDNCH.

94 Bradley, Mark P. (2009), *Vietnam at War.* Oxford: Oxford University Press, 174–176.

95 Kerkvliet, Benedict J. (2005), *The Power of Everyday Politics: How Vietnamese Peasants Transformed National Politics.* Ithaca: Cornell University Press, 146.

96 Dang, Trung Dinh (2010), 'Post-1975 land reform in Southern Vietnam: How local actions and responses affected land policy', *Journal of Vietnamese Studies*, 5(3), 85–86.

97 Dalrymple, Dana G. (1986), 'Development and spread of high-yielding rice varieties in developing countries'. <http://pdf.usaid.gov/pdf_docs/pnaav435.pdf> [accessed 27 February 2014].

98 Elliott (2003), 1242.

99 Elliott (2003), 1242.

100 Kerkvliet (2005), 177–179; Long (2006), 136–142.

101 Kerkvliet (2005), 180–183.

102 Kerkvliet (2005), 184.

103 Taylor, Phillip (2001), *Fragments of the Present: Searching for Modernity in Vietnam's South*. Honolulu: University of Hawaii Press, 76–82.

Key texts

Biggs, David. (2010). *Quagmire: Nation-Building and Nature in the Mekong Delta*. Seattle: University of Washington Press.

Cullather, Nick. (2010). *The Hungry World: America's Cold War Battle Against Poverty in Asia*. Cambridge, Mass.: Harvard University Press.

Elliott, David. (2003). *The Vietnamese War: Revolution and Social Change in the Mekong Delta, 1930–1975*. Armonk, N.Y.: M.E. Sharpe.

Kerkvliet, Benedict J. (2005). *The Power of Everyday Politics: How Vietnamese Peasants Transformed National Policy*. Ithaca, N.Y.: Cornell University Press.

Miller, Edward G. (2013). *Misalliance: Ngo Dinh Diem, the United States, and the Fate of South Vietnam*. Cambridge: Harvard University Press.

CHAPTER 3
EXPORT PROCESSING ZONES, SPECIAL ECONOMIC ZONES AND THE LONG MARCH OF CAPITALIST DEVELOPMENT POLICIES DURING THE COLD WAR

Patrick Neveling

On 1 November 1950, two Puerto Rican males tried to shoot their way into the provisional White House in Washington, aiming to kill President Harry S. Truman. A report to the US House of Representatives Committee on Interior and Insular Affairs identified the assassins as members of the Puerto Rican Nationalist Party (PRNP), said to be an underground resistance movement opposed to US colonialism. Reflecting the mindset of contemporary US Cold Warriors, the report described the PRNP as 'a handful of independence fanatics … replete with terror' and supported by the US Communist Party.[1]

Given this harsh tone, it is surprising that the report did not see any need for direct political action. Instead, the battle against communism in Puerto Rico was considered won because the US federal government had already extended social security to Puerto Rico, and an extension of the US Employment Service agency had been approved. Such measures, the report boldly declared, would eradicate the roots of terror, since 'It is a historical fact that communism thrives where people are hungry and unemployed'.[2] The recent Washington shooting was portrayed as a desperate response because local Puerto Rican policies had served a 'deadly blow … to the collectivist colossus of Moscow' with 'Operation Bootstrap'. The latter was called an 'intelligent and scientific application of a tax incentive program' that had increased employment numbers and tripled the value of production and services within a few years. A letter to President Truman signed by approximately 300,000 Puerto Ricans was presented as evidence for the success of recent US policies. This condemned the attempted assassination, saying that 'during 450 years never before we have seen such an arbitrary act of violence'.[3] The report also juxtaposed the 450 years of colonization with the recent past, citing a speech by Puerto Rico's first democratically elected Governor, Luis Muñoz-Marín, who had declared that 'The decade which has elapsed between 1940 and 1950 marked the end in Puerto Rico, long before achieved in the rest of Latin America and Anglo-Saxon America, of the colonial period.'[4]

Places such as Puerto Rico rarely take centre stage in academic studies of the Cold War's economic history. There is an 'either-or' in such studies: the focus is either on economic competition in the heartlands of the capitalist and communist blocs, respectively, or on the policies of the two blocs towards the 'Third World'. This chapter aims to provide insights beyond this dichotomy. Instead, it shows that strategies in the

US dependency of Puerto Rico served as a blueprint for US development policies in the era of decolonization. The Puerto Rican tax incentive scheme, identified above as the 'deadly blow to the collectivist colossus of Moscow', was transmitted globally under labels such as 'export processing zone' (EPZ), 'free trade zone' (FTZ), 'foreign trade zone' (also FTZ) or, more recently, 'special economic zone' (SEZ). For most of the period under consideration in this chapter, the standard label used for such zones was 'export processing zone' (EPZ).[5] Today these zones are the predominant locations for light-industrial manufacturing, with around seventy million workers in 3,500 EPZs in more than 130 countries.[6]

This chapter follows the spread of EPZs, from US Cold War foreign policy to export-oriented industrialization efforts promoted by the United Nations Industrial Development Organisation as well as the World Bank in the 1970s and the 1980s. The first section reconstructs the establishment of the world's first EPZ in Puerto Rico and highlights the emerging relations among capital, state and labour. It shows that one central debate of the Cold War – how to achieve 'industrial productivity and eventually the good life' – already informed Puerto Rico's choice of export-oriented development policies over import-substitution.[7] Section two considers how, once the EPZ scheme had produced impressive growth rates, the island's political leadership supported US Point Four and Alliance for Progress missions, helping promote export-oriented development policies as well as US benevolence. Section three focuses on the way EPZs served to undermine a change in development policies promoted by the non-aligned movement. It addresses the United Nations Industrial Development Organisation (UNIDO), one of the new UN agencies that emerged due to the non-aligned movement's agenda but nevertheless became a driving force in the global spread of EPZs in the 1970s. Section four provides concluding remarks about how the analysis of the global spread of EPZs as central theatres of the Cold War introduces seemingly peripheral places into the analysis and how an understanding of what was at stake in the entangled eras of decolonization and the Cold War is advanced if it is framed within the longer history of capitalist exploitation.

Capitalist development in Puerto Rico before and after the Second World War

Puerto Rico came under the control of the United States in 1898. Until then, the island had been under Spanish rule and had produced a range of cash crops such as tobacco and coffee. The Foraker Act of 1900 laid the foundations for a US-style two-chamber political system; the US dollar was introduced as currency; and Puerto Rico became part of the US tariff system. James L. Dietz, a leading economic historian of Puerto Rico, has called the Foraker Act 'an economic instrument designed to control Puerto Rico's economic life'.[8] It facilitated the entry of US business interests, particularly those of agricultural trusts, which turned a diversified but hardly prosperous economy under Spanish rule 'into a classic monocultural economy' driven by sugar.[9] 'Exports' to the mainland quickly rose, while imports from competing cane-sugar producers on other Caribbean islands remained subject to licensing and tariffs. The export-value of Puerto Rican sugar jumped from $5.8 million (USD) in 1902 to $53.7 million in 1930; the area under cane cultivation increased fourfold; and milling technology and production processes were significantly modernized. While one could speak of a rapid modernization of local agriculture, in reality US trusts earned the lion's share of profits, as they controlled the most productive mills. The number of local millers declined rapidly as centralization kicked in, and workers' wages were kept low to compete with Cuba and the Philippines, where production costs were supposedly lower. Other industries in the agricultural sector went through similar trajectories, and once the global recession hit Puerto Rico in the 1930s, wages in the agricultural sector were largely insufficient to buy 'adequately nutritious food'.[10]

Puerto Rican industrialization is often seen as occurring after the 1940s. But already in the 1920s, the crisis of the local agricultural workforce facilitated the rise of a new, non-agricultural sector that would soon outmatch the growth rate of sugar. Cotton goods produced in the local needlework industry, such as dresses, skirts, blouses and underwear, fetched less than $800,000 in export revenues in 1920. In 1929, earnings had risen twenty-fold to $15.3 million. US manufacturers dominated this industry and were supported by educational policies that compelled girls to spend half of their lessons in elementary schools acquiring needlework skills.[11] The labour force for 'needlework' in the early 1930s was estimated to be around 60,000, and was spread throughout 166 small shops and households subcontracted by labour agents.[12] However, the rise of this single export-oriented manufacturing industry was insufficient to support population growth. From 1899 to 1930, the population grew from just under one million inhabitants to over 1.5 million, reaching 2.3 million by 1957.[13]

Finding ways to feed and employ the rapidly increasing population was the first in a series of crucial lessons that US policymakers learned in Puerto Rico that would find their way into Cold War policies towards Third World development. Before 1930, Puerto Rico already foreshadowed what would later be known as the 'Malthusian trap' of increasing birth rates, ensuing population increase, a lack of available wage labour and, ultimately, gloomy prospects for a growing and increasingly young population.[14]

The Cold War was most violent in the Third World, but the apex of paranoia was arguably reached on the US homefront during the McCarthy era. During the 1920s, Puerto Rican migrants provided rightwing Americans with a sense of what it meant to have increasing socio-economic problems that nurtured anti-capitalist sentiments at their doorstep. More than 45,000 Puerto Ricans lived in large US cities. New York became the central focus for the diaspora community, where public protests focused not only on miserable housing and working conditions, but also protestors' critique of colonial rule in Puerto Rico. Anti-colonial ideas originating in India, Latin America and the Soviet Union spread from New York to Puerto Rico, where they coincided with Wilsonian self-determination ideology taught at local universities.[15]

In this climate, a new generation of Puerto Rican politicians rose to prominence. During the Great Depression, while more radical political movements found a large support base, the moderates of this generation, led by later Governor Muñoz-Marín, called for an extension of the Roosevelt administration's New Deal policies to the island. Muñoz-Marín was elected as a US Senator for the Liberal Party in 1933, and his Washington office gave him access to the highest political circles, including Rexford Guy Tugwell in the Department of Agriculture and ultimately Eleanor Roosevelt, the president's wife. In 1934, the First Lady visited Puerto Rico shortly after a brutal police crackdown on a general strike, which had discredited the Socialist Party's claim to represent all local unions.

At the time, the Socialist Party governed as part of a coalition that included the US sugar trust-driven Republican Party, and both parties opposed the extension of New Deal policies to the island. As the coalition's popularity waned following the failed strike, the Chardón Plan, named after a scientist from the University of Puerto Rico, was launched. This plan proposed the expansion of labour-intensive production in agriculture and manufacturing, as well as government acquisition of one of the large sugar mills to free small planters from having to sell their produce to the large US trust-owned mills. A New Deal-style colonial administration began work on housing projects, poor-relief programmes and food-for-work employment programmes.[16]

With the entry of the United States into the Second World War in 1941, further core concepts of the Chardón Plan were implemented. Muñoz-Marín now led the newly founded Partido Popular Democrático (PPD) that had won local elections in 1940. The PPD opted to remain a US dependency until the development agenda bore fruit. Washington, keen to ensure a friendly environment for US military posts on the island, appointed Tugwell as governor in 1941. With his support, excise taxes on imports of Puerto Rican liquor, cigars and sugar to the mainland, which the federal government used as annual funding for local development projects, were placed under local government auspices. With this money, the PPD established a planning board, a government bank and an industrial development company.[17] The Puerto Rico Industrial Development Company (PRIDCO) became operational in 1942. Several million dollars were spent on the construction of factories to produce otherwise expensive import-commodities. New factories for shoes, pulp and paper, glass bottles and cement created 'ten thousand jobs at the cost of US $21 million'.[18] As we shall see, early Puerto Rican development policies equalled what came to be called import-substitution-based development in the 1950s.

However, the New Deal had powerful opponents on the mainland and in Puerto Rico. After the war, these opponents became very vocal. Business circles and various political parties criticized the amount of money spent per job created as a sign of failure. Strike action in government-owned factories and consultancy reports highlighting better growth prospects from private-sector investment provided a pretext for the leadership of the PPD and PRIDCO to change development policies radically.[19]

In the words of the *Wall Street Journal*, a 'Puerto Rican lure' was established.[20] This lure was the tax incentive programme, which featured boldly in the report on the assassination attempt summarized in the introduction to this chapter, and laid the foundations for the modern-day EPZ/SEZ development regime. PRIDCO now offered mainland investors customs-free and tax-free production for ten years alongside other government subsidies such as cheap leases for industrial plots, low rents for state-owned factories and, of course, a cheap, docile labour force, which was policed with a heavy hand. Arthur D. Little, a Boston-based consulting company, was hired to promote relocations. A newly founded Office of Information for Puerto Rico in Washington embarked on a vibrant promotion campaign. In 1946 alone, 14,000 copies of a monthly newsletter were distributed. Another 35,000 brochures were sent to manufacturers, bankers, business writers and so on, promoting 'Puerto Rico's Potential as a site for textile apparel and other industries'.[21]

PRIDCO also reversed its spending policy. Now, the local state invested federal money coming from the excise-tax refund to provide fixed capital assets for private investors; an example was the $7 million construction of a luxury hotel for the Hilton Hotels Corporation. Agreement for this with PRIDCO was reported as an outstanding success in the corporation's 1946 Report to Stockholders. PRIDCO shouldered all construction expenses. In return, the Hilton Hotels Corporation signed a twenty-year lease for the building, during which the corporation 'had to provide working capital for the efficient and uninterrupted operation'. Annual payment was two-thirds of 'gross operating profits' plus a sum no higher than 5 per cent of the 'cost for installed furniture and fixtures'.[22] In other words, had the hotel not made any profit, PRIDCO would have recuperated no more than the expenses for furniture and fixtures at the end of the twenty-year lease. Evidently, the turn away from development driven by state-owned corporations and factories was radical and risky.

Another $4.7 million of PRIDCO's money went into the construction of a textile plant in Ponce, a larger city on the southern coast. The factory brought a very particular, ruthless form of US capitalism to Puerto Rico, and made the island an important asset for the growing mainland coalition of businessmen opposing the New Deal.[23] Such businesses already had relocated within the US from northern to southern states, where unions were weaker and labour was cheap.[24] Relocations of production sites on a global scale would become the hallmark of EPZs across the globe in the 1960s and after. As with the planning infrastructure, Puerto Rico was exemplary for the relations among state, capital and labour that nurtured the emergence of such 'runaway shops'.

The lease for the Ponce textile factory went to Royal W. Little. Little was not only one of the first mainland investors to come to Puerto Rico under the new tax incentive scheme, but also the nephew of Arthur D. Little, the owner of the consulting company working for PRIDCO. In his 1979 published autobiography, Royal Little portrayed himself as a self-made man who became one of the leading US textile and garment manufacturers in the 1940s. Wartime production of textiles and garments for the US Army increased his fortune. In 1943, he set up the first vertically integrated company, Textron, Inc., producing synthetic fibre-based textiles. Textron expanded rapidly, buying out several spinning mills and other plants in New England to obtain their quota of raw materials that the wartime federal state had allocated per plant. The brand became a nationwide success, not least because Textron spent $1 million annually on advertising.[25] Acquisitions in the US northeast had included manufacturers, such as Lonsdale and the Nashua Manufacturing Company, whose operations dated back to the early nineteenth century. After the war, these were subjected to time-motion studies intended to measure and possibly increase the productivity of workers. When Royal Little realized that the ratio of worker productivity to wages in the southern US mainland states and in Puerto Rico produced a higher yield, he shut down several New England plants. Firing 10,000 workers did not go down well with the Textile Workers Union of America or certain local senators: a US Senate Subcommittee hearing in 1948 investigated the relations between the closures and Textron's recent establishment in Ponce.[26]

At the opening of the hearing, the presiding senator confronted Little with a letter from the Textile Workers Union of America, which stated that the 'management's judgement cannot always be in the workers' interest. But we do not believe management should be free to wreck an entire community to further its own narrow objective'.[27] Referring to the time-motion studies, Little responded bluntly that per-man productivity in New England prevented Textron from competing with other companies.[28]

With the radical change in development policies, Puerto Rican leaders attempted to raise the living standard of the population by attracting mainland investors. But only substantial incentives could persuade mainland capital to move to the island. On the other side of the relocation chain initiated by Puerto Rican EPZ policies, companies such as Textron were happy to accept the compensation offered. However, this required them to shut down operations on the mainland, since, they argued, production in Puerto Rico was more profitable.

This narrative of entangled histories provides the background for EPZs in the Cold War and in the era of decolonization. Such zones facilitated relocation of industrial manufacturing from one region to another. Relocations served to limit the bargaining power of workers in the abandoned locations of the capitalist bloc, while providing a tool to fend off socialist and communist political tendencies in the receiving Third World regions. The Puerto Rican EPZ regime has had enduring implications for the global debate over development policies. Puerto Rico was a colony, and it remained one in many ways despite the granting of limited sovereignty in 1947: a regime change was unlikely or could have been contained easily with the deployment of the US troops stationed on the island. Therefore, the island and its inhabitants provided a safe laboratory and accordingly served as a training ground for US officials to master the challenges that decolonization posed during the Cold War.

Particularly instructive in this regard was a debate preceding the approval of Act No. 184 in 1948, which granted new investors full exemption from income, property, excise and municipal taxes. Promoting this bill, Teodoro Moscoso, head of PRIDCO and a rival of Tugwell, argued that tax exemption should not be seen as an investor subsidy, as his opponents claimed, but as compensation for costs incurred by operations in Puerto Rico. Large-scale employment, meanwhile, would generate local revenues from workers' income taxes. Soon, the debate over mainland investors became tied to calls for independence. As stated above, the PPD had publicly announced in 1940 that colonial dependency was temporary, and would be waived once economic progress had been achieved. After the Second World War, some political parties rallied for independence again.

The US Tariff Commission supported Moscoso's agenda with a report that established a cost-benefit analysis of US colonialism for Puerto Rico. Mainland support, the report concluded, kept the fast-growing population alive, since it was part of a mainland tariff system that granted Puerto Ricans certain benefits, including: access to goods that might be otherwise unaffordable, revenues from agriculture that went to local shareholders as well as US corporations, and an excise tax rebate from the federal government that allowed the local government to pay for industrial development.[29] Dependency even worked both ways, the report emphasized, because an independent Puerto Rico with a starving population would harm the United States' image as a benevolent country.

From an analytical angle, Puerto Rico indeed enjoyed privileged access to the mainland market because it was a US dependency. This access was central for abandoning the initial project of import-substitution: before 1947, government-owned factories had been built to replace imports of shoes, cement and glass bottles. Afterwards, an export-oriented development policy was pursued, with private investors producing goods for the mainland market. Instead of independence, then, the limited sovereignty granted to Puerto Rico in 1947 included a shift from import-substitution to export-oriented development.

Of course, there is an irony to this story: the truly burdensome investments in fixed capital were shouldered by the Puerto Rican state. Similar to the Hilton Hotel Corporation, Textron did not build or buy the Ponce plant. In his autobiography, Little lauds himself for convincing PRIDCO to put up $4 million for the factory *and* for machinery. Textron entered the business with $1 million as working capital. For this, an annual return on investment of 100 per cent was projected. Because such a return did not materialize, Textron received additional PRIDCO money in the early 1950s.[30] Still, operations were closed down in 1957.[31] Coincidentally, 1958 would have been the first year for Textron to pay taxes on Puerto Rican operations.

Textron was an early success story for Operation Bootstrap – in Spanish 'Operación Manos a la Obra' – as the wider framework of PRIDCO's export-oriented development programme was called, and its closure foreshadowed general decline. In the 1960s, many US investors left. Large-scale investment in industrial infrastructures such as oil refineries briefly succeeded in keeping the economy afloat. But by the 1970s, an impoverished population queued for food stamps. The mainland government did not provide any support, possibly because domestic economic crises, with skyrocketing unemployment and stagflation, took up all resources. But in the 1950s, those days were not yet visible. Based on these theoretical considerations, this chapter will now describe the global spread of EPZs from Puerto Rico.

Turning the Puerto Rican EPZ into a showcase for capitalist development

The Puerto Rican EPZ regime became a hotspot for global diffusion. US Cold War propaganda about Puerto Rico did not necessarily highlight the particular relations among capital, state and labour that were a defining feature of early EPZs. Neither did propagandists emphasize that manufacturing relocation was an excellent tool to undermine workers' bargaining power, or anything else suspicious administrators in Washington took for activities aligned with the 'communist colossus'. Instead, what US propaganda focused on was high growth rates in Puerto Rico to convey a twofold message: The first was that export-oriented, capitalist development could indeed produce rapid growth and therefore deliver on the promise of the good life. As Cold War tensions increased, such a message became essential to the survival of the many anti-communist regimes that the United States maintained or sought to set up across the developing world. As the following will show, many of these regimes, including Egypt and Taiwan (then Republic of China), set up their own EPZs.[32] The second message concerned the United States itself: promoting the superpower as a benevolent nation that treated obedient dependencies, such as Puerto Rico, with utmost care was crucial in the global climate of decolonization.

A Ford Foundation-funded biography of Teodoro Moscoso, the founding director of PRIDCO, recorded 10,000 visits by foreign officials since 1947 to inspect and learn from the Puerto Rican 'miracle'.[33] This high number is realistic, given that successive US administrations promoted the island as a blueprint for successful, capitalist development policies. Puerto Rico was a crucial representative of the Truman administration's Point Four programme and the Kennedy administration's Alliance for Progress. The reliance of these initiatives on Puerto Rico was grounded not only in sheer numbers, but also in two types of personae: Puerto Rican politicians and US consultants. In particular, the Arthur D. Little (ADL) consulting company played a pivotal role in Point Four, while a networking relationship between ADL and Puerto Rican officials became one of the backbones of the Alliance for Progress.[34]

In the first fifteen years after 1947, Operation Bootstrap did indeed produce high growth rates and substantial employment. As the island attracted increasing relocations from the US mainland in textiles, garments, switchboard assembly and other electronics manufacturing, Puerto Rican officials were sent around Latin America to give testimony of US benevolence. As early as October 1951, Puerto Rican Senator Ernesto Juan Fonfrías toured Latin American capitals. Initially heading a Puerto Rican delegation to the Inter-American Press Association conference in Montevideo, the senator stopped in Rio de Janeiro, Lima, Quito and Bogota to give public speeches and press conferences.[35] Another stop was Santiago de Chile, where the local US ambassador sent a cable to Muñoz-Marín praising the senator's 'most attractive personality', which had helped inform Chileans and American residents 'about the true relationship existing between the people of Puerto Rico and their fellow citizens of continental United States'.[36]

Promotion activities also targeted audiences with significant leverage in regional development policy. In February 1952, the Caribbean Commission held its annual 'Industrial Development Conference' in Puerto Rico. Delegations from the French Caribbean Department, the Dutch Antilles, the UK territories of Barbados, Jamaica, Trinidad and Tobago, and the US territories, Puerto Rico and Virgin Islands, were present. 'Observers' included delegations from ADL, Canadian *Caisse Central de la France d'Outre-Mer*, the Chambers of Commerce of Guadeloupe and Trinidad, Britain's Colonial Development Corporation, the Dominican Republic, the Economic Development Administration of Puerto Rico, the French Consulate in San Juan, the French Embassy in Cuba, the Puerto Rico Manufacturers' Association, the United Kingdom & British Co-Chairman of the Caribbean Commission and the University College of the West Indies.[37]

In his opening speech to the conference, Muñoz-Marín was keen to highlight the similarities between Puerto Rican problems and those of other Caribbean islands in terms of population growth, unemployment and establishing an industrial manufacturing base.[38] After an eight-day exchange, the conference came up with dozens of recommendations, all of which suggested export-oriented development as the key to industrialization. The Puerto Rican organizational model – comprising a development corporation, a government development bank and a planning board – was highlighted in the final Commission report, as were suggestions for zoning industrial estates, introducing industrial standards and quality controls, promoting industrial relocation, increasing labour productivity, government-funded factories and a range of tax incentives to attract investors.[39] Additional research in British and Caribbean archives is required to determine the extent to which this Puerto Rican conference was a hallmark for the region. But certainly Jamaica and Trinidad, at the time both still British colonies, accordingly intensified their export-oriented policies in the 1950s. Jamaica set up a development corporation in 1952, and the colony became a role model for development efforts in other British dependencies such as Mauritius.[40]

As early as 1951, PRIDCO celebrated the signing of its 100th contract with an investor – in this case US mainland corporation Beacon Textiles, Inc. – and turned this into a large celebration of its own achievements and Puerto Rico's progress more generally. A local newspaper, *Diario de Puerto Rico*, concluded that 'the Puerto Rican people have "fabricated" a superior economy against all the obstacles of its destiny'.[41] The US marketing agency, Hamilton Wright, made feature-length, documentary-style movies about Puerto Rico – one entitled 'Island of Progress' – that were screened in Puerto Rican cinemas, on the mainland and across the Americas.[42]

ADL chairman Raymond Stevens joined the celebrations in Puerto Rico, holding press conferences and visiting factories and the PRIDCO housing project. His schedule also included swimming, sightseeing, night clubbing and a pig-roast at popular Luquillo Beach.[43] This may well have been the blueprint for Latin American delegations' visits that made the island a useful tool for Point Four, as well as for mainland journalists, flown in at the expense of Hamilton Wright, to pen positive reports about Puerto Rico's lighthouse effect for the free world.[44]

For ADL, the Puerto Rican success was excellent business. In 1950, ADL became the sole auditor for investors approaching the local Government Development Bank for a loan.[45] On holiday in Jamaica, one senior ADL member followed up contacts with the local government, and secured a contract for ADL to advise on establishing Jamaica's first national development agency; ADL held board membership and line-managed staff in Jamaican investment promotion offices in New York and London. Among other EPZ measures, an ADL memorandum suggested ten-year tax exemptions for investors as a central feature for Jamaican development policies.[46]

Business opportunities soon stretched to other continents, as ADL was put in charge of the industrialization branch within the Point Four office in Egypt.[47] In 1960, ADL joined forces with the Asia Foundation to work on industrial development projects in East Pakistan. Joint plans for a travelling institute for industrial development promotion in Asia were also drawn up, and Thailand was chosen as the first showcase.[48] Of course, not all ADL projects endured successfully. In 1960, the *Wall Street Journal* printed a feature-length piece and the influential German weekly *Die Zeit* devoted three pages to ADL's delivery of 'ideas on demand'.[49] Both newspapers emphasized one potential pitfall of Cold War development policies that neither Point Four nor later US development projects could surmount: as the *Wall Street Journal* only half-jokingly mentioned, regime changes in Honduras, Cuba and Egypt had forced ADL to abandon projects that incoming socialist (leaning) governments could then use for their own purposes.[50]

However for ADL, such developments were no less lucrative. During the 1960s, the frontier of capitalist industrial manufacturing actually expanded. In the early part of the decade, the Kennedy administration set up the Alliance for Progress, and many Puerto Rican politicians and bureaucrats became US envoys to Latin America. Former PRIDCO Director Moscoso had an exceptional career. He was appointed US Ambassador to Venezuela before moving on to an appointment as US Coordinator of the Alliance in 1962.[51] Once the Alliance turned sour, an ADL stockholders meeting on 26 March 1965 elected him to the board of directors, and, on the same day, Moscoso sat in on the Annual Directors Meeting at the headquarters in Cambridge, Massachusetts.[52] This may well have been a reward for ADL's highly beneficial relationship with PRIDCO. ADL's Puerto Rican business had further increased in 1956 after Moscoso had set a new target during PRIDCO's celebration of the 400th factory opening. Soon, the aim was to double the number of factories from 500 to 1,000. To help with this, ADL was contracted to set up a permanent office in San Juan in 1957.[53]

When that office was closed in 1962, its director, Richard Bolin, moved to Mexico to set up a new ADL resident office. The historical record on Bolin's work in Mexico is somewhat contradictory. Bolin himself claims that his was a singular effort based on successful collaboration with Mexican officials, while historians have portrayed him as an ADL employee.[54] It seems, however, that ADL obtained a consultancy and recommended the establishment of bonded factories for border cities with standard EPZ incentives such as tax and customs exemptions, state-funded industrial estates, oppressive anti-unionization policies and so forth. This was then implemented under the Mexican government's Border Industrialisation Programme, which became operational on 1 January 1965, just one day after the forced return migration of millions of Mexicans working under the Bracero programme in the US agricultural sector had begun. Similar to the needlework industry in Puerto Rico, EPZs were not necessarily a watershed for Mexican export-oriented development policies.[55] The zones were rather 'the last in a series of systematic efforts' to industrialize the Mexican border region, dating back to the granting of free-trade privileges for bonded warehouses in the 1930s.[56] But in terms of growth rates and employment figures, the Border Industrialisation Programme was far more successful.

Similar to Textron's relocations to the United States south and then Puerto Rico, US industrial relocations to Mexico soon met strong criticism from unions. As the capitalist bloc underwent stagflation during the 1970s, a US Congress hearing considered whether two clauses in the US tariff system, which promoted the partial manufacturing and assembly of textiles, garments and electronics abroad, were actually detrimental to the national economy. Bolin had set up the Flagstaff Institute in the early 1970s, offering research and consultancy to US companies seeking to relocate to northern Mexico. At that hearing in 1976, Bolin helped US industrialists successfully defend their interests against the unions.[57]

This section has focused on the way the EPZ model was promoted to developing nations via the example of Puerto Rico and the services of ADL during the first decades of decolonization. The 1976 US Congress hearing offered a first indication of how events in international politics were increasingly caught up with the EPZ promotion business in the 1970s. The following section reconstructs the importance of 1970s' international politics for EPZs as well as the prelude and the aftermath to that decade.

Turning US development policy against the non-aligned movement

Following the Bandung Conference in 1955, a number of developing nations formed what came to be called the non-aligned movement. This movement would become a powerful alternative to the capitalist and socialist blocs during the 1960s and the 1970s. One of its main achievements was the establishment of new UN agencies for the promotion of Third World development in the 1960s. The UN Commission on Trade and Development (UNCTAD) was headed by the famous Latin American economist, Raúl Prebisch, who had been fighting for greater national autonomy in development policies since the 1950s. His work is often associated with the rise of import-substitution policies, as opposed to export-oriented development policies. Section two of this chapter has shown that a dispute over such policies in Puerto Rico actually preceded this debate of the 1950s. Nevertheless, the policies promoted by the non-aligned movement conflicted with the EPZ regime that had spread across the decolonizing world since the late 1940s.[58]

Besides UNCTAD, the UN Development Programme and the UN Industrial Development Organisation (UNIDO) were established in the 1960s to cater to the needs of the Third World. Tense negotiations within the UN Economic and Social Council (ECOSOC) between the capitalist bloc, the communist bloc and the non-aligned movement over industrial development preceded the creation of UNIDO. The capitalist bloc initially opposed the establishment of a UN agency devoted to industrial development. ECOSOC resolution 751 (XXIX) of April 1960 therefore established an Industrial Development Committee. Four years later, the tables had turned, and the fourth IDC session unanimously recommended the creation of UNIDO to the UN General Assembly.[59] The following thus describes a historical irony: that is, soon after its foundation, UNIDO, an organization intended to strengthen national sovereignty in an era of export-oriented development policies, became the driving force in global EPZ promotion, delivering the triumph of EPZs in global light-industrial manufacturing from the 1970s onwards and strengthened multinational corporations instead.

Setting up UNIDO meant, however, that the policies of all UN member-states towards industrial development were considered part of the new agency's agenda. This posed a decisive obstacle to the non-aligned movement's wishes to establish a new international economic order. Instead, in the 1970s what sociologists labelled a 'new international division of labour' emerged, in which EPZs brought increasingly exploitative labour relations to developing countries, while relocations triggered structural unemployment in the capitalist bloc.[60]

In preparation for a decision on UNIDO's organizational structure and tasks, the UN Industrial Development Committee's associated Centre for Industrial Development (CID) sought models of industrialization. A questionnaire that was distributed to member-states via the UN Secretary General in September 1966 pointed to the potential of export industries in accordance with ECOSOC resolution 1178 (XLI). By then, and as the sections above have shown, several countries and colonial dependencies had EPZs up and running. Others, such as the Philippines, were developing EPZs with funding from USAID and other sources.[61] Therefore, EPZs figured prominently in the CID progress report to the first session of UNIDO's general assembly, the Industrial Development Board, in 1967. Accordingly, the board suggested that UNIDO promote EPZ-like regimes, and a group for export promotion was established as part of the Industrial Policies and Programming Division.[62]

This group quickly went to work. Headed by William Tanaka, whose home country Japan had substantial interests in EPZs by that time, the export promotion team conducted a global survey on EPZ activities in 1970. The correspondence for this survey also became the centrepiece for promoting UNIDO's export promotion services to national development agencies and ministries.[63] An early technical assistance mission to Mauritius in 1969 was regularly mentioned in marketing-style letters, as Tanaka sought to acquire further technical assistance requests from member-states.[64]

Tanaka and his export promotion team had a substantial sum of money at their disposal. Their challenge was to spend it, rather than deciding which requests for technical assistance to accept or decline. UNIDO's export promotion team was not only looking for 'customers' for its TA missions: it also needed expertise on EPZs. Similar to PRIDCO in Puerto Rico, existing EPZs across the world were run by agencies that enjoyed significant independence from government ministries. And similar to Moscoso, such agencies' personnel were well trained to spot lucrative opportunities.

The Kaohsiung Export Processing Zone Authority in Taiwan was the first agency to recognize that with UNIDO's export promotion, consultancy could make a fortune. Much like Puerto Rico, Jamaica and Mauritius, Taiwan's economy had long been reliant on agriculture, particularly sugar. As one of the main allies of the United States since the onset of the Cold War, Taiwan received substantial US development funding and, with this, US approaches to economic development. First plans for an EPZ had been drawn up in the mid-1950s and were realized when the first EPZ opened in 1965 as part of a new container harbour in Kaohsiung.[65] Kaohsiung EPZ Authority's responses to the 1970 global EPZ survey strongly impressed Tanaka, who responded that few of the 'more than a hundred free zones ... are indicating a success, [but] we feel that the KEPZ is showing the best results in its contribution to the industrialization of the country and the promotion of exports'.[66]

It is surprising at first that Tanaka expressed such strong doubts about the performances of EPZs when he sought to become key to their global spread. This is important to note: first, Tanaka's motive was to position UNIDO's export promotion as paramount among the agencies promoting the spread of EPZs. Private consultancy firms such as ADL or Bolin's Flagstaff Institute were options, as were national development promotion agencies from the United States and other capitalist bloc nations. Dismissing what these had achieved so far may have been in Tanaka's interest. Second, this exchange is revealing about the origins of EPZs. The survey that Tanaka and his group conducted covered not only EPZs: the vast majority of the 'more than a hundred free zones' mentioned were free port and free trade zones. Such regimes mainly concerned the duty-free storage and customs-free trans-shipment of goods, and had a much longer history than EPZs. Recently historians have sought to establish a historical continuity that connects the US free zone system that became operational in ports in the 1930s to the global spread of EPZs.[67] International development agencies have sometimes pointed to historical continuities dating to the Hanseatic League port cities of medieval days, or, more recently, to one free port in Roman Antiquity.[68] Because there was no production and, hence, no industry in the many free ports and free zones that UNIDO's export promotion team surveyed, Tanaka dismissed their workings as unsuccessful in the above quote. This demonstrates why it is advisable to establish clear categories for comparison in world history and delineate the trajectories of historical phenomena such as EPZs and SEZs accordingly.[69]

The cooperation between UNIDO's export promotion team and the Kaohsiung EPZ perfectly illustrates how the Cold War international political arena shaped the operations of UNIDO. The large funding that the export promotion team had for promoting export-oriented development policies with EPZ regimes came from a special fund that enabled UN member-states to donate to UNIDO with a specified purpose. Many capitalist nations thus gave money for the spread of EPZs.[70] Plans for a close collaboration between UNIDO's export promotion and Kaohsiung EPZ Authority were drawn up, and an international training workshop on EPZs was planned for 1971. This was advertised repeatedly in the UNIDO newsletter, a monthly publication distributed globally.[71] But just three weeks before the workshop was to be held, the Taiwanese delegation walked out of the UN Council to protest against the possible inclusion of the People's Republic of China (PRC), which seemed imminent after many UN member states had recognized the PRC in the 1960s and the United States established relations with the PRC after the Sino-Soviet border conflict in 1969.

Now that Taiwan was no longer a UN member, the UNIDO workshop had to be moved elsewhere quickly. This was a stroke of luck for the Shannon Free Airport

Development Corporation (SFADCo), a partly state-owned development agency in the Republic of Ireland running an EPZ attached to Shannon airport.[72] SFADCo leadership not only secured the hosting of this workshop in early 1972 but also placed an affiliate, Peter Ryan, as Tanaka's successor. From 1972 until well into the 1990s, a significant percentage of UNIDO's EPZ consultancy contracts went to SFADCo. One beneficiary was Shannon entrepreneur Tom Kelleher, who wrote the first *Handbook on Export Processing Zones*, published by UNIDO in 1976. This handbook was a comprehensive guide to establishing an EPZ; it included templates for organizational structures from EPZs in Shannon; Bataan, Philippines; and Masan, South Korea, as well as a blueprint act for setting up an EPZ by national law.[73] That handbook is possibly most emblematic of the inexorable global spread of EPZs from the early 1970s onwards; it remains UNIDO's second best-selling publication ever, and many national EPZ laws strikingly resemble its suggestions.

Even an escalation of the non-aligned movement's demands for a new international economic order at UNIDO's second general conference in Lima in 1975 could stop neither the process initiated by the export promotion team nor the general global spread of EPZs. In Lima, a ballot of eighty-two against one, with seven abstentions, voted for a fifty-seven-point declaration demanding sovereignty over natural resources, the right to nationalize economic activities 'in accordance with its laws', and strict guidelines for multi-national corporations operating in foreign countries.[74] Such measures, if applied, would have contradicted most of what EPZs were about: for example, they would have restricted the free hand given to multinational corporations. But the Lima Declaration hardly informed political and economic policies on the ground. In 1975, twenty-seven of the seventy-seven non-aligned nation states had EPZs operational or in an advanced planning stage: if Third World nations wanted to find an entry point into the world market for industrial manufacturing, they had little choice but to follow the policies established in Puerto Rico in 1947. With the Third World debt crisis emerging in the late 1970s and escalating in the 1980s, this situation became aggravated and the choices of Third World nations were depleted further.

The export promotion team could not foresee those events and thus took measures to make the EPZ business independent. At a working group meeting in Barranquilla, Colombia, in 1974, Ryan proposed an independent umbrella organization of EPZs worldwide. This World Export Processing Zones Association was inaugurated at a UNIDO-funded expert working-group meeting in Bataan's EPZ by delegations from thirty-two EPZs in 1978.[75] Three years later, former ADL staff member, Richard Bolin, was elected president, and World EPZ Association operations merged with the operations of Bolin's Flagstaff Institute. World EPZ Association consultants started taking a large cut of UNIDO and World Bank consultancy contracts. As this business grew, World EPZ Association and Irish consultants associated with Shannon, rather than competing, closely collaborated.

In the 1980s, the World Bank made the establishment of EPZs a condition for many of the structural adjustment programmes that indebted Third World nations had to sign up to. In this, the Bank could rely on the pioneering work started in Puerto Rico in the late 1940s, spread by Point Four and the Alliance for Progress and brought to perfection by UNIDO's export promotion in the 1970s. Following harsh measures introduced by the World Bank's structural adjustment programmes, the number of operational EPZs rose from 79 in 1975 to 197 in 1986, and further to 845 in 1997. The number of workers in EPZs worldwide also grew exponentially in that period: from 700,000 in 1975, to approximately 2 million in 1986, to 22.5 million in 1997.[76]

Several nations established EPZs in that period, and EPZ employment rose rapidly, even in nations with socialist-leaning governments, which often had little choice but to sign up to the World Bank structural adjustment programmes. An excellent example for this is Mauritius, where an EPZ was set up by the pro-Western Mauritius Labour Party in 1970. Exploitation in the zone fuelled anti-imperialist sentiments that triggered two general strikes on the island and helped the socialist Mouvement Militant Mauricien to a landslide victory in 1982. By then, Mauritius had been tied to structural adjustment programme measures for three years already, and the incoming government soon realized that the actual sovereign was the World Bank and the International Monetary Fund.[77]

Still, much of that exponential growth happened because the PRC, which did not have to shoulder a structural adjustment programme, reversed its development policy radically. A visit by Jiang Zemin to Shannon obviously influenced these reforms, which included the opening of four SEZs in 1980. Jiang was then 'senior Vice Minister in charge of the State Import and Export Administration', and many years later, he told the Irish Ambassador to China how important his stay in Shannon had been for policy measures introduced in the 1980s.[78] Jiang's statement was to some extent a polite misrepresentation, since plans for the PRC's zones had been drawn up in 1977, and the first foreign companies set up shop in the Shenzhen SEZ in 1979.[79] However, the measures introduced throughout the 1980s resembled the Irish zones, involving the absence of corporate tax waivers in favour of a flat corporate tax of 15 per cent, as well as administrative control of local EPZ authorities that extended beyond the industrial areas to workers' settlements.[80]

The operations of UNIDO's export promotion in the 1970s importantly tied many developing nations to local and multinational capital, and made labour increasingly dependent on postcolonial patterns of exploitation. The triumph of the EPZ model in global light-manufacturing industries and export-oriented development agendas was finally sealed with the opening of EPZs in the PRC.

Conclusion: Capitalism in understanding decolonization and the Cold War

This chapter has shown that during the Cold War and the era of decolonization, EPZs were an indispensable tool for the United States – and the capitalist bloc in general – for promoting capitalist development policies in the Third World. As noted in the introduction, much economic history explicitly focusing on the Cold War explains the 'victory' of capitalism via the socialist bloc's failure to create a consumer culture comparative to the heartlands of the capitalist bloc. The race for prosperity between the German Democratic Republic and the Federal Republic of Germany is often identified as a global stage, where competition between the two blocs was obvious and visible.[81] That race also informs more complex analyses that consider the socialist bloc's growing debt to the capitalist bloc in the 1970s and the upheaval that the neoliberal counterrevolutions by Thatcher, Reagan and others caused in the global economy.[82] Yet there is a blind spot in these works. As this chapter shows, the capitalist bloc could secure abundant supplies of ever-cheaper consumer goods made by industrial workers in the Third World via EPZs. At the same time, relocations from the industrial heartlands of the capitalist bloc such as New Hampshire and from important production centres in the Federal Republic of Germany and Britain provided the political means for the neoliberal crackdown on trade unions and workers in old and new core industrial sectors such as textiles, garments and electronics and increasingly services such as data processing.

Such capitalist engagement with the Third World has been noted since the 1970s by social scientists who have identified EPZs as arenas of 'super-exploitation' where wages have been insufficient for workers to reproduce their labour power. However, these analyses pay little attention to the early Cold War roots of these policies.[83] For this and other reasons, academics, trade unionists, politicians, workers and many others see a close connection between the spread of EPZs and imperialism, old or new.[84] Others, such as the father of the Taiwanese economic miracle, former minister and renowned member of various neoliberal think tanks, Kuo-Ting Li, or the Mauritian economist and later UNIDO EPZ-consultant, Eduard Lim-Fat, have heralded EPZs as a complete cure to the pitfalls of development in the era of decolonization.[85]

To reconstruct the global spread of EPZs through the lens of the entangled, global phenomena of the Cold War and decolonization allows for a broader analytical scope of post-1945 global economic history and Cold War history. Those who wish to analyse the world's history in recent centuries inevitably position themselves within the range of general principles that have been proposed as the elementary structures of capitalism.[86] Writing about the global spread of EPZs, then, is also an invitation to go beyond the capitalist bloc's notion that such zones could offer decisive blows to the 'collectivist colossus in Moscow' or that Puerto Rico offered 'dramatic proof to the world that enlightened government planning and free enterprise are not incompatible'.[87] Such mindsets have been commonplace since the heyday of neoliberal development economics in the 1970s. But in many cases they can be contrasted with the realities of the global EPZ and SEZ regimes, past and present, that have kept the life-expectations of workers in postcolonial countries low and the fiction of capitalist progress alive in the heartlands of the capitalist bloc. Beginning in Puerto Rico, a new structure of dependent independence for developing nations was established in 1947. Developing nations that sought to build up industries to overcome dependency on selling raw materials now had a fast-forwarded road into industrialization; they only had to open EPZs/SEZs and invite in multinational corporations. When the non-aligned movement sought to tame these newcomers in the 1970s, they were outplayed again through the export promotion working group in UNIDO.

Although this might not have been intended during the Puerto Rican development programme of 1947, EPZs have helped sustain the image of capitalist growth and progress even through the crisis of the 1970s. In this way, the zones surely contributed to the Berlin Wall coming down in 1989. But the end of the Cold War did not mean the end of EPZ regimes. Instead, zones have spread ever more rapidly, as the governments of former socialist countries opened national economies and privatized public assets such as factories and machinery. In the 1990s and early 2000s, another obstacle for EPZ promoters emerged when trade unions joined a global campaign against the zones, listing the many killed trade unionists and workers' inhumane labour conditions. Their calls were echoed by the global anti-sweatshop movement, part of which was a large student campaign to prevent the sale of campus wear produced in EPZs. UNIDO, and even the World Bank, stopped promoting EPZs in the late 1990s and early 2000s. But with the recent global economic recession and what is called the 'second neoliberal revolution' in development economics, influential research groups in the Bank's public–private partnership bodies now support EPZs under the new label SEZ, claiming that such zones are part of a 2,500-year-long history of free trade.

This forging of world history and the persistence of EPZs after 1989 ultimately demonstrates that the confrontation between the capitalist and the socialist blocs, which was a defining feature of the Cold War, is an episode in a much longer and possibly much more global struggle over the distribution of wealth that has affected the lives of almost all households in the world.

Notes

1   Crawford, Fred L, 'Letter of submittal', in William H. Hackett, 'The Nationalist Party: Report to the Committee on Interior and Insular Affairs. US Congress. House of Representatives, Washington', 25 May 1951, Tarea 96–20, Caja 368, Folder 'Miss Crosby, Emily (Miss)', Oficina del Gobernador (OdG), General Archives of Puerto Rico (GAPR).

2   Hackett, William H. (1951), 'The Nationalist Party: A factual study of the Puerto Rican insurrectionists under Albizu Campos, the Blair House shooting, various assassination attempts, and of the communist praise and support for these seditionists', US Congress Report to the Committee on Interior and Insular Affairs, House of Representatives, Washington, Tarea 96–20, Caja 368, Folder 'Crosby, Emily (Miss)', ODG, GAPR, 23.

3   Hackett (1951).

4   Hackett (1951), 21.

5   On changing uses, see Neveling, Patrick (2015), 'Imperialism's new shades and long shadows: Free trade zones, export processing zones and special economic zones after World War II', in Saer M. Bâ and Immanuel Ness (eds.) (2015), *The Palgrave Encyclopedia of Imperialism and Anti-Imperialism*. Basingstoke: Palgrave Macmillan.

6   Boyenge, Jean-Pierre Singa (2007), 'ILO database on export processing zones (Revised)', *ILO Working Papers*, 251, <http://www.ilo.org/public/english/dialogue/sector/themes/epz/epz-db.pdf> [accessed 10 April 2009]; Akinci, Gokhan, Crittle, James and FIAS/The World Bank Group (2008), *Special Economic Zones: Performance, Lessons Learned, and Implications for Zone Development*. Washington: The World Bank Group, 7.

7   Engerman, David C. (2004), 'The romance of economic development and new histories of the Cold War', *Diplomatic History*, 28(1), 23–54, p. 51.

8   Dietz, James L. (1986), *Economic History of Puerto Rico. Institutional Change and Capitalist Development*. Princeton: Princeton University Press, 89.

9   Dietz (1986), 99.

10 Dietz (1986), 103–111.

11 Dietz (1986), 117–119.

12 Ayala, César J. and Bernabe, Rafael (2007), *Puerto Rico in the American Century: A History since 1898*. Chapel Hill: University of North Carolina Press, 47.

13 Stead, William H., (1958), *Fomento – The Economic Development of Puerto Rico (A Staff Report)*. Planning Pamphlet No. 103. Washington: National Planning Association, 4–5.

14 On the scientific origins and the consequences of these later policies, see Connelly, Matthew (2008), *Fatal Misconception: The Struggle to Control World Population*. Cambridge, MA: Belknap Press; Cullather, Nick (2007), 'The foreign policy of the calorie', *The American Historical Review* 112(2), 337–364.

15 Ayala and Bernabe (2007), 88–94.

16 For an in-depth analysis of economic and political developments, see Dietz (1986), 143–181.

17 Ayala and Bernabe (2007), 138–146.

18 Maldonado, A.W. (1997), *Teodoro Moscoso and Puerto Rico's Operation Bootstrap*. Gainesville: University of Florida Press, 32–45.

19 See Dietz (1986), 191–194.

20 Neveling, Patrick (2015), 'Export processing zones and global class formation', in James Carrier and Don Kalb (eds.) (2015), *Anthropologies of Class: Power, Practice, and Inequality*. Cambridge: Cambridge University Press, 171–199.

21 Office of Information for Puerto Rico/Washington (1946), 'Annual report', San Juan, Puerto Rico, Tarea 96–20, Caja 444, OdG, GAPR. Such promotional offices interestingly date back to 1930, when Theodore Roosevelt Jr. was governor of Puerto Rico, and opened an office in New York to promote mainland investment in Puerto Rico. Dietz (1986), 145.

22 Hilton Hotels Corporation (1947), 'Annual report to stockholders: Seven months ended December 31, 1946, Chicago, Ill.; Wilmington, Delaware', San Juan, Puerto Rico, Tarea 96–20, Caja 430, OdG, GAPR, 7.

23 On this movement, see Phillips-Fein, Kim (2009), *Invisible Hands: The Businessmen's Crusade against the New Deal*. New York: W.W. Norton.

24 Baca, Georg (2005), 'Legends of Fordism: Between myth, history, and foregone conclusions', in Bruce Kapferer (ed.) (2005), *The Retreat of the Social: The Rise and Rise of Reductionism*. New York: Berghahn Books, 31–46; Cowie, Jefferson (1999), *Capital Moves: RCA's Seventy-Year Quest for Cheap Labor*. Ithaca: Cornell University Press.

25 Little, Royal (1979), *How to Lose $100,000,000 and Other Valuable Advice*. 1st ed. Boston: Little, Brown, 63–76, quote from p. 74.

26 Little (1979), 63–76.

27 Subcommittee of the Committee on Interstate and Foreign Commerce (1948), 'Investigation of Closing of Nashua, N.H., Mills and Operations of Textron, Incorporated', United States Senate, Eighteenth Congress. Washington: United States Government Printing Office, 2

28 'Textron President Gives Reasons for Closing Nashua Textile Plants; South Offers More Workers; Per-Man Output in New England Low', *Wall Street Journal*, 18 September 1948, 2.

29 Maldonado (1997).

30 Little (1979), especially 82–83.

31 Cappa, Luis Sánchez, 'Accionistas de Textron pueden perder dinero', *El Mundo*, 29 March 1957.

32 The cases are too numerous to list here. A first EPZ became operational in Indonesia in 1970, just five years after the Suharto regime had established itself by killing several hundred thousand alleged communists, and another in Chile in 1975, two years after the US-backed coup by General Pinochet. Plans to set up an EPZ in Saigon were pursued even in the final weeks of the war in 1975. See Neveling, Patrick (in preparation), 'Relocating Capitalism: Export Processing Zones and Special Economic Zones since 1947', Chapter 7.

33 Maldonado (1997), xiii.

34 Little research has been done on these connections so far. Importantly, ADL might have been instrumental in preparing for an EPZ in Taiwan, which is often falsely claimed as an independent invention. On some literature on ADL's global EPZ ventures, see Schrank, Andrew (2003), 'Foreign investors, "flying geese", and the limits to export-led industrialization in the Dominican Republic', *Theory & Society* 32(4), 415–443.

35 Secretary to the Governor Louis Laboy, 'Cable to James P. Davies, Director, Office of Territories, Department of the Interior, Washington', San Juan, 27 September 1951, Tarea 96–20, Caja 1435 ('Conventions, Congresses, Meetings, Lectures'), OdG, GAPR.

36 John M. Webber, US Embassy, Santiago, 'Cable to Louis Munoz Marin, Governor of Puerto Rico' San Juan, 19 October 1951, Tarea 96–20, Caja 1435, OdG, GAPR.

37 Caribbean Commission (1952), 'Report of the Industrial Development Conference held by the Caribbean Commission in Puerto Rico, February 11–19', San Juan, Caja 2, Administracion De Fomento Economico/Div. Economia y Of. Desarollo Industrial (hereafter ADFEDEODI), GAPR, 1–3.

38 Caribbean Commission (1952), 4.

39 Caribbean Commission (1952), 11–12.

40 Patrick Neveling (2012), 'Manifestationen der Globalisierung: Kapital, Staat und Arbeit in Mauritius, 1825–2005', D.Phil thesis, Halle, Germany: Martin-Luther-University Library, 220–227.

41 Editorial, 'La Industria Num. 100', *Diario de Puerto Rico*, 16 February 1951. That newspaper also surely had reason to celebrate: Large advertisements congratulating PRIDCO for the signing of contract no. 100 by Beacon Textiles and PRIDCO-owned Crane China filled the pages before that editorial.

42 For the work of Hamilton Wright see Tarea 96–20, Caja 1435, OdG, GAPR.

43 Stevens, Raymond (1951), '100th Industry Celebration, Program of Activities', Boston, Series II, Box 2, MC 579, Trip to Puerto Rico, 1951, Arthur D. Little, Inc. Collection (hereafter ADL), Massachusetts Institute of Technology Archives (hereafter MITA).

44 E.g. (1950), 'The Atlantic Report on the World Today: Puerto Rico', *The Atlantic*, 186(1).

45 L. Manek, (ADL vice-president), 'Draft agreement sent to government development for Puerto Rico, attention of Mr. Esteban A. Bird, Executive Vice President', Boston, 3 April 1950, Series II, Box 2, MC 579, Trip to Puerto Rico, 1951, ADL, MITA.

46 Halden, Alexander G., 'Attachment to memorandum on trip to Jamaica'. Boston, 4 October 1951, Series II, Box 2, MC 579, Trip to Jamaica, 1951, ADL, MITA, 7.

47 ADL Staff Egypt, 'ADL on the Nile', Boston, January 1954, Series 7, Box 5, MC 579, History Earl Stevenson, ADL, MITA, 8.

48 See Arthur D. Little Inc. (1960), 'Various', Boston, Series II, Box 3, MC 579, The Asia Foundation, ADL, MITA.

49 Gresmann, Hans, 'Ideen auf Bestellung, Arthur D. Little macht Phantasie zu Geld', Sonderdruck *Die Zeit*, Hamburg, 17 November 1961, Series VII, Box 3, MC 579, ADL, MITA.

50 Staff reporter, 'Yankee Concern Sells Business Know-How To Underdeveloped Nations; Clients Grow', *The Wall Street Journal*, 14 September 1960, Series VII, Box 2, Puerto Rico-History, ADL, MITA.

51 'Ambassador Moscoso's Experience Seen Helpful to U.S.-Venezuelan Relations', statement by President Kennedy, Boston, 22 May 1961, Papers of Teodoro Moscoso, Box 2, 9/35/A/5/7, John F. Kennedy Library Archives (JFKL).

52 Arthur D. Little Inc. (1965), 'Annual Directors Meeting, March 26', Cambridge, MA, Series II, Box 1, MC 579, ADL, MITA.

53 Arthur D. Little Inc. (1957), 'New Puerto Rican Office is Opened', Series 7, Box 5, MC 579, Folder: History Earl Stevenson, ADL, MITA.

54 For a version where Bolin appears as an ADL employee, see Cowie (1999), 111–113. For Bolin's take on his work as an individual consultant, see Bolin, Richard (2000), 'Interview', in Samuel Schmidt (ed.) (2000), *In Search of Decision: The Maquiladora Industry in Mexico*. Flagstaff: Flagstaff Institute, 221–264.

55 McHeyman, Josiah (1991), *Life and Labor on the Border: Working People of Northeastern Sonora, Mexico, 1886–1986*. Tucson: University of Arizona Press.

56 Fernández-Kelly, María Patricia (1983), *For We Are Sold, I and My People: Women and Industry in Mexico's Frontier*. Albany: State University of New York Press, 23–26.

57 Subcommittee on Trade of the Committee on Ways and Means (1976), *Special Duty Treatment or repeal of Articles Assembled or Fabricated Abroad, Second Session on Items 806.30 and 807.00 of the Tariff Schedules of the United States (Provisions for Special Duty Treatment of Articles assembled or Fabricated Abroad) and Bills to Amend or Repeal Such Provisions*, US House of Representatives, Ninety-Fourth Congress. Washington: US Government Printing Office.

58 For a more detailed explanation, see Neveling (2014) in Carrier and Kalb (2014); also Christopher Miller (this volume).

59 Lambert, Youry (1993), *The United Nations Industrial Development Organization: UNIDO and Problems of International Economic Cooperation*. Westport, Conn.: Praeger.

60 See Neveling, Patrick (forthcoming), 'The global spread of Export Processing Zones and the 1970s as a decade of consolidation', in Knud Andersen, Stefan Müller and Ralf Richters (eds.) (forthcoming), *Changes in Social Regulation: State, Economy, and Social Protagonists since the 1970s*. Oxford: Berghahn Books.

61 Neveling (forthcoming).

62 Neveling (forthcoming).

63 For the correspondence, see Folder TS 221/2 (21), United Nations Industrial Development Organisation Archives, Vienna (UNIDOA).

64 See Tanaka, William H., 'Letter to Teodore Q. Pena, Commissioner and Executive Officer, Foreign Trade Zone Authority, Port Area, Manila', 16 April 1970, Folder TS 221/2 (21), UNIDOA.

65 Neveling (forthcoming).

66 Tanaka, W.H., 'Letter to Wu (KEPZ)' Vienna. 16 March 1970, Folder TS 221/1 (21), Economic Affairs, UNIDOA.

67 See Orenstein, Dara (2011), 'Foreign-trade zones and the cultural logic of frictionless production', *Radical History Review*, 2011(109), 36–61.

68 Farole, Tom (2011), *Special Economic Zones in Africa: Comparing Performance and Learning from Global Experiences*. Washington: The International Bank for Reconstruction and Development/The World Bank.

69 For a survey of free zones, EPZs and SEZs in world history along these lines see Neveling, 'Imperialism's new shades'. Miller (this volume) offers another perspective.

70 Neveling, (forthcoming).

71 For example, UNIDO Newsletter. 'UNIDO Calendar/15–27 November, Kaohisung, Taiwan, Training Workshop on Industrial Free Zones as Incentives to Promote Export-oriented Industries', Vienna, August 1971, UNIDO Newsletter Vol. I (1971–1976), UNIDOA.

72 On the history of Shannon Airport, the Shannon Free Trade Zone and of SFADCo, see Neveling, (2014).

73 Kelleher, Tom (1976), 'Handbook on export processing zones', Vienna, 007125, UNIDOA, Industrial Development Abstracts, Appendix 5.

74 UNIDO Newsletter. 'Conference adopts 57-point declaration', Vienna, May 1975, UNIDO Newsletter Vol. I (1971–1976), UNIDOA, 1–2.

75 United Nations Industrial Development Organisation (1978), 'Establishment of a World Export Processing Zones Association (WEPZA), Report of an Expert Working Group, Manila, Philippines, 30 January–4 February 1978', Vienna, ID/205 (ID/WG. 266/8), UNIDOA, Industrial Development Abstracts.

76 Neveling (2015). These data are to be treated as indicative rather than accurate.

77 For details, see Neveling (2012), Chapter 10. See Miller (this volume) for a different position on the Mauritian EPZ.

78 Embassy of Ireland, PRC, 'Letter from Joe Hayes to Paul Sheane, Chief Executive, Shannon Free Airport Development Corporation Ltd'. 1 December 1995, Archives of the Shannon Free Airport Development Corporation Ltd, Shannon Town, Republic of Ireland.

79 Political Adviser's Office, 'Shenzhen Special Economic Zone', 16 February 1982, HKRS 1056-1-316, Hong Kong Special Administrative Region, Government Records Service (GRS).

80 Senzhen Industrial Development Service Company, 'A brief introduction to the recent industrial investment projects in the Shenzhen Special Economic Zone in Guangdong Province (English Translation)', September 1982, HKRS 1056-1-316, Hong Kong Special Administrative Region, GRS.

81 Engerman (2004); Loth, Wilfried (2010), 'The Cold War and the social and economic history of the twentieth century', in Melvyn P. Leffler and Odd Arne Westad (eds.) (2010), *The Cambridge History of the Cold War*. Cambridge: Cambridge University Press, 503–524. Similar problems arose for Indian development policies. The lighthouse effect of Puerto Rican policies was such that the Indian government granted guarantees against nationalization to oil refineries and considered tax breaks and other investment incentives for foreign investors in the 1950s. Bowles, Chester (1952), 'New India', *Foreign Affairs*, 31(1), 79–94. Plans for the first Indian EPZ date back to the same period. Neveling, Patrick (2014), 'Structural contingencies and untimely coincidences in the making of neoliberal India: The Kandla Foreign Trade Zone, 1965–1991', *Contributions to Indian Sociology*, 48(1), 17–43.

82 Arrighi, Giovanni (2010), 'The world economy and the Cold War, 1970–1990' in Leffler and Westad (2010), 23–44.

83 Fröbel, Folker, Heinrichs, Jürgen and Kreye, Otto (1981), *The New International Division of Labour: Structural Unemployment in Industrialised Countries and Industrialisation in Developing Countries*. Cambridge: Cambridge University Press.

84 For an overview on this, see Neveling (2015).

85 This is one of the aspects in which my historical narrative differs from that of Miller's (this volume).

86 O'Brien, Patrick K. (2001), 'Review: metanarratives in global histories of material progress', *The International History Review*, 23(2), 345–367.

87 (1950), 'The Atlantic Report'.

Key texts

Cowie, Jefferson. (1999). *Capital Moves: RCA's Seventy-Year Quest for Cheap Labor*. Ithaca: Cornell University Press.

Heyman, Josiah M. (1991). *Life and Labor on the Border: Working People of Northeastern Sonora, Mexico, 1886–1986*. Tucson: University of Arizona Press.

Neveling, Patrick. (2015). 'Export processing zones and global class formation', in James Carrier and Don Kalb (eds), *Anthropologies of Class: Power, Practice, and Inequality*, Cambridge: Cambridge University Press, 171–199.

Neveling, Patrick. (2015). 'Flexible capitalism and transactional orders in colonial and postcolonial Mauritius: A post-occidentalist view', in Jens Kjaerulf (ed), *Flexible Capitalism: Exchange and Ambiguity at Work*, Oxford: Berghahn.

Ong, Aihwa. (1987). *Spirits of Resistance and Capitalist Discipline: Factory Women in Malaysia*. Albany: State University of New York Press.

Rosen, Ellen Israel. (2002). *Making Sweatshops: The Globalization of the U.S. Apparel Industry*. Berkeley: University of California Press.

Safa, Helen Icken. (1995). *The Myth of the Male Breadwinner: Women and Industrialization in the Caribbean*. Boulder: Westview Press.

Sklair, Leslie. (1988). *Foreign Investment and Irish Development: A Study of the International Division of Labour in the Midwest Region of Ireland*. Oxford: Pergamon Press.

PART II
INTELLECTUAL ASSERTIONS IN THE ANTI-COLONIAL ERA

This part incorporates individuals and groups who asserted their own perspectives and ideas into the major, often clashing, ideologies of the period: communism, human rights and self-determination, among others. It addresses how intellectuals coming from a background of oppression – both in the decolonizing world and within the superpowers – were attentive to, and also wary of, the potential to create a new social order. It considers how intellectuals situated themselves at the crossroads of the Cold War and decolonization; how they navigated the prominent institutions and ideas of the era; and how they ultimately sought to challenge normative ideas despite institutional and social constraints.

CHAPTER 4
CLASS STRUGGLE AND SELF-DETERMINATION AT *POLITICAL AFFAIRS*: AN INTELLECTUAL HISTORY OF COMMUNIST ANTI-COLONIALISM IN THE UNITED STATES, 1945–1960
John Munro

The Cold War and decolonization were neither external to the superpowers nor exactly contemporaneous. Given the swath of scholarship on Cold War domestic politics within the United States and the Soviet Union after the Second World War, not to mention the bookshelves of literature on colonialism and decolonization's longer durée, neither of these claims should seem particularly controversial.[1] Yet although the larger picture is established, we know less about what the interaction between the longer story of decolonization and the domestic dimensions of the Cold War looked like on the ground within the superpowers. By way of a reading of *Political Affairs*, the monthly journal of the Communist Party of the United States (CPUSA or CP), during the decade and a half after 1945, this chapter will devote attention to the details of one slice of anti-colonial Cold War culture within the United States. Along the way, it will make three principal arguments for the importance of ideas to histories of decolonization and the Cold War: that self-determination was a key concept in terms of solidarity between the African American freedom movement and struggles against formal colonization; that anti-communism was powerful but ultimately unable to totally silence the left in the United States in the 1950s; and that the post-war United States was theorized as an imperial force by intellectuals within the country. After some historical stage setting and contextualization of *Political Affairs* amid other publications of the period in question, I will take up a closer reading of three themes within the journal itself: self-determination, intersectionality and the idea that the combination of capitalist accumulation, white supremacy and an expansive foreign policy rendered the United States an imperial power, although one not in possession of a far-flung, formal empire.[2]

Popular front, anti-colonial front

In the United States and its antecedents, histories of resistance to what political theorist Cedric Robinson has generatively called 'racial capitalism', or the structural entanglement of white domination and capital accumulation, long precede the twentieth century.[3] Nonetheless, 1935 proved to be pivotal in the acceleration of opposition against the system that Robinson describes. That year alone, the founding of the trade union Congress of Industrial Organizations, the mass mobilization of African Americans against Italy's invasion of Ethiopia and the publication of *Black Reconstruction* by towering intellectual and co-founder of the National Association for the Advancement of Colored People (NAACP), Dr. W.E.B. Du Bois, all signalled an upsurge of militant, activist critiques of existing hierarchies. Also in 1935, the Soviet Union, in response to fascism's European ascent, called for liberals and leftists across the globe to unite in a 'Popular Front' against the forces of reaction. This Popular Front line marked a shift in world communist strategy, one that would have an important impact on politics in the United States.

Before 1935, the CPUSA, like other Moscow-aligned communist parties, argued that those parties occupying the liberal centre through to the far right of the political spectrum represented allied shades of support for the ruling class. Anything short of a demand for the overthrow of capitalism, accordingly, gave sustenance to the imperialist system that projected the reach of powers such as Britain or the United States in the search for profits and markets. The Popular Front, which dominated left politics for most of the following decade, revised this doctrine to downgrade opposition to imperialism in favour of left-liberal solidarity against the fascist danger. As Nazism's ascendancy predisposed many African American activists towards antifascism, and with more leftists recognizing that race mattered, the Black freedom movement became intertwined with the Popular Front during the Depression and after the United States formally entered the military contest with fascism in 1941. The result was not that the formal left was subsumed into the Black freedom struggle, or vice versa, but that each maintained a mutual relative autonomy. US communists tended to focus on defending the Soviet Union and its policies, while African American activists kept their eyes on defeating the racial logic that justified white supremacy, fascism and imperialism. Of course, 'Black' and 'Red' were often overlapping designations. In this context, the CPUSA was able to win renewed credibility and influence in the Black community through its support for anti-racist causes, but the party also engendered suspicion through its insistence on submission to its undemocratic, Stalinist mode of organization and by prioritizing Popular Front antifascism above ending Jim Crow segregation.

When victory over fascism in 1945 eliminated the enemy common to capitalist West and communist East, the US and USSR faced each other as increasingly inimical global rivals. Not surprisingly, the CPUSA got in line behind the Soviet Union in ending its Popular Front policy and in once again adopting an unaccommodating attitude towards capitalism and the empire-building that, following Marxist theory, it inexorably necessitated. US liberals, meanwhile, increasingly shied away from notions of diplomatic cordiality with the Soviets and from the further regulation of domestic capitalism inaugurated under Roosevelt's New Deal. These developments had contradictory effects.[4] The late 1940s and the 1950s were not auspicious years for the US left. The political culture of McCarthyism intensified anti-communism within the United States, while the CPUSA's own Stalinist milieu disenchanted organizations such as the NAACP. Stalinism was also well in evidence on the pages of *Political Affairs*. The result of this political culture – one not new to the post-war period – was a lack of democracy and substantive debate, especially on the topic of the waves of murderous purges that the Soviet government had carried out against its own citizens.[5] But a critique of US Stalinism absent a discussion of race can only produce an impoverished analysis. Civil rights organizer and contributor to *Political Affairs*, Jack O'Dell, for one, 'never met a black person who was in the Communist Party because of the Soviet Union. We joined the Communist Party because they fought against racism and they were dependable in that fight'.[6] O'Dell's interpretation exemplifies a tension within CP circles, one that historians have too often tried to resolve by exchanging examples of, on the one hand, dogmatism, centralism and ideological succour to the murderous excesses of Soviet policy, and on the other, a proud, fighting history of the oppressed against the beneficiaries of that oppression.

In any case, critiques of colonialism or white supremacy that emphasized the structural relationship between race and class were afforded less and less room in public life as the Cold War got under way, as the case of the Council on African Affairs (CAA) made clear. The CAA, led by Du Bois, artist-intellectual Paul Robeson and scholar-activist Alphaeus Hunton, was formed in 1937 and took advantage of the Popular Front spirit of antifascist cooperation to put forward an agenda that called for imperialism's dismantlement and Jim Crow's retirement. A decade into its existence, the CAA came under sustained attack as an alleged tool of the communist conspiracy, and a decade later the group collapsed under ongoing political pressure.[7]

The CAA was in part an outgrowth of the Popular Front. It was also the product of an anti-colonial front that spanned the depression and persisted well into the Cold War. The anti-colonial front was a political formation that opposed fascism but did not jettison support for self-determination in doing so. In the tradition of Du Bois' magnum opus of 1935, the anti-colonial front fused analyses of racism and capitalism (and later patriarchy, as we will see below) to argue that imperialism was the product of interlocking inequalities. Cold War anti-communism notwithstanding, such a productive tension that considered and contested the junctions of race, class and empire persisted. In terms of its intellectual production, *Political Affairs* represented something more than an ever-shrinking venue for Stalinist diatribes. The journal was a site of anti-colonial continuity where such themes as the co-constitution of multiple axes of oppression or the raced and gendered components of US empire, themes that would come to the fore in social movements and scholarly analysis in the coming decades, were able to develop. In doing so, *Political Affairs* joined a range of texts engaged in the same pursuit. The Old Left, as it came to be called, printed voluminous instructions for its generational successor, the New Left of the 1960s.[8]

Empire's opponents write back

Political Affairs devoted considerable space to the relationships between capitalist exploitation, racial oppression and colonial subjugation. The journal, however, was not unique. Several groundbreaking works published before, during and just after the Second World War by such figures as Du Bois, leftist historian Herbert Aptheker and novelist Howard Fast focused on African American resistance to racial and economic structures, as well as the deep roots of European imperialism that ultimately precipitated the world wars.[9] With titles such as *Color and Democracy* and *Freedom Road*, these were not the last books to highlight structural interconnections. A survey of but a few representative texts conveys a sense of the intellectual and literary world in which *Political Affairs* existed after 1945, while indicating that the journal was not singular, but part of an oppositional undercurrent within the United States that included and also transcended the CP-affiliated left.[10]

Racial capitalism, including its gendered and imperial components, was subject to rigorous critique in a range of important early Cold War titles. In 1946, as world war became Cold War, novelist Ann Petry's *The Street* offered a fictionalized account of how poverty, patriarchy and racism combined to thwart protagonist Lutie Johnson's efforts to make a decent life for herself and her son in wartime Harlem. In 1948, as Cold War realities tilted the political spectrum rightward within the United States, Trinidad-born Lincoln University sociologist Oliver Cromwell Cox published *Caste, Class, and Race*. Cox's comparative study took as its scope the world capitalist system to argue that 'racial antagonism is essentially political-class conflict', thereby carrying on Popular Front thinking that intertwined race and political economy.[11] Lloyd Brown did likewise in *Iron City*, a novel about Black communists organizing a defence campaign within prison for an African American millworker held on death row after being framed for murder. Written in 1951, *Iron City* was a defiant challenge to the racial order and the assault on the left at the pinnacle of McCarthyism's defence of both. Three years later, John Oliver Killens's profound novel *Youngblood* expressed how white supremacy policed all women's sexuality and exposed the brutal violence and daily indignities of Jim Crow Georgia. Killens also explored the possibilities of collective interracial solidarity between African Americans and poor whites.[12]

Meanwhile, sociologist E. Franklin Frazier, emphasizing the economics of white supremacy, turned his attention to African American leaders and was frustrated by what he saw as their willingness to conform to the limited parameters that anti-communism placed upon the freedom agenda. In 1957, Frazier excoriated the Black middle class for inhabiting what he called 'the world of make believe', where African American leaders abandoned Black workers, emulated the white propertied classes and accepted a form of racial integration that mandated political subordination to the demands of US Cold War policy. Among its targets, Frazier's polemic took aim at mainstream African American newspapers, singling out *Ebony* and *Jet* in particular, which he faulted for their shallow coverage of decolonization struggles internationally.[13] This critique was in keeping with Frazier's extensive, interdisciplinary impact on anti-colonial discourse within and beyond the United States during the 1950s and the 1960s.[14] Also in 1957, Alphaeus Hunton published *Decision in Africa*. Written in the wake of the demise of the Council on African Affairs, Hunton's volume chronicled the history of Africa's economic exploitation by Europe and the United States, and it proposed continental revolt as the solution to Africa's ills.[15]

In 1958, two additional titles appeared, which, although drawing on opposing political traditions within the larger left, further exemplified the semi-subterranean existence of an anti-colonial front in the United States. Independent leftist intellectual C.L.R. James had been deported from the United States to England in 1953, but he remained a voice of left opposition to the Stalinist and vanguardist ingredients that had often flavoured Popular Front politics. The small political organization, Correspondence, of which James, Grace Lee (Boggs), Martin Glaberman and until 1955 Raya Dunayevskaya were central figures, emerged from Trotskyist parties and tendencies in the early 1950s. James continued to advise the group from London, and under his leadership they published *Facing Reality*. This book took as its subject the creation of a new, more just society through international struggles against state power, union bureaucracies and racism. Arguing that 'it is the Negro people and Negro workers in particular who have brought home to white workers the importance of the colonial question, in Africa, but also in the Far East', *Facing Reality* indicated that an optimistically toned anti-colonialism that critiqued Popular Front strategy from the left existed at the moment when Old Left was becoming New.[16]

Similarly optimistic about the will of social movements to create social justice, although much closer to CP circles than *Facing Reality*, was Paul Robeson's *Here I Stand*. By 1958, Robeson was very familiar with the personal tolls that could tax domestic critics of US foreign policy: his passport had been revoked, his performing career undermined and his newspaper, *Freedom*, suppressed. Robeson could well have become totally cynical by the late 1950s, yet the sentiment in *Here I Stand* was directly reminiscent of the hopefulness that accompanied the defeat of fascism in 1945:

> Here, then, in the changing bases of power abroad, is the main source of that pressure for changes at home. The era of White Supremacy, the imperialist domination of the East by a handful of Western nations, is rapidly coming to an end. A new era is being born. We, the Negro people of the United States, and of the Caribbean area as well, are a part of the rising colored peoples of the world. ... Freedom is a hard-bought thing and millions are still in chains, but they strain toward the new day drawing near.[17]

With words that clearly connected the theme of formal empire's demise to that of domestic racial liberation, Robeson added to a published conversation that sought to describe and defy the imperial system in which aggregations of power along racial, economic and international lines were structurally linked. This critical discussion of racial capitalism did not lapse into silence, despite the very real influence of Cold War anti-communism. Rather, this body of work formed part of a vital intellectual bridge over the supposed McCarthyite void that might otherwise have severed the anti-colonial front from the

New Left era, when white supremacy, capitalism, patriarchy and imperialism would also constitute central themes of radical theory and praxis.

Leninism, Stalinism, journalism

In addition to such substantive, often scholarly, volumes, readers following left politics in the United States could turn to journals and magazines. Some of the largest journalistic contributions to anti-colonial discourse between the Second World War and the 1960s were produced by the CPUSA press and those friendly to it. The political constellation influenced by Leninism in the post-war United States saw the consistent dissemination of left ideas through magazines and journals as a paramount task, all the more so during a period of political reaction: their daily, weekly, monthly and quarterly undertakings in the late 1940s and the 1950s were a central part of the fight against empire at home and abroad. V.I. Lenin's influence on the CPUSA was apparent not only in his conception of imperialism as a special stage in the history of capitalism, but also in his insistence that professional revolutionaries remain in contact with each other and potential supporters by maintaining regular publications.[18] As the Cold War began, CP politics shifted from antifascist coalition towards class war, anti-imperialism and a more militant anti-racism; the published word was deemed essential to promoting that new vision.[19]

Beyond *Political Affairs*, the CP press maintained an anti-colonial forum for its left-wing readership through the *Daily Worker* and *Masses & Mainstream*. The main CPUSA paper, the *Daily Worker*, provided news reporting as well as renewed explications of the Party line, once every twenty-four hours. To the extent that the CPUSA opposed racism and empire, the *Daily Worker* did likewise. As we have seen, CPUSA's anti-colonial credentials were not impeccable, yet the *Daily Worker* contained numerous challenges to the imperial system of racial capitalism. The paper's campaigns against government harassment of Black anti-colonial activists Ferdinand Smith, Claudia Jones, Robeson, James Jackson and Du Bois, or William Patterson's and Herbert Aptheker's columns on the ways in which lynching, police brutality and the prison system functioned as interlocked tools of US empire exemplified the *Daily Worker*'s opposition to a transnational imperialism from which the United States was not exempt.[20]

Masses & Mainstream was a direct descendant of the *New Masses*. Itself connected to the early twentieth-century US left through the *Masses* (1911–1917), *New Masses* was a rather non-dogmatic communist arts and culture magazine that ran from 1926 to 1948.[21] In the early days of the Popular Front, with a circulation of 25,000, it outsold the liberal mainstays *New Republic* and the *Nation* combined. *New Masses* merged with the CP's literary journal *Mainstream* to form *Masses & Mainstream* in February 1948, which provided another platform for Du Bois in the late 1940s and the 1950s.[22] At the time of the publication's founding, Du Bois agreed to become a contributing editor at the request of Aptheker.[23] But such affiliations did not mean that Du Bois became a pawn of the communists. When Aptheker asked Du Bois to defend the CPUSA leadership in court by drawing a comparison between the historic oppression of African Americans and that of leftists fighting for the proletariat, he declined, stating bluntly that 'I think the analogy between the American Negro, whose position I know fairly well, and the Marxists is not good.'[24] Du Bois did not break with his communist allies, but such a rebuke reminded them of both the distinctiveness of African American struggles and of his political independence. Indeed, Du Bois took the opportunity afforded by his association with *Masses & Mainstream* to explain to a wider audience that 'with my particular type of thinking and impulse to action, it was impossible for me to be a party man.'[25] This publication allowed Du Bois to publish his arguments about the imbrications of race, class and empire, while associating the communist movement in the United States with the old sage and thus his prestige in the Black community.

The *Daily Worker* and *Masses & Mainstream*, then, joined the broad aggregation of publications that kept leftist politics in print, and in part comprised the milieu in which *Political Affairs* existed. As the theoretical journal of the CPUSA, *Political Affairs* produced a monthly statement of, and some debate about, the Party line in its coverage of politics and culture in the United States and internationally. In contrast to the *Daily Worker*'s relative brevity and *Masses & Mainstream*'s cultural orientation, *Political Affairs* delved into the issues of the day at length, and thus recorded the most fully developed theoretical analyses of the communist camp. Although the significance of the CP to the US left declined after the late 1940s and was further diminished after 1956, *Political Affairs* remained a point of contact for the Party and those it influenced. Given the declining fortunes of the CP during the 1950s, the journal was perhaps more important than ever in functioning as a vehicle for political continuity. Subscription rates indicated as much, with Aptheker reporting in December of 1957 that circulation had increased by more than 1,500 copies in the preceding four months. In 1958 he stated that circulation in July was up 750 copies over that of May. By 1962, Aptheker disclosed to then-Party leader Gus Hall that although individual subscriptions were on the increase, overall printing of *Political Affairs* was down due to a decline in bundle orders. The printing for that June was 5,000 copies.[26]

Tracing the documented record of anti-colonial ideas in *Political Affairs* reveals an unresolvable tension within a political culture where a Stalinist democratic deficit combined with the anti-racist promise of racial capitalism's abolition. In the world of the communist left, Moscow's influence was real, but it was not embraced in equal measure by all within the CPUSA orbit. After the Second World War, the CP rededicated itself to struggles against racism, patriarchy and imperialism in dogmatic ways that obliged its supporters to adhere strictly to the Party line. At times this tendency put Soviet priorities first and alienated communists from their traditional base among the white proletariat while driving away other sympathetic leftists.[27] Stalinism was authoritarian, but this did not prevent activists connected to the Party from carving out critical space in which to contest the dominant politics of the early Cold War; thus, significant anti-racist and anti-colonial work during this period was carried out under the banners of the CPUSA. At *Political Affairs*, those contributions occurred through ongoing attention to what was called the 'national and colonial question', through numerous articles that brought a gendered analysis to questions of race and class and through pieces specifically focused on US imperialism.

Renewing pre–Cold War debates about class, colony and nation

Debates on the left about class struggle and self-determination had taken on extra significance in 1917 when the Bolsheviks seized power in Russia and thus removed their approach to these issues from the realm of theoretical abstraction. Some Marxists, namely Rosa Luxemburg, had championed a proletarian internationalism. She insisted that imperialism would only temporarily extend capitalism's dominance, but 'even before this natural economic impasse of capital's own creating', workers should not capitulate to bourgeois nationalist detours but foment proletarian revolution without delay.[28] Lenin disagreed. By 1920 he promoted a nationalist-Marxist alliance in which 'Communist parties must assist the bourgeois-democratic liberation movement' in colonized territories.[29] Lenin's position won the day within Soviet Marxism, with Joseph Stalin pronouncing three months after Lenin's death that 'victory of the revolution in the West lies through a revolutionary alliance with the liberation movement of the colonies and dependent countries against imperialism'.[30] These Comintern debates also led, in 1928, to the 'Black Belt thesis', a position initially put forward by African American theorist and CPUSA member Harry Haywood. The thesis argued, following Stalin's definition, that African Americans in the southern United States constituted a nation. Beyond strengthening the anti-racist commitment of the CPUSA, this political line infused 'the national and colonial question' within US Marxism, where, as 'the Negro question', it attributed characteristics of nationality to the Black community within the United States.[31] The rise of fascism and consequent call for left-liberal unity sent the Black Belt thesis into decline. But with the onset of the Cold War, the thesis made a high-profile return in a series of articles in *Political Affairs*, thus creating new space for anti-racism to exist and be debated in the CP.

Party Educational Director Doxey Wilkerson touched off this conversation as the war was nearing its end in 1945 with a self-critical piece that was typical of the general reconsideration of the antifascist alliance. Wilkerson challenged the Party's wartime record, pointing to a lack of anti-racist initiative in the war industries, the segregated military and the US south. Looking ahead towards reconversion, Wilkerson urged 'a broad, militant counter-attack against reaction all up and down the Negro freedom front'.[32] However, for another CPUSA journalist, Claudia Jones, Wilkerson had not adequately clarified the political situation. Concerned that the fragile alliance between organized labour and the African American community, to the extent that it existed at all, would be divided and smashed by a wave of post-war reaction, Jones argued that the need to work diligently against white supremacy was now greater than ever. The Party was compelled to develop the theoretical tools equal to that task.

For Jones, dreams of racial freedom were not subsumable to working-class aspirations. It was for this reason that the national question loomed large in the struggle against US imperialism and its homologous European counterparts: 'It is our understanding of the Negro question as a *national* question, that is, as the question of a nation oppressed by American imperialism, in the ultimate sense as India is oppressed by British imperialism and Indonesia by Dutch imperialism.'[33] Jones argued that this did not mean that the CP ought to focus its energy on winning a Black nation in the US south, but that the notion of self-determination should remain a 'programmatic demand', a guiding principle around which anti-racist work could be organized.[34] In his response, Wilkerson argued that any revival of the 'Self-Determination in the Black Belt' slogan would be 'theoretically incorrect and, therefore, tactically disastrous'.[35] He saw Black national characteristics as only rudimentary in form, and characterized the African American population as a distinct national minority, seeking neither disintegration nor separation from the larger US nation. The national line would only impede the Marxist imperative of fostering maximum unity between Black and white masses.

Others, including Aptheker, joined the debate. For him, African American history confirmed the thesis of nationality.[36] And in 1950, James Jackson, who was then rising to a position of theoretical eminence within communist circles on this question, also argued that the Black Belt had some of the characteristics of a colony, but what was more important was to recognize that the severity of oppression in the region never bred docility. Instead, domination gave rise to 'a potentially democratic and revolutionary force, the oppressed and imprisoned Negro nation, which is fighting, and will fight, on a scale as yet unimagined, for its liberation from the imperialist bondage of Wall Street-Dixiecrat slavemasters'.[37] Jackson identified proletarian class war, Black self-determination and land reform as the key points of struggle in the 1950s' south.

The persuasiveness of Jones's and Jackson's articles, combined undoubtedly with pressure from the Party apparatus to get into ideological line, brought Wilkerson around. In 1952 he wrote a general article on race for the journal that upheld the logic of the national self-determination position, while providing a historical overview of the history of racism that brought colonialism to the fore. In an argument then in circulation via historian Eric Williams and which would later be amplified by scholars such as Edmund Morgan and Theodore Allen, Wilkerson claimed that racism was bound up with the evolution of capitalism and imperialism on both sides of the Atlantic in the sixteenth through nineteenth centuries. In his terms, there existed a 'causal relationship between the development of capitalist colonial exploitation and the rise of racism'.[38]

The original author of the self-determination line, Harry Haywood, also took part in this discussion, and unsurprisingly came down in favour of a national notion of the Black Belt. He also placed this conception in an international context with an argument that foreshadowed what was later called 'tricontinentalism'. Connecting the Americas to Africa and Asia, Haywood concluded that 'The intimate ties binding together the Negro peoples of the world constitute a great source of strength in the national liberation struggles in three continents. They are great weapons in the battle against the imperialists, especially those of the United States and Great Britain'.[39] Once again, *Political Affairs* made connections between the Black freedom struggle in the United States and anti-colonial movements throughout the global South.

Analysing the intersections of gendered racial capitalism

By the end of the 1950s, with the African American movement against racial segregation capturing the imagination of a new generation, the CP finally retired its self-determination slogan.[40] But through its attention to the national and colonial question, *Political Affairs* served as a conduit for debates about the relationship among race, class and empire that had preceded the Cold War and even the Popular Front. The journal also helped introduce new anti-imperialist perspectives, such as those that brought gender and empire into one field of vision. As was the case with the Party's renewed efforts against white supremacy, women's oppression took on new urgency as the CP embarked on its post-war shift to the left. This focus was signalled in *Political Affairs* by the CPUSA's upper echelon, with Party leaders Elizabeth Gurley Flynn and William Foster both taking up the issue of 'male supremacy'.[41] In parallel to the strain of anti-colonial thought maintained during the McCarthyite years, feminist activists within the CP likewise struggled against patriarchy.[42] No one brought these two streams together as forcefully and astutely as Claudia Jones.[43]

Born Claudia Cumberpatch in Port-of-Spain, Trinidad, in 1915, Jones immigrated to New York with her mother and three sisters in 1922. Inspired by the CP's Depression-era defence in the Scottsboro case, she joined the Young Communist League in 1936; in 1945 she 'graduated' into the CPUSA itself, moving quickly up the ranks to emerge as a major Party theorist after 1945.[44] She was arrested in 1951 with sixteen other CP leaders charged under the anti-communist Smith Act, and was ultimately deported to Britain in 1955. These harrowing experiences with McCarthyite repression did little to silence her. Instead, Jones organized against white racism within London's burgeoning Black community while continuing to publish critical analyses of US and British imperialism.[45] In the United States, in addition to writing for *Political Affairs*, Jones also worked as a CP journalist in other venues, especially the *Daily Worker*.[46] During the Second World War, she dutifully called for unity around Franklin Roosevelt that 'transcends creed or color, political belief or social standing'.[47] But after the war, the turn in Party direction enabled her to hone her considerable critical skills on the intersecting oppressions of the day.

At the *Daily Worker*, Jones contributed pieces advocating for civil rights for Black veterans and an ongoing federal commitment to the Fair Employment Practices Commission, as well as articles indicative of a parting of the ways between communists and liberals, such as critiques of the National Urban League's Lester Granger and labour leader A. Philip Randolph.[48] As the Cold War brought the repressive apparatuses of the US state down upon the Party, Jones used the *Daily Worker* to attack the government's foreign and domestic policy.[49] But as a publication dedicated to theoretical matters where she could develop her ideas at greater length, it was *Political Affairs* that circulated her most brilliant, original ideas.

As we have seen, Jones was one of the interlocutors in the discussion of the self-determination slogan. She also took the CP's post-war move away from the Popular Front as an opportunity to criticize the Party's wartime emphasis on African American integration into 'the existing American system'. After all, she pointed out, if such was the Black community's goal, 'what need to mobilize and heighten the fight against white chauvinist ideology? What need to mobilize independent and militant struggle against … Hitler-like discriminatory practices … ?'[50] After posing these questions, which revealed the fallacy that progressive unity could itself adequately address racial oppression, Jones criticized the Party's wartime record of uncritically supporting Roosevelt, ignoring daily Black struggles against white racism and failing to support the 'Double V' campaign for victories over both international fascism and domestic white supremacy. These retrospective criticisms represented more than another twist in the communist political line. They demonstrated that Party members could now voice their opposition to imperialism without the restrictions imposed by the terms of the wartime Grand Alliance.

Jones then turned to the salience of gender. She highlighted the reality in which women's wartime work was often reverted to homemaking, and for many Black women, the making of white women's homes. Jones also called attention to how women being sent back to the kitchen lacked adequate social services, contended with reduced workplace nursery programmes and faced rising milk prices. These developments ought to concern members of the Communist Party and readers of *Political Affairs*, Jones proposed, because they were issues around which left activists could mobilize women to fight for their rights within the United States. At the same time, these supposedly personal matters were clearly political in that they connected the ways in which support for imperial allies abroad through the Marshall Plan and Truman Doctrine brought few benefits to women and people of colour at home.[51]

Race and gender met empire in an article that made a notable contribution not only to the journal but also, in ways that would become clearer as anti-racist feminism developed over the coming decades, to social theory more generally. 'An End to the Neglect of the Problems of the Negro Woman!' was a response to the lack of racial nuance in the Party's attention to gender.[52] Jones underscored the hypocrisy of claims that women in the United States enjoyed relative workplace equality, boasts that stopped 'at the water's edge where Negro and working-class women are concerned. Not equality, but degradation and super-exploitation: this is the actual lot of Negro women!'[53] Constructing a multi-layered portrait of power, 'An End to the Neglect' posited race, class and gender as the intersecting sources of Black women's triple oppression. Jones surveyed the history of this oppression and the militancy and resilience with which it had been contested, then emphasized areas such as trade union activity, domestic service and interracial social gatherings where, across the political spectrum, Black women's contributions were consistently undervalued or worse. The responsibility for rectifying this deplorable situation, Jones contended, lay 'squarely on the shoulders of white men and white women'.[54] From this perspective, the Party's work on gender would be self-defeating absent a commitment to anti-racism, since 'only to the extent that we fight all chauvinist expressions and actions as regards the Negro people and fight for the full equality of the Negro people, can women as a whole advance their struggle for equal rights'.[55]

Jones took her readers through a complex argument about how multiple dimensions of social domination overlapped with and constituted one another, then demonstrated how all of this was entangled with imperialism. 'An End to the Neglect' concludes with the argument that the struggle against US imperialism could be waged effectively only if the intricacies of oppression were borne in mind. Thus, this article's contribution to anti-colonial thought in the United States encapsulated comparative literature scholar Carole Boyce Davies' later observation that 'Claudia Jones saw her various struggles, and her role in them, not as contradictory but as elements in an ongoing challenge to imperialistic domination at local and global levels'.[56] The perspective of 'An End to the Neglect' was taken up by other authors in countless subsequent articles in the *Daily Worker*, making Jones's insights accessible to an audience on the communist left broader than those who read the more abstract formulations of *Political Affairs*.[57] Her arguments also influenced the Sojourners for Truth and Justice, an anti-colonial and anti-racist organization headed by several leading Black women on the left. Although short-lived, the group's campaigns against apartheid in South Africa as well as racial terrorism within the United States made them a rare expression of Black feminist anti-imperialism in the 1950s.[58]

Conclusion: Theorizing US imperialism

Jones followed 'An End to the Neglect' with several other articles in *Political Affairs* that took up the relationship between capitalism, white supremacy, patriarchy and US foreign policy, but she was not the only communist writer worried about US imperialism, nor was she the only one who connected US foreign policy with hierarchies at home.[59] In one CP-produced pamphlet, for instance, Aptheker placed US expansion during the 1890s alongside the nation's long history of racial oppression to conclude that 'white chauvinism is organically connected, from its origin, with American imperialism'.[60] Aptheker's choice of decade, though, presented a tragic narrative in which a genuinely anti-colonial national founding was followed by a fall into the temptations of empire a century later. In the mid-1950s, Aptheker argued that compared to the ideas that attended the nation's founding, US Cold War policy was 'violative of these splendid traditions' and 'besmirches the noble heritage of our country'.[61] It was at such moments – hearkening as they did to the 'Communism is Twentieth Century Americanism' slogan of the late 1930s – that CP theorizing lacked attention to the connectivity between settler colonialism, racial slavery and US imperialism.[62]

There was, nonetheless, a range of communist interpretations of US empire. Foster, as the main representative of the Party's post-war turn, led the charge. Surveying the global political scene as the war drew to a close, he argued that 'the present world situation presents an unequalled opportunity for the United States to acquire domination internationally'.[63] For Foster, fascism in Europe and Asia was dead, and North America seemed its most likely post-war continental destination, with the Soviet Union constituting the major obstacle to a US-led fascist-imperialist resurgence. This argument represented an economically oriented understanding of fascism that pervaded much of the left in the Second World War era, in which fascism was a tool of big business rather than any kind of social phenomenon. Given the influence of Lenin's concurring account of imperialism as a manifestation of economics, analyses of US imperialism in *Political Affairs* sometimes lacked sharpness: US empire was at times equated with fascism or with capitalism, without drawing careful distinctions or particular attention to how culture, race and gender had also shaped the colonial past and present.

Throughout the 1945–1960 period, US empire-building remained in the spotlight at *Political Affairs*. Although not always with the intersectional nuance of Claudia Jones, the journal published numerous pieces that drew parallels and points of connection between US and European imperialism, as well as the African American freedom struggle and decolonization.[64] *Political Affairs* also paid attention to the ways in which Latinos within the United States and points south experienced and challenged Washington and Wall Street's imperial project, while the journal kept its readers conversant with US imperialism on the African continent.[65] Taken together, the journal's many articles devoted to empire in the Cold War added to the extensive, if not always highly visible, body of ongoing anti-colonial thought that made the 1940s and the 1950s more than merely Stalinist prologue to left history in the next decade.

Reading the issues of *Political Affairs* of the post-war period helps revise notions of the 1950s as a decade that completely ruptured radicalism within the United States. What comprised the main themes of communist intellectual history of the late 1940s and the 1950s – self-determination, intersectionality and US empire – continues to generate considerable attention and debate, and although they are not only a product of the mid-century communist left, the historical parallel is more than coincidental. *Political Affairs*, though, points to more than the partial failure of McCarthy-era anti-communism. The journal also provides evidence of one strand of solidarity politics that linked struggles against racial capitalism in the US and Europe's colonies; it substantiates the argument that decolonization has its own periodization longer than and autonomous from that of the Cold War; and it demonstrates the ways in which decolonization and the Cold War interacted within one of the superpowers. For several reasons, it remains an important text of its time.

Notes

1 Good starting places for the former include McEnaney, Laura (2010), 'Cold War mobilization and domestic politics: The United States', in Melvyn P. Leffler and Odd Arne Westad (eds.) (2010), *The Cambridge History of the Cold War, Volume I: Origins*. New York: Cambridge University Press, 420–441; Priestland, David (2010), 'Cold War mobilization and domestic politics: The Soviet Union', in Melvyn P. Leffler and Odd Arne Westad (eds.) (2010), *The Cambridge History of the Cold War, Volume I: Origins*. New York: Cambridge University Press, 442–463. For the latter, examples include Young, Robert J.C. (2001), *Postcolonialism: An*

Historical Introduction. New York: Blackwell; Bradley, Mark Philip (2010), 'Decolonization, the global south, and the Cold War, 1919–1962', in Leffler and Westad (2010), 464–485; Simpson, Brad (2012), 'The United States and the curious history of self-determination', *Diplomatic History*, 36(4), 675–694; Prashad, Vijay (2013), *The Poorer Nations: A Possible History of the Global South*. New York: Verso.

2 The voluminous historiography on the topic of US empire and the many complex issues it raises are given particularly insightful and comprehensive treatment in Kramer, Paul (2011), 'Power and connection: Imperial histories of the United States in the world', *American Historical Review*, 116(5), 1348–1391.

3 Robinson, Cedric J. (1983; 2000), *Black Marxism: The Making of the Black Radical Tradition*. Chapel Hill: University of North Carolina Press, especially Chapters 2 and 3; Quan, H.L.T. (2005), 'Geniuses of resistance: Feminist consciousness and the Black radical tradition', *Race & Class*, 47(2), 39–53.

4 Useful, and contrasting, starting places for these dynamics include Horne, Gerald (1996), 'Who lost the Cold War? Africans and African Americans', *Diplomatic History*, 20(4), 613–626; Plummer, Brenda Gayle (1996), *Rising Wind: Black Americans and U.S. Foreign Affairs, 1935–1960*. Chapel Hill: University of North Carolina Press, especially Chapter 5; Anderson, Carol (2003), *Eyes Off the Prize: The United Nations and the African American Struggle for Human Rights, 1944–1955*. New York: Cambridge University Press.

5 The enormity of the purges within the Soviet Union is covered vividly throughout Snyder, Timothy (2010), *Bloodlands: Europe Between Hitler and Stalin*. New York: Basic Books. For their impacts on the US left, see Isserman, Maurice (1993), *If I Had a Hammer: The Death of the Old Left and the Birth of the New Left*. Chicago: University of Illinois Press, 1–34; Wald, Alan M. (2012), *American Night: The Literary Left in the Era of the Cold War*. Chapel Hill: University of North Carolina Press, 292–318.

6 O'Dell, Jack (1956), 'The political scene in Louisiana', *Political Affairs*, 35(8), 13–23; O'Dell (1993), ' "I never met a black person who was in the Communist Party because of the Soviet Union:" Jack O'Dell on fighting racism in the 1940s', *History Matters*, <http://historymatters. gmu.edu/d/6927/> [accessed 20 December 2013]. For O'Dell's significance to the Black freedom movement, see Singh, Nikhil Pal (ed.) (2010), *Climbin' Jacob's Ladder: The Black Freedom Movement Writings of Jack O'Dell*. Berkeley: University of California Press.

7 Von Eschen, Penny M. (1997), *Race Against Empire: Black Americans and Anticolonialism, 1937–1957*. Ithaca: Cornell University Press.

8 On the relationship between Old and New Lefts in the United States, see Isserman, Maurice (1987; 1993), *If I Had a Hammer: The Death of the Old Left and the Birth of the New Left*. Chicago: University of Illinois Press; Gosse, Van (2005), *Rethinking the New Left: An Interpretative History*. New York: Palgrave Macmillan.

9 Du Bois, W.E.B. (1935; 1962), *Black Reconstruction in America, 1860–1880*. New York: Atheneum; Aptheker, Herbert (1943; 1993), *American Negro Slave Revolts*. New York: International Publishers; Fast, Howard (1944), *Freedom Road*. New York: Amsco School Publications; Du Bois, W.E.B. (1945; 1975), *Color and Democracy: Colonies and Peace*. Millwood, NY: Kraus-Thomson; Du Bois (1946; 1965), *The World and Africa: An Inquiry Into the Part Which Africa Has Played in World History*. New York: International Publishers.

10 There are several excellent and comprehensive studies of the context I am gesturing towards here. See Denning, Michael (1997), *The Cultural Front: The Laboring of American Culture in the Twentieth Century*. New York: Verso; Smethurst, James Edward (2005), *The Black Arts Movement: Literary Nationalism in the 1960s and 1970s*. Chapel Hill: University of North Carolina Press; Wald, Alan M. (2007), *Trinity of Passion: The Literary Left and the Antifascist*

Crusade. Chapel Hill: University of North Carolina Press; Jackson, Lawrence P. (2011), *The Indignant Generation: A Narrative History of African American Writers and Critics, 1934–1960*. Princeton: Princeton University Press; Wald, Alan M. (2012), *American Night: The Literary Left in the Era of the Cold War*. Chapel Hill: University of North Carolina Press.

11 Petry, Ann (1946), *The Street*. Boston: Houghton Mifflin; Cox, Oliver Cromwell (1948; 1959), *Caste, Class, and Race: A Study in Social Dynamics*. New York: Monthly Review Press, 333. Also see McAuley, Christopher A. (2004), *The Mind of Oliver C. Cox*. Notre Dame: University of Notre Dame Press, especially 54–58, 97–117.

12 Brown, Lloyd L. (1951; 1994), *Iron City*. Boston: Northeastern University Press; Killens, John Oliver (1954; 1982), *Youngblood*. Athens: University of Georgia Press.

13 Frazier, E. Franklin (1957), *Black Bourgeoisie: The Rise of a New Middle Class*. New York: Free Press, especially 191–192.

14 Gaines, Kevin K. (2005), 'E. Franklin Frazier's revenge: Anticolonialism, nonalignment, and black intellectuals' critiques of western culture', *American Literary History*, 17(3), 506–529.

15 Hunton, William Alphaeus (1957; 1960), *Decision in Africa: Sources of Current Conflict*. New York: International Publishers.

16 James, C.L.R., and Boggs, Grace Lee (1958; 2006), *Facing Reality: The New Society, Where to Look for It and How to Bring It Closer*. Chicago: Charles H. Kerr, 157.

17 Robeson, Paul (1958; 1988), *Here I Stand*. Boston: Beacon Press, 84–85.

18 Lenin, V.I. (1916; 1939), *Imperialism: The Highest Stage of Capitalism*. New York: International Publishers; Lenin (1902; 1947), *What Is To Be Done? Burning Questions of Our Movement*. Moscow: Progress Publishers.

19 Hill, Rebecca (1998), 'Fosterites and feminists, or 1950s ultra-leftists and the invention of AmeriKKKa', *New Left Review*, 228, 66–90.

20 See, for example, 'Ferdinand Smith held at Ellis Island by gov't', *Daily Worker*, 23 May 1952; 'Defend Claudia Jones!', *Daily Worker*, 10 November 1955; 'Paul Robeson heard despite state dep't', *Daily Worker*, 4 May 1955; 'Jackson's statement on Smith Act fight', *Daily Worker*, 7 December 1955; 'State dep't bars Du Bois from Ghana', *Daily Worker*, 1 March 1957; Patterson, William L. (1953), 'Official US prison data bare persecution of Negro people', *Daily Worker*, 20 May 1953; Aptheker (1953), 'The jail as a special weapon in oppression of Negro people', *Daily Worker*, 1 July 1953.

21 On the *New Masses*, see Wald, Alan M. (2002), *Exiles from a Future Time: The Forging of the Mid-Twentieth-Century Literary Left*. Chapel Hill: University of North Carolina Press, Chapter 4.

22 ' "Masses & Mainstream" off press today', *Daily Worker*, 27 February 1948; Kelley, Robin D.G. (2000), 'Interview of Herbert Aptheker', *Journal of American History*, 87(1), 151–171, especially 160; Wald (2002), 108.

23 W.E.B. Du Bois to Herbert Aptheker, 25 February 1948, reel 62, frame 352, W.E.B. Du Bois Papers (Special Collections, W.E.B. Du Bois Library, University of Massachusetts, Amherst).

24 W.E.B. Du Bois to Herbert Aptheker, 11 April 1949, reel 63, frame 690, Du Bois Papers.

25 Du Bois, W.E.B. (1948), 'From McKinley to Wallace: My fifty years as a political independent', *Masses & Mainstream*, 1(6), 3–13, p. 7.

26 Herbert Aptheker to John Pittman, 10 December 1957, box 1, folder 30, John Pittman Papers (Tamiment Library and Robert F. Wagner Labor Archives, New York University); Herbert Aptheker to William Alphaeus Hunton, 25 July 1958, box 5, folder 31, Herbert Aptheker

Papers (Department of Special Collections, Stanford University Libraries); Herbert Aptheker to Gus Hall, 22 May 1962, box 8, folder 24, Aptheker Papers.

27 Three useful explorations of these dynamics are Anderson, Carol (2003), 'Bleached souls and red Negroes: The NAACP and black communists in the early Cold War, 1948–1952', in Brenda Gayle Plummer (ed.), *Window on Freedom: Race, Civil Rights, and Foreign Affairs, 1945–1988*. Chapel Hill: University of North Carolina Press, 93–113; Healey, Dorothy Ray and Isserman, Maurice (1993), *California Red: A Life in the American Communist Party*. Champaign: University of Illinois Press, 125–129; and Zahavi, Gerald (1996), 'Passionate commitments: Race, sex, and communism at Schenectady General Electric, 1932–1954', *Journal of American History*, 83(2), 514–548.

28 Luxemburg, Rosa (1913; 1964), *The Accumulation of Capital*. New York: Monthly Review Press, 446–453, 467, p. 467.

29 Lenin, (1920), 'Draft theses on national and colonial questions'. <http://marxists.anu.edu. au/archive/lenin/works/1920/jun/05.htm> [accessed 20 December 2013]. For a discussion of how Lenin's thinking on this point evolved as a result of his debate with Indian Marxist intellectual M.N. Roy, see Haithcox, John Patrick (1971), *Communism and Nationalism in India: M.N. Roy and Comintern Policy, 1920–1939*. Princeton: Princeton University Press, Chapter 1. For the impact of Lenin's rhetorical allegiance to self-determination on anti-colonial movements at the end of the First World War, see Manela, Erez (2007), *The Wilsonian Moment: Self-Determination and the International origins of Anticolonial Nationalism*. New York: Oxford University Press, 37–38, 195–196.

30 Stalin, Joseph (ed.) (1924; 1936), 'The national question', in (1936), *Marxism and the National and Colonial Question*. London: Lawrence and Wishart, 192. Within the Soviet Union, Lenin's and Stalin's ideas about the utility of nationalism legitimated Soviet nationalities policies that reified minority identities and had their own imperial elements, including ethnic cleansing. See Martin, Terry (2001), *The Affirmative Action Empire: Nations and Nationalism in the Soviet Union, 1923–1939*. Ithaca: Cornell University Press; Brown, Kate (2004), *A Biography of No Place: From Ethnic Borderland to Soviet Heartland*. Cambridge, MA: Harvard University Press; Edgar, Adrienne (2006), 'Bolshevism, patriarchy, and the nation: The Soviet "emancipation" of Muslim women in pan-Islamic perspective', *Slavic Review*, 65(2), 252–272.

31 Stalin, Joseph (1913), 'Marxism and the national question', in Stalin (1936), 8; Haywood, Harry (1978), *Black Bolshevik: Autobiography of an Afro-American Communist*. Chicago: Liberator Press, 218–240, 268–269; Horne, Gerald (1993), 'The red and the black: The Communist Party and African-Americans in historical perspective', in Michael E. Broen et al. (eds.) (1993), *New Studies in the Politics and Culture of U.S. Communism*. New York: Monthly Review Press, 199–237; Solomon, Mark (1998), *The Cry Was Unity: Communists and African Americans, 1917–1936*. Jackson: University Press of Mississippi, 68–91.

32 Wilkerson, Doxey A. (1945), 'Speech by Doxey A. Wilkerson', *Political Affairs*, 24(7), 619–623, p. 623.

33 Jones, Claudia (1946), 'On the right to self-determination for the Negro people in the Black Belt', *Political Affairs*, 25(1), 67–77, p. 69, emphasis original.

34 Jones (1946), 77.

35 Wilkerson (1946), 'The Negro and the American nation', *Political Affairs*, 25(7), 652–668, p. 652.

36 Aptheker, Herbert (1949), 'Consciousness of Negro nationality: An historical survey', *Political Affairs*, 28(6), 88–95.

37 Jackson, James (1950), 'Theoretical aspects of the people's struggle in the south', *Political Affairs*, 29(7), 66–82, p. 68.

38 Wilkerson (1952), 'Race, nation and the concept "Negro"', *Political Affairs*, 31(8),13–26 pp. 19–20. Also see Williams, Eric (1944; 1994), *Capitalism and Slavery*. Chapel Hill: University of North Carolina Press; Morgan, Edmund S. (1975), *American Slavery, American Freedom: The Ordeal of Colonial Virginia*. New York: W.W. Norton; Allen, Theodore W. (1994), *The Invention of the White Race, Volume One: Racial Oppression and Social Control*. New York: Verso; Allen, Theodore W. (1997), *The Invention of the White Race, Volume Two: The Origin of Racial Oppression in Anglo-America*. New York: Verso.

39 Haywood, Harry (1952), 'Further on race, nation and the concept "Negro"', *Political Affairs*, 31(10), 47–59, p. 59. 'Tricontinentalism' was introduced in Havana in 1966, at the first conference of the Organization of Solidarity of the Peoples of Africa, Asia and Latin America, and subsequently became a concept that brought together anti-colonial struggles and postcolonial theory. See Young (2001), especially 4–5.

40 Lightfoot, Claude (1960), 'The Negro question today', *Political Affairs*, 39(2), 84–90.

41 Flynn, Elizabeth Gurley (1948), '1948 – a year of inspiring anniversaries for women', *Political Affairs*, 27(3), 259–265; Foster, William Z. (1948), 'On improving the Party's work among women', *Political Affairs*, 27(10), 984–990.

42 Weigand, Kate (2001), *Red Feminism: American Communism and the Making of Women's Liberation*. Baltimore: Johns Hopkins University Press; Cobble, Dorothy Sue (2004), *The Other Women's Movement: Workplace Justice and Social Rights in Modern America*. Princeton: Princeton University Press, especially 28–31.

43 While Jones's individual brilliance is not difficult to detect, it must be noted that her analysis and her anticipation of intersectionality were also the products of collective debate and discussion among Black left feminists. This dynamic is readily apparent in three excellent recent studies: Gore, Dayo F. (2011), *Radicalism at the Crossroads: African American Women Activists in the Cold War*. New York: New York University Press; McDuffie, Erik S. (2011), *Sojourning for Freedom: Black Women, American Communism, and the Making of Black Left Feminism*. Durham: Duke University Press; Higashida, Cheryl (2012), *Black Internationalist Feminism: Women Writers of the Black Left, 1945–1995*. Champaign: University of Illinois Press.

44 For more on Scottsboro, see Pennybacker, Susan (2009), From Scottsboro to Munich: Race and Political Culture in 1930s Britain. Princeton: Princeton University Press.

45 Sherwood, Marika (1999), *Claudia Jones: A Life in Exile*. London: Lawrence & Wishart; Davies, Carole Boyce (2007), *Left of Karl Marx: The Political Life of Black Communist Claudia Jones*. Durham: Duke University Press.

46 Jones's journalistic output is surveyed in Davies (2007), Chapter 2.

47 Jones, Claudia, 'Concord at Crimea', *Spotlight*, April 1945, 8–10, p. 10.

48 Jones, Claudia, 'Vets form outfit to fight for Negroes' rights', *Daily Worker*, 9 April, 1946; Jones, Claudia, 'Some queries to FEPC "leaders"', *Daily Worker*, 25 February 1946; Jones, Claudia, 'Fight for FEPC needs support', *Daily Worker*, 24 June 1946; Jones, Claudia, 'The shrewd strategy is unity', *Daily Worker*, 3 July 1946; Jones, Claudia, 'Truman, Randolph stage love fest over remains of Senate FEPC bill', *Daily Worker*, 22 February 1946: Jones, Claudia, 'How Randolph aided filibuster', *Daily Worker*, 23 February 1946.

49 Jones, Claudia, 'Un-American committee and the Negro people [in three parts]', *Daily Worker*, 1, 2 and 3 August 1949; Jones, Claudia, 'Claudia Jones writes from Ellis Island', *Daily Worker*, 8 November 1950; Jones, Claudia, 'The rising peace demand at women's conventions', *Daily Worker*, 15 June 1951; Jones, Claudia, 'Warmakers fear America's

women', *Daily Worker*, 7 August 1951; Jones, Claudia, 'Her words rang out beyond the walls of the courthouse', *Daily Worker*, 21 November 1952.

50 Jones, Claudia (1945), 'Discussion article by Claudia Jones', *Political Affairs*, 24(8), 717–720, p. 719.

51 Jones, Claudia (1948), 'For new approaches to our work among women', *Political Affairs*, 27(8), 738–743.

52 Weigand (2001), 101.

53 Jones, Claudia (1949), 'An end to the neglect of the problems of the Negro woman!', *Political Affairs*, 28(6), 51–67, p. 52.

54 Jones (1949), 62.

55 Jones (1949), 63.

56 Davies (2007), 60.

57 Weigand (2001), 108.

58 McDuffie (2008), 'A "new freedom movement of Negro women": Sojourning for truth, justice, and human rights during the early Cold War', *Radical History Review*, 101, 81–106; Castledine, Jacqueline (2008), '"In a solid bond of unity": Anticolonial feminism in the Cold War era', *Journal of Women's History*, 20(4), 57–81.

59 Jones, Claudia (1950), 'International women's day and the struggle for peace', *Political Affairs*, 29(3), 32–45; Jones, Claudia (1951), 'Foster's political and theoretical guidance to our work among women', *Political Affairs*, 30(3), 68–78; Jones, Claudia (1951), 'For the unity of women in the cause of peace!', *Political Affairs*, 30(2), 151–168; Jones, Claudia (1952), 'The struggle for peace in the United States', *Political Affairs*, 31(2), 1–20.

60 Aptheker, Herbert (undated), 'American imperialism and white chauvinism', box 1, folder 6, Jefferson School of Social Science Records (Tamiment Library).

61 Aptheker (1954), 'The Declaration of Independence', *Political Affairs*, 33(7), 10–22, p. 18.

62 On the Americanism line, see Isserman, Maurice (1982), *What Side Were You On? The American Communist Party During the Second World War*. Middletown, CT: Wesleyan University Press, 9–14.

63 Foster, William Z. (1945), 'The danger of American imperialism in the postwar period', *Political Affairs*, 24(6), 493–500, p. 495. Also see Foster, William Z. (1946), 'American imperialism, leader of world reaction', *Political Affairs*, 25(8), 686–695.

64 Pittman, John (1946), 'The Negro people spark the fight for peace', *Political Affairs*, 25(8), 724–433; Berry, Abner (1948), 'Cotton patch imperialism and Negro freedom', *Political Affairs*, 27(11), 1129–1136; Ford, James W. (1949), 'The Communist Party: Champion fighters for Negro rights', *Political Affairs*, 28(6), 38–50; Patterson, William L. (1950), 'In memory of Sacco and Vanzetti', *Political Affairs*, 29(7), 83–85; Davis, Benjamin J. (1950), 'On the colonial liberation movements', *Political Affairs*, 29(11), 37–49; Jackson, James (1951), 'The effect of the war economy on the south', *Political Affairs*, 30(2), 106–123; Davis, Benjamin J. (1951), 'Foster's contributions to the cause of national and colonial liberation', *Political Affairs*, 30(3), 36–50; Patterson, William L. (1951), 'We charge genocide!', *Political Affairs*, 30(12), 42–52.

65 J.D. (1952), 'On chauvinism against the Mexican-American people', *Political Affairs*, 31(2), 51–56; Perry, Pettis (1952), 'Puerto Rico and the fight for its independence', *Political Affairs*, 31(6), 30–37; Foster, William Z. (1953), 'The explosive situation in Latin America', *Political Affairs*, 32(7), 8–14; Hunton, William Alphaeus (1959), 'Central Africa and freedom', *Political Affairs*, 38(4), 44–48; Lumer, Hyman (1960), 'U.S. imperialism and the Congo', *Political Affairs*, 39(9), 1–12.

Key texts

Gore, Dayo F. (2011). *Radicalism at the Crossroads: African American Women Activists in the Cold War*. New York: New York University Press.

Higashida, Cheryl. (2012). *Black Internationalist Feminism: Women Writers of the Black Left, 1945–1995*. Champaign: University of Illinois Press.

McDuffie, Erik S. (2011). *Sojourning for Freedom: Black Women, American Communism, and the Making of Black Left Feminism*. Durham: Duke University Press.

Robinson, Cedric J. (1983; 2000). *Black Marxism: The Making of the Black Radical Tradition*. Chapel Hill: University of North Carolina Press.

Smethurst, James Edward. (2005). *The Black Arts Movement: Literary Nationalism in the 1960s and 1970s*. Chapel Hill: University of North Carolina Press.

Von Eschen, Penny M. (1997). *Race Against Empire: Black Americans and Anticolonialism, 1937–1957*. Ithaca: Cornell University Press.

Wald, Alan M. (2002). *Exiles from a Future Time: The Forging of the Mid-Twentieth-Century Literary Left*. Chapel Hill: University of North Carolina Press.

CHAPTER 5
'A UNIQUE LITTLE COUNTRY': LEBANESE EXCEPTIONALISM, PRO-AMERICANISM AND THE MEANINGS OF INDEPENDENCE IN THE WRITINGS OF CHARLES MALIK, c. 1946–1962

Andrew Arsan

The Lebanese philosopher and politician Charles Malik was a reluctant diplomat. Cherry-picked to be Lebanon's envoy to the United Nations Conference on International Organization in San Francisco of April 1945 by the president of the newly independent state, Bishara al-Khuri, he returned to his hotel after one round of meetings to record in his diary his distaste with the niceties of diplomatic life: 'Power politics and bargaining', he insisted, 'nauseate me. There is so much unreality and play and sham that I can't swing myself into this atmosphere and act'. His 'heart', he wrote to his former doctoral supervisor, the British-born Harvard philosopher A.N. Whitehead, lay 'definitely in teaching and speculation'; his 'interest in politics and diplomacy' was a mere 'temporary' distraction, which he would abandon 'as soon as I find my mission reasonably fulfilled'.[1]

Protest though he might, Malik would spend much of the subsequent decade and a half in the glare of the diplomatic limelight, whether as a representative of Lebanon or as one of the key participants in the debates on human rights, self-determination and the meaning of freedom and sovereignty that unfolded in the 1940s and the 1950s, as political movements across Africa, Asia and the Middle East sought their independence from colonial rule. He served as Lebanese ambassador to the United States during 1945–1955, juggling this appointment with a succession of roles at the United Nations. After a brief return to academia as a professor of philosophy at the American University of Beirut, he was appointed Lebanese foreign minister by President Kamil Sham'un in November 1956, a position he would hold until 1958.

Malik's spell in office proved both tumultuous and fraught with controversy. In March 1957, the Sham'un government declared its adherence to the Eisenhower doctrine. Enunciated by the American president in a speech to Congress that January, this undertook 'to secure and protect the territorial integrity and political independence of such nations, requesting such aid against overt armed aggression from any nation controlled by international communism'.[2] This move appeared the culmination of a

I would like to thank the volume editors, Elisabeth Leake and Leslie James, and Cyrus Schayegh for their close readings of this chapter, and Susan Pennybacker, Paul Anderson, Toby Matthiesen and Will Carruthers for their helpful comments on various incarnations.

rapprochement between Western governments casting about for a sympathetic and reliable ally in the Eastern Mediterranean, and the Sham'un's government, increasingly rattled by domestic opposition and the seemingly inexorable swell of pan-Arabism in the wake of the Suez crisis of 1956. To many Arab nationalists in Lebanon, Syria and Egypt, it seemed further confirmation of Sham'un's treacherous drift or 'deviation' away from the Arabist principles he had espoused in the late 1940s and the early 1950s, a process that had begun with his refusal to condemn the Baghdad pact of 1955, and to break diplomatic ties with Britain and France during Suez. The latter, in particular, had rendered him complicit, in the eyes of his ideological foes, in the 'tripartite aggression' against Egypt.

For those who opposed this decision, regarding it as a capitulation to the forces of reaction and imperialism, Malik appeared just as culpable as Sham'un. Indeed, many contemporaries regarded Malik as America's man in the Middle East, treating his sympathy for the United States as the natural pendant to his hostility towards pan-Arabism. George McClintock, American ambassador to Beirut in the late 1950s, described Malik as the 'apostle of Americanism'.[3] To his predecessor, Donald Heath, he was the 'public figure in the Middle East most vocally in favour of cooperation with America' and 'chief source attack on Nasser-type Arab nationalists and communists'. For his part, the British ambassador to Beirut, George Middleton, was certain that Malik's affections were fully reciprocated, observing that Malik 'is persona gratissima in Washington and can always count on a sympathetic hearing'.[4] Such opinions were hardly closely guarded secrets, but mere echoes of widely held perceptions. In the months after his appointment, Malik served as a focus for 'anti-American opinion', a lightning rod for Lebanese opponents of the Sham'un government and its decision to adhere to the Eisenhower doctrine.[5] For those who sought greater integration into the Arab world, and eventual incorporation into an Arab union, Malik seemed the very embodiment of 'deviationism' – a figure so lost in his passionate embrace of American empire that he failed to notice the inexorable historical change unfolding all around him. So close was Malik's association with the United States in the minds of contemporaries that Kamil Sham'un's decision to appoint him foreign minister was widely seen as a 'declaration of policy', an unequivocal show of the government's 'pro-Western' – and particularly, pro-American – inclinations, borne out by its adherence to the Eisenhower doctrine a few months later.[6]

Ad hominem attacks on both Sham'un and Malik as traitors to the Arab cause, full of imprecations and dark mutterings, became frequent on the radio station Sawt al-'Arab, the mouthpiece of Egyptian pan-Arabism. Malik only grew more unpopular when he was elected to parliament in the legislative elections of 1957, condemned by Sham'un's opponents as mired in flagrant gerrymandering and fraud. He thus came to symbolize all that was wrong with the Sham'un administration in the eyes of figures like the Sunni politician Sa'ib Salam or the Druze notable Kamal Junblat. On the one hand, Malik, parachuted into parliamentary life, seemed to stand for Christian high-handedness and Sham'un's overweening disregard for due process and the desires of the Lebanese people. On the other, he appeared to embody the refusal of Christian Lebanese to acquiesce in the seemingly irrepressible growth of pan-Arab sentiment. When latent tension between Sham'un's supporters and the opposition erupted into street fighting in July 1958, Malik was charged with taking the government's case to the United Nations, accusing the newly created United Arab Republic (UAR) of a dangerous infringement of Lebanese sovereignty. The UAR, he argued, had fomented unrest through relentless propaganda, had channelled weapons and funds to the rebels, and had let its agents loose to commit terrorist acts on Lebanese soil. All of this, he fulminated, amounted to a foreign-sponsored coup against Lebanon's legitimate government.

The many faces of Malik

Much of the growing scholarly attention Malik has received in recent years has glossed over his national engagements, focusing firmly on his role as an advocate of human rights, both at the United Nations and at the Bandung conference of 1955. There is ample justification for this, for as Sam Moyn has pointed out, he was 'perhaps the key figure' in the negotiations that led to the adoption of the Universal Declaration of Human Rights in 1948: it was Malik who helped secure unanimous approval for the draft as president of the Economic and Social Council, and who took on the back-breaking work of steering it through eighty-one meetings of the General Assembly's Committee on Social, Economic and Cultural Affairs – or Third Committee – and some 168 amendments.[7] To Roland Burke, meanwhile, Malik – 'one of the leading human rights advocates in the world' – helped find a platform for these rights at Bandung, where he distinguished himself by his deep knowledge of UN procedure and diplomatic nous.[8]

This chapter seeks to turn the lens of scholarly inquiry back upon Malik's other roles in these years, first as Lebanon's ambassador to the United States, then as the country's foreign minister. In doing so, it seeks to examine afresh, and complicate, Malik's historiographical reputation as an unquestioning proponent of American interests. Historians have often followed contemporary perceptions of Malik to cast him in the role of a broker beyond compare, doing America's bidding in the Middle East. Citing his education, his time in Washington and his close ideological and personal rapport with John Foster Dulles – who shared both Malik's deep personal piety and profound animus for communism – as evidence of his role in facilitating the tentacular extension of US power through the region in the first decade of the Cold War. To Caroline Attié, Malik, whose 'hatred of Communism echoed that of Dulles', was 'fervently pro-American' and 'pro-Western'.[9] Likewise, Irene Gendzier describes him as a staunch 'exponent of a Lebanese-US political rapprochement', who made repeated overtures to State Department officials from the late 1940s onwards, beseeching them to pay greater attention to Lebanon and its place in the Middle East. Despite initial American wariness, he came in due course to be recognized as a crucial 'ally' and 'interlocutor', who helped shape 'Washington's thinking on Lebanon and the region in a manner compatible with US interests', in large part because of his close personal relations with the CIA bureau chief in Beirut, Wilbur Eveland, and his 'personal, ideological, and theological rapport' with Dulles himself.[10]

However, this chapter argues that we must strive to understand his undoubted sympathy for the United States as the product of a protracted, inconsistent and sometimes fraught process of political reflection. Why did Malik come to be, by the mid-1950s, such an ardent proponent of rapprochement with the United States? And how did his attitude towards the United States change over the course of the late 1940s and the 1950s, and for what reasons? The answers to these questions, this chapter contends, are far from self-evident. Contrary to received opinion, they are not to be found in a long-standing and deep-seated predisposition towards America on Malik's part. Rather, his embrace of America was at first distinctly ambivalent, before becoming increasingly full-throated, if not full-hearted, in the mid-1950s. The motives for this turnabout can be found in his deep and unwavering commitment to Lebanese sovereignty and his fondness for a political entity he regarded as both precious and inherently precarious, surrounded as it was by hostile neighbours jealous of its independence and eager to infringe upon its freedoms. This attachment was only bolstered by Malik's virulent antipathy for communism and pan-Arabism, threats he regarded as intimately bound together. With its 'dialectical materialism', the former was the 'enemy of freedom and man', and the latter, little more than an expression of the 'dark and blind craving of the masses', with their 'clamor for social and economic justice'.[11] To this list, finally, we must add his complex and ambivalent understanding of self-determination. To Malik, this notion was at once full of the potential for genuine individual and collective liberation, and open to manipulation by those whose expansionist appetites and oppressive propensities threatened to reproduce the imperial inequalities independence had seemingly promised to undo. We should be wary, then, of treating Malik either as a champion of the rights of the person, a committed universalist free of national moorings, or as a mere comprador of American empire. More useful than these rigid frames of interpretation would be an eventful history of Malik's political thought, capable of tracking the ways in which it shifted in the face of the ascendancy of an increasingly assertive pan-Arabism.

There is no doubt that Malik did seek to impress upon officials in Washington the importance of Lebanon to 'American long-range interest' in the Middle East as early as 1949, or that he came, in due course, to serve as a crucial intermediary between Lebanese and American officials.[12] Moreover, he had by the late 1950s taken upon himself the role of defender of 'Western civilization'. Expounding upon the uniqueness of this 'pearl beyond all price', he portentously urged 'the individual in modern Western society ... to realize that he is the heir of a tremendous heritage ... the cumulative tradition of Greece, Rome, the Near East, and Western Europe', which it was his duty to uphold. Upon this, Malik insisted, depended '[n]ot only his own fate, but the fate of other individuals in other societies'; the destiny of the world, in his view, rested upon the survival and fulfilment of this singular inheritance.[13] It would be difficult to deny, then, that Malik was indeed, by the mid-1950s, sympathetic to the projection of American power in the Middle East, and a man who spoke in Manichean terms of a confrontation between Western civilization and its enemies.

Furthermore, Malik – like many children from the Greek Orthodox villages of the Kura, in what is now northern Lebanon, where he was born in 1906 – was educated from a young age in American establishments. After completing his schooling at the American Mission School for Boys in Tripoli, he studied mathematics and physics at the American University of Beirut. While living in Cairo in the late 1920s, he developed an interest in philosophy; resolving to undertake graduate study, he eventually completed his doctorate on the philosophy of time in the writings of A.N. Whitehead and Martin Heidegger at Harvard, after an abortive spell at Freiburg under Heidegger's supervision. He then returned to Beirut, where he once again took up a berth at the American University, helping establish its philosophy department and settling down to a life of teaching and discussion. The temptation to treat Malik as a figure raised, from a young age, to think sympathetically of the United States, its intellectual culture and political objectives are understandable.

However, this is to overlook the other formative influences upon his thought, from the process philosophy of the British-born Whitehead to Heideggerian phenomenology and the writings of Lebanese thinkers such as Michel Chiha, who sought to elaborate in the 1930s exceptionalist narratives of their nation as a polity defined by its openness, a site of cultural interchange and a haven for successive streams of refugees from across the Middle East. Moreover, we must be careful not to flatten out Malik's ideas and telescope his intellectual development, regarding him as a hardened Christian cold warrior who saw the Middle East and the world as beset by a cataclysmic 'clash of civilisations, [a] war between East and West, communism and freedom, Christianity and all the other lesser religions'.[14] As Joel Isaac and Duncan Bell have warned, this is to take things the wrong way round, to treat the *explanandum* as *explanans* and effect as cause. By qualifying Malik in such terms, in other words, we treat the Cold War as an 'all-purpose', all-encompassing phenomenon providing a ready-made explanation for his political worldview, rather than asking what circumstances led him to adopt the rhetoric of a global struggle for the soul of mankind.[15] Likewise, it is undoubtedly true that, as Moyn has argued, the 'ideology closest' to Malik's heart came in time to be a 'Western one'. However, we cannot simply consider him as the member of a 'global diplomatic elite, often schooled in Western locales', and whose political thoughts were derived from European models and precedents. To argue that Malik's 'strong anticommunist leanings' and 'hopes for a Christian future in the Middle East' sprung entirely from his conversion to the European ideas of 'Christian personalism' is to overlook the deeply contingent and particular nature of his thought.[16] For his long flirtation – and eventual infatuation – with the United States was born of a consideration of Lebanon's place in a decolonizing and increasingly polarized world. As strategic as it was sentimental, this commitment was by no means predetermined.

Moreover, an examination of Malik's stances allows us to reflect upon the heuristic possibilities and pitfalls born of regarding the writings of non-Western intellectuals in the post-1945 period as the products of the Cold War. In endowing the latter with explanatory power as a 'frame for ... all kinds of events and processes ... here and there and yonder', we run the risk of putting too much analytical weight on this 'overdeterminant structure', and straining it such that it loses all exploratory use.[17] Nevertheless, we cannot treat it as a term inapplicable outside of American history; as Odd Arne Westad has pointed out, there were 'other rationalities, other political and social agendas, [and] other intentions at work' in the world of the 1950s, which could sometimes be made to match the expectations and calculations of Washington officials. More helpful would be an approach that considers the ways Malik – and others like him – sough to adopt, refashion and manipulate the discursive and material forces of the Cold War as they attempted to negotiate their states' newfound independence.

Indeed, we cannot discount the importance decolonization played in Malik's thought. This was not just an 'end point', a full stop punctuating the twentieth century and marking the break between the colonial and the postcolonial, or a 'moment' whose outcome was self-evident and predetermined.[18] What's more, self-determination and self-rule were causes not just for jubilation, but also for trepidation for a small state like Lebanon, built – in Malik's view – upon a particular social compact and surrounded by hostile neighbours. We should not forget, then, that decolonization prompted much intellectual labour, as political actors devised 'competing strategies and complex visions' to make sense of the new realities of independence.[19] For Malik, one such strategy was to call upon external protection of Lebanon's precarious sovereignty, and particular social and political systems, from the depredations of Zionism, communism and Arab nationalism. As the United Nations failed to live up to its apparent promise, and old allies like France became bogged down elsewhere and lost their significance, he increasingly turned towards the United States.

As a consequence, Malik's writings can present us with an opportunity to examine further America's place in the post-1945 Middle East. Irene Gendzier has persuasively argued that Lebanon came to represent a 'hospitable and invaluable' bridgehead for the wider ambitions of American policymakers in the Middle East, a region that rapidly came to assume a central place in their global strategic thinking.[20] However, we still need a clearer, more sophisticated sense of the ways local actors understood, and sought to deflect and manipulate, American power.[21] While historians have recently paid increasing attention to Middle Eastern attitudes towards the United States in the mid-twentieth century, their accounts often have a downcast, elegiac tone about them. Bemoaning the lost hope of veritable understanding between the United States and the Arab world, they strive to show the ways in which American policy led Arab sympathy to sour into suspicion and resentment. These are sad tales of betrayal and despair, of unfulfilled expectations and broken promises.[22] Such narratives often hinge in a mechanical fashion upon particular turning points, momentous events that radically recast Arab perceptions of America. If the creation of the state of Israel and the first Arab-Israeli war in 1948 was one such turning point, then the promulgation of the Eisenhower doctrine and US intervention in Lebanon in 1958 was another. To Maurice Labelle, the despatch of American marines to Lebanese beaches 'contributed to the consolidation of a popular perception that a new age of empire was emerging in the region', cementing the association in the minds of many between 'US global power', the 'perceived threat of empire' and the authoritarian policies of local rulers.[23] Malik's writings point to a rather more complex chronology, full of hesitations, breaks and tentative moves, than much of this work has suggested.

Malik and the perils of Zionism

In February 1949, Malik wrote a lengthy 'report on the current situation' to the Lebanese Ministry of Foreign Affairs, discussing the predicament confronting Lebanon and the Arab states in the wake of the first Arab–Israeli war. Despite the effusion that had greeted national independence, deep disenchantment had already set in with the *nakba*, or catastrophe – as Malik's friend and one-time AUB colleague, the Syrian historian and thinker Qustantin Zurayq, was quick to call the loss of Palestine.[24] But 'all that has happened till now, in Palestine and beyond', Malik warned, 'is only the beginning'. The 'Arab world' faced two fates: 'colonisation by the Jews' or 'resurgence anew as a modern, respected [region], participating, in concert with the active civilisations, in the creation and preservation of all that is valuable'. For 'just as the Near East had known … the Roman, Byzantine, Turkish, and Mandate eras, so the Zionists wanted the current era to be known as the Jewish or Israeli era'. However, the success of the Zionist movement was not born simply of its own strength or international support, but also of 'Arab backwardness and disunity'. Palestine was at once the 'pivot' of the Arab world and its 'mirror'; its fate was but the 'faithful reflection' of the 'catastrophe' of Arab life, in all its 'weakness' and 'ruin'. This was a bleak appraisal of the dangers and challenges that came with decolonization. To Malik, the time of the nation had not brought with it emancipation from foreign overrule, but the new – and potentially greater – threat of Zionist 'colonialism'.[25]

What is more, the trappings of national sovereignty were not sufficient to confront the expansionist designs of the Israeli state, which was merely 'preparing for the execution' of the 'coming phase, in which it would complete its colonisation and enslavement of the Arab world'. The 'largest disaster' confronting the Arabs, Malik warned, was not military defeat or political disarray, but that 'thought is not free amongst us'. For 'freedom guarantees the expression of the truth, and the truth is the ultimate guarantee of freedom'. What was needed, then, was 'the diffusion of learning, impartial analysis, and the encouragement of thought'. But 'our countries' were so 'backward', so 'tardy' in embarking upon such 'reform' that it amounted to nothing short of a 'fundamental renewal of our intellectual life'.[26]

Lebanon was, for Malik, at the centre of this undertaking. 'More than any other Arab country, it was called upon' to lead the way in this 'renovation'. While other Arab states might have greater capacity to lend their 'armies, their wheat or financial wherewithal' to the task, Lebanon was 'qualified to provide intellectual activity and mental renewal'. It was essential, then, that its 'full … independence' be preserved in the face of growing 'political and economic pressure for its incorporation into Syria'. Lebanon was, Malik insisted, an 'intrinsic part of the Arab world', and its 'destiny' remained inextricably bound to that of its neighbours. However, the vision Lebanon 'presented, for itself, for the Arabic world, and for the world as a whole' – one of a 'free, enlightened spirit, connected to tradition, giving rise to institutions and movements, organised for material life, and exploding with knowledge and truth' – could only be realized under conditions of 'full freedom and political independence'. Its 'erasure' would not just make a travesty of the pieties of self-determination; it would also be a loss to the Middle East and the world. The crux of Malik's argument was clear. Lebanon had to be accepted on its own terms; 'if the Arab world opened its breast to an independent Lebanon … providing complete safeguards against Arab unity', the 'economic and cultural development' of the Middle East could be ensured, and any Lebanese 'slide' towards Israel prevented.[27]

However, another question hovered in the background. What assistance could Lebanon expect from 'Western countries' should it be 'attached' against its will 'to Syria or a larger Arab coalition'? Writing from Washington, Malik's assessment was as stark as it was surprising. In the event of such a development, 'the United States would remain a bystander'. Only if 'such a movement led to chaos and disturbances, born of the determination of a large part of the Lebanese to ensure their country's absolute independence' would the United States 'take an interest in the matter'. 'For America, this was a question of force and violence, and not one of principle'. More than this, there were 'circles in America which remained uneasy at Lebanon's independence from Syria, and saw no use in it'. This did not bode well for Lebanon's sovereignty. Should a 'crisis arise, and were it to appear that the only solution was to sacrifice Lebanon, then these circles would assert their weight', easily 'decid[ing] the matter' with disastrous consequences. Malik's answer to this quandary was as unexpected as his disavowal of American support. Of the three great Western powers with an interest in the Middle East, only France could be counted upon by the Lebanese, despite the resentment and mutual recrimination that had surrounded its withdrawal from the Middle East in the mid-1940s. For only France, Malik insisted, 'wished to see Lebanon remain independent, and would truly act should its independence be threatened, serving as a determined and principled intermediary', impressing upon the United States and Britain the importance of Lebanese sovereignty.[28]

This assessment confounds conventional narratives of decolonization, and complicates our understanding of Malik's relationship to the United States. Independent statehood did not signal freedom from foreign threats for Lebanon, whose sovereignty remained compromised by Zionist appetites and pan-Arabism's driving search for unity. More than this, Lebanon's independence remained, in a sense, dependent upon the goodwill of others. A mere six years after Lebanon and Syria had unilaterally declared their independence in a deeply acrimonious split from France, Malik insisted that only the former Mandatory power genuinely sought to uphold Lebanon's sovereignty because of its deep sentimental commitment to the existence of this territorial entity. The United States, by contrast, was no reliable ally. Seeing the world through the lens of power politics, its leaders remained far too sympathetic towards Israel, and far too dependent upon the votes of Jewish Americans, to be counted upon to intervene in Lebanon's favour in its hour of need.[29] This was no blind commitment to a West conceived of in vague and monolithic terms, but a careful game of strategic calculus, in which Malik disaggregated and disentangled differing interests and commitments.

The national and the universal

Far from being a universalist, committed in the abstract to the rights of the human person and indifferent to the variations of culture, Malik appears from this account to be a thinker deeply concerned with the protection of national sovereignty against the depredations of inherently expansionist ideologies. This may seem, on the face of it, difficult to square with his pronouncements at the United Nations, where he warned in February 1947 against 'the claims of groups today – especially the political group, the nation embodying itself in the institution called the state', and their 'tendency to dictate to people what they ought to think, [and] do'. Malik seems here an anti-national thinker – indeed, one opposed to any kind of collective imposition, with his forceful insistence that 'people's minds and consciences are the most inviolable and sacred things about them, not their belonging to this or that class, ... nation, or ... religion'.[30] But the contradiction is more apparent than real. Just as his vision of an Arab 'awakening' founded upon 'light, knowledge, truth, and liberty' drew deeply upon the distinctive blend of Heideggerian phenomenology and Christian theology, which led him to argue that 'only the truth can set free', so Malik's espousal of personal rights grew out of his commitment to preserving a particular vision of Lebanese sovereignty and society.[31]

Thus, Malik repeatedly invoked Lebanon in his early appeals for a legally binding Bill of Human Rights. In May 1946, he declared that while 'it is easy ... to speak of freedom in general', 'what we care for in Lebanon, what we endeavour to realize above everything else is freedom of thought and conscience, freedom of expression and being'. This was Lebanon's 'distinctive historical contribution' to the world. Without respect for this 'fundamental freedom' to 'be what you are' and what 'your conscious requires you to become', Lebanon could simply not survive. For the 'history of my country', Malik declared,

> Is precisely that of a small country struggling against all odds for the maintenance and strengthening of real freedom of thought and conscience. Innumerable persecuted minorities have found, throughout the ages, a most understanding haven in my country, so that the very basis of our existence is complete respect of differences of opinion and belief.

He went further still in early 1947. Without freedom of thought, Lebanon was 'simply inconceivable'. From the particular case of Lebanon, he derived a more general attack on what he called 'the tyranny of the masses, which seems ultimately to have an inevitable tendency of embodying itself in what I might call the tyranny of the state. If there is any danger to fundamental human rights today', he declared, 'it is certainly from that direction'.[32] This declaration is particularly important. One can begin to see here an overlooked source for Malik's strident anti-communism and vision of human rights. For his commitment to protecting the singular human person in its particularity from the writ of the many was profoundly entangled with his desire to preserve an independent Lebanon, free of totalizing forces – whether communism, Zionism or Arab nationalism – which strove for collective identification and stymied the individual's potential for transformation.

This concern was more apparent still in Malik's stance towards self-determination. Malik recognized the 'zest generated' by this idea amongst people in 'non-Western lands'. However, he insisted upon the 'formidable complexities' of self-determination, against those who 'would brush [them] aside … in favor of a simple, direct affirmation that every people and every nation has a natural right to self-determination'. Amongst the issues that threatened to fall by the wayside in the unseemly rush towards independence, Malik noted, were fundamental questions. Was self-determination, 'to which all agreed in principle … an individual or a group right'? 'How is self-determination related to freedom, independence, self-government? What constitutes a "people"? When are "minorities" entitled to this right?' And, finally, 'are people … entitled to suppress freedom of thought, conscience and enquiry in the name of "cultural self-determination?"'[33] A global regime of personal human rights, Malik suggested, allowed not just for the expression of individual thought through the clamouring din of the collective, but also for the protection of minorities against majorities, and of small states against their larger neighbours' appetites.

An eventful history of exceptionalism

By the early 1950s, however, Malik was rapidly growing disillusioned with the obstacles the 'troubled world situation' had thrown in the way of his project.[34] Returning from the United Nations to the Harvard Club one night in late 1954, he noted in his diary:

> Interest now in human rights has subsided at the UN, and even in the world. The political issues of the cold war, of war or peace, of what mode of coexistence, if any, can be envisaged and should be worked for between the communist bloc and the rest of the world, and of the liberation of the still dependent peoples of Asia and Africa; these political issues, as well as the economic and material issues of the vast social revolution raging in every country in the world … – it is these problems today, and not questions of human rights, that seem to occupy the minds of men.

Malik regarded this, on one level, as a deep loss, the shallow concerns of 'the social, economic and political revolution throughout the world overwhelming any sense of independent human dignity'.[35] But on another, he had already begun to adapt his own rhetorical strategies to these altered circumstances. Talking rather less of rights and rather more of Lebanon and the Middle East, he gradually came to abandon the United

Nations as a forum in which to make his claims, redoubling his efforts to win over American policymakers and public opinion to Lebanon's cause. His 1953 appearance on the American television programme 'Longines Chronoscope' was representative of this new approach. Lebanon, he explained gravely, is a 'very small country … both in size and in population', 'yet its importance both in the Near East and … the world at large cannot be measured by either its size or its population'. For this was a land in which 'East and West meet together in freedom and in perfect mutual respect'. Indeed, it was 'famous for its freedom … People can think what they like, they can express what they think, they can live as they please'. What is more, Lebanon was well placed, as a meeting point of civilizations, to 'play a moderating and mediating role', 'whether in the Arab League … or in the United Nations or in any international gathering'. Lebanon, then, was at once a haven of freedom and a hyphen holding together East and West; as such, 'it really is a unique little country in the world'.[36] Malik had once embedded his defence of the Lebanese social compact within a broader discourse of human rights, using the particular to inform and illustrate the universal. Although the national and the global remained folded together in his words, he now insisted more baldly than ever on the importance of this exceptional construct in and of itself. Lebanon mattered, not as an exemplar, but for its own sake. Built around the exceptionalist narrative he had long espoused, this was an undisguised appeal for American interest in Lebanon.

Malik's enduring commitment to safeguarding Lebanese sovereignty became firmer still in the wake of the Suez crisis, finding vociferous expression during the short bout of civil strife that broke out in Lebanon in May 1958. Like the Lebanese president, Kamil Sham'un, who charged the UAR with seeking to extend 'its control' over the domestic politics of neighbouring countries with a view to 'dominating the Arab world', Malik was persuaded that this was the work of foreign conspirators determined to sap the structure of the Lebanese state.[37] Speaking before the UN Security Council on 6 June, he accused the UAR of 'massive, illegal and unprovoked intervention in the affairs of Lebanon'. This, Malik argued, 'threaten[ed]' the country's 'independence', before producing a long list of evidence designed to demonstrate that the government of the UAR had supplied 'arms on a large scale … to subversive elements'; trained these 'elements' 'in subversion'; participated, and allowed its citizens to participate, in 'subversive and terrorist activities' and 'in the direction of rebellion'; and waged a 'violent and unprecedented' campaign in state-controlled newspapers and radio stations, 'inciting the people of Lebanon to overthrow their government'. 'There is no war', Malik noted, 'between Lebanon and the United Arab Republic', and yet for two years the 'Government of Lebanon' had been 'called by every conceivable and inconceivable name' – a campaign, he contended, in which the UAR had 'lavishly' used language of 'unrestrained violence', the likes of which had not been witnessed even in the 'darkest hours of the Second World War'. What is more, '[d]uring 1957 and 1958 many terrorist and subversive activities were carried out by agents of the Governments of Syria and Egypt' on Lebanese soil, including 'bombings, assassinations and kidnappings'. The case, then, was clear: this amounted to a systematic attempt 'to overthrow the present régime [sic]', whose 'only sin' was its independence and desire to follow a 'policy of friendship towards and co-operation with the Western world', 'and to replace it with one... more subservient to the will of the United Arab Republic'.[38]

But Malik saw something of greater magnitude still in the UAR's purported actions. Far from a trivial neighbourhood dispute of no significance to the wider world, 'unprovoked massive intervention' in the domestic affairs of Lebanon endangered 'international peace and security' by destabilizing the precarious 'equilibrium of interests in the Near East'. Furthermore, by taking no heed of the realities of Lebanese sovereign statehood, the UAR seemed to make a mockery of the commitment of the United Nations to protect the independence of its members from foreign meddling and interference. The case of Lebanon, then, was a 'test case'. The Security Council's decision mattered to 'every small country in the world'. For if 'intervention in the affairs of one small country should be allowed to work its way without let or hindrance, how can any other small country feel secure again?' It was simply inconceivable that the United Nations should stand idly by; its duty was, 'above all', to 'protect the small nations'. Failure to take action threatened to set a very grave precedent indeed. Not only did the 'fate' of Lebanon, its 'independence', 'peace in the area and perhaps even in the world' all rest in the balance; more than this, the United Nation's very integrity, its purpose even, depended on the Security Council's decision.[39]

In laying out this argument, Malik returned to, and revised, the question he had first raised some six years earlier: how was self-determination related to independence? In other words, how might the competing claims of various national ideologies be weighed up and given precedence? And, Malik now added, how might the sovereignty of small states be protected from the unwelcome attention and interference of their larger, more assertive, more imposing neighbours? As we have seen, this was an issue that had preoccupied Malik as early as 1949, when he identified both Zionism and pan-Arabism as threats to Lebanese independence. By 1958, his anxiety about Israeli expansionism had grown muted, but his fear of Arab nationalism and communism only more pronounced. He had considered, over the years, several protectors: the old colonial power, France; the international community, embodied in the UN; and the United States. By 1958, Malik had grown entirely disillusioned with the United Nations, whose findings on the Lebanese crisis the Sham'un government angrily dismissed as 'clearly either inconclusive, misleading or unwarranted' for having failed to concur with their charges of sustained UAR infringements upon Lebanese sovereignty.[40] The United States was, in the minds of Malik and Sham'un, the only place to turn. On 15 July 1958, the first US Marines landed at Khaldeh, in response to Sham'un's invocation of the Eisenhower doctrine.

Conclusion

There was nothing inconsistent, in the end, about Charles Malik's apparent drift from serving 'during the late 1940s as an Arab spokesman for Palestine at the U.N.' to ending his career 'as the anti-Palestinian architect of the alliance with Israel during the

Lebanese Civil War'.[41] Underlying his various commitments, some enduring, others more transitory, was an adamantine, unwavering commitment to Lebanese sovereignty. Malik's lasting hostility to communism, but also the anti-Zionism and Arabism that characterized his writings of the late 1940s, and the condemnations of pan-Arabism and encomia of the United States that came to the fore from the mid-1950s, can all be traced, in part, to his exceptionalist understanding of Lebanon. This helped shape the vision of absolute personal freedom of thought and belief that he sought to promote at the United Nations, the particular underwriting the universal. But it also made him, somewhat paradoxically, ambivalent about the new age of self-determination. For the formidable contagion of sovereignty that spread through the world in the decades after 1945 brought with it not just welcome independence, but also – as Christopher Lee has noted – sometimes intractable 'existential predicaments'.[42] Far from redrawing the map of the world along national lines, the time of independence threatened to recast old patterns of imperialist domination in new forms, as expansionist ideologies rode roughshod over hard-won freedoms. For Malik, then, the Cold War offered a means of escaping the quandaries of decolonization. Only in America's arms, he came to conclude, could Lebanon find respite from the unwelcome attentions of its neighbours.

Notes

1   Glendon, Mary Ann (2011), *The Forum and the Tower: How Scholars and Politicians Have Imagined the World, from Plato to Eleanor Roosevelt*. Oxford: Oxford University Press, 200–201.

2   'The Eisenhower Doctrine, 1957', <http://history.state.gov/milestones/1953-1960/eisenhower-doctrine> [accessed 14 March 2014]. See Yaqub, Salim (2004), *Containing Arab Nationalism: The Eisenhower Doctrine and the Middle East*. Chapel Hill: University of North Carolina Press.

3   Glendon (2011), 236.

4   Attié, Caroline (2004), *Struggle in the Levant: Lebanon in the 1950s*. London: IB Tauris, 108.

5   Gendzier, Irene (2006), *Notes from the Minefield: United States Intervention in Lebanon and the Middle East, 1945–1958*. New York: Columbia University Press, 236.

6   Salibi, Kamal (1958), 'The Lebanese Crisis in perspective', *The World Today*, 14(9), 376.

7   Moyn, Samuel (2010), *The Last Utopia: Human Rights in History*. Cambridge, Mass.: Belknap, 65.

8   Burke, Roland (2010), *Decolonization and the Evolution of International Human Rights*. Philadelphia: University of Pennsylvania Press, 25.

9   Attié (2004), 116, 106.

10 Gendzier (2006), 123, 10.

11 Malik, Charles (1957), 'Introduction', in Philip W. Thayer (ed.) (1957), *Tensions in the Middle East*. Baltimore: Johns Hopkins University Press, xiii, xi; Malik, Charles (1961), 'The tide must turn'. Saint Louis: Saint Louis University, n.p.

12 Gendzier (2006), 131.

13 Malik, Charles (1962), 'The individual in modern society', in John Brooks (ed.) (1962), *The One and the Many: The Individual in the Modern World*. New York: Harper & Row, 154–156.

14 Said, Edward (2009), *Out of Place: A Memoir*. London: Granta, 265.

15 Isaac, Joel and Bell, Duncan (2012), 'Introduction', in Joel Isaac, and Duncan Bell, (eds.) (2012), *Uncertain Empire: American History and the Idea of the Cold War*. Oxford: Oxford University Press, 3–4.

16 Moyn (2010), 65–66.

17 Stephanson, Anders (2012), 'Cold War degree zero', in Isaac and Bell (2012), 21, 42.

18 Shepard, Todd (2006), *The Invention of Decolonization: The Algerian War and the Remaking of France*. Ithaca: Cornell University Press, 4; Lee, Christopher J. (2005a), 'Introduction: Between a moment and an era: the origins and afterlives of Bandung', in Christopher J. Lee (ed.) (2005b), *Making a World After Empire: The Bandung Moment and Its Political Afterlives*. Athens: Ohio University Press, 5.

19 Lee (2005a), 9.

20 Gendzier (2006), 7.

21 For a notable exception, see Citino, Nathan (2012), 'The "crush" of ideologies: the United States, the Arab World, and Cold War modernisation', *Cold War Studies*, 12(1), 89–110.

22 Makdisi, Ussama (2010), *Faith Misplaced: The Broken Promise of U.S.-Arab Relations, 1820–2001*. New York: Public Affairs.

23 Labelle, Maurice (2013), 'A new age of empire? Arab "anti-Americanism", US intervention, and the Lebanese Civil War of 1958', *International History Review*, 35(1), 21.

24 Zurayq, Qustantin (1948), *Ma'na al-Nakba*. Beirut: Dar al-'Ilm l-il-Malayin.

25 Malik, Charles (2008; 1949 reprint), *Isra'il… Amirka… wa al-'Arab: Tanbu'at min Nisf Qarn*. Beirut: Dar al-Nahar, 27, 24.

26 Malik (2008; 1949 reprint), 28–29, 19, 90–93.

27 Malik (2008; 1949 reprint), 95, 143, 156, 145.

28 Malik (2008; 1949 reprint), 146–148.

29 Malik (2008; 1949 reprint), 57–86.

30 Malik, Charles (2000), *The Challenge of Human Rights: Charles Malik and the Universal Declaration*. Ed. Habib C. Malik. Oxford: Centre for Lebanese Studies, 27–29.

31 Malik (2008), 18.

32 Malik (2000), 15–16, 23, 26.

33 Malik, Charles (1952), *Human Rights in the United Nations with Text of Draft Covenants*. New York: UN Department of Public Information, 5–6.

34 Malik (1952), 2.

35 Malik (2000), 234–235.

36 (1953), 'Longines-Wittnauer with Dr. Charles Malik', <http://archive.org/download/gov. archives.arc.95856/gov.archives.arc.95856_512kb.mp4> [accessed 14 March 2014].

37 Agwani, M.S. (ed.) (1965), *The Lebanese Crisis, 1958: A Documentary Study*. London: Asia Publishing House, 90–91.

38 Agwani (1965), 122–123, 138, 134.

39 Agwani (1965), 144–147.

40 Agwani (1965), 218.

41 Said (2009), 264.
42 Lee (2005a), 3.

Key texts

Attié, Caroline. (2004). *Struggle in the Levant: Lebanon in the 1950s*. London: IB Tauris.
Burke, Roland. (2010). *Decolonization and the Evolution of International Human Rights*.
    Philadelphia: University of Pennsylvania Press.
Gendzier, Irene. (2006). *Notes from the Minefield: United States Intervention in Lebanon and the
    Middle East, 1945–1958*. New York: Columbia University Press.
Louis, Wm. Roger and Owen, Roger (eds). (1989). *Suez 1956: The Crisis and Its Consequences*.
    Oxford: Clarendon Press.
Louis, Wm. Roger and Owen, Roger (eds). (2002). *A Revolutionary Year: The Middle East in
    1958*. London: IB Tauris.
Malik, Charles. (2000). *The Challenge of Human Rights: Charles Malik and the Universal
    Declaration*. ed. Habib C. Malik. Oxford: Centre for Lebanese Studies.
Moyn, Samuel. (2010). *The Last Utopia: Human Rights in History*. Cambridge, MA: Belknap.

PART III
CONTESTING HERITAGE AND IDENTIFICATION

This part focuses on the production of national identities. Within the volume, it also introduces some of the less literal – but no less important – interactions between decolonization and the Cold War. Involving the Soviet 'empire', Chinese international ambitions and Egypt (only unofficially a colony), it examines how national identity was constructed through cultural production; the ways it harnessed particular narratives of heritage; and how it engaged levels of racial, ethnic and cultural diversity. In particular, it considers how and why modes of identification competed and clashed, whether Malayan versus Chinese 'ethnicity', Soviet metropole versus periphery or Egyptian colonial and postcolonial cultural practices.

CHAPTER 6
THE MALAYAN COMMUNIST PARTY AND THE MALAYAN CHINESE ASSOCIATION: INTERNATIONALISM AND NATIONALISM IN CHINESE OVERSEAS POLITICAL PARTICIPATION, c. 1920–1960
Anna Belogurova

Two ethnically Chinese political organizations, the Malayan Communist Party (MCP) and the Malayan Chinese Association (MCA), played key roles in Malaya's road to independence from the British Government, which was achieved in 1957.[1] The MCP, established in 1930 and an overwhelmingly ethnic Chinese organization until 1941, is now best known for its role in the Malayan Emergency of 1948–1960, an insurgency against the British Government.[2] During the same period, the pro-British MCA, established in 1949, successfully led negotiations with the British for national independence. The sensitive nature of the involvement of ethnic Chinese in Malaysia has until now precluded comparisons between the MCP and the MCA. The MCA is credited with producing a Malaya-centred view among ethnic Chinese and coalition politics as a way of enhancing Malayan unity, whereas both MCP Malayan and China-centred nationalism have been perceived negatively.[3] In contrast, this paper argues that continuity between the MCP in the 1930s and the MCA in the late 1940s and the early 1950s reveals an important story about multi-ethnic politics and the potential for continuity as well as dissonance.

What can be called 'internationalist nationalism' created this continuity in the patterns of political participation among Chinese migrants, both communist and non-communist, in Malaya during the first half of the twentieth century. This originated in the internationalism of the Chinese Nationalist Party, the Guomindang (GMD), and was strengthened by the Comintern and its allied Chinese Communist Party (CCP), as well as in the fact that both the MCP and the MCA were Chinese overseas associations. The MCP and the MCA had the same two needs: to embed themselves in the local environment (that is to indigenize by involving locals in a Chinese organization) and, at the same time, to maintain the connection with China through their Chinese nationalism.[4]

The first part of this chapter will discuss the emergence of the discourse of a multi-ethnic Malayan nation and the idea of an alliance between ethnic parties within the MCP. It demonstrates that it was the MCP that first encouraged multi-ethnic Malayan nationalism; it aspired to create a multiparty union representing the interests of three major ethnic groups among the multi-ethnic population of Malaya: Malays, Indians and Chinese. A similar alliance, but led by the MCA, eventually would carry out negotiations for Malayan independence with the British in the 1950s. The second half of this chapter will demonstrate the continuities between the MCP in the early 1930s and the MCA in the 1940s. This MCP–MCA comparison suggests the importance of bridging the historiographies of pre-war and post-war institutions and discourses in understanding the Cold War period beyond the communist–non-communist divide. As an ideological struggle, the Cold War had its roots in the interwar period, and the efforts of the Comintern and the CCP to establish communist parties, such as the MCP, in Southeast Asian colonies certainly belonged to the longer Cold War: local communist parties and their alliances provided political alternatives to Western models for anti-colonial resisters. The same markers of anti-imperial resistance and 'nationalist internationalism' that characterized the MCP counter-insurgency threat during the Malayan Emergency, which is viewed as a marker of the traditional early Cold War period, are visible from its earliest Comintern origins in 1930. This chapter further contextualizes decolonization in longer processes, further complicating the dominant narrative of a successful, British-led decolonization and unification of Malaya into a nation-state guided by a multi-ethnic government.[5] The conjuncture of Chinese migration and globalization created an indigenous nationalism that shaped the decolonization process.

The Malay land: Ethnic tensions and the Malayan Emergency

The Malayan Emergency was rooted in tensions between two major ethnic groups, the Malays and the Chinese, at a time when Malaya consisted of several sultanates under British dominion. Southeast Asia, known as *Nanyang*, or the South Seas, in Chinese, historically has been an area of Chinese migration. Mass relocation of Chinese labourers to the Malay peninsula – which today has the largest proportional Chinese population outside China – began after the British-imposed rule in the western Malay states in 1874 in order to profit from feuds among Chinese tin mine owners.[6] From the turn of the twentieth century, the British banned troublesome Chinese organizations, such as secret societies and the GMD, denied Chinese political rights as 'aliens' and restricted 're-Sinicization' measures undertaken by the Chinese government through Chinese-language education and the press.[7] In contrast, the British recruited Malays in lower administrative ranks, protected Malay land rights and preserved Malay peasant customs.[8] The Chinese in Malaya viewed British actions as oppressive, and leaders of commercial, clan and provincial associations promoted their own political rights. The Chinese dominated the cities of the Malay Peninsula and comprised the majority of the population in most of the states. According to the 1921 census, nearly half the Malayan population – around 3,358,000 – was Indian (14.2 per cent) or Chinese (35 per cent), and in 1931 this increased to 16 and 39 per cent, respectively.[9] At this time, 65 per cent of the Chinese in Malaya worked in tin mines, small rubber holdings and farms, whereas 75 per cent of Indians worked on European rubber estates.[10]

During the Japanese occupation of Malaya between 1941 and 1945, the predominantly Chinese wartime resistance experienced increased ethnic tensions with the Malays, many of whom collaborated with the Japanese. With the war in China in mind, the Japanese military occupational authorities imposed penalties on and massacred thousands of Chinese in Malaya as punishment for their anti-Japanese stance. The MCP led the guerrilla resistance against the Japanese occupation, and after the war it emerged as a strong party that expanded its support base even as it was denied political representation in reoccupied British Malaya.

The fall of Singapore to the Japanese in 1942 had prompted a British reassessment of its policy in Malaya, including the need to promote a united, strong Malayan state that would embrace non-Malays and deprive local sultans of sovereignty.[11] After the Pacific war, the British Government promoted the idea of ethnic cooperation and requested the formation of a multiracial government, including non-Malays, to which they would grant the rule of independent Malaya.[12] In 1949, Malcolm MacDonald, Commissioner-General for Southeast Asia, established the Communities Liaison Committee (CLC), the forerunner of multiracial political coalitions such as Malaya's Alliance and National Front (*Barisan Nasional*). The United Malays National Organisation (UMNO) and MCA leaders worked with British representatives. There were six Chinese, six Malays and one representative each from the Indian, Eurasian, Ceylonese and European communities on the CLC. The CLC mainly concerned itself with questions of citizenship for non-Malays and special rights for Malays. The CLC became defunct in 1951, after concluding that interracial cooperation would be impossible to achieve on a grassroots level.[13] Another attempt at multiracial cooperation included the multiracial United Malaya National Party, conceived in 1949 by Malay leader Dato' Onn Jaafar, with the encouragement of Tan Cheng Lock, the founder of the MCA. However, this was not put into practice because the MCA leadership did not support Tan in his attempts to de-communalize the MCA. Later, Jafaar, supported by Tan, established the Independence of Malaya Party.[14] In 1952, the MCA formed an alliance with the UMNO on a nationwide scale and jointly participated in the elections. The Malayan Indian Congress joined the alliance, which contested and won the elections, ultimately leading Malaya to independence in 1957.[15]

However, simultaneous to these negotiations, the Emergency also included significant British counter-insurgency efforts. Although efficient – and, indeed, later used elsewhere as a model – British counter-insurgency measures had the opposite of their intended effect during the first years of the Emergency. In an effort to deprive the MCP of their (often forced) support, counter-insurgency tactics actually ended up encouraging those who feared arrest or were angered by the forced resettlement of Chinese squatters into guarded camps to join the guerrillas. Squatters had first moved into rural areas due to urban unemployment caused by the Great Depression of the early 1930s; the British Amendment of the Malay Reservation Act of 1933 prevented squatters from obtaining land titles. By 1940, there were 150,000 squatters, and their numbers increased dramatically during the Japanese occupation.[16] After the Emergency began in 1948, the interests of the mostly rural guerrillas, who drew on the traditions of anti-Japanese warfare and on the prestige of a force that had resisted invaders and were inspired by communist successes in China and Indochina, ran counter to the urban, commercially and traditionally oriented Chinese, who had organized into clan associations and chambers of commerce.

Because of the aggravated relationship between the Chinese community and the British, historians have portrayed the MCP as exploiting Chinese nationalism and 'failing to appreciate' Malay nationalism, thus not truly engaging with Malayan problems.[17] Chinese nationalism, it has been noted, was further compromised in the eyes of the British and Malays because the MCP was viewed as fighting for the cause of the CCP, not Malaya.[18] Even the MCP viewed its own Chinese nationalism and exclusively Chinese membership as an embarrassing cause of its failure to attract non-Chinese membership to an ostensibly 'national' party, which was supposed to include members of all communities.[19] Indeed after the 1989 peace agreement with the Malaysian government, MCP general secretary Chin Peng ascribed the failure of the MCP insurgency to a lack of Malay support, as well as to unsuitable geography and premature conditions for Marxism in Malaya.[20] The MCP's failure during the Emergency thus reflected the challenges of attracting non-Chinese members into a Chinese organization, which was necessary for successful MCP nation-building. In other words, it reflected a broader failure of the Party's historical internationalist nationalism.

The rise of the Malayan Communist Party

However, contrary to the dominant narrative outlined above, the involvement of non-Chinese in a Chinese revolutionary organization – a process that can be termed 'indigenization' – was actually promoted in Malaya from the late 1920s. The need to indigenize local organizations was shaped by the interwar internationalist moment, including the internationalizing efforts of the Chinese Nationalist Party (GMD), as well as the beginnings of the Cold War ideological battleground, with the global activities of the Chinese communist organization (the CCP) and the Soviet Comintern.[21] This expansion required increased local membership, as well as the localization of messages that also connected to the international cause.[22] With the establishment of the CCP and the Comintern-aligned Malayan National Communist Party (MCP) in 1930, local migrant Chinese communists employed the Comintern and its message to imagine a Malayan nation along the lines of a multi-ethnic 'soviet union' within the borders of the Malayan Peninsula.[23]

The Comintern's need to localize the 'world revolution' through promotion of indigenous membership matched the impulse of the CCP in British Malaya to indigenize as an overseas Chinese association.[24] Since 1927, left-wing GMD members in Malaya had promoted unity between overseas Chinese and the 'weak nations' of the Nanyang region, as colonial people were referred to in the social Darwinist discourse of the Chinese revolution. The Malayan branch of the GMD argued that unity would advance the cause of self-determination for these 'nations' and help resist discrimination against local Chinese by the colonial governments.[25] The CCP similarly had harboured plans to involve non-Chinese in its Nanyang Provisional Committee headquartered in Malaya since 1927.[26] This sentiment was voiced by a prominent labour organizer and de facto leader of the CCP, Li Lisan, whose participation in the CCP and Comintern congresses in Moscow in 1928 made him well aware of the Comintern's interest in establishing communist parties in the colonies.[27] Li also wanted to separate the CCP organization in Nanyang from the local GMD outpost and formulate different goals, since the GMD had suppressed the CCP in 1927. In early 1929, Li criticized the Nanyang communists for focusing on 'a Chinese revolution' by conducting anti-Japanese campaigns and protesting British measures to control Chinese education.[28] Li instead promoted a Nanyang-centred revolution as the 'beginning of the national movement', and placed responsibility for Nanyang's emancipation on the local Chinese, making the colonial liberation of the Chinese and the local population inseparable:

> It is the fundamental task of our party to tighten the relationship of all the oppressed nations and to make the Malay people understand that in order to release them from the yoke of the imperialists, the unity of the oppressed is absolutely necessary. If the Chinese want to claim for emancipation, it is possible only when all the oppressed nations are released. It is absolutely impossible to release any single nation separately. ... Thus, the principle task of our party is first of all to make all the oppressed unite and strive for the goal of the national emancipation.[29]

Based on its 1928 line, the Comintern helped reorganize the Nanyang Provisional Committee of the CCP into the separate MCP, Indochinese and Siamese parties, and established other parties in Southeast Asian colonies, such as Taiwan and the Philippines, as a way of undermining European imperialism through their 'weakest link'.[30] Hence, the MCP's establishment has been considered by some historians as promoting Soviet interests.[31] Indeed, by 1928, the Comintern had begun encouraging the CCP to establish connections with Java in order to re-establish the *Partai Komunis Indonesia*, which had been destroyed by the Dutch after the disastrous communist uprising of 1926.[32] However, according to documentary evidence, the foundation of 'an independent party of the Nanyang [Southeast Asia], directly instructed by the Third International' was a CCP initiative that wanted to attract Comintern attention and resources to Nanyang; it was not ordered by the Comintern.[33]

Reflecting Li Lisan's earlier critiques, the founding conference of the MCP on 22 and 23 April 1930 also criticized the existing party for being a 'narrow national [ethnic Chinese] movement'. The conference was attended by 'a Malay' (a representative of Malays) and a representative from East India (Indonesia). There were reportedly 1,130 party members (including five Malays) and more than 4,250 members of the communist-influenced 'red' trade union.[34] According to another report, the MCP's membership was 10 per cent 'Malaysian and Indian', a figure likely exaggerated in response to Comintern criticism.[35] Despite its ambitions, the MCP was still perceived to be 'exclusively Chinese' and appeared to have 'no plan to involve non-Chinese other than [through] vulgar conversation and politeness' because of difficulties with their different 'languages and custom'.[36] The MCP's problems in engaging Malays were unsurprising, given the party's typically condescending attitudes that perpetuated nineteenth-century European stereotypes of Malays as being lazy, superstitious and backward.[37] An MCP report stated, 'All aborigines are lazy. Though they have fertile land, they do not persevere to till it but spend their fatal time in sexual abuses, idleness and superstition ... .'[38] In December 1931, there were only forty-six non-Chinese members in the MCP.[39]

Beginning with minutes taken at its establishing conference, the MCP focused on Malaya as a future nation-state. Terms used included 'emancipation of the Malay oppressed nationalities' (*Malai beiyapo de minzu jiefang*) or a 'Malay people' (*Malaide renmin*) consisting of 'complex nationalities' (*fuza de minzu*).[40] This discourse emerged through a semantic slippage between the multiple meanings of *minzu* as 'country', 'people', 'nation' and 'nationality' that occurred when the Comintern tried to establish a Malayan 'national' party in a country that did not yet exist.[41] The MCP was established as a Comintern-affiliated 'national' party by Comintern representatives such as Ho Chi Minh (Vietnam) and Fu Daqing (China). The discussions regarding how the MCP should handle the multi-ethnic population of Malaya and establish this 'national' party were carried out by the CCP members (who became MCP members) in accordance with their understanding of 'national'. The Comintern intended to create a 'national' communist party, in accordance with point seventeen of the Comintern's twenty-one requirements for accepting a party as a Comintern section, which required the naming of a countrywide party (*partiya etoi strany*).[42] However, the CCP communists imagined a different 'national' party. In 1929, the CCP first promoted the creation of a unified Nanyang party consisting of communist parties, which were to be organized along ethnic lines. This party would manage communist activities across Southeast Asia, including Malaya. The 'Communist Party of Nanyang Nationalities' (*kommunisticheskaya partiya nan'yanskih narodnostey*) was to cover the 'Indian islands': the Malayan archipelago, Burma and the Annam and Siam committees.[43] At the MCP founding conference, the Nanyang party was to be renamed 'the Nanyang various peoples communists' joint secretariat' as a transitional organization to 'the communist party [of] the various oppressed peoples of Nanyang', and would include a 'Malay Communist Party' or 'Communist Committee of Malay Peninsula'.[44] To expand the party's membership beyond Chinese communities, the MCP members-elect suggested that the CCP 'establish [a] nucleus in each people, in order to establish independent party of each people ... .'[45] The MCP's political resolutions stated the following in English:

> Some members insist to organise [sic a union] Party embracing all people in Malaya. This organisational line is also contradictory to the organisational principle of international party, for the unit of organisation is people. Each native people should organise a national Party ... To organise an unity Party consisting of various peoples is incorrect ... [46]

The Chinese communists interpreted the Comintern's 'national' party as being based on an 'ethnic group' ('people') because of *minzu*'s multiple meanings, and likely because the communist cells in mainland Southeast Asia functioned as ethnic organizations, with separate communist organizations for the Chinese, Vietnamese and Indonesian Malay.[47] In 1929, the CCP had already planned to unite these ethnic cells into unified parties.[48] This was against the Comintern's policy of having only one communist party per country: 'The idea of creating several communist parties based on the nationalities in Malaya must be energetically combated.' The Comintern directive stated that there must be only one party in 'the Malayan State' that 'includ[ed] workers of all nationalities'.[49]

The newly established MCP, which primarily consisted of CCP members, chose the Comintern version of the 'national' party in order to acquire Comintern recognition and funding. The ethnic Chinese party was to become a 'national Malayan' party, and the Chinese communists were to lead Malaya to colonial liberation on behalf of the Malayan 'nation'. In CCP documents from 1928 to 1929, the term 'Malaya' was not used, and in the MCP's founding conference minutes, the 'Malaya' party and 'Nanyang' party were used interchangeably to mean a national party. The goal of the revolution was to achieve 'a united front of the oppressed peoples' and to organize 'the Democratic Republic by free union among the various people on Nanyang', which the MCP, in the same paragraph, called the 'Democratic Republics in the Malaya States'.[50]

In 1926, the call for 'a true Malayan spirit and consciousness' and a united Malaya had been made by Tan Cheng Lock, the future founder of the MCA who was then associated with neither the GMD nor the MCP.[51] It could be argued that both the Comintern's introduction of the idea of a national party and the CCP's idea of the alliance of ethnic parties provided practical ways to carry out this plea. The double meaning of *minzu* as both nation and nationality in GMD discourse has been linked to the emergence of the discussion of '*minzu* as communities within a [Malaysian] nation', which was later promoted by various Chinese associations, such as the MCA, in the 1950s.[52] Between 1932 and 1934, the MCP and Tan both promoted Malayanization (*Malaiyahua*). The emerging MCP discourse regarding a Malayan nation, involving both immigrant and indigenous populations and policies based on local conditions, occurred in conjunction with the changing social experience of immigrants, who felt a growing need to identify with Malaya.[53] Reasons for this included a dramatic increase in the locally born Chinese population, from 20.9 per cent in 1921 to 29.9 per cent in 1931, as well as the British 'pro-Malay' policy that discriminated against Chinese political and landownership rights.[54] Malayanization did not necessarily entail becoming Malay. Instead, Tan's goal was to 'Malayanise the children of the permanent population, i.e., to make them true citizens of Malaya', and 'to unite all races in Malaya'.[55] This was likely a reaction to the introduction of an Alien Registration Ordinance of 1933 that curbed Chinese immigration, as well as a 1933 amendment to the 1913 Malay Reservation Enactment, which ensured that non-Malays were excluded from the ownership of land traditionally held by Malays.[56] An inclusive Malayan identity needed to be forged so that immigrants could enjoy equal rights with indigenous Malays.

This double nationalism reflected the MCP's need as a Chinese association to be rooted in both its place of origin and its host country – China and Malaya, respectively – and this became obvious in the double meaning of *minzu* in MCP texts during the late 1930s, in which the 'nation' referred to both Malaya and China.[57] The MCP promoted Malayanization of the party to mobilize support from the Malay and Indian communities against the Alien Registration Ordinance, which mainly affected and was protested by Chinese immigrants.[58] MCP Malayanization was based on fighting the Ordinance in the interests of the Malayan revolution (*Malaiya gongnong laoku qunzhong de geming yundong*) and the Malay nation (*Malai minzu*), since many suspected Chinese communists were deported alongside those Chinese who lost their jobs as the result of the Great Depression.[59]

The MCP rationale for involving non-Chinese in the anti-Ordinance movement appropriated Comintern internationalism and inherited the pan-Asianism of another Chinese association, the GMD. Malaya's multi-ethnic population presented a potential, miniature model of pan-Asian liberation under Chinese leadership. The GMD promoted the involvement of non-Chinese in colonial liberation, drawing on the pan-Asianist ideas of Sun Yatsen, which described the resistance of 'suffering Asian nations' against the 'powerful nations of Europe'.[60] Interestingly, then, the structure and discourses of the MCP – the multi-ethnic revolutionary organization established by the CCP in Southeast Asia – can be traced to the earlier GMD anti-imperialist leagues of the 1920s in Europe and China and to the societies of Asian intellectuals in the early 1900s in Japan and Shanghai. The first anti-imperialist league was established in the United States to protest the annexations of the Philippines and Cuba, whose anti-colonial struggles had inspired Chinese nationalists.[61] Anti-imperialist leagues established in 1925–1927 had high GMD participation. One-fifth of the representatives at the establishment congress of Brussels' League Against Imperialism were GMD members.[62] In Canton, Ho Chi Minh established an anti-imperialist league together with the GMD; in Hankou and Shanghai, the GMD created the Union of the Oppressed Peoples of the East (*Dongfang bei yapo minzu lianhe hui*) among migrants from East Asia.[63] Hu Hanmin, chosen by Sun Yatsen as his successor, planned for the GMD to convert itself into a global organization of *Minzu Guoji*, the International of Nationalities, after it joined the Comintern; it would 'lead the international national revolutionary movement [*lingdao guojide minzu geming yundong*]'.[64] In the 1930s, the idea of a pan-Asian *Minzu Guoji*, an 'International of the East' headed by China and aspiring to liberate the 'weak races of the East', was first advocated by left-wing GMD members, and it became a key discourse in GMD policy countering Japan's expansion in Southeast Asia.[65] These ideas were echoed in the MCP; one member, Ma Ning, a Chinese writer and teacher and head of propaganda in the Malaya Anti-Imperialist League (*Malaiya fandi datongmeng*), participated in a conference of representatives of 'Chinese immigrants' (*qiaomin*) from India, Vietnam, Burma, Malaya and China. This was held in the jungle near Johor Bahru, and was referred to as the All-Nanyang Colonial Peoples Delegate Congress (*Quan Nanyang ge zhimindi ge minzu daibiao da hui*).[66] The MCP aspired not only to free the multi-ethnic Asian population of Malaya, but also pan-Asian liberation beyond Malaya's borders.

Hu Hanmin's imagined International of Nationalities provides a glimpse into not only China's long-term vision of its role in Southeast Asia, but also its ambitions to lead the world anti-colonial movement in the second half of the twentieth century.[67] The Comintern preoccupation with the Chinese revolution in the late 1920s was in tune with CCP *and* GMD pan-Asian aspirations for Chinese leadership in the colonial liberation. This was amplified, as the two Chinese parties and the Comintern embraced, for a time, the internationalism of the interwar years. The failure of the Comintern policy of cooperation between the CCP and GMD, which witnessed the bloody suppression of CCP members by the GMD in 1927, resulted in the exodus of many CCP members to Southeast Asia, where they persisted in establishing their organizations, continuing the process that had started in the early 1920s. In 1930, both Hu Hanmin and Li Lisan encouraged international propaganda to support the Chinese revolution.[68] In 1930, the Comintern promoted the mobilization of Malaya's three major ethnic communities through the MCP, calling for support for the Chinese and Indian 'revolutions' and 'the liberation of Malaya'.[69] Malaya was a unique place for these kinds of slogans, since Indians and Chinese comprised the majority of the population. The Comintern thus provided a new, global justification for the internationalism of the Chinese Revolution of Sun Yatsen's time, and merged Chinese nationalism and internationalism (pan-Asianism) in the MCP's Malayan nationalism. This perspective subsequently allows us to consider the emergence of MCA internationalism and Malayan nationalism in a fresh light.

The Malayan Chinese Association

Despite being on opposite sides of the Cold War 'communist/anti-communist' dichotomy, the MCP and MCA shared a common goal in advocating for the interests of Malaya's Chinese community. This is reflected in the ambiguous class politics of both parties. This interest shaped their participation in the discourse of a Malayan multi-ethnic nation and their desire for the colonial liberation of all ethnic communities of Malaya as a whole to ensure the prosperity of overseas Chinese and other communities. This goal was also reflected in their political alliances with ethnic parties of the time.

Tan Cheng Lock had conceived of the MCA as a Malaya-centred Chinese party since 1943, when he fled to India during the Japanese occupation of Malaya. He envisioned an association that would assist the British in dealing with post-war problems upon their reoccupation of Malaya.[70] The MCA was formed in February 1949 by Chinese community leaders from across Malaya as a response to the Malayan Emergency, and Tan became the first MCA president (1949–1958). The MCA launched activities to assist the British Government in handling the Emergency and dealt with the consequences of the Emergency among the Chinese population. The MCA worked to acquit the wrongly detained, persuading the British against the deportation of rural community members accused of supporting the MCP and advocating for the rights of Chinese rural squatters. It also organized community defence groups for protection from MCP harassment, as well as engaging in philanthropy.[71]

Although the MCP and the MCA were opposed in their attitudes towards the British and theoretically represented competing classes, in reality they had comparable membership that included both 'workers' and 'businessmen', albeit in different proportions at different times. Because of the adoption of an anti-bourgeois discourse by the MCP in 1939, the number of 'businessmen' in the MCP had dropped from 20 per cent of the 1,400 party members in 1930 to apparently none on the eve of the Japanese occupation.[72] In 1947, the MCP-led Pan-Malayan Federation of Trade Unions claimed to control 80 per cent of all trade unions in Malaya with a membership of over 263,000, comprising more than 50 per cent of the workforce.[73] However, the number of MCP guerrillas was much smaller. In 1952, the Malayan National Liberation Army, led by the MCP, had 7,000–8,000 members – a number that would drop dramatically within the following few years.[74] In 1949, the MCA claimed a membership of 103,000 after boosting its membership with welfare work, thereby including members of the Chinese provincial lodges (*huiguan*). In 1962, when the Emergency had quieted down, while 35 per cent of the MCA's (now declined) 67,700 members were 'businessmen' and 3 per cent were shopkeepers, 48 per cent belonged to the 'working class', including such people as rubber tappers, mine and construction workers, hawkers, miscellaneous labourers and handicraftsmen. Interestingly as well, many MCA and MCP members were former GMD members.[75]

Thus MCP and MCA membership cannot be divided neatly along traditional class lines. The MCA contained elements of the 'working class', and on the other side, while the membership of 'businessmen' in the MCP dropped by the time of the occupation, in the period before this, the MCP also was concerned with the well-being of affluent members of the Chinese community. Wealthier members had been an important source of the Chinese communists' budget in Nanyang since the late 1920s.[76] According to a Comintern report, in 1939 the MCP reported a dramatic decline in Chinese ownership of rubber plantations (from a 'majority' down to 16 per cent) and tin mines (80–34 per cent since the 1910s), citing British oppression of the Chinese.[77] Where the MCP obtained these figures is unclear. But based on secondary sources, the MCP likely blamed British efforts, as well as the effects of the Great Depression, for undermining Chinese capitalists' connections with Chinese labour, outlawing Chinese self-regulating organizations such as secret societies, regulating and codifying the labour contract system and monopolizing a lucrative trade in opium, spirits and tobacco; the colonial government further banned gambling, which had previously made mining lucrative for Chinese owners even on poorer-yielding tin land.[78] Thus both the MCP and MCA advocated for the well-being of a diverse array of members of the Chinese Malayan community; however, the MCP's strong anti-bourgeoisie and anti-British language lost the party support on the eve of the Japanese occupation.[79]

The MCP and MCA had similar operational and communication modes: circulars sent from the centre to local branches (provincial lodges and Chinese chambers of commerce), loose, decentralized organization and poor discipline. The MCA central headquarters in Kuala Lumpur did not have a firm hold over state branches, since many did not consider the MCA a political organization but rather an umbrella association because it focused on welfare work and often shared premises with leaders of local chambers of commerce and provincial lodges. Tan solved the problem of poor discipline just as the CCP in Malaya had done in 1928: by reorganization.[80] In 1951, in order to take part in the elections in preparation for Malayan independence, the MCA was changed from a welfare organization, which was no longer necessary as the issue of squatter resettlement had been resolved, into a centralized political organization.[81]

The MCP and MCA further shared national aspirations. As was discussed earlier, Tan's discourse on Malayan consciousness likely influenced the MCP's evolving perceptions of the Malayan nation. After the start of the Emergency, Tan embraced the same discourse of a 'Malayan nation' or 'Malayan people' consisting of all ethnic communities that had been coined over a decade previously by the now-banned MCP. In 1949, Tan said,

> The people of Malaya can only constitute a Nationality if the different Communities making up its mixed population are united among themselves by common sympathies, and fellow-feeling and reconcile themselves to living together in peace and harmony under equal rights and laws.

Moreover, 'the Chinese in Malaya have come to stay and must Wake up and Unite not only among themselves but also with the Malays and other Communities to make this land, which feeds, nourishes and sustains us, one country and one nation and the object of their loyalty, love and devotion'.[82] In 1951, Tan emphasized that the MCA had been formed to

> foster and to engender a truly Malayan outlook, consciousness and patriotism among the domiciled Malayan Chinese in order to forge and fortify their ties with this country and unity as an integral part and parcel of the Malayan people, and to help develop their sense of civil responsibility, duty and obligation to their country of adoption.[83]

Tan thus used the words 'nationality', 'people' and 'nation' in the same way as the MCP in 1930. The MCP and MCA also spoke similarly about achieving prosperity for the local Chinese and others in a unified Malaya through internationalism (the unity of the local Chinese community with the locals). Tan's planned National Unity Organization was to embrace 'all races, parties, and classes' in order 'to promote a Malayan ideal of unity, goodwill and cooperation among all who have made or desire to make Malaya their permanent home'.[84] In his speech of 1949, Tan stated,

> It is in that spirit and primarily with that end in view that representatives of the Chinese community from the various component parts of Malaya have assembled here today to launch into existence an organisation on a Pan-Malayan basis with the twin fundamental objectives of bringing about cohesion and unity among the Malayan Chinese of all classes and promoting interracial good will, harmony and cooperation for the sole good of this country and its inhabitants as a whole.[85]

Tan's focus on uniting local Chinese with other Malayan communities, Chinese indigenization and the common organization of these communities was identical to that suggested by the CCP members at the founding of the MCP. Tan advocated the same inclusion of immigrants in the Malayan nation as the MCP had, and supported equal rights for the Chinese in a multi-ethnic Malayan nation. Tan's discourse of a Malayan nation was connected to his goal of achieving citizenship rights on behalf of the Chinese majority, who had been deprived in the citizenship provisions of 1948.[86] He argued that the political transformation of the Chinese into true Malayans could only come about if they were accorded constitutional rights equal to those of the Malay community.[87] While both the MCA and the MCP were concerned with the Malayanization of their organizations in the post-war period, however, both struggled in this process.[88] The MCP and the MCA both measured their success by activities that fostered a united Malaya, a Malayan consciousness and cooperation between the Chinese and other ethnic communities. One form of indigenization was the welcoming of non-Chinese into Chinese organizations. Tan advised that the MCA 'must interest itself in the masses, whether Malays, Chinese or Indians' and that the MCA had to work for all and be broadminded. He explained that the MCA's motto could not be 'For Chinese only'.[89] Much like local GMD members and the MCP, who earlier had aspired to involve non-Chinese but were unsuccessful, the MCA added non-Chinese associate members in 1951–1953. However, while these associate members had voting rights, they could not hold office, and in 1953 associate members were denied voting rights. After 1967, the category was withdrawn altogether, and the MCA again became closed to non-Chinese.[90]

Ultimately, despite the failure of both the MCP and the MCA to attract non-Chinese into their organizations in significant numbers, it can be argued that unlike the MCP, MCA indigenization was successful. After all, the MCA headed the multi-ethnic political alliance that led Malaya to independence. However, the model of the alliance between ethnic parties that the MCA led was the same as that of the Nanyang CCP in 1929: it mirrored the CCP's vision for the organization of the MCP. Moreover, the MCP's 'national' status, as required by the Comintern, resonated with Tan's idea of a Chinese association that would be the basis of a broader, unifying Malayan party. In 1951, Tan echoed the dialogue that had surrounded the formation of the MCP:

Perhaps what is needed, and the first and most practical step to be taken under existing conditions and in the present stage of the development of Malayan consciousness among the people of this land, would be to create a new united Malaya national organisation or party with a new constitution in which members of all the races are assembled and meet on a common ground and on an equal footing to discuss the affairs of the country purely as Malayans ... This would be the way to prepare the ground for the merging of the existing communal associations into the proposed non-communal and national organisation.[91]

As this chapter has shown, the mutually influential development of the MCP and MCA nationalist organizations had a long history. In the 1920s, MCP members had been exposed to Tan's speeches and activity, which had aimed to promote the political participation of the Chinese. This influenced their appropriation of the Comintern's idea of Malaya as a nation. In the same way, Tan was likely aware of the MCP discussion of a 'Malayan nation' and adopted it. Both Tan and the MCP had the same goals of promoting Chinese rights, and they embraced the idea of Malayan unity and nation, which was encouraged by the British government as well. Tan embraced the MCP's historic line because the British increasingly identified a unified, multiracial government as the form through which they would grant self-government. MCA language was pragmatic in response to the British, but it also drew on a longer history.

The alliance of Chinese, Malay and Indian political parties that led Malaya to independence exemplified the mode of organization that the CCP had envisioned in 1930 when it created the Malayan *National* Communist Party, as required by the Comintern. However, through the MCA, Tan encouraged and blended the agendas of Chinese overseas joint political action with other Malayan ethnic communities; the localization of the internationalist Chinese nationalism espoused by MCA forerunners, such as the GMD and CCP, and the MCP's Malayan nationalism.

The dual Chinese and Malayan nationalism of the MCA, as in the case of the MCP and the GMD, was expressed not only in the discourse of the 'Malayan nation', but also in regional internationalism. Specifically, in 1943 Tan promoted a regional pan-Pacific and East Asian security organization led by the United States, Britain and China, which was reminiscent of the *Minzu Guoji*:

> One feels justified in anticipating that what has happened in the past and the circumstances in the future may induce the two great Anglo-Saxon nations, viz. the United States of America and Great Britain, together with China, as the three leading Powers and vitally interested parties, to form as part of a world organisation for security, the central core of a Confederation of the countries in East Asia and the Pacific Basin for the purpose of promoting their economic collaboration and common prosperity as well as for the protection and defence and to act as guardians of the peace of these regions, especially as the Pacific Ocean bids fair in the future to constitute the centre of gravity of human civilisation and security and the great theatre of human events for all centuries to come.[92]

This MCA concept of a multi-ethnic Malayan nation had the imprint of the historical pattern of the domestic and overseas Chinese historical 'internationalist nationalism'.

Conclusion

Establishing the genealogy of pre–Second World War internationalism is important for understanding its legacy in the later Cold War period. In the nationalism and internationalism of two Malayan Chinese organizations, the MCP and the MCA, the larger historical continuity of internationalism and nationalism (in terms of the meaning of the 'nation') can be observed without compartmentalizing them according to the ideological pronouncements and affiliations of the Cold War, which colour scholarly understanding and historiography. MCA internationalism can be viewed in the context of post-war regionalist internationalism, such as the Bandung initiative, pan-African, Pan-American and pan-Arab movements, as well as the Colombo plan, which Australian politicians defined as new internationalism, neither communist nor capitalist. [93]

The internationalism of the MCP and the MCA was rooted in the pan-Asian ethos of the Chinese Revolution and in Sun Yatsen's definition of the nationalist origins of internationalism (*shijie zhuyi*), as well as in long-held Chinese ideas about a global world, such as those of *Tianxia* ('All under heaven') or *Da Tong* ('Great Unity').[94] The convergence of nationalism and internationalism was arguably a feature of interwar globalization. Slavic, Islamic, African and European 'pan-movements' emerged with twentieth-century globalization, and by the 1930s, they had become crucial in channelling anti-colonial resistance that was based on emerging national identities sustained by transnational organizations, such as the CCP and GMD.[95] Both the GMD's *Minzu Guoji* and the MCP's support for an internationalist liberation of multi-ethnic Malaya were the zeitgeist of the regionalist 1930s. Unlike the Japanese pan-Asianism and Enver Paşa's pan-Islamism – which, after a short-lived concord with Bolshevik internationalism, clashed with Soviet interests in Central Asia, Manchuria and Siberia – the Chinese and Comintern internationalisms remained in harmony until after the Second World War in China proper and were productive in Malaya.[96]

In 1930, the Malaya of the MCP was propelled into being a 'nation' with a 'national' communist party consisting of Chinese immigrants. The MCP's discourse on the Malayan nation emerged from interpretive opportunities provided by ambiguities in the translation of keywords in authoritative documents and the multiple meanings of the word *minzu*. These were opportunities created by Comintern involvement, and the Chinese communists in Malaya embraced them to their advantage.

The Comintern's creation of a 'national' party facilitated this slippage in meaning, creating the discursive foundation of a multi-ethnic Malayan nation. *Minzu* came to refer to the Malayan nation as a multi-ethnic community residing in the territory of British Malaya bound by a 'Malayan' identity. The Comintern provided a new justification for Chinese communists located in Singapore and Malaya to take a leading role in, and offered an organizational model for, the emancipation of the oppressed Nanyang people, which had been the goal of Chinese pan-Asianism since the time of Sun Yatsen. Through a revolution on behalf of the nation, MCP dual Malay(an)/Chinese identity provided a way for a Chinese association, the MCP, both to embed itself in the host environment of Malaya and to remain rooted in China by advocating for the rights of the Chinese. The Comintern altered the political participation patterns of Chinese organizations by transforming the process of indigenization through the involvement of non-Chinese into an internationally valid Malayan nationalism, which was needed locally. The MCA, like the MCP, adopted this 'enhanced' version of indigenization.

The MCP played a key role in Malayan decolonization, but perhaps not in the way Chin Peng, the long-time General Secretary of the MCP, later claimed. The key influence of the MCP may not have been its pressure on the British through insurgency, but rather the implementation of the MCP discourse of Malayan nationalism and its related model of political participation by the MCA.[97] The model of a political union of parties organized on ethnic principles, first espoused by the CCP members who formed the MCP, became a model for the political structure of an independent Malaysia.

Notes

1 My thanks to Dr Martin Thomas for his feedback on an earlier draft of the essay. I gratefully acknowledge the support of the Nanyang Technological University, Singapore, and of the University of Oregon where I was based while working on this chapter.

2 Cheah, Boon Kheng. (1983), *Red Star over Malaya: Resistance and Social Conflict During and After the Japanese Occupation of Malaya, 1941–1946*. Singapore: Singapore University Press, 15.

3 Heng, Pek Koon (1988), *Chinese Politics in Malaysia: A History of the Malaysian Chinese Association*. Singapore; New York: Oxford University Press, 54.

4 See Kuhn, Philip A. (2008), *Chinese Among Others: Emigration in Modern Times*. Lanham, MD: Rowman & Littlefield, 45–52.

5 Hack, Karl (2003), 'Theories and approaches to British decolonization', in Marc Frey, Ronald W. Pruessen and Tan Tai Ong (eds.) *The Transformation of Southeast Asia. International Perspectives on Decolonization*. Armonk: M.E. Sharpe, 106; Harper, T.N. (1999), *The End of Empire and the Making of Malaya*. New York: Cambridge University Press, 2.

6 Kuhn (2008), 148, 160–161.

7 Wang Gungwu (1976), 'The limits of Nanyang Chinese nationalism, 1912–1937', in C.D. Cowan and O.W. Wolters (eds.) *Southeast Asian History and Historiography*. Ithaca: Cornell University Press, 405–423, esp. 418–421.

8 Roff, William (1967), *The Origins of Malay Nationalism*. New Haven: Yale University Press, 118, 122.

9 Cheah (1983), 3; Roff (1967), 208.

10 Yeo, Kim Wah (1982), *The Politics of Decentralization: Colonial Controversy in Malaya, 1920–1929*. Kuala Lumpur: Oxford University Press, 33–35.

11 Hack, Karl (1995), 'Screwing down the people: The Malayan Emergency, decolonisation, and ethnicity', in Hans Antlöv and Stein Tønesson (eds.) *Imperial Policy and Southeast Asian Nationalism, 1930–1957*. London: Curzon Press, 98.

12 Heng (1988), 200–201.

13 Heng (1988), 147–148.

14 Heng (1988), 157–159.

15 Heng (1988), 179–250.

16 Heng (1988), 101–102.

17 Leong, Stephen Mun Yoon (1976), 'Sources, agencies and manifestations of overseas Chinese nationalism in Malaya, 1937–1941', unpublished PhD dissertation, University of California, Los Angeles, 819; Ng, Sin Yue (1981), 'The Malayan Communist Party and overseas Chinese nationalism in Malaya, 1937–1941', unpublished MA dissertation, University of Hull, 55; Wang Gung Wu (1970), 'Chinese politics in Malaya', *China Quarterly*, 43, 1–30, 18, 29.

18 See Wang (1970).

19 CCP Central Committee, 'A letter from the Central Committee of CCP to Nanyang Provisional Committee. A draft resolution of the Central Committee of the Chinese Communist Party on the revolutionary movements and policies of our party in the Nanyang', 22 January 1929, Russian State Archive of Socio-Political History, Moscow (*Rossiyskiy Gosudarstvenniy Arhiv Sotsio-Politicheskoy Istorii*; RGASPI) 514/1/532/8-13.

20 Hack (2000), 226.

21 Manela, Erez (2007), *The Wilsonian Moment: Self-Determination and the International Origins of Anticolonial Nationalism*. New York: Oxford University Press.

22 I draw inspiration in this view of globalization from Robert, Dana L. (2008), 'The first globalization? The internationalization of the Protestant missionary movement between the World Wars', in Ogbu Kalu (ed.) *Interpreting Contemporary Christianity: Global Processes and Local Identities*. Eerdmans: Curzon, 93–130.

23 Anderson, Benedict (1991), *Imagined Communities: Reflections on the Origin and Spread of Nationalism*. London: Verso. C.C. Chin has called this the MCP's Malayan 'nation of intent' as reflected in 'All-Malaya' organizations. Chin, C.C. (2004), 'The revolutionary programmes and their effect on the struggle of the Malayan communist party', in C.C. Chin and Karl Hack (eds.) *Dialogues with Chin Peng: New Light on the Malayan Communist Party*. Singapore: Singapore University Press, 261.

24 Far Eastern Bureau of the Comintern, 'To the Malayan Comrades', 17 December 1930, RGASPI 495/62/12/3-4ob.

25 The 7th sub-branch [of the GMD] in Singapore, 'Message to the Overseas Chinese in respect of the Second Anniversary of the death of Sun Chung San [Sun Yatsen]', 1927, Straits Settlements Original Correspondence, CO 273/538, p. 5, TNA.

26 Yong, C.F. (1997), *The Origins of Malayan Communism*. Singapore: South Sea Society, 78, 160.

27 Perry, Elizabeth J. (2012), *Anyuan: Mining China's Revolutionary Tradition*. Berkeley: University of California, 148.

28 Nanyang Provisional Committee of the CCP, '*V tsentral'nyi komitet*', 19 July and 22 August 1928, RGASPI 495/62/1/1-17.

29 This is the language of the original document. I have established Li's authorship of the document based on the identical language in his diary and a CCP letter to the Nanyang communists. CCP Central Committee, 'A letter from the Central Committee', 9–10; Li Lisan, 1 January 1929, *Zhonggong zhongyang dangshi yanjiu shi di yi yanjiubu bian* (eds.) (1999), *Li Lisan bainian dancheng jinianji. The Publishing House of the History of the Chinese Communist Party*, 68–69.

30 Comintern (1929), *Shestoi kongress Kominterna, Stenograficheskiy otchet. Vyp. 4, Revolutsionniye dvizheniye v kolonnialnyh i polukolonial'nyh stranah*. Moscow-Leningrad, 24.

31 Yong (1997); Cheah, Boon Kheng (1992), *From PKI to the Comintern, 1924–1941: The Apprenticeship of the Malayan Communist Party, Selected Documents and Discussion*. Ithaca: Cornell University Press; McLane, Charles B. (1966), *Soviet Strategies in South East Asia: An Exploration of Eastern Policy under Lenin and Stalin*. Princeton: Princeton University Press; Quinn-Judge, Sophie (2003), *Ho Chi Minh: The Missing Years, 1919–1941*. Berkeley: University of California Press.

32 Eastern Secretariat of the Comintern, Letter to the Far Eastern Bureau, 23 October 1930, RGASPI 495/62/2/1-2.

33 CCP Central Committee, 'A letter from the Central Committee', 10.

34 'The Minutes of the Third Representative Conference of Nanyang', 1930, RGASPI 514/1/634/93-158, esp. pp. 109, 130, 136–137; 'Resolutions adopted at the Third Congress of Malaya Party', 1930, RGASPI 495/62/3/1-10, pp. 3–4; '*Protokol der.3.Delegierten Konferenz von Nanyang (Malayische Jureln.)*', undated 1930, RGASPI 514/1/634/86-92, esp. pp. 86, 88, 90; CC CCP, 'A letter from the Central Committee', 13, 8–9.

35 'Informatsiya o Malaiskih Shtatah', 3 October 1930, RGASPI 495/62/7/2-4.

36 Ho Chi Minh, 18 November 1931, RGASPI 534/3/549/25-27. Ho Chi Minh's authorship is established based on the contents of the text; MCP, 'Report from Malay', 2 January 1931, RGASPI 495/62/11/27-29; Anonymous, 'To the CC of the Chinese party and Comintern', undated, RGASPI 495/62/11/1-4; 'Informatsiya o Malaiskih Shtatah'.

37 Milner, Anthony (1994), *The Invention of Politics in Colonial Malaya: Contesting Nationalism and the Expansion of Public Sphere*. Cambridge, MA: Cambridge University, Chapter 3, esp. 64; Anonymous, 'To the CC of the Chinese party'.

38 Anonymous, 'To the CC of the Chinese party', 2.

39 Monthly Review of Chinese Affairs, December 1931. CO 273/572, pp. 41, 44, TNA.

40 MCP Central Committee, '*Zhongyang tonggao disi hao*', 10 August 1930, RGASPI 495/62/13/31-32; MCP Central Committee, 'Gongren ying zuo shenmo shiqing', 15 November 1930, RGASPI 495/62/23/84-93.

41 The MCP had no connection with the short-lived *Belia Malaya* (Young Malaya, 1930–1931), which was established by a group of Malay student teachers, including Ibrahim Yaacob (who is credited with coining the discourse of multi-ethnic Malayan nation in 1937), and inspired by the idea of unity with Indonesia. See Roff (1967), 224–225, 255; Tan, Liok Ee (1988), 'The rhetoric of Bangsa and Minzu: Community and nation in tension, the Malay Peninsula, 1900–1955', working paper, Centre of Southeast Asian Studies, Monash University.

42 Comintern (1934), *21 usloviye priyema v Komintern*. Second Edition, Introduction by Pyatnitskiy, Izdatelstvo TsK VKP(b). Central Committee of the All-Russia Communist Party.

43 Nanyang Provisional Committee, *Otchet o polozhenii v Nanyane*', January 1930, RGASPI 514/1/632/7-28, p. 16.

44 'The Minutes of the Third Representative Conference of Nanyang', 120.

45 'Resolutions adopted at the Third Congress of Malaya Party', 8.

46 This is the original language of the source. 'Resolutions adopted at the Third Congress of Malaya Party', 4.

47 Goscha, Christopher E. (1999), *Thailand and the Southeast Asian Networks of the Vietnamese Revolution, 1885–1954*. Richmond, Surrey: Curzon Press.

48 CCP Central Committee, 'A letter from the Central Committee', 12.

49 Far Eastern Bureau of the Comintern, 'To the Malayan Comrades'.

50 'The minutes of the third representative conference of Nanyang', 118–119.

51 'Extract from Mr. Tan Cheng Lock's speech at the meeting of the legislative council held on 1st November 1926', in C.Q. Lee (ed.) (1947), *Malayan Problems from the Chinese Point of View*. Singapore: Tannsco, 90.

52 Tan (1988), 27–28, 34.

53 Far Eastern Bureau of the Comintern, 'To the Malayan Comrades'; Wu, Yin Hua (1983), *Class and Communalism in Malaysia*. London: Zed Books, 51; I borrow conceptualization from Koselleck, Reinhart (1985), Begriffsgeschichte and social history', in Reinhart Koselleck (ed.)

Futures Past: On the Semantics of Historical Times. Cambridge, MA: Massachusetts Institute of Technology Press.

54 Ratnam, K.J. (1965), *Communalism and the Political Process in Malaya.* Kuala Lumpur: University of Malaya Press, 9; Roff (1967), 208.

55 Tan Cheng Lock, Address at the meeting of the legislative council at Malacca on 12 February 1934, in Lee (1947), 95–97.

56 Loh, Francis Kok-Wah (1988), *Beyond the Tin Mines: Coolies, Squatters, and New Villagers in the Kinta Valley, Malaysia, c. 1880–1980.* Singapore: Oxford University Press, 33.

57 MCP, '*Magong dier ci zhong zhihui yi yijuean*', 20 February 1940, RGASPI 495/62/28/18-36, pp. 29–30.

58 'United Chambers of Commerce. Malayan Chinese topics. Alien registration. Proposed new bill opposed', *The Straits Times,* 20 September 1932, 18.

59 MCP Central Committee, '*Magong lianzi tonggao di yi hao. Dantuan zhongyang guanyu waiqiao dengji lülie yu womende gongzuo de jueyi*', 12 October 1932, RGASPI495/62/20/1-6, p. 6.

60 Sun Yatsen, '*Dui shenhu shanghuiyisuo deng tuanti de yan shuo*', 28 November 1924, in Sun Yatsen (1986), *Sun zhongshan quan ji.* vol. 11. Beijing: Zhong hua shuju, 409. For studies approaching the GMD as a Chinese overseas association, see Li Minghuan (1995), *Dangdai haiwai Huaren shetuan yanjiu.* University of Xiamen publishing house; Fitzgerald, John (2007), *Big White Lie: Chinese Australians in White Australia.* Sydney: University of New South Wales Press.

61 Harrington, Fred H. (1935), 'The anti-imperialist movement in the United States, 1898–1900', *Mississippi Valley Historical Review,* 22, 211–230; Karl, Rebecca E. (2002), *Staging the World: Chinese Nationalism at the Turn of the Twentieth Century.* Durham: Duke University Press.

62 Piazza, Hans (2002), 'Anti-imperialist League and the Chinese Revolution', in Mechthild Leutner et al. (eds.) *The Chinese Revolution in the 1920s: Between Triumph and Disaster.* London: Routledge, 167–169.

63 Quinn-Judge (2003), 83–84; The union of the oppressed peoples of the East, '*Dongfang beiyapo lianhehui shang zhongzhihui cheng*', 23 July 1927, reel 64, file 7625.1, Hankou Collection, Hoover Archives, Stanford University.

64 Hu, Hanmin, '*Minzu Guoji yu disan guoji*', in Cuncui xueshe (ed.) (1980), *Hu Hanmin shiji ziliao huji.* vol. 4. Hong Kong: Publishing Company Datong, 1400–1401.

65 Li, Yinghui (1997), *Huaqiao zhengce yu haiwai minzuzhuyi (1912–1949).* Taibei: Guoshiguan, 506–507; Yu, Yujin, 'A review of the misery of the weak races of the East', 'Culture Biannual (Wenhua banniankan)', February 1931, Monthly Review of Chinese Affairs, June, CO 273/572, pp. 49–51, TNA. For left-leaning GMD ideas about the Eastern International, see So, Wai Chor (1991), *The Kuomintang Left in the National Revolution, 1924–1931: The Leftist Alternative in Republican China.* New York: Oxford University Press, 84, 85, 92, 234.

66 Yu, Yueting, '*Ma Ning yige beiyiwang de liao bu chao de 'zuoyi' zuojia*', in Zhao, Ting (ed.) (1994), *Shifan qun ying guanghui zhonghua (diershi juan).* vol. 20. The Publishing House of the Peoples' Education of the Province of Shaanxi, 181–182.

67 Cook, Alex (2010), 'Third world Maoism', in Timothy Cheek (ed.) *A Critical Introduction to Mao.* New York: Cambridge University Press.

68 Li, Lisan, '*Pismo Li Lisanya Zhou Enlayu i Tsu Tsubo*', 17 April 1930, in M.L.Titarenko and M. Leutner (eds.) (2003), *VKP(b), Komintern i Kitai. Documenty. VKP(b), Komintern i soventskoye dvizheniye v Kitae. 1931–1937. T.3 Chast 2,* Moscow: ROSSPEN; Hu (1980).

69 Far Eastern Bureau of the Comintern, 'To the Malayan Comrades'.

70 Heng (1988), 56.

71 Heng (1988), 54.

72 Anonymous, 'To the CC of the Chinese party'. According to Yong, in the early 1930s, party leaders were petty bourgeoisie, intellectuals and working class. Yong (1997), 167.

73 Yong, C.F. (2004), 'An overview of the Malayan communist movement to 1942', in Chin and Hack (2004), 250.

74 Chin, C.C. (2004) 'In search of the revolution: a brief biography of Chin Peng' in Chin and Hack (2004), 366.

75 Heng (1988), 78, 81–82.

76 Anonymous, '*Nanyang gongzuo baogao*'. February 1929, RGASPI 533/10/1818/55-68, p. 56.

77 Li, Tun-go, '*Sokrashcenniy perevod broshury Malaya segonya sostavlennoi na kitayskom yazyke*', 23 December 1941, RGASPI 495/62/29/65-86, pp. 71–72; Vilkov, Zyuzin, Dashevskyi, '*Spravka o rabote sredi kitaiskih emigrantov v Malaye. sostavlena na osnove materialov 1939–1940 g.g)*', 4 February 1942, RGASPI 495/62/30/10a-54, pp. 18–19, 46.

78 Nonini, Donald M. (1992), *British Colonial Rule and the Resistance of the Malaya Peasantry, 1900–1957*. New Haven: Yale University Southeast Asia Studies, 67.

79 '*Maijin*', December 1939 through early 1941, RGASPI 495/62/28/53-84, esp. p. 81.

80 Nanyang Provisional Committee, '*V tsentral'nyi komitet*'.

81 Lim, Bee Khim (1991), 'Tan Cheng Lock, Tan Siew Sin and the MCA (1949–1974)', unpublished BA honours dissertation, National University of Singapore, 19–20; Leong, Yew Koh, Letter to Tan Cheng Lock, 1 June 1950, and Letter from Tan Cheng Lock to Leong Yew Koh, 24 June 1950, both cited in Lim (1991), 21–23.

82 Tan Cheng Lock, 'Speech on the 27th February 1949 at the Inaugural Meeting of the Proposed Malayan Chinese Association at Kuala Lumpur', in Lee (1947), 1.

83 Tan Cheng Lock's speech at the MCA annual Central General Committee meeting, 21 April 1951, cited in Heng (1988), 86.

84 National Unity League' Plan, *The Straits Times*, 4 May 1948, 7.

85 Tan Cheng Lock, 'Speech on the 27th February 1949', in Lee (1947), 1.

86 Only in 1957 did the MCA fight off these citizenship provisions. Heng (1988), 46–50.

87 Heng (1988), 86.

88 Cheah (1983), 68.

89 Tan Cheng Lock, 'Malayan Mirror' 1, 2, 28 June 1953, cited in Lim (1991), 19.

90 Heng (1988), 159.

91 Tan Cheng Lock (1951), *We need a new Malayan national party*. Pamphlet reprinted from Sunday Standard, 22 April 1951. Singapore: Tiger Press, 1, 6–7.

92 '1943, Tan Cheng Lock's Memorandum on the future of Malaya', in Lee (1947), 24.

93 Amrith, Sunil S. (2005), 'Asian internationalism: Bandung's echo in a colonial metropolis', *Inter-Asia Cultural Studies*, 6(4), 557–569; James, Leslie (2015), *George Padmore and Decolonization from Below: a Transnational Anti-colonial Strategy, 1939–1959*. London: Palgrave; Lowe, David (2013), 'Journalists and the stirring of Australian public diplomacy: The Colombo Plan towards the 1960s', *Journal of Contemporary History*, 48(1), 175–190.

94 Sun Yatsen, '*Sanminzhuyi, Minzuzhuyi*, lecture 4', 17 February 1924, in Sun Yatsen (1986), 226; Wu Jianshu (1997), 'Cong da Yazhou zhuyi zouxiang shijie datong zhuyi: luelun Sun

Zhongshan de guoji zhuyi sixiang', *Jindaishi yanjiu*, 3, 183–198; Karl (2002), 113–114, 169–173.

95 Aydin, Cemil (2007), *The Politics of Anti-Westernism in Asia: Visions of World Order in Pan-Islamic and Pan-Asian Thought*. New York: Columbia University Press, 4, 201–203.

96 Aydin (2007), 145–149.

97 Chin and Hack (2004), 234–235.

Key texts

Cheah, Boon Kheng. (1992). *From PKI to the Comintern, 1924–1941: The Apprenticeship of the Malayan Communist Party, Selected Documents and Discussion*. Ithaca: Cornell University Press.

Chin, C.C. and Hack, Karl (eds). (2004). *Dialogues with Chin Peng: New Light on the Malayan Communist Party*. Singapore: Singapore University Press.

Harper, T.N. (1999). *The End of Empire and the Making of Malaya*. New York: Cambridge University Press.

Heng, Pek Koon. (1988). *Chinese Politics in Malaysia: A History of the Malaysian Chinese Association*. Singapore, New York: Oxford University Press.

Karl, Rebecca E. (2002). *Staging the World: Chinese Nationalism at the Turn of the Twentieth Century*. Durham: Duke University Press.

Tan, Liok Ee. (1988). 'The rhetoric of Bangsa and Minzu: Community and nation in tension, the Malay Peninsula, 1900–1955'. Working Paper, Centre of Southeast Asian Studies, Monash University.

Yong, C.F. (1997). *The Origins of Malayan Communism*. Singapore: South Sea Society.

CHAPTER 7
NEGOTIATING RUSSIAN IMPERIAL ARYANISM: SOVIET ORIENTAL STUDIES IN THE COLD WAR

Hanna Jansen

The introduction to the classic history of Tajikistan, *The Tajiks: an Ancient, Classical and Medieval History* (1972), reads, 'Theories claiming that so-called "pure" races dominate others are speculative and contradicted by scholarly findings'.[1] It was the director of the prestigious Institute for Oriental Studies (IVAN) in Moscow, Bobodzhan Gafurovich Gafurov (1908–1977), who introduced this 'socialist' perspective on Soviet Central Asian history. He aimed to show the cultural unity of Central Asian nations, and thus to refute the 'futile efforts of bourgeois emigrant historians' that presented the 'history of the peoples of Central Asia as nothing but an arena of conflict between ethnicities and races'.[2]

Gafurov's suggestion that Soviet historians, in contrast, were freed from such a racist bias underscored Soviet self-representations in Cold War diplomacy and propaganda as a postcolonial and post-racist state. According to the Soviets, socialism had proven that under the proper socio-economic circumstances, people from all cultures and races were equally capable of progress and, by providing the optimal context for human development, the Soviet state had strengthened the intercultural and interracial unity between people. The biography of Gafurov himself added symbolic weight to such self-representations: while born under Tsarist colonial rule as the son of a poor Muslim family in the rural areas in the Ferghana Valley, he benefited from opportunities under Soviet rule, which allowed him to chart a brilliant career in both academic and Party hierarchies from the 1930s onwards. This in itself seemed to confirm the decolonized character of the Soviet state.

For much of the Cold War period, the dominant interpretation among Western historians would have been that Gafurov's statements masked the 'true' face of Soviet rule, which was that of a totalitarian and neocolonial state that used socialism to legitimate the suppression of national minorities' right to self-determination. In recent years, however, many authors have successfully challenged such simplifying views. Authors such as Francine Hirsch, Terry Martin and Ronald Suny have taken the drive for national emancipation as an essential aspect of Soviet state-building. While perhaps disagreeing on the Soviet intentions for doing so, they argue the Soviet Union should not be simply understood as a 'breaker of nations', but rather as a state that aimed to modernize its population progressively through nation-building.[3] Authors such as Douglas Northrop, Marianne Kamp, Adrienne Edgar and Stephane Dudoignon have added to this a Central

Asian perspective: placing Soviet rule and its excesses in Central Asia in the context of Soviet modernization aims.[4]

This chapter aims to situate Soviet modernizing strategies of nation-building in Central Asia in the broader contexts of globalization and Cold War. It seeks to reconsider Soviet decolonization by relating it to Soviet strategies of 'national liberation' in the Third World during the Cold War. And it shows how, paradoxically, throughout the Cold War, imperial Russian practices were continued in the Soviet drive to 'liberate' Soviet minority nations from imperial cultural and political oppression. Drawing on works such as that of Vera Tolz and Adeeb Khalid, it highlights that scholars and intellectuals of the pre-revolutionary generation were involved in the construction of the Soviet state as a union of ethnic nations, and in the mind of these early Soviet state-builders, nations did not stand on their own. Rather than viewing the construction of independent nation-states as an end-goal in itself, the Soviet intellectuals of the interwar period understood decolonization and ethnic minority nation-building as a stage in the process of strengthening and modernizing international civilizations. These intellectuals presented no isolated case, as such ideals were internationally widespread as is illustrated, for instance, by the wide array of 'Pan-' ideologies that globally manifested themselves in this period.

This chapter traces the continuities with pre-revolutionary thought in the work of Soviet Orientalists. The terms 'Oriental Studies', 'Orient' and 'Orientalist' are used primarily in a localized, descriptive sense.[5] As Tolz has convincingly shown, Soviet Orientalists were aware of the imperial bias underlying the pre-revolutionary tradition of Russian Orientology, but nevertheless continued to use these terms for self-reference. To their minds, the term had lost its overtones of colonial oppression since socialist revolution, and nation-building had effectively 'decolonized' the Tsarist empire. Orientalists provided the Soviet Union with scholarly findings that allowed for the identification and construction of the history and cultural traditions of Oriental nationalities. This chapter will turn specifically to the career of Bobodzhan Gafurov, a Soviet Orientalist and Tajik historian, in order to assess the political function of Soviet academic discourses on Central Asian nation-building, particularly Tajikistan. In the traditional understanding of Russian and Soviet Orientalists, the Tajik 'Indo-European' cultural tradition provided Soviet Central Asia with links to Persianate countries such as Afghanistan, Iran and India, and also to the Russian Slavs since Slavic had been categorized as an Indo-European language in the second half of the nineteenth century.

The focus on academic negotiations of ethno-national identity and development allows this chapter to move beyond the confines of Cold War polarizations. The idea that national liberation would support a process of international cultural integration irrespective of Cold War alliances remained central to the tradition of Oriental Studies for most of the Soviet period. Nevertheless, this chapter also shows the great influence Cold War competition had on such notions of international unity. To illustrate this, the emergence of notions of Indo-European and 'Aryan' civilization as a central characteristic to both the Tajik cultural heritage and that of the Soviet Union at large will be traced. The embrace of 'Aryanism' in the late 1960s is explained as part of Moscow's strategy to present itself as a centre of world civilization in response to the changing relations between the Soviet Union, China and India. In this context of Cold War superpower competition, Gafurov became an unofficial diplomat for 'Aryan' civilization, which he framed in terms of decolonization. On the level of the Soviet peripheries, however, Moscow's embrace of 'Aryanism' created new international and intercultural hierarchies. The unintended consequence of this was that these led to resistance that came to be framed in national terms, thus constituting a discourse of national oppression rather than liberation.

Soviet Oriental Studies and ethno-national liberation

Ever since 1917, socialist revolutionaries advanced the ideal of ethnic nation-building ('national liberation') in the former Tsarist Empire as part of a worldwide socialist mission against bourgeois and imperial oppression. Soviet Comintern agitators at the same time propagated the message of ethno-national liberation abroad, thus seeking to expand Soviet influence at the cost of traditional regimes by reaching out to minority nations. Traditionally, Russian imperial administrators and policymakers had referred to notions of shared religion in order to legitimate foreign intervention, for instance in the case of Christian Armenia in the Ottoman Empire.[6] In the Muslim areas of 'Russian Turkestan' (present-day Central Asia), Russian colonizers justified their conquest by emphasizing shared cultural and religious heritages. Russian imperial scholars and administrators viewed Central Asian Muslims as 'unorthodox' Muslims who had converted to Islam only half-heartedly. Russian scholarship also supported the idea that Central Asian Muslims were still strongly committed to pre-Islamic traditions that they shared with other people inhabiting the Russian Empire.[7]

Furthermore, Russian ideals of 'Aryanism' also supported such imperial discourses. 'Aryan' idealism upheld the idea that the Russian Slavs were the direct descendants of Indo-European civilizations found in Asia rather than Western Europe.[8] To claim 'Aryan' descent for Russia served several purposes in foreign affairs. First, it granted the Russian Slavs an ancient Aryan noble origin that challenged European claims to civilizational leadership. Second, Aryanism supplied the Russians with a means to justify interventionism in Asia. To claim Aryan ties allowed Russia to present the annexation of Muslim Central Asia as a 'liberating' campaign that freed Central Asian Aryans from 'Turkic-Mongolian' dominance (the 'Tatar yoke') and allowed them to repatriate to the Russian Indo-European homeland.[9] In this sense, the trope that Central Asian Muslims were strongly committed to pre-Islamic traditions allowed for the embrace of Central Asian Muslims speaking Indo-European languages as 'Muslim Aryans'.[10]

When in the course of the nineteenth century Euroscepticism spread, some Russian Orientalists came to criticize the dominant tradition within Russian Orientology of harbouring a Western culturally chauvinist bias.[11] Often advancing from romantic anti-imperial positions, these Orientalists rejected the preoccupation with global imperial civilizations, propagating instead the value of locally rooted, ethnic cultures

(*Volkskultur*).[12] The most influential Soviet Orientalist working on Soviet Central Asian studies was the internationally authoritative scholar of Central Asian history, Vasily Vladimirovich Barthold (1869–1930). To Barthold and his colleagues, it was not cosmopolitan dynastic rulers but locally rooted merchants and missionaries who were the primary agents advancing progressive cultural integration between people and nations. At the same time, they believed that progressive empires played a role as benefactors of civilization, since imperial infrastructures greatly facilitated processes of international and intercultural interaction.[13] Criticizing Russian 'Aryanism', Barthold claimed that the great empires of the East, such as the Arabic Caliphate and the Mongol Empire, also had brought about the progressive cultural integration of Eastern and Western people.[14] He nevertheless held on to the idea (also adhered to by Russian 'Aryanists') that special cultural ties existed between Russian Slavs and Central Asian Muslims, arguing that the specifics of the Central Asian tradition of Islam had allowed Central Asians to transmit ancient and pre-Islamic traditions and customs well into the Islamic period.[15]

After the Revolution, the Eurosceptic tradition in Oriental Studies that Barthold represented acquired state backing. During the 1920s, academic Orientalists actively cooperated with Soviet policymakers and administrators in order to grant all ethnic groups of the former Tsarist realm territorial and cultural autonomy. Taking part in large-scale multidisciplinary expeditions, they set out to uncover the identities and complex ethnogenesis of local minority nations.[16] Early Soviet ethnographers viewed language as the main, albeit not the only, marker of ethno-national identity.[17] Prior to Soviet rule, much of the urban population in the area of Soviet Central Asia had been bilingual, speaking both Indo-European (Persian, Eastern Iranian) and Turkic languages. As the Bolsheviks viewed vernacular languages rather than languages of Imperial culture, rule or religion as the 'core' identifiers of nationhood, most of the Soviet Central Asian ethno-national administrative units set up in October 1924 had Turkic as their titular language. Only the Tajik Autonomous Soviet Socialist Republic (Tajik ASSR), that was situated as an Autonomous Republic within the confines of the larger Uzbek Union Soviet Socialist Republic (Uzbek USSR) and encompassed the relatively uncultivated mountainous areas to the East of the urban centres of the Uzbek Republic, had Persian as its titular language.[18] Since the Persian linguistic tradition in Central Asia was strongly associated with Islamic court culture and the rule of traditional elites, it was now at a disadvantage.

When in the 1930s Stalin began to build a grand cultural tradition for the Soviet Union that established the USSR as direct heir to the universal civilizations of the past, he granted the Russian culture a dominant, centrifugal role within the larger Soviet tradition.[19] In their accounts of the history of Central Asia, Soviet Orientalists thus gave prominent civilizational roles to predecessors of the Russian Slavs: the Scythian nomads of the Eurasian steppes.[20] While traditionally, civilization was related to urban societies and traced in linguistic findings (monuments and manuscripts), Soviet ethnographers argued that cultural traditions could also be found in material culture, primarily pottery.[21] This allowed Soviet scholars to situate 'primitive peoples' and nomadic cultures at the origin of civilization. Accordingly, when in the late 1930s the first histories of the new Soviet Republics began to be written, the Turko-Nomadic Muslims of Central Asia were viewed as deeply rooted in the pre-Islamic cultural heritage of the early Indo-European settlers in Central Asia.[22]

Tajik 'national liberation' and communist agitation among Iranian minorities

The work and career of Bobodzhan Gafurov illustrate that, throughout the Cold War, Soviet support of anti-colonial nation-building remained strongly tied to the ideal of transnational cultural integration. In the 1930s, Gafurov became the protégé of Iosif Samuilovich Braginsky (1908–1989), a Persian-speaking Jewish Ukrainian Comintern veteran, who was a leading figure in the Soviet foreign propaganda apparatus and had been active among Persian-speaking minorities in the East (primarily in the Trans-Caucasus and Northern Iran, but later also in Afghanistan). Braginsky had worked as a teacher at the Communist University for Toilers of the East and taught many of the early Tajik Party elites who later had successful careers in Soviet cultural relations abroad.[23] When Braginsky was installed as head of the Ideological Department of the Tajik Communist Party in 1937, Gafurov became his Deputy Director for Printed Materials. From that moment on, his career flourished. In 1939 he was installed as head of the Department for Cultural Enlightenment, in 1941 as Tajik Party Secretary for Propaganda and in 1946 as First Secretary of the Tajik Communist Party, thus acquiring the highest political rank within the Tajik Republic. Under Braginsky's patronage, Gafurov was groomed as a spokesperson for Tajik ethnic and socialist nation-building, and the official national history of Tajikistan was published under his name. That Gafurov was granted sole authorship while, in fact, all Republican histories were written by collectives indicates that he was a useful figure for Soviet policymakers and administrators. Gafurov's first publications appeared during the Second World War when Soviet troops occupied Northern Iran. (Iran was subdivided into a British and Soviet zone in 1941, the year that Gafurov was installed as Secretary for Propaganda.)

Gafurov served Soviet prospects in the East in his status as a former colonial subject, liberated and educated under socialism, adding symbolic weight to socialist agitation among national minorities in Iran. Gafurov's first book, *The Fall of the Bukharan Emirate* (written together with a certain N.N. Prokhorov), appeared in 1940 and celebrated the socialist achievements of Soviet decolonization, taking the Tajik Republic as the example.[24] To Gafurov, 'only Soviet power could offer liberation from the national yoke', 'destroy colonialism' and 'offer minority nations independent statehood'.[25]

Gafurov's writings during the Second World War created an image of the Soviet Union as an ideologically committed protector of Oriental minority nations. Gafurov claimed that the Nazis sought to destroy the culture not only of Eastern Europeans and the Slavic 'brotherly' people but also of the 'people from the Orient in the Crimea and in the Northern Caucasus'.[26] Suggesting that the Nazi threat legitimated Soviet interventions abroad, he argued, 'The German fascists wanted to carry the Tajik culture to its grave', and during the war the Soviet 'sense of responsibility ... for their home country and for the fate of all of humanity' had grown.[27] His work thus offered ideological justification for Soviet intervention in Northern Iran and for Soviet involvement in the national liberation and the construction of Soviet-friendly Kurdish and Azerbaijani national minority republics on Iranian soil. Furthermore, his work also provided cultural arguments for Soviet interventionism abroad on behalf of national minorities.

Throughout the war, Gafurov's propaganda also explicitly presented the Tajik nation as embedded in an international cultural tradition that it shared, in particular, with Iranian people, treating the great figures of the Persio-Islamic civilization, such as Ferdowsi, Hafiz, Saadi, Jami and Ibn Sina, as part of a specific 'Tajik-Iranian' heritage.[28] In his second book, *The Tajik People in the Struggle for the Freedom and Independence of their Homeland* (published in 1944, also with Prokhorov as co-author), Gafurov criticized imperial Iranian elites in the past for having divided the Iranian people inhabiting northern Iranian territory and Central Asia, presenting such divide-and-rule strategies as the rationalization for the 'Aryan' ideology. To his mind, ancient Persian imperial elites already had 'driven a wedge' between the Central Asian 'Iranians' and their brethren in Persia. By categorizing only Western Iranians as 'Aryan', the Persian kings had excluded the Tajiks from the 'Aryan' realm.[29] Depicting Tajiks and Iranians as cultural brethren, he thus continued the imperial strategy that justified foreign intervention based on shared traditions.

To emphasize the cultural ties between Soviet national republics and foreign minority nations strengthened the image of the Soviet Union as a benefactor of foreign diaspora communities and as a homeland for 'liberated' minority nations abroad. This imagery was actively realized by the Soviet regime: in 1945, Stalin invited the Armenian populations in the Middle East and Anatolia to repatriate to the Soviet homeland.[30]

Post-war culture building and Stalin's anti-cosmopolitanism

After the war, Tajik cultural traditions acquired more prominence in Gafurov's writings. From 1945 onwards, the project of Soviet culture-building was reinvigorated, and the themes addressed in Gafurov's writings became more conservative, shifting towards the glorification of Soviet cultural traditions. Gafurov urged Tajik elites to take the lead in the process of 'elevating' the Tajik-Iranian culture, in particular Tajik writers. He argued:

> All the best [products] of our people in the realm of society, culture, literature, and way of life should be studied more in depth, and propagated more widely, not only within our Republic, but also beyond the borders of Tajikistan, and its contribution should be integrated into the universal treasury of Soviet culture, into the character of the Soviet man.[31]

His work of this period presented Soviet Tajikistan as leading a process of cultural enlightenment that, considering the transnational cultural ties of the Tajik people, was inherently international: 'To work for the growth of the vigour of our intelligentsia is one of the important tasks of this day, and indispensable for the elevation of our culture as a whole.'[32] He emphasized that Tajik elites should know 'foreign languages' and suggested, paraphrasing Stalin, that Tajik culture spread to the Orient beyond Soviet borders: 'If we really want to develop Tajikistan into a civilized country at the gate of the Oriental countries ... we have to work with tripled energy at the development of culture.'[33]

Nevertheless, in the immediate aftermath of war, Gafurov's focus on internationally shared Tajik-Iranian cultural traditions came under critique. By August 1944, Sergei Pavlovich Tolstov, a leading Soviet ethnographer and director of the Institute of Ethnography in Moscow from 1942–1965, criticized Gafurov's 1944 outline of Tajik history, arguing that 'some Tajik historians' had driven a 'wedge' between the Turkic Central Asians and their Indo-European ancestors by claiming the ancient Iranian culture of Central Asia exclusively for the Tajiks.[34] Indeed, Gafurov had argued that the Turkic people in Central Asia had only been 'slowly susceptible to Iranian culture', and instead remained attached to their 'nomadic traditions'.[35] By the time the first edition of the official Tajik national history, *The History of the Tajik People* (1949), was published, Gafurov had changed his position. He now argued that the ancient Iranian culture of Central Asia was shared by Central Asian Turkic and Iranian people alike, and he argued that all Central Asian people had made 'original contributions to the universal treasury of human culture'.[36]

Soon after the appearance of this first edition, yet another shift in the evaluation of the ancient cultural heritage of Central Asian people took place. In response to rising Cold War tensions and growing fears of capitalist aggression, Stalin broke off friendly relations with the West, shifting his attention towards socialist bloc-formation.[37] Central to this was Stalin's aim to strengthen and purify local ethno-national traditions. He launched a series of purges in order to eradicate all 'cosmopolitan', non-native cultural and academic traditions from the Soviet public sphere, particularly targeting Russian Jews.[38]

Soviet historians were given the task of celebrating examples of military vigour and political leadership in history rather than episodes of cultural brilliance. For instance, the medieval Turko-nomadic warlord Timur was portrayed as a national hero for the Soviet Uzbeks in 1946, and he was praised for his personal charisma, political skills and military achievements.[39] In a defining article of 1926, Barthold had distinguished four ancient Central Asian cultural traditions or civilizations: Khorezmia, Sogdia, Bactria and Parthia. Of these ancient cultures, Barthold argued, Khorezm had developed the strongest political traditions and state structures of all ancient Central Asian cultures. Barthold identified the Sogdians as the direct predecessors of the modern Tajiks, and he claimed that in contrast to the Khorezmians, the Sogdians had developed weak states. Culturally, on the other hand, Barthold argued the influence of the Sogdians had been great, as they had played a historic role as transmitters of culture, thus contributing greatly to the progressive development of civilization.[40] In 1948, Tolstov published a work on ancient Central Asian history, entitled *On the Trail of the Ancient Civilization of Khorezm*, and it was rewarded with the prestigious

Stalin premium.[41] The book placed the ancient Khorezmians, who were regarded as the ancient predecessors of the Central Asian Uzbeks rather than Sogdia, at the core of Central Asian civilization.[42] In response to Cold War pressures, then, Turko-nomadic military and state traditions acquired a more prominent place within Central Asian historiography.

Bloc formation and communist cultural integration

In line with the new emphasis on native traditions, all editions of Gafurov's *The History of the Tajik People* (1949, 1952, 1955) – the official national history of Tajikistan – explicitly rejected 'Aryanism' as a *racist* ideology.[43] Gafurov argued that 'Aryan' categories were used by 'Western historians' to obstruct the integration of people on the basis of 'racist positions'. He criticized such perspectives claiming that the 'Iranian speaking peoples were never a "pure race" or "pure-blooded Aryans"', and that 'the theory of a "pure race" was a reactionary fabrication, a myth'.[44]

In response to Stalin's rejection of bourgeois civilization as a means to acquire cultural unity, Tajik historiography had to repudiate the progressive influence of international civilizations on local Tajik historical development. Thus in the second revised edition of *The History of the Tajik People* (1952), laudatory accounts of Tajik-Iranian bourgeois cultural heritages were muted. This rejection of the heritages of imperial civilizations, however, did not bring the ideal of cultural integration between people in the Soviet Union to its end. As Francine Hirsch has shown, in the Soviet understanding, ethnicity was not a fixed, biologically determined given, but subjected to socio-economic change. As such, it was believed that ethno-national native traditions could merge with one another.[45]

In the second edition of *The History of the Tajik People*, accounts of mutually beneficial cultural exchange figured prominently, but were now restricted to communist states. As part of Soviet communist bloc-formation strategies, Soviet scholars were urged to participate in the construction of national histories of allied states.[46] The establishment of the People's Republic of China (PRC) in 1949 led to great hopes for an anti-Western Sino-Soviet bloc, and the writings of Tolstov were widely disseminated in communist China.[47] Chinese revolutionaries eagerly absorbed Soviet theories of the ethnogenesis of 'primitive societies', and in October 1950, the year that the USSR signed a Treaty of Friendship with the PRC, the Chinese declared that scholarship in China should be based on the principle of anti-imperialism.[48] In the 1952 edition of *The History of the Tajik People*, accounts of Sino-Tajik cultural interaction consistently granted the Soviet people leading roles in this process. For instance, in Gafurov's discussion of beneficial cultural exchanges between the Soviet Union and China, the Chinese adopted cotton-production skills from the Ferghana Valley, so the Soviet Central Asian people thus had 'supported both [Chinese] silk-production and irrigation'.[49] Arguing that Buddhism was spread to China by Central Asians, Gafurov concluded that 'the forefathers of Tajiks, Uzbeks, Turkmen and other people of Central Asia in the ancient period played a leading role in the development of universal human civilization'.[50]

In this process of cultural integration within the communist bloc, the most prominent leading role was granted to the nomadic Scythian predecessors of the Russian Slavs. All volumes of *The History of the Tajiks* maintained that the dominant element in the ethnic composition of Central Asians was Scythian, thus rooting Russian cultural dominance over Central Asia in ancient history. Moreover, Gafurov emphasized that ancient ethno-cultural links existed between the Soviet Republics and Eastern Europe: 'the material culture of the Pamiri-Semirechiye [Tajik-Uzbek] Scythians in the Gissar Mountains' corresponded to 'monuments of Scythian culture in Eastern Europe'.[51] *The History of the Tajik People* thus conceived of an international Scythian cultural whole that stretched from northeastern Europe towards South Asia. Gafurov claimed ' … we have come across objects that can be exclusively found in the areas of the Baltics and the Indian Ocean'.[52] Apparently, within the larger transnational Scythian 'civilization', the specifically Tajik cultural realm 'reached from the Pyrenees to the Indian Ocean'.[53]

Khrushchev's dual diplomacy: Revolutionary idealism and culture

After Stalin's death in March 1953, the new Party leader, Nikita Khrushchev, strove to de-Stalinize inter-ethnic relations within the communist bloc, undertaking a strategy of internal political decentralization.[54] In international affairs de-Stalinization involved the re-establishment of diplomatic ties with non-communist countries. Central Asian writers and propagandists were sent off to Asia to rekindle ideas of Soviet-Asian cultural unity.[55] Illustrative of the new importance attributed to cultural integration in the establishment of good foreign relations with Eastern non-communist countries were the debates held within the Soviet Committee for Solidarity with the Countries of Asia (SKSSA). The SKSSA was established in May 1955, apparently at India's urging.[56] At a Presidium meeting of November 1956, one SKSSA member suggested that when speaking to an international audience, it was better to focus on Soviet achievements in economic development rather than culture, since cultural enlightenment was a 'sensitive' subject abroad. Most committee members, however, agreed with the Kazakh literary writer and scholar, Mukhtar Auezov, that Asian countries faced a cultural challenge, and it was the task of the SKSSA to address it. A.A. Guber, an Indonesia specialist, claimed to agree with the president of the committee, Mirzo Tursun-Zade (a Tajik revolutionary poet and one of the Tajik elites trained by Braginsky) that the SKSSA had to strive for the construction of a 'new culture'. Both Tursun-Zade and Auezov suggested that literature might serve as a means to show how the cultural traditions of Soviet Asia were compatible with Soviet modernity.[57]

However, with Cold War pressures growing, Soviet manoeuvring space for emphasizing Asian cultural unity shrank, as Asian states began to argue that Soviet Central Asia had 'lost' its Asian cultural specifics as a consequence of Soviet modernizing strategies.[58] In his attempt to woo the decolonizing states in the Third World, Khrushchev adopted a culturally neutral policy towards the East that emphasized socialist ideological commitments to decolonization and Soviet economic development rather than ancient national roots and shared cultural heritages.[59] In August 1955, the Institute of Oriental Studies of the Soviet Academy of Sciences in Moscow (IVAN) was reorganized. Plans to rehabilitate the study of ancient civilization by setting up sectors for ancient manuscripts and monuments at the IVAN were removed from the agenda.[60] The instalment of Guber as director indicated Soviet sympathies for the non-aligned states. Research at IVAN came to be directed particularly towards the modern Orient, and focused on issues of economic development and national liberation.[61] At the 20th Party Congress in 1956, Politburo member Anastas Mikoyan stressed the importance of modern Oriental Studies:

> …especially in this period when our contacts with the East are growing and becoming stronger, and when, as a consequence of the extension of our economic, political and cultural ties with the countries of the East, the interest displayed in them by Soviet people has grown immeasurable.[62]

In subsequent years, the IVAN became one of the largest research institutes within the Soviet Academy of Sciences, expanding its staff and increasing its output.

At the non-governmental level, however, narratives of cultural integration and enlightenment continued to frame Soviet negotiations of transnational alliances with recently decolonized Asian countries, and they intersected with Cold War polarizations.[63] An important factor in the continuation of Soviet strategies for the advancement of Asian cultural enlightenment and integration was the growing friendship between India and the Soviet Union.[64] Indian Prime Minister Jawaharlal Nehru was actively involved with the organization of international academic networks, propagating cultural integration between East and West and international cultural enlightenment on the basis of ancient Asian spiritual traditions.[65] Rejecting Cold War ideological polarizations, Nehru regarded the Soviet Union as an important ally in this process. Rather than denying the 'Asian' identity of the Soviet Central Asian Republics, he took them as a showcase for the integration of Western modernization and Asian cultural traditions.[66]

According to Nuriddin Mukhitdinnov, First Secretary to the Uzbek Republic at the time of Nehru's visit to the Soviet Union in the summer of 1955, Nehru criticized Khrushchev for failing to appreciate the cultural connections between India and Central Asia.[67] Nehru's tour of the Soviet Union began in Dushanbe, the capital of Tajikistan. According to Soviet India specialist E.P. Chelyshev, Gafurov, who in 1955 was First Secretary of the Tajik Republic, heralded Nehru's visit as the beginning 'of an era of Tajik-Indian relations', claiming that the Indian and Tajik people 'were spiritually, ethnically and cultural-historically closely connected'.[68] In July 1956, Gafurov replaced Guber as Director of the IVAN, indicating increased Soviet support for diplomacy in Asia based on cultural ties shared at least by Soviet Central Asia and India.

An open policy emphasizing ancient cultural traditions that united India and the Soviet Central Asian Republics, in particular, was hampered by the Cold War alliance between the PRC and the Soviet Union. But in the late 1950s, relations between the PRC and the Soviet Union and India soured. Sino-Soviet disagreements over communist development – in particular Mao's Great Leap Forward that was launched in 1957 – gave rise to criticism on both sides, and in June 1960 Khrushchev and Mao openly fell out at the Congress of the Romanian Communist Party. Disputes between India and the PRC over their shared Himalayan border broke into open warfare in 1962.[69] Against this background, a trend to rehabilitate cultural themes began to show in the work of Soviet Orientalists. The Soviets participated in an international project to rewrite the history of 'Asia', proposed by the Delhi-based Indian Council of World Affairs (ICWA) in 1957. The ICWA had as its aim to construct an integrative history of Asia, uniting the historical paths of the Arabic world, India and China.[70] IVAN Indologist (and founder of Soviet Afghanistan studies) I.M. Reisner was a member of the project coordinating council.[71]

At the IVAN, the instalment of Gafurov was only one of the structural changes indicating a shift in Soviet Oriental Studies towards embracing cultural themes that emphasized the unity between the Soviet Union and India. In 1957, Yuri Rerikh, son of the famous imperial Orientalist, Nikolai Rerikh, was invited to the IVAN to head the Department of Indian Philosophy and Religion.[72] In 1959, the IVAN launched two series of ancient source publications, one on the *Literary Monuments of the Peoples of the East* and one on *Written Monuments of the East*. These volumes served as diplomatic gifts and supported Soviet self-presentations as an ancient civilization abroad.[73] In 1960, when Moscow hosted the 25th International Congress for Orientalists, most Soviet speakers presented papers on ancient and medieval history, to the surprise of Western observers who expected highly politicized presentations.[74] This renewed emphasis on ancient traditions took place beyond the confines of the IVAN. As Vladislav Zubok has shown, in Soviet society at large, ancient cultural and spiritual traditions also were rehabilitated. In his words, the 1960s witnessed the rise of Soviet 'preservation enthusiasm'.[75]

Nevertheless, as long as Khrushchev remained in power, official state diplomacy towards the East remained culturally unspecific. The opening speech to the 1960 Congress for Orientalists was made by Mikoyan, and his words contrasted markedly with the presentations of the majority of Soviet scholars. He spoke strictly of modern developments, emphasizing the successes of Soviet decolonization and state-building when he declared that 'There were some among the Soviet scholars presenting a paper, who before had hardly possessed a written language; and others whose fathers had not been able to read or write.'[76] In 1960, the Institute of Sinology was integrated into the IVAN and renamed the Institute of the Peoples of Asia (INA – *Institut Narody Azii*); this name emphasized decolonization.

The embrace of cultural unity between the Soviet Union and India manifested itself primarily in institutional contexts removed from the central Soviet decision-making bodies. Moscow Orientalists did not publish their work at the central publishing house of the Soviet Academy of Sciences (NAUKA), but at a separate publishing house for Eastern Literature set up in 1957.[77] The ICWA conference on the 'History of Asia' materialized not as part of a Soviet academic program, but under the wings of UNESCO. Thus, distance between Soviet official foreign policy and the unofficial diplomacy of academic exchanges was created, which allowed the Soviet Union diplomatic manoeuvring space in the academic realm. In his position as director of the IVAN (INA after 1960), Gafurov's figure had symbolic value for both the official and unofficial international strategies. To have a formerly colonized Muslim direct one of the most prestigious Soviet research institutes showcased both Soviet ideological commitments to decolonization and Soviet Asian cultural identity.

Brezhnev, the Sino-Soviet split and the Soviet Union as Aryan civilization

After Leonid Brezhnev replaced Khrushchev as First Secretary in October 1964, a more straightforward critique of the Chinese became possible. In November of that year, Gafurov gave a secret speech before the Soviet Academy of Sciences that showed how far the Soviet Union had moved away from the position it had taken on China in the Stalin period. In 1949 the Soviet Union had assured China that they would refrain from cultural minority propaganda on Chinese territory and allow Kazakhs, Uighurs and Mongols 'to find their place within the new Chinese community of peoples'.[78] Now Gafurov presented the Soviet Union as a protector of minority nations in China, claiming that in China, 'Uyghurs – the Kazakh intelligentsia in Xinjiang – were subjected to relentless repression'. Gafurov argued that Chinese promises to grant 'minorities the right to self-rule' were false, depicting the Chinese leadership as an oppressor of minority nations. This change in discourse suggests that with Brezhnev's ascension, the Soviet leadership no longer considered itself bound by its promises to refrain from minority agitation among Soviet diaspora communities on Chinese soil.[79]

Gafurov's attack on the PRC was reminiscent of his wartime critique of Iran. He claimed the PRC harboured a racist national policy, which he understood once more as an ideology aimed to obstruct the historical process of unification between culturally related people. To his mind, the Chinese were 'racists' because they presented the world as divided between 'white and yellow' races and because they aimed to claim 'Asia for the Asians'. He argued that Chinese communism was 'anti-Marxist', as it sought to exclude 'Eastern-European socialists' from the worldwide decolonization movement. He blamed the Chinese for disregarding 'the interaction between two continents' and accused them of presenting world history as a 'clash between civilizations'.[80] In a later report on the 24th Party Congress in 1972, Gafurov further argued against such a perspective. He argued against the idea of the world as divided into Eastern and Western civilizations, dismissing such views as 'Eurocentrism' (*Europotsentism*) and 'Orient-centrism' (*Vostopotsentrism*).[81]

In the early 1960s, Mao criticized the Soviet Union on cultural grounds, arguing that despite its communist state organization, the Soviet Union should be regarded as a member-state of the 'First World' based on its cultural loyalties.[82] When in the late

1960s the Sino-Soviet split reached its peak, the Soviet Union came to present itself openly as an Indo-European centre of world civilization that explicitly aimed to integrate traditions of both East and West.[83] In the Soviet Academy of Sciences, experts on Turkic-nomadic cultures were replaced by Indo-Europeanists from 1964 onwards. In 1964, Boris Borisovich Piotrovsky, an expert on the ancient West Asian Armenian kingdom of Urartu, replaced Mikhail Illiarionovich Artamonov, a specialist in the West Asian Turkic nomadic Khazars, as Director of the Hermitage. In 1966, Tolstov was succeeded as Director of the Institute for Ethnography by Yulian Vladimirovich Bromley, a specialist on Southern Slavs, particularly the Ukrainian Khorvats, who were believed to have ancient Iranian roots.[84] The fluctuating career of the former First Secretary of the Uzbek Republic, Nurriddin Mukhitdinnov, also can be understood in the context of gradual Soviet rehabilitation of Indo-European cultural identity. Khrushchev had installed Mukhitdinnov as Secretary for Soviet relations to the Third World at the Presidium of the Central Committee in December 1957, thus choosing a 'Turko-nomadic' Uzbek as the highest politically visible representative of Soviet Central Asia in the Soviet Party hierarchy. But in the early years of the Sino-Soviet split, Mukhitdinnov was removed from the ranks of the Party Presidium (at the 22nd Party Congress in 1961).[85] In 1968, the same year that Gafurov (an Iranian, Indo-European representative of Central Asian culture) acquired full membership in the Soviet Academy of Sciences, Mukhitdinnov was sent to Syria as an ambassador.[86]

At the Academy of Sciences, Gafurov was installed as chair for general history, a position he shared with Boris Piotrovsky. In 1967, Piotrovky's major work, *Urartu: the Kingdom of Van and its Art*, was republished in English, and Gafurov approached his former co-worker at the Tajik Academy of Sciences, the archaeologist Boris Litvinski, to rewrite *The History of the Tajik People*.[87] Litvinsky and his wife, Elena Davydovich, an expert on medieval numismatics, had been outspoken critics of Tolstov during the 1940s and were forced to move from Tashkent to Dushanbe during the anti-cosmopolitan campaigns.[88] The new edition was completed in 1970 and published in 1972, and as its title *The Tajiks: An Ancient, Classical and Medieval History* suggested, it devoted special attention to ancient history. As in his earlier work, Gafurov accused the West of drawing artificial boundaries between the people of Asia. But while blaming Western scholars for taking up 'racist positions', the new edition no longer equated racism with 'Aryanism'.[89] In fact, in the 1972 edition, Gafurov embraced 'Aryan' categories. Claiming that the ancient Tajik language belonged to the 'Aryan branch' of the 'Indo-European family of languages' that also 'include the Slavic, German, Keltic, Roman, Greek, Armenian and other languages', Gafurov situated the language in a cultural tradition that also incorporated the West. To his mind, however, the Asian tradition of Indo-European culture shared by the 'Indo-Aryan' and 'Iranian or Aryan' people 'was particularly close and long lasting'.[90] The Indo-European identity adopted by the Soviet Union thus situated the Soviet Union at the centre of a cultural tradition that spread East and West but was particularly strongly represented by India and Soviet Tajikistan.

Soviet 'decolonization': Liberating the history of Asian civilization

In the same period as the new edition of Gafurov's Tajik national history, Gafurov also became involved with the coordination of a pilot programme of a new UNESCO project that eventually came to be named 'The Program for the Study of the Civilizations of the Peoples of Central Asia'.[91] It was launched at the height of the Sino-Soviet split in 1967 on the initiative of the National Committees to UNESCO of the Soviet Union, India, Iran, Afghanistan and Pakistan.[92] Its declared aim was to research the cultural heritages of countries related to the Central Asian centres of ancient Indo-European culture, Bactria, Sogdia and Khorezm.[93]

For Soviet scholars, using the name 'Central Asia' meant a break with the past; since 1924, it had been custom to call the region that united the Soviet Central Asian Republics (with the exception of Kazakhstan) 'Middle Asia' (*Sredniaia Aziia*).[94] As the new name 'Central Asia' (*Tsnatral'naia Aziia*) was understood also to encompass Eastern Asian countries such as Mongolia, China and Tibet, the adoption of this name widened the historical cultural realm attributed to the Soviet Central Asian Republics.[95] As such, the programme's set-up reflected Gafurov's critique of Chinese 'Orient-centrism', as it placed the Soviet Central Asian Republics at the centre of a larger transnational Asian civilization that also integrated China.[96] Soviet scholars claimed, 'Central Asia was the cradle of one of the most ancient civilizations, a cross-road where the culture of many Oriental people's mixed and mingled'.[97] In response to the Sino-Soviet split, they thus presented the Indo-European culture of Central Asia as a source of Chinese civilization.

While coordination of the 'Central Asian Civilization' project was in the hands of the Paris office, in 1967 a special directing committee was organized at the INA in Moscow, and local research centres were created in New Delhi, Tehran, Kabul and Islamabad.[98] Gafurov distinguished the new project from the former UNESCO East-West Program, claiming that in the framework of the 'Central Asian Civilization' programme, research was no longer conducted by 'Orientalists' but by 'the people of Asia' working from their own national research centres. On this basis, he presented the programme as an achievement in decolonization, claiming it had 'opened up hardly known or forgotten civilizations to the world'.[99] The new edition of Gafurov's history of Tajikistan, *The Tajiks*, also seemed effectively 'decolonized': the book no longer granted the leading role in Tajik ethnogenesis to the Slavic Scythians, but rather to the Tajiks themselves, claiming that the Scythians had arrived on Central Asian territory much later than the eastern Iranian Aryans.[100]

Gafurov's anti-colonial pretences, however, stood in sharp contrast with the self-image the INA adopted in the period when the 'Central Asian Civilization' programme was launched. By the late 1960s, the INA came to present itself as heir to the pre-revolutionary imperial tradition of Russian Orientology. In 1968, the editorial of a Soviet-friendly Calcutta-based journal argued that 'Soviet Orientalists' were 'the direct inheritors of the grand tradition of ... Indology studies set up in St. Petersburg'.[101] In 1969, the INA readopted its traditional name: the Institute for Oriental Studies (IVAN).[102] Also the research of Russian/Soviet ancient civilization returned to the agenda. A new department for 'Manuscripts and Monuments' was established, besides a department for the 'Study of Soviet Central Asia'.[103] At the first conference held in the programme for 'Central Asian Civilization', India specialist Grigory Bongard-Levin introduced the ancient Central Asian Kushan Kingdom as a major historical empire, claiming the Kushan Kingdom had ' ... ranked with the great powers of that time – Rome, Parthia and China under the Hans'.[104] In line with Barthold, Bongard-Levin celebrated empires for their ability to facilitate progressive cultural integration: 'The unification of diverse areas in the framework of one kingdom brought various cultures and peoples into close proximity. The Kushan period is an integral part of the history of peoples of India, Central Asia, Afghanistan, Pakistan and Iran.'[105]

While embracing certain elements of imperial rule as progressive, Soviet Orientalists followed several strategies to show that they remained also committed to ideals of socialist liberation from bourgeois oppression. First, the narratives of empire produced by Soviet Orientalists in the late 1960s all emphasized popular agency. Gafurov introduced the UNESCO 'Central Asian Civilizations' programme as a study of the culture of 'the peoples of Asia'.[106] Bongard-Levin stressed that the Kushan Kingdom was 'built by the people from Central Asia'.[107] The Calcutta-based journal on Soviet Indology claimed that Soviet Orientalists possessed a 'passionate love for the Indian people' and 'an intensely human interest in their subject'.[108] Second, Soviet scholars moved discussions of Central Asian ethno-cultural transnational unity – such as the conferences organized as part of the UNESCO 'Central Asian Civilizations' programme – from the central political organs in Moscow to the Soviet Union's peripheries. The first international conference within the 'Central Asian Civilizations' programme was held in Dushanbe, and by the late 1960s the Tajik Republic also acquired its own Institute for Oriental Studies. In 1973 it was also agreed that a new international research centre should be set up for the study of Central Asian culture in Dushanbe. Finally, these discussions were hosted by Gafurov as director of the INA/IVAN, a former subject of Tsarist colonial oppression.

Now, the real heroes of Central Asian history became the cultural figures of Indo-European civilization rather than the charismatic warlords and statesmen of the Turkic-nomadic past.[109] As a consequence, the early 1970s witnessed a growing critique by Soviet Orientalists of the positive evaluations of the Uzbek national hero and Turko-nomadic warlord Timur. Gafurov's *The Tajiks* depicted Timur as an 'aggressor' whose 'destructive activities' were contrasted to the progressive development of culture.[110]

Within Soviet Central Asia, Moscow's revisions of Central Asian history gave rise to a flood of publications that aimed to appropriate Central Asian civilization for either the Uzbek or Tajik Republics. In Tajikistan, scholars derogatorily rejected the notion that Turkic traditions had brought progress to Central Asian civilization as 'Pan-Turkism'.[111] In Uzbekistan, the 1970s and the 1980s saw the emergence of a nationalist narrative that claimed Central Asian culture was essentially Turkic.[112] As such, in the Soviet peripheries Moscow's celebration of Central Asian civilization created a new power dynamic that could be framed in terms of imperialism and colonization, centring on questions of international cultural dominance and ethno-national oppression.

Conclusion

This chapter has shown that throughout the Cold War, Soviet commitments to 'decolonization' in Asia remained strongly intertwined with pre-revolutionary, imperial ideals of ethno-national liberation. The early generation of Soviet Orientalists did not advance ethno-national liberation within the former Russian Empire in order to establish separate, mutually exclusive nation-states, but rather with the aim to reform progressively international civilization. The work of Bobodzhan Gafurov has illustrated how Soviet Orientalists used ethno-national histories to support Soviet foreign policy and as tools for minority agitation in the East (in many cases, Soviet diplomats to the East were trained Orientalists). Soviet ideological commitments to decolonization and socialist nation-building during the Cold War also allowed for the continuation of a pre-revolutionary ideal of international cultural integration that intersected with Cold War polarizations.

Cold War tensions and competition for influence in the Third World affected and reshaped imperial ideals of cultural unity. In the age of Stalin's anti-cosmopolitanism, for instance, the progressive role of bourgeois cultural heritages and civilizations was rejected and the value of pagan and nomadic traditions in the progress of world history and culture was propagated instead. Similarly the embrace of Indo-European 'Aryanism' in the late 1960s occurred under the influence of the growing Soviet-Indian friendship, on the one hand, and the Sino-Soviet split, on the other, and allowed the Soviet Union to present itself as a centre of world culture, rehabilitating the idea that empires could play progressive roles as benefactors of cultural development.

At the level of Central Asia, Gafurov explicitly phrased the embrace of civilization in terms of decolonization and the achievement of socialist cultural harmony between people. This chapter has shown, however, that Soviet views of what constituted progressive Central Asian civilization were, to a great extent, the result of Moscow's political Cold War strategies and had an exclusivist effect when scaled down to the level of international relations in the Soviet peripheries. An unintended consequence of Soviet commitments to ethno-national liberation was that in the context of Soviet Central Asian international relations, 'Aryan' civilization became invested with particular *national* characteristics. Thus, Moscow's embrace of Aryan civilization in the context of Cold War power politics threatened to deny the Soviet Central Asian Uzbeks access to the heritage of Central Asian civilization that they traditionally shared with the Soviet Central Asian Persian speakers. As such, these commitments came to constitute new subjectivities in the peripheries.

Thus, to regard Soviet rule as simply obstructive to national self-determination obscures many aspects of Soviet postcolonialism. Discourses of national liberation and nation-building were intertwined with discourses of national integration and supranational regionalism throughout the Cold War. This chapter suggests that to understand national conflict in the Soviet Central Asian peripheries, we should look at them not just as the result of Moscow's domestic 'neo-imperial' policies, but rather as the result of an entirely more complex process of negotiations over power and identity within a multipolar, transnational Central Asian regional whole that also involved Third World agents.

Notes

1   This article was written on the basis of PhD research conducted within the framework of a larger research project entitled *The Legacy of Soviet Oriental Studies : Networks, Institutions, Discourses*, directed by Prof. Michael Kemper (University of Amsterdam) and Dr. Stephane A. Dudoignon (l'École des hautes Études en Science Sociales, Paris) and funded by the Dutch Scientific Council (NWO).

2   Gafurov, B.G. (1972), *Tadzhiki: Drevneishaia, drevniaia I srednevekovaia istoriia*. Moscow: Nauka, 4.

3   See Hirsch, Francine (2005), *Empire of Nations: Ethnographic Knowledge and the Making of the Soviet Union*. Ithaca: Cornell University Press; Martin, Terry (2001), *The Affirmative Action Empire: Nations and Nationalism in the Soviet Union, 1923–1939*. Ithaca: Cornell University Press; Suny, Ronald and Martin, Terry (2001), *A State of Nations: Empire and Nation Making in the Age of Lenin and Stalin*. New York: Oxford University Press. For the term 'breaker of nation' see Hirsch (2005), 3.

4   Northrop, Douglas (2004), *Veiled Empire: Gender and Power in Stalinist Central Asia*. Ithaca: Cornell University Press; Edgar, Adrienne (2004), *Tribal Nation: The Making of Soviet Turkmenistan*. Princeton: Princeton University Press; Kamp, Marianne (2006), *The New Woman in Uzbekistan: Islam, Modernity, and Unveiling under Communism*. Seattle: University of Washington Press; Dudoignon, Stephane A. (2013), 'From revival to mutation: the religious personnel of Islam in Tajikistan (1955–1991)', in John Heathershaw and Edmund Herzig (ed.) *The Transformation of Tajikistan: The Sources of Statehood*. London: Routledge, 67–94.

5   This chapter nevertheless builds upon Edward Said's famous argument that Western scholarship produced a biased image of the Orient that legitimated the European colonial mission, placing it in the context of Soviet Oriental Studies in the Cold War. See Said, Edward (1978), *Orientalism*. London: Routledge.

6   See Laycock, Jo (2009), *Imagining Aremania. Orientalism Ambiguity and Intervention.* Manchester: Manchester University Press; Herzig, Edmund and Kurkchiyan, Marina (2005), *The Armenians: Past and Present in the Making of National Identity*. London: Routledge; Suny, Ronald (1993), *Looking toward Ararat: Armenia in Modern History*. Bloomington; Indianapolis: Indiana University Press.

7   See DeWeese, Devin (2002), 'Islam and the legacy of Sovietology: a review essay on Yaacov Ro'I's Islam in the Soviet Union', *Journal of Islamic Studies*, 13(3), 298–330; Frank, Allen (2001), *Muslim Religious Institutions in Imperial Russia: The Islamic World of Novouzensk District and the Kazakh Inner Horde, 1780–1910*. Leiden: Brill; Kemper, Michael and Conermann, Stephan (2011). *The Heritage of Soviet Oriental Studies*. London: Routledge.

8   See Laruelle, Marlene (2005), *Mythe Aryen et Rêve Impérial dans la Russie du XIXe Siècle*. Paris: CNSR editions.

9   Laruelle, *Mythe Aryen et Rêve Impérial dans la Russie du XIXe Siècle*.

10 For use of the term 'Aryan Muslim', see for instance Koplik, Sara (2008), 'The experience of Bukharan Jews outside the Soviet Union in the 1930s and 1940s', in Ingeborg Baldauf, Moshe Gammer and Thomas Loy (2008), *Bukharan Jews in the 20th Century: History, Experience, Narration*. Wiesbaden: Reichert Verlag.

11 See Tolz, Vera (2011), *Russia's Own Orient: The Politics of Identity and Oriental Studies in the Late Imperial and Early Soviet Periods*. Oxford: Oxford University Press.

12 Such reappraisals of local cultures rather than transnational civilizations took place on an international scale. For the case of Europe, see Leerssen, Joep (2006), *National*

Thought in Europe: A Cultural History. Amsterdam: Amsterdam University Press; Smith, Woodruff (1991), *Politics and Sciences of Culture in Germany, 1840-1920*. Oxford: Oxford University Press. For the case of Asia, see Stolte, Carolien (2013), 'Orienting India: interwar internationalism in and Asian inflection, 1917-1937', unpublished PhD dissertation, University of Leiden; Sartori, Andrew (2008), *Bengal in Global Concept History: Culturalism in the Case of Capital*. Chicago: University of Chicago Press.

13 For nineteenth-century critiques of 'Aryanism' in the German tradition of Orientology, see Marchand, Suzanne (2009), *German Orientalism in the Age of Empire: Religion, Race, and Scholarship*. Cambridge, MA: Cambridge University Press.

14 See Bregel, Yuri (1980), 'Barthold and modern oriental studies'. *International Journal of Middle East Studies* 12(3), 385-403.

15 See Bartol'd, Vasilii (1966a), 'Mistitsizm v islame', in B.G. Gafurov and I.N. Vinnikov (eds.) *V.V. Bartol'd: Sochinennia*. Vol. 6. Moscow: Vostochnaia Lituratura, 114-120; Bartol'd (1966b), 'Barmakidy', in *V.V. Bartol'd: Sochinennia* 669-674; Bartol'd (1966c), 'Neskol'ko slov ob ariiskoi kul'ture v Srednei Azii', in *V.V. Bartol'd: Sochinennia* 322-332.

16 See Gafurov, B.G., Vinnikov, I.N. and Gankovski, Y.V. (1967), 'Archeological study of Soviet Central Asia', in Gafurov, B.G., Vinnikov, I.N. and Gankovski, Y.V. (1967), *Fifty Years of Soviet Oriental Studies: Brief Reviews*. Moscow: Nauka; Laruelle, Marlene (2008), 'The concept of ethnogenesis in Central Asia: Political context and institutional mediators (1940-1950)', *Kritika: Explorations in Russian and Eurasian History*, 9(1), 169-188.

17 Hirsch, 50, 51.

18 Rzehak, Lutz (2001), *Vom Persischen Zum Tadschikischen: Sprachliches Handeln und Sprachplanung in Transoxanien Zwischen Tradition, Moderne und Sowjetmacht (1900-1956)*. Wiesbaden: Reichert Verlag.

19 For Stalinist culture-building, see David-Fox, Michael (2012), *Showcasing the Soviet Experiment: Cultural Diplomacy and Western Visitors to the Soviet Union, 1921-1940*. Oxford: Oxford University Press; Clark, Katerina (2011), *Moscow, the Fourth Rome: Stalinism, Cosmopolitanism, and the Evolution of Soviet Culture, 1931-1941*. Cambridge, MA: Harvard University Press.

20 Shnirelman, Victor (1995), 'From internationalism to nationalism: Forgotten pages of Soviet archaeology in the 1930s and 1940s', in Philip Kohl and Claire Fawcett (eds.) *Nationalism, Politics and the Practice of Archaeology*. Cambridge, MA: Cambridge University Press, 132-137; Curta, Florin (2002), 'From Kossinna to Bromley: Ethnogenesis in Slavic Archaeology', in Andrew Gillett (ed.) *On Barbarian Identity: Critical Approaches to Ethnicity in the Early Middle Ages*. Turnhout: Brepols, 201-218.

21 Shnirelman (1995). For a contemporary critique on traditional interpretations of nomadic culture as primitive, see Golden, Peter B. (2011), *Central Asia in World History*. Oxford: Oxford University Press.

22 For more on the search for Soviet Central Asia's ancient roots, see Shnirelman, Victor (2010), 'A symbolic past: the struggle for ancestors in Central Asia', *Russian Politics and Law* 48(5), 48-64.

23 See Komissarov, D.S. (1966), 'Vstupitel'naia stat'ia', in Radzhabov Z. Sh. (1966), *Iosif Samuilovich Braginskii: materialy k biobibliografii uchenykh Tadzhikistana, vyp. 8*. Dushanbe; Braginskii, I.S. (1986), *Zapadno-Vostochnyi literaturnyi sintez i tvorchestvo S. Aini (problem i portrety)*. Dushanbe: Izdatel'stvo IRFON.

24 Gafurov, B.G. and Prokhorov, N.N. (1940), *Padenie Bukharskogo Emirata*. Stalinabad: Gosizdat.

25 Gafurov and Prokhorov (1940), 6, 38, 43.

26 Gafurov, B.G. (1945a), 'Glubzhe izuchat' bogatoe istoricheskoi proshloe tadzhikskogo naroda', in E.N. Pavlovskii (ed.) *Nauka v Tadzhikistane: pervaia nauchnaia sessiia k XV-letiiu Tadzhikskoi SSR*. Stalinabad: Akademiia Nauk Tadzhikskii Filial, 16, 17.

27 Gafurov, B.G. (1945b), 'Kakim dolzhen byt' partiinyi i sovetskii rabotnik', *Kommunist Tadzhikistana*, 4 September 1945.

28 Gafurov, B.G. and Prokhorov, N.N. (1944), *Tadzhikskii Narod v Bor'be za Svobodu i Nezavisimost' Svoei Rodiny*. Stalinabad: Gosizdat.

29 Gafurov and Prokhorov (1944), 35.

30 See Laycock (2009).

31 Gafurov, B.G. (1945c), 'O nekotorykh voposakh kul'tury i nauki: okonchanie', *Kommunist Tadzhikistana*.

32 Gafurov (1945c).

33 Gafurov, B.G. (1945d), 'Soveshchanie Pisatelei', *Kommunist Tadzhikistana*; Gafurov (1945c).

34 Tolstov, S.P. (2007), 'Dokladnaia zapiska', *Etnograficheskoe obozrenie*, 5, 165.

35 Gafurov and Prokhorov (1944), 136.

36 Gafurov, B.G. (1949), *Istoriia Tadzhikskogo Naroda v kratkom Izlozhenii*. Dushanbe: Tadzhikskogo Filiala Akademii Nauk SSSR, 26–27. For Stalin's use of 'universal treasury of culture', see Van Ree, Erik (2007), 'Heroes and merchants: Stalin's understanding of national character', *Kritika: Explorations in Russian and Eurasian History*, 8(1), 41–65; Clark (2011).

37 See Hopf, Ted (2012), *Reconstructing the Cold War. The Early Years, 1945–1958*. Oxford: Oxford University Press.

38 Slezkine, Yuri (1996), 'N. Ia. Marr and the National Origins of Soviet Ethnogenetics', *Slavic Review*, 55(4), 826–862; Van Ree, Erik (2002), *The Political Thought of Joseph Stalin: A Study in Twentieth-Century Revolutionary Patriotism*. London: Routledge, 199–207; Slezkine, Yuri (2004), *The Jewish Century*. Princetossn: Princeton University Press.

39 See Iakubovskii, A. (1946), 'Timur. Opyt Kratkoi Kharakteristiki', *Voprosy Istorii*, 8 (9), 42–74. For an account of Soviet evaluations of Timur's historical legacy, see Manz, Beatrice (2002), 'Tamerlane's career and its uses', *Journal of World History*, 13(1), 1–25.

40 See Bartol'd, Vasilii (1925), 'Tadzhiki. Istoricheskii ocherk', in B.G. Gafurov (ed.) *V.V. Bartol'd: Sochinenniu*. Vol. 2(1), pp. 449–468. Moscow: Vostochnaia Lituratura.

41 Tolstov, S.P. (1948), *Po sledam drevne Khorezmiiskoi Tsivilizatsiei*. Leningrad: Izd'vo Akademii Nauk SSR.

42 Tolstov (1948). For the book's reception, see Germanov, V.A. (2002), 'S.P. Tolstov: maître, docteur, commandeur, ou l'histoire à travers l'archéologie et l'ethnographie', *Cahiers d'Asie Centrale*, 10, 193–215.

43 Gafurov (1949). This official history of the Tajiks was meant for a popular audience, and was used as a textbook in schools. The book was re-edited twice: the second edition appeared in 1952 and the third in 1955.

44 Gafurov (1949), 26.

45 See Hirsch (2005).

46 Editorial Board (1949), 'Neotlozhnye zadachi Sovetskoi istorikov-vostokovedov', *Voprosy Istorii*, 4, 8.

47 See Westad, Odd Arne (2013), *Restless Empire: China and the World since 1750*. London: The Bodley Head. For the reception of Tolstov's work in China, see Guldin, Greg (1992),

'Anthropology by other names: The impact of Sino-Soviet friendship on the anthropological sciences', *The Australian Journal of Chinese Affairs*, 27, 133–149.

48 Guldin (1992), 134.

49 Gafurov, B.G. (1952), *Istoriia Tadzhikskogo Naroda v kratkom Izlozhenii*. Moscow: Nauka, 79.

50 Gafurov (1952), 88.

51 Gafurov (1952), 14; Gafurov (1955), *Istoriia Tadzhikskogo Naroda v kratkom Izlozhenii*. Moscow: Nauka, 22.

52 Gafurov (1952), 88.

53 Gafurov (1949), 14.

54 Kalinovsky, Artemy (2013), 'Not some British colony in Africa: The politics of decolonization and modernization in Soviet Central Asia, 1955–1964', *Ab Imperio*, 2, 191–222.

55 See Braginskii (1986).

56 'Predislovie', undated, F9540.op.1, State Archive of the Russian Federation, Moscow (*Gosudarstvennyi arkhiv Rossiiskoi Federatsii*, GARF).

57 'Stenogramma Zasedaniia Sovetskogo Komiteta Solidarnosti Stran Azii', 1 November 1956, F9540.op1.d2. GARF.

58 Stolte (2013), 188–189.

59 Westad, Odd Arne (2005), *The Global Cold War: Third World Interventions and the Making of Our Times*. Cambridge, MA: Cambridge University Press. On Khrushchev's vision of Asia, see Kirasirova, Masha (2011), ' "Sons of Muslims" in Moscow: Soviet Central Asian Mediators to the foreign East, 1955–1962', *Ab Imperio*, 4, 106–132; Kalinovsky (2013).

60 'Postanovlenie o dal'neischem razvitii sovestskogo vostokovedeniia'. 21 February 1958, F5.op35.d78, Russian State Archive of Contemporary History, Moscow (*Rossiiskii gosudarstvennyi arkhiv noveishei istorii*, RGANI).

61 Shastitko (2009), 72–73.

62 Mikoyan, Anastas (1956), 'Speech by A.I. Mikoyan, Member of the Presidium of the Central Committee of the C.P.S.U., and First Vice-Chairman if the Council of Ministers of the USSR at the 20th Party Congress of the Communist Party of the Soviet Union, Feb 16 1956'. *Soviet News* 8, 21.

63 On continuing Indian strategies to negotiate Asian cultural unity on the sub-state level after Bandung, see Stolte (2013), 193–195.

64 On deteriorating relations with China, see Westad (2013), 336 ff. On the growing Soviet-Indian friendship and the Soviet diplomatic mission to the East, see Shastitko (2009), 70–71.

65 See Stolte (2013); Toynbee, Arnold (1967), *Acquaintances*. Oxford: Oxford University Press.

66 See Wong, Laura Elizabeth (2008), 'Relocating East and West: UNESCO's major project on the mutual appreciation of eastern and western cultural values', *Journal of World History*, 3(8), 349–374, p. 358.

67 Mukhitdinnov, Nuriddin (1994), *Gody provedennye v Kremle. Vosmopinaniia veterana viuy, truda u Kommunisticheskoi partii, rabotavshego so Stalinym, Malenkovym, Brezhnevym, Andropovym*. Tashkent: Narodnogo Naslediia im. A. Kadyri, 153.

68 Chelyshev, E.P. (2009), 'Vostochnyi Mudrets', in E.P. Chelyshev (2009), *Akademik Bobdzhan Gafurov: k 100-letiiu so dnia rozhdeniia*. Moscow: Vostochnaia Literatura, 7.

69 Westad (2013), chapters 8 and 9.

70 'Memorandum of the "History of Asia" Project', 18 November 1957, File 008(470) MP 03, United Nations Educational, Scientific and Cultural Organization Archives, Paris (UNESCO).

71 On the basis of this proposal by the ICWA made in 1957, an Asian History Congress was organized in New Delhi in 1961 that lasted from 9 to 13 December; see File 008(470) MP 03, UNESCO.

72 Dylykova,Vilena (2002), 'On "povernul koleso" otechestvennoi Tibetologii', in Knizhnik, T.O. (ed.) *Vospominaniia o Iu.N. Rerikhe*. Moscow: Mezhhdunarodnyi Tsentr Rerikhov, 44.

73 Shastitko (2009), 66.

74 See MacFarquhar, Roderick (1960), 'The 25th International Congress of Orientalists', *The China Quarterly*, 4, 114–118.

75 Zubok, Vladislav (2009), *Zhivago's Children: The Last Russian Intelligentsia*. Cambridge, MA: Harvard University Press, 251.

76 As quoted in Shastitko (2009), 68.

77 Chelyshev (2009), 8.

78 Here I quote Westad (2013), 318.

79 'Doklad', 17 June 1964, F1731.op1.d30, Archive of the Russian Academy of Sciences, Moscow (*Arkhiv Rossiiskoi Akademii Nauk*, ARAN).

80 'Doklad', 17 June 1964, F1731.op1.d30, Archive of the Russian Academy of Sciences, Moscow (*Arkhiv Rossiiskoi Akademii Nauk*, ARAN).

81 Gafurov, B.G. (1972), *XXIV KPSS i ideologicheskaia bor'ba v razvivaiushikhsia stranakh na sovremennom etape. Tom 1 & 2*. Moscow: Akademiia Nauk SSSR Institut Votsokovedeniia.

82 Westad (2005), 162.

83 Shastitko (2009), 71. For more on the pro-Indo-European Slavic turn in Soviet scholarship under Brezhnev, see Curta (2002), 201–218.

84 Kozlov, S. Ya. (2003), *Akademik Iu.V. Bromlei i otechestvennaia etnologiia 1960–1990-e gody*. Moscow: NAUKA.

85 Mukhitdinnov (1994), 6.

86 Mukhitdinnov (1994), 6.

87 'Otchet IVAN za 1967', 1968, Institute of Oriental Studies of the Russian Academy of Sciences, Moscow (*Institut Vostokovedeniia Rossiskogo Akademii Nauk*, IVRAN); Litvinskii, B.A. (1999), 'Bobodzhan Gafurovich Gafurov – osnovopolozhnikj Tadzhikskoi istoricheskoi nauki', in M.S. Lebedev (ed.) *V makhshtabe veka. Sbornik vospominanii o B.G. Gafurove – uchenom, politike, grazhdanine*. Moscow: Posol'stvo Respubliki Tadzhikistan v Rossiiskoi Federatsii, 57.

88 Interview by the author with Boris Litvinskii and Elena Davydovich, Moscow, May 2010.

89 Gafurov (1972), 4.

90 Gafurov (1972), 28.

91 See Gafurov, B.G. and Miroshnikov, L.I. (1976), *Izuchenie tsivilizatsii Tsentral'noi Azii. Opyt mezhdunarodnogo sotrudnichestva po proektu Iunesko*. Moscow: Glavnaia redaktsiia vostochnoi literatury.

92 Gafurov and Miroshnikov (1976), 32.

93 Gafurov and Miroshnikov (1976), 33.

94 Sultanov, T.I. (2006), *Chingizkhan i chingizidy: Sud'be i vlast'*, St. Petersburg, 134.

95 Miroshnikov, L.I. (1971), 'Les Civilisations d'Asie centrale et leur étude', *Cahiers d'Histoire Mondiale*, 631–646, p. 634.

96 Gafurov and Miroshnikov (1976), 32.

97 Chattopadhyaya, Debiprasad (1970), 'Kushan Studies in the USSR', *Soviet Indology Series*, 3, 29.

98 Gafurov and Miroshnikov (1976), 79, 80.

99 Gafurov and Miroshnikov (1976), 31.

100 Gafurov (1972), 36.

101 Chattopadhyaya (1970), editorial.

102 'Otchet IVAN za 1969', 1970, IVRAN.

103 'Otchet IVAN za 1969', 1970.

104 As quoted in Chattopadhyaya (1970), i.

105 As quoted in Chattopadhyaya (1970), i.

106 Gafurov and Miroshnikov (1976), 31.

107 Chattopadhyaya (1970), i.

108 Chattopadhyaya (1970), editorial.

109 Manz (2002).

110 Gafurov (1972), 7–8.

111 For a discussion of Russian revisionism of the Timurid legacy, see Manz (2002); on Tajiks blaming Uzbeks for 'Pan-Turkism', see Atkin, Muriel (1992), 'Religious, national and other identities in Central Asia', in Jo-Ann Gross (ed.) *Muslims in Central Asia: Expressions of Identity and Change.* Durham: Duke University Press, 46–72.

112 See Laruelle (2008).

Key texts

Barghoorn, Frederick. (1960). *The Soviet Cultural Offensive: The Role of Cultural Diplomacy in Soviet Foreign Policy.* Princeton: Princeton University Press.

Heathershaw, John and Herzig, Edmund. (2013). *The Transformation of Tajikistan: The Sources of Statehood.* London: Routledge.

Hirsch, Francine. (2005). *Empire of Nations: Ethnographic Knowledge and the Making of the Soviet Union.* Ithaca: Cornell University Press.

Laruelle, Marlene. (2008). *Russian Eurasianism. An Ideology of Empire.* Washington: Johns Hopkins University Press.

Martin, Terry. (2001). *The Affirmative Action Empire: Nations and Nationalism in the Soviet Union, 1923–1939.* Ithaca: Cornell University Press.

Tolz, Vera. (2011). *Russia's Own Orient: The Politics of Identity and Oriental Studies in the Late Imperial and Early Soviet Periods.* Oxford: Oxford University Press.

CHAPTER 8
GROUNDING IDEOLOGIES: ARCHAEOLOGY, DECOLONIZATION AND THE COLD WAR IN EGYPT

William Carruthers

Discussions of Egypt's political place in the world tend to come attached to fairly standard narratives. For example, scholars working in the field of international relations have often described the period connected to Egyptian decolonization in terms of a particular chain of events. The story goes that, in the years following the Free Officers' coup of July 1952, the British occupation of Egypt finally ended, and the United States jostled for influence in the country at the same time as the Cold War grew in resonance. Meanwhile, after Gamal Abdel Nasser had usurped Muhammad Nagib as the Free Officers' leader in 1954, the coup started to become constructed as a revolution. Eventually – and particularly after the Bandung conference in 1955, the cataclysm of Suez in 1956 and the creation of the United Arab Republic in 1958 – Soviet planners moved in, the Egyptian state became massively centralized and Third World and Pan-Arab identities increased in importance. Simultaneously, in addition to histories of his eventual undoing after the Arab–Israeli War of 1967, studies of the increasing consolidation of Nasser's political power abound.[1]

However, as Laura Bier has noted, there are alternatives to this (fairly linear) decolonization narrative. Discussing the set of practices that she terms Egyptian state feminism, Bier asserts that 'what such studies leave out are the countless struggles to define the content and meaning of the [Nasserist] project that occurred in other arenas'.[2] This chapter deals with one such arena. Archaeological practice – and the representation of archaeological remains more generally – helped define Egyptian state projects during the post-1952 period and also forged connections between Egypt and wider political processes: the spread of the Cold War, for example. In this manner, archaeological work comprised one of 'the countless struggles' to constitute the meaning of Egyptian decolonization, and unlike certain political narratives, the history of archaeology in Egypt makes clear that the process of defining and dispersing decolonized political power in the country not only occurred from the top down. This process also occurred, perhaps literally, from the ground up as archaeological fieldwork took place. After briefly discussing archaeological representations from Egypt's decolonizing era and discussing the historical background to the practice of archaeology in Egypt, this chapter illustrates this thesis by concentrating on an excavation carried out just south of Cairo in the mid-1950s at the site of Mit Rahina (ancient Memphis). This case study emphasizes the necessity of bringing the role of archaeological work, hitherto barely discussed, into wider discussions about decolonization and the Cold War.[3]

Archaeological representations in the Egyptian media

A vastly contradictory set of political spheres engulfed Egypt and its archaeological remains, and representations of archaeological tourism during the period of Egyptian decolonization provide a convenient introduction to them. The drive to attract foreign visitors to Egypt's archaeological sites had long played a role in defining the country's place vis-à-vis the rest of the world.[4] After 1952, this drive would also become a potent indicator of the complexity of Egypt's decolonization narrative, at least in terms of the touristic representations that circulated around Egypt's archaeological spaces and the heterogeneous political narratives to which these representations could be connected. These representations attest to a country with a constantly – and perhaps purposefully – fluid relationship with various political contexts. This complex situation belies the meta-narratives imposed upon Egypt in histories of international relations, and starts to suggest how people actually mediated those meta-narratives, at least in the press.

For instance, the *Egypt Travel Magazine* attempted to attract an English-speaking audience to the country.[5] However, the representations contained within the publication also indicate the heterogeneous discourses being mobilized around Egyptian archaeological sites. Take issue number 75 of November 1960: the publication carried the name of the *Egypt Travel Magazine*, but the front cover of this issue also carried the discreet reminder – as a subtitle in a much smaller font – that Egypt officially constituted the southern region of the United Arab Republic (a political union with Syria that had begun in 1958). Egypt, as the cover made clear, possessed multiple identities, and inside this issue, stories relating to archaeology further attested to this situation. At a time (just two years after the Suez Crisis) when British relations with Egypt had apparently suffered, an article entitled 'First British cruise arrives' had a remarkably upbeat tone. The article noted that 'this is the first time that a cruise composed entirely of British tourists and organized by the Royal Mail Lines has touched port at Alexandria since the *Iberia* in 1955'. The article also discussed how 'all [the passengers] were able to visit the Pyramids and Sphinx'.[6]

While clearly a promotional ruse, this transparent attempt to woo further British visitors demonstrates how the lure of Egypt's archaeology placed the country within multiple conflicting international spheres: whether the pan-Arab United Arab Republic or a Britain attracted by the romantic lure of Egyptian antiquities. Other articles also melded discussions of archaeology and the attraction of other international constituencies to Egypt. For instance, one piece discussed the visit of Hamengkubuwono IX, the Sultan of Yogyakarta and the Minister and Chair of the Superior Council of Tourism in Sukarno's Indonesia. The article noted that the Sultan had come to Egypt to inspect the country's tourist facilities, and he had also visited archaeological sites in Luxor.[7] Meanwhile, another article reported the visit of the (American) Chairman of Rotary International and his wife, who visited the pyramids, located in 'Egypt, the crossroads of a new world'.[8] They also attended a dinner in Cairo's Nile Hilton, which, after its construction during the second half of the 1950s, was the pre-eminent establishment for visitors to the country's archaeological sites. The Nile Hilton potently signified Egypt's contradictory relationship with the American power structures that the country's revolutionary leadership had apparently rejected: as Annabel Wharton has noted, Conrad Hilton tied his growing hotel network to 'Free World' ideals circulating within the United States.[9] Thus, from the front cover of the *Egypt Travel Magazine* onwards, there is a political ambiguity in the articles that the publication contains that is hard to reconcile with any straightforward narrative of Egypt's non-aligned place in the world.

The Arabic language press also indicated the complex political spheres enveloping Egypt's archaeological sites. Every time celebrities or international dance and theatre troupes visited Egypt, it seemed that the press corps – presumably in collusion with state tourism representatives – would make the visitors undergo a photo opportunity at the pyramids and ask them for some positive words about the country. Yet these opportunities also revealed the deep ambiguities of Egypt's place in the world. In January 1958, for instance, *Akhir Sa'a*, a weekly illustrated magazine, pictured the Hollywood star Linda Christian in front of the pyramids. The accompanying report emphasized Christian's more local background ('the woman born in Palestine and who lived in the East').[10] However, the accompanying pictures also made clear the apparent allure of Hollywood glamour to readers in Egypt, illustrating the star beaming in the spotlight atop a camel. Even at a time when the Soviet Union had taken an apparently increased role in Egyptian life, then, America's influence over Egypt never entirely faded. Press representations provide a convenient, if not necessarily very deep, introduction to such a contradictory political whirl as it manifested itself around archaeological sites. However, events at the sites themselves were significantly more meaningful.

Practising the modern in archaeology

Archaeological practices on the ground echoed, and perhaps helped to constitute, this political ambiguity. One excavation, a collaborative exercise between the University of Pennsylvania Museum of Archaeology and Anthropology (University Museum) and the Egyptian Department of Antiquities, provides a particularly helpful example. Beginning in 1953 and ending in 1957, these two institutions negotiated, carried out and closed down their work at the site of Mit Rahina.[11] This process, including the act of excavation itself, attempted to come to terms with and also influence the political direction a decolonized Egypt would take – from both the American and the Egyptian sides. On one level, as the excavation's quick termination suggests, this attempt failed. However, on another level, archaeological practices indeed aided the constitution of Egypt's now-revolutionary future. Away from meta-narratives of international relations, the definition of Egypt's future place in the world thus took place on, and also in, the (archaeological) ground.

Some historical context makes clear why this political act of archaeological definition occurred. After, but also prior to, the Free Officers' coup of July 1952, archaeological work in Egypt existed within a state of more general political flux. The coup was one event in a much longer anti-colonial struggle, and among the matters comprising that struggle, antiquities had proven a long-standing source of contention. After 1922, when the discovery of Tutankhamun's tomb had coincided with Britain's unilateral granting of nominal (if not actual) independence to Egypt, Egyptian claims to ownership and control of antiquities found in the country became increasingly vocal. More importantly, they also became increasingly successful.[12] Egyptian government officials now placed the representatives of the largely Western infrastructure of institutions dedicated to excavating in, and removing artefacts from, Egypt on the defensive by threatening their ability to carry out these acts.[13] Among other institutions related to the Egyptian past, officials worked hard to make sure that the Department of Egyptian Antiquities (or *Maslihat al-Athar al-Misriyya*), the government body in charge of administering ancient archaeological sites and the Museum of Egyptian Antiquities in Cairo, comprised an increasingly Egyptian staff. Since its foundation in the nineteenth century, members of the Department, many of whom were foreign, had worked under a French director. That director would remain French until after the Free Officers' coup of 1952. However, the institution's (often British) mid-level employees were increasingly embattled, as more Egyptians laid claim to their jobs in the period from 1922 onwards.[14]

Debates about Egyptian modernity, as well as its gradual construction, helped constitute this process. Indeed, the establishment of a thoroughly *Egyptian* Department of Egyptian Antiquities occurred at the same time as the modern Egyptian nation-state became an increasingly manifest entity.[15] Thus, the enactment of this process made the country's past a central part of its move towards decolonization. From 1925, the newly founded (and explicitly modern and secular) Egyptian University in Cairo started to train the state's citizens in various facets of Egyptian archaeology, institutionalizing the past as a phenomenon that an appropriately educated group of Egyptian citizens could tackle. Meanwhile, the Ministry of Education took charge of the Department of Egyptian Antiquities, alongside various other institutions that dealt with Coptic and Arab antiquities. Placed under the appropriate Ministry, antiquities administration became a field within which Egyptian citizens could not only claim appropriate, trained understanding: now, they could assert the ability to work in this field, too, by citing the authority of rational, even technocratic, expertise in administering archaeological work in their country.[16] In turn, this action helped realize the possibilities of decolonized Egypt by pointing to the inevitability of a wholly Egyptian-run country.

The events of July 1952 confirmed the potency of this specifically Egyptian body of modernist technocrats. For the first time, an Egyptian, Mustafa Amer, previously Rector of Faruq University in Alexandria, became Director of the Department of Egyptian Antiquities. Subsequently, in 1953, a change in the law centralized all government departments related to Egypt's ancient past into one new Department of Antiquities, also under Amer's control.[17] In this context of national modernization, the cooperative work at Mit Rahina took place, representing one, but certainly not the only, attempt by archaeological practitioners from elsewhere to stake their claim to continued relevance within this modernizing (and soon to be revolutionary) Egyptian world. Significantly, then, this attempt also illustrates how archaeological work that took place in this decolonizing context could become entwined with much wider political ideals, helping define what decolonization in Egypt actually meant.

Developing Egypt from the ground up

The University Museum's representatives purposefully tied the excavation at Mit Rahina to discourses of development and modernization. At least in the US context, these discourses had become increasingly incorporated into Cold War policies.[18] At this stage, tying archaeological work to such modernizing practices also provided the perfect point for American entry into Egypt, particularly as many of the technocrats now employed by the Egyptian Department of Antiquities had themselves appropriated discourses of modernization over the previous few decades. Thus, the practice of archaeology in Egypt led to the potential materialization of conflicting political ideals in the country as Egyptian and American experts met.

Egyptians such as Mustafa Amer had gained their positions of leadership by mobilizing the rationalizing discourses from which contemporary theories of development and modernization had gained prominence. Originally trained in Egypt, but also possessing a Master's degree in geography from the University of Liverpool, Amer emphasized the need for Egyptians to produce modern scientific knowledge: he believed that such knowledge constituted 'a prerequisite for Egypt's entry into the modern world'.[19] Embodying the increasing prominence of discourses of expertise (*khibra*) and scientific and technical development in Egypt, technocrats like Amer were deeply amenable to furthering this work on the ground as a national, and now revolutionary, project directed towards constituting Egypt's future modernity.

Meanwhile, the University Museum's representatives had other reasons to take serious heed of development and modernization discourses beyond their obvious applicability to the Egyptian context. These reasons, inherently tied to American conceptions of the early Cold War, varied from institutional self-interest to the apparently altruistic. They also indicated how, even when not set forward by official US government programmes, such Cold War discourses still made their way into the decolonizing world.[20] In the United States, government policy linked development and modernization practices, which had historically coalesced in the Tennessee Valley Authority of the interwar New Deal, to the promotion of the national (and thus also 'Free World') interest. Point Four, the US technical assistance programme announced by President Truman in his January 1949 inaugural address (and renamed and reconstituted several times, eventually becoming USAID), aimed to show the 'underdeveloped' world the worth of American values of democracy and political community. Government officials viewed this work as a means of building the right sort of decolonized nation: one that subscribed to liberal democracy and capitalism, which would welcome the arrival of those values through the transfer of scientific and technological expertise offered by Point Four representatives.[21]

Such values possessed obvious appeal for the employees of the University Museum most closely involved with the Mit Rahina work. For instance, Rudolf Anthes, Curator of the University Museum's Egyptian Section and in charge of the work at Mit Rahina on behalf of the institution, believed in the cultivation of a certain type of modernist liberty. A German *émigré*, Anthes was a trained Egyptologist who had worked in Berlin's collection of Egyptian antiquities, held at the city's Neues Museum. During the Second World War, the Nazi regime persecuted him due to his opposition to their ideologies; however, at the end of the conflict, he had ended up as Director of the Berlin collection. But due to the division of the city, Anthes then had to work in East Berlin while living in its West. He eventually seized the opportunity to move to Philadelphia and work for the University Museum, and also became a quiet proponent of certain, although certainly not all, Free World ideologies.[22] A supporter of liberal ideals of citizenship, US development work clearly appealed to him.

The University Museum's Director, the archaeologist Froelich Rainey, also had great interest in American development policy. Rainey had worked for the State Department during the Second World War and had links to the fledgling CIA and broader US foreign policy circles. Now, as Rainey planned a massively increased programme of international research work for his Museum's employees, his movement within these official and quasi-official foreign policy networks clearly aided the formulation of his agenda. At one point, Rainey even placed CIA operatives among his excavation staff.[23] More potently, however, Rainey formulated the University Museum's potential Mit Rahina work extensively in the style of US development policy. Rainey clearly saw – and believed in – the potential benefits of this policy for the promotion of his institution and his country. At the time of the initial Mit Rahina suggestion, he had apparently proposed similar work in Iraq, Turkey and Afghanistan.[24]

Indeed, a consideration of the initial proposals for the excavation put together by Rainey and Anthes during 1953 and 1954 reflects how efficacious the two men found constructing an archaeological project that could make use of development and modernization policy. At the same time as US development experts worked with Egyptians on a land reclamation programme known as the Egyptian American Rural Improvement Service, so the University Museum proposal suggested naming the forthcoming excavation work the 'Egyptian-American archaeological research programme'.[25] This new programme echoed the cooperative nature of US development initiatives, a collaboration initially proposed by Rainey in a letter to the Egyptian historian Shafiq Ghurbal, Undersecretary of the Ministry of Education.[26] The project called

for work under the direction of Egyptians and Americans, [the] publication of results in both English and Egyptian [*sic*] if technically possible, agreement of the cooperating institutions on the site or sites to be excavated, and a division of [excavated] objects within the terms of the current Egyptian Antiquities Law.[27]

After a visit to Egypt in the first half of 1954, during which he discussed these proposals with government representatives including Amer, Anthes further refined these goals. The two organizations would still work together; additionally, the expert practitioners that the Museum promised to provide would also train Egyptians in the field, aiding the development of the Department of Antiquities' workforce (if also in a way that suited the University Museum). Finally, the Museum agreed to bear much of the financial burden of the work, including publication, although the refined proposal did not make clear whether any excavated artefacts would ever return to America, leaving the possibility temptingly open.[28]

The proposed Egyptian-American archaeological research programme represented a compromise solution buried in the contradictions of contemporary politics. On one level, through its adoption of development discourse, the programme opened archaeological work in Egypt to non-governmental cooperation with American institutions and practices at the same time as American political leaders worked to assert their, and their country's, influence in the Middle East more generally. However, on another level, the proposed work allowed Egyptians to assert their own national development prerogatives, in particular by making use of the resources offered by the University Museum, at a time when decolonization proceeded swiftly. In practice, the two sides never completely resolved this issue, reflecting the problems encountered as US diplomats and technical assistance representatives sought to bring decolonizing states on side during the early stages of the Cold War. As much as the official levels of the political world, archaeological practice was an arena in which the wider meanings of Egyptian decolonization became real.

Shaping land, shaping people at Mit Rahina

As work at Mit Rahina took shape on the ground, problems related to the excavations became increasingly clear. In particular, when translated onto the ground the work highlighted the practical limitations of US-style development aims. Indeed, the ground on which the project took shape played a central role in this situation. Land occupied a major place in development and modernization projects: as earlier examples like the Tennessee Valley Authority had shown, the use and shaping of land could potentially mould the actions of the people who lived and worked on it.[29] Similar, then, to other US development projects such as the land reclamation scheme carried out by the Egyptian American Rural Improvement Service, the programme at Mit Rahina transparently attempted to mould people through controlling the ways they lived and worked on the archaeological site. Rudolf Anthes himself noted in April 1954 that 'the Egyptians[,] if they are going to be efficient [archaeologists] in the future ... can't do that without adapting themselves to the methods of European researchers'.[30]

The work at Mit Rahina attempted to achieve this aim by shaping the practices and views of its Egyptian trainees as they carried out their work in the field along these 'European' (or, more broadly, Western) lines. This regulation, as became clear throughout the excavations, was to take place through the University Museum field team's guidance of their trainees' excavation, recording and timekeeping practices, in addition to some of their domestic habits.[31] Archaeologists working in Egypt long had understood the possibilities their field practice possessed for forming such disciplined subjects: the

British archaeologist William Matthew Flinders Petrie, for instance, had connected such regulated work to his early twentieth-century eugenicist ideals.[32] Now, the linking of the Mit Rahina work to Cold War ideals of modernization provided a new, up-to-date justification for this practice. Furthermore, the University Museum, which was also offered other potential sites, had excavated at Mit Rahina both during and for a few years after the First World War.[33] Beyond regulatory practices, then, returning to the site provided another chance to demonstrate what the University Museum could do in Egypt.

However, making the work collaborative made implementing Western ideals at the site significantly harder. Chronologically parallel to the Egyptian American Rural Improvement Service and the Mit Rahina excavations, the Egyptian government had set up its own land reclamation programme, which it named Tahrir (or 'Liberation') Province. The programme attempted to demonstrate that Egypt could undertake modernization projects without foreign aid, and also undertake them on a large, even totalizing, scale by not only reclaiming land, but also using that process to construct an idealized Egyptian community. As Egypt's new leaders began to reshape the country as a revolutionary nation-state, so the shaping of the land through its reclamation played a vital part in this process, much as it did at Mit Rahina.[34]

Thus, beyond the other reasons that played a role in the choice of Mit Rahina, after meeting with Amer, Anthes noted that the 'site anyhow must be done since the area is claimed by the peasants'.[35] The work at Mit Rahina closely fit evolving modernization plans in Egypt. Indeed, Anthes' use of the word 'peasants' aligned closely with this policy, which characterized the peasantry and the land they worked as an object of reform. As in Tahrir Province, that land could now be reclaimed and redistributed for the peasantry's agricultural use.[36] Choosing to work with this Egyptian modernization process was not necessarily problematic *per se*. However, the diplomatic choice of Mit Rahina as an excavation site caused significant problems, since the land there presented considerable difficulties in terms of its archaeological excavation.

Indeed, the problems that the University Museum team encountered at the site made the demonstration of their expertise there almost impossible, rendering their proposed application of American development objectives increasingly difficult. Mit Rahina was located in the waterlogged earth of the Nile Valley's floodplain, unlike many other archaeological sites in Egypt, which were more normally located on the country's desert fringes. Anything extracted from the site was therefore found in something of a congealed mess, and during the excavations, diary entry upon diary entry illustrates how these circumstances, in addition to the way in which they created odd patterns of archaeological remains, made it difficult for the University Museum team to understand the material that they excavated. Indeed, in one particularly memorable instance in 1955, Anthes bemoaned:

> But why, for God's sake, did they use these brick built squares as a deposit of broken (and fragmentary) pots? It may have some meaning that so many bottom pieces were found; did they use these as flower pots?? But no flowers are found![37]

Anthes' exclamation verges on the meaningless, which in itself is telling: none of the University Museum team could understand the site where they had volunteered to work. For most of their time there, they simply could not give the site meaning. Ironically, the work at the site coincided with an increasing awareness among archaeologists elsewhere of the importance of understanding the earth itself, whether waterlogged or otherwise, for constructing interpretations of the past. In particular, the stratigraphic relationships of archaeological remains visible in the vertical 'sections' at the side of excavation trenches had started to take on new meaning at this point in time as a means of understanding the relative chronologies of past human action that those sections embodied. In the post–Second World War era of decolonization and the Universal Declaration of Human Rights, archaeologists outside of Egypt claimed that their work could be applied around the world to an extent never before possible, helping them understand the entirety of the human past in all of its variation. One archaeologist in particular, Mortimer Wheeler of the University of London's Institute of Archaeology, even went so far as to claim that 'there is no method proper to the excavation of a British site which is not applicable – nay, must be applied – to a site in Africa or Asia'.[38] Wheeler subtly suggested that his own stratigraphic technique could be applied exactly where many of the world's decolonizing nations were located, and it thus seems unsurprising that Anthes would later, in 1965, note in relation to Mit Rahina that:

> we learned by our own experience the fact which is elementary outside of Egypt, that only a coordinated system of horizontal and vertical cuts [in the ground] is adequate for the understanding of a site which has accumulated under changing living conditions ... [39]

Unfortunately, Anthes and his co-workers only realized the applicability of new forms of archaeological stratigraphy at Mit Rahina at the very end of the second excavation season, when the method's inadvertent application in one particular trench allowed them finally to understand the relative chronology of the remains they had uncovered at the site.[40] After two seasons of scrabbling around Mit Rahina, and particularly after a second season during which the team took time to read material that highlighted the importance of stratigraphic sections in understanding complex archaeological remains, a section was eventually applied to the site that helped make sense of what the team found within their excavation trenches. However, even then the team only applied this section accidentally: one excavation trench at Mit Rahina was so large that in order to undertake work there it became necessary to leave a central baulk, a 'relief wall', standing inside it until the very last minute.[41] This baulk, when finally prepared for clearance so that the entire trench could be understood as a whole, revealed how the complex assortment of remains in the site had become formed and connected over time. Thus, only after staring at this section did Anthes realize, 'our site now stands in a more significant position with regard to the whole Memphis area than could be realised before'.[42] Only at the end of the second season of work could this claim to authority be made, and only then could the team's expertise be justified.

Indeed, notes made by Anthes make clear that despite efforts to assert the University Museum's control, in addition to Western ideals, at Mit Rahina, local cultural forms seem to have consistently made themselves felt during the excavation. On-site practices reinforced Egyptian working hierarchies that had developed over the previous few decades. The group of skilled archaeological workers known as Quftis, who hailed from the town of Quft in Upper Egypt and who had formed a powerful comprador body since the time of Petrie's excavations in Egypt in the late nineteenth and early twentieth centuries, seem (from the available evidence) to have taken charge of much of the excavation work and also of the local villagers who laboured for the project.[43] Excavation practices thus mobilized field-based social practices that had developed throughout the decades prior to 1952, lending a significantly more 'local' flavour to the proceedings than had perhaps initially been imagined.

Meanwhile, Egyptian insubordination also became an issue. Possessing little authority on the site, the University Museum team had little control over those individuals who the Department of Antiquities presented for training. In 1956, for example, the Department offered up Ibrahim 'Abd el-Aziz, one of its employees, yet 'Abd el-Aziz did not adapt well to the team's disciplining practices. On 17 March, Anthes complained that 'Abd el-Aziz 'does not appear before breakfast'.[44] By 19 March, he pointedly noted that ''Abd el Aziz [sic] has not shown up'.[45] By 5 April, Anthes commented that 'he is clever enough, but you can't rely on him'.[46] Later in the month, 'Abd el-Aziz had not arrived again, and Anthes phoned Amer to tell him that 'I should like to have him ['Abd el-Aziz] removed because we do not need him and do not want him any longer'.[47] At Mit Rahina, the American development work that the excavation so obviously reflected received short shrift. In the archaeological sphere, attempts to influence the course of Egyptian decolonization from the Western side therefore appeared inconclusive.

Cancellation and continuation

After two seasons at Mit Rahina, both partners in the excavation wanted to cancel their involvement. Indeed, the University Museum's management had consistently expressed doubt about the efficacy of sponsoring the dig. Certain individuals who sat on the institution's Board of Managers suggested that the excavations had not produced the artefacts that the Museum had so desired in its initial proposal. Therefore, the Board, together with Rainey, whose motivation for supporting the work also seemed to dwindle as Mit Rahina failed to produce what he perceived as any useful results, used the 1956 Suez crisis and its aftermath as a pretext not to continue with the renewed excavations that Anthes had planned, much as on certain levels, US involvement with Egypt itself slightly declined at this point in time. Indeed, Anthes' inadvertent success at the site at the end of the second season, and also his connected hope for improved work there, won him little institutional favour under these circumstances.[48] The work at Mit Rahina seemed not to have produced anything of much value, whether in terms of artefacts or in terms of appropriately trained Egyptians.

The attitude behind this cancellation also demonstrated a striking disconnect from changing Egyptian discussions about antiquities, which emphasized that Egyptian relations with the wider world were as influenced by fields such as archaeology as political practice more generally. In particular, these discussions, reflecting the manner in which US-style practices at Mit Rahina had failed to counter various Egyptian assertions of power, started to mirror the Egyptian state's own increasing assertiveness. Despite the presence of international excavation teams in the country, discussions increasingly attempted to make certain that Egyptian hands would take total control of Egypt's material past, whether in the field or elsewhere, at the same time as Egyptian officials took increasing control of the country's future, particularly after Suez. Such control did not merely extend to the Egyptianization of the Department of Antiquities. Debates also took place in the Egyptian press, influenced by policy rumblings emanating from the state's structures of governance, as to whether the government should further regulate the country's antiquities trade.[49]

Meanwhile, under the terms of a cultural exchange agreement with Egypt, Polish archaeologists had also recently started excavation in Egypt.[50] Members of Western institutions perceived this move as a rejoinder to their own work. Indeed, Anthes and certain members of his excavation staff expressed concern that Western influence in Egypt would dwindle and Soviet influence increase if Western archaeological work did not continue uninterrupted.[51] The excavations at Mit Rahina may not have formed an explicit part of US policy in Egypt. They may not even have been that successful by 1957. However, it is clear that at least some of the University Museum's Mit Rahina team were distraught not to have the further chance to influence the practices of Egyptians in the way that had originally been set out. Yet, as they voiced this desperation, it was also starting to become clear that that chance would not exist.

The Egyptian government did not wish the Mit Rahina work to continue, and the Department of Antiquities' communication with the University Museum mirrored the state's increased assertiveness post-Suez. Indeed, a bluntly purposeful letter arrived in Philadelphia in October 1957. Written by the new Director of Egypt's Department of Antiquities, Muharram Kamal, the letter, distinctly underwhelmed by anything Rainey's failed institution had done or now had to say for itself, stated that the Department could not renew the University Museum's excavation permit, because it now wanted archaeological excavation work to take place in the Egyptian region of Nubia: the soon-to-be-initiated construction of the new Aswan High Dam would lead to the flooding of the region's antiquities.[52] Post-Suez, the Egyptian government began entirely to dictate terms to Western archaeological missions, even as it apparently did the Poles a significant favour by allowing them to take home certain antiquities. The University Museum's archaeologists would be welcome in Nubia, but their efforts at Mit Rahina had clearly served little purpose.

Indeed, the planned construction of the new Aswan High Dam had already led to a 1955 report, prepared by the Department of Antiquities and distributed internationally, outlining which Nubian sites would need to be excavated before flooding occurred.[53] However, while the Department of Antiquities had previously requested international assistance, representatives of the institutions that might have provided this help had also felt more or less free to ignore the plea. Excavation in Egypt had historically taken place north of Nubia, and work outside of the more southerly, and potentially much more artefact poor, region represented a far more attractive prospect to institutions such as the University Museum, even at a site like Mit Rahina.[54] Before Suez, the Egyptian state could not get foreign archaeologists to listen to its message.

Afterwards, however, this situation changed: Egyptian assertiveness following Suez dramatically altered events. Indeed, Kamal's written order for directed archaeological excavation in Nubia reflected wider state policy and the consolidation of the power of an Egyptian technocracy: the ideal order of the day had become modernization work directed by Egyptian state experts. Under Amer's directorship, the Department of Antiquities had gone some way towards this outcome, but under Kamal's lead, the institution went further. Could archaeologists from countries like the United States find a way once again to attempt to assert their own priorities and ideologies? Only time would tell.

Conclusion

Archaeological work in Egypt reflected the country's wider decolonizing experience, suggesting that postcolonial Egypt was constituted as much through an apparently innocuous field like archaeology as through top-level political discussions. The University Museum attempted to use the Mit Rahina work not only to foster its own influence in Egypt, but also to bring American political ideals into Egypt as the Cold War gathered pace. However, the particularities of the Egyptian situation meant that those involved with implementing these ideals found them hard to practice, much as other US attempts to work with the country seemed to fail. Eventually, too, the Egyptian government took a much firmer stance with the University Museum, cancelling its work and directing further archaeology towards Nubia. This assertive move echoed post-Suez political realities, as Egypt became an increasingly assertive state on the world stage.

On some level, then, archaeology adds little new insight to the story of Egyptian decolonization: the course of archaeological events seems to reflect political meta-narratives of the era more generally. However, events at Mit Rahina illustrate the particular ways in which this meta-narrative could emerge: in this reading, failure in cooperative fieldwork contributed to the path of Egyptian decolonization as much as events surrounding the Suez Canal. In a different, more successful, situation, the Museum may have kept working at the site, and the development programme it attempted to put into practice may have been implemented. The realities of decolonization in Egypt thus did not come about in as straightforward a manner as has otherwise been suggested, hinting that a more nuanced historical investigation of this historical period is necessary.

Notes

1 I conducted the research for this article as part of my doctoral work at the University of Cambridge, funded by the UK's Arts and Humanities Research Council; additional travel support to research the material featured in this article came from Darwin College, Cambridge, and the Royal Historical Society. I would like to thank Eleanor Robson and Jim Secord for their helpful supervision, and also Elisabeth Leake and Leslie James for both the original chance to present the paper and also the chance to publish it in this volume.

2 Bier, Laura (2011), *Revolutionary Womanhood: Feminisms, Modernity, and the State in Nasser's Egypt*. Cairo: The American University in Cairo Press, 4. Rather more linear narratives tend to occur in volumes written within an international relations frame, including: Hahn, Peter L. (1991), *The United States, Great Britain, and Egypt, 1945–1956: Strategy and Diplomacy in the Early Cold War*. Chapel Hill, NC: University of North Carolina Press; Holland, Matthew F. (1996), *America and Egypt: From Roosevelt to Eisenhower*. Westport, CT: Praeger.

3 The only other discussion of archaeology in this historical context seems to be Bloembergen, Marieke and Eickhoff, Martijn (2011), 'Conserving the past, mobilizing the Indonesian future: Archaeological sites, regime change and heritage politics in Indonesia in the 1950s', *Bijdragen tot de Taal-, Land- en Volkenkunde*, 167(4), 405–436. Given the lack of literature on archaeological practices in the Middle East and North Africa in this period, it is currently difficult to understand the extent to which archaeological practices in Egypt at this time were in any way exceptional for the region.

4 See in particular Reid, Donald Malcolm (2002), *Whose Pharaohs? Archaeology, Museums, and Egyptian National Identity from Napoleon to World War I*. Berkeley: University of California Press.

5 The publication also had a French edition, albeit with the same (English) name.

6 Abdel-Sayed, Samira (1960), 'First British cruise arrives', *Egypt Travel Magazine*, 75 (November), 34–37.

7 Anonymous (1960), 'Visit of the Sultan of Jog Jakarta', *Egypt Travel Magazine*, 75 (November), 45.

8 Anonymous (1960), 'The President of Rotary International in Cairo', *Egypt Travel Magazine*, 75 (November), 38.

9 Wharton, Annabel Jane (2001), *Building the Cold War: Hilton International Hotels and Modern Architecture*. Chicago: The University of Chicago Press.

10 Unknown author (1958), 'Sāriqat al-Azwāj Taʿtarifu bi-Ṣarāha (The Husband Stealer Confesses Sincerely)', *Akhir Saʿa*, 22 January, 30.

11 The excavation reports comprise: Anthes, Rudolf (1956), 'A first season of excavating in Memphis', *University Museum Bulletin*, 20(1), 3–25; Anthes, Rudolf (1957), 'Memphis (Mit Rahineh) in 1956', *University Museum Bulletin*, 21(2), 3–34; Anthes, Rudolf (1959), *Mit Rahineh 1955*. Philadelphia: The University Museum, University of Pennsylvania; Anthes, Rudolf (1965), *Mit Rahineh 1956*. Philadelphia: The University Museum, University of Pennsylvania.

12 Colla, Elliott (2007), *Conflicted Antiquities: Egyptology, Egyptomania, Egyptian Modernity*. Durham, NC: Duke University Press.

13 See Reid (2002) for infrastructure details.

14 Reid, Donald Malcolm (1997), 'Nationalizing the pharaonic past: Egyptology, imperialism, and Egyptian nationalism, 1922–1952', in Israel Gershoni and James P. Jankowski (eds.) *Rethinking Nationalism in the Arab Middle East*. New York: Columbia University Press, 127–149.

15 For various elements of this modernizing process, see Goldschmidt, Arthur, Johnson, Amy J. and Salmoni, Barak A. (eds.) (2005), *Re-Envisioning Egypt, 1919–1952*. Cairo: The American University in Cairo Press.

16 Carruthers, William (2014, forthcoming), 'Egyptology, Archaeology and the Construction of Revolutionary Egypt, c. 1925–1958', unpublished PhD dissertation, University of Cambridge, ch. 1, addresses this process of Egyptian institutional reform as it related to antiquities.

17 On Amer, see El Shakry, Omnia (2007), *The Great Social Laboratory: Subjects of Knowledge in Colonial and Postcolonial Egypt*. Stanford: Stanford University Press.

18 For modernization and development work in general, see Ekbladh, David (2010), *The Great American Mission: Modernization and the Construction of an American World Order*. Princeton: Princeton University Press; Escobar, Arturo (1995), *Encountering Development: The Making and Unmaking of the Third World*. Princeton: Princeton University Press. For this work in Egypt, see Alterman, Jon B. (2002), *Egypt and American Foreign Assistance, 1952–1956*. Basingstoke: Palgrave; El Shakry (2007); Mitchell, Timothy (2002), *Rule of Experts: Egypt, Techno-Politics, Modernity*. Berkeley: University of California Press.

19 El Shakry (2007), 68 (her words, not his).

20 Cf. Ekbladh (2010), 154.

21 Alterman (2002); Ekbladh (2010).

22 O'Connor, David B. (1985), 'In memoriam: Rudolf Anthes', *Expedition*, 27, 34–36.

23 Rainey, Froelich G. (1992), *Reflections of a Digger: Fifty Years of World Archaeology*. Philadelphia: University Museum of Archaeology and Anthropology.

24 Froelich Rainey to Shafiq Ghurbal, 21 April 1953, Expedition Records: Egypt, Box 38, Folder 3, Archive of the University of Pennsylvania Museum of Archaeology and Anthropology, Philadelphia (UMA).

25 Froelich Rainey to Shafiq Ghurbal, 21 April 1953, Expedition Records: Egypt, Box 38, Folder 3, UMA.

26 On Ghurbal, see Di-Capua, Yoav (2009), *Gatekeepers of the Arab Past: Historians and History-Writing in Twentieth-Century Egypt*. Berkeley: University of California Press.

27 Froelich Rainey to Shafiq Ghurbal, 21 April 1953, Expedition Records: Egypt, Box 38, Folder 3, Archive of the University of Pennsylvania Museum of Archaeology and Anthropology, Philadelphia (UMA).

28 Copy of (presumably final) Mit Rahina proposal, 15 June 1954, Expedition Records: Egypt, Box 38, Folder 3, UMA.

29 Ekbladh (2010).

30 Alterman (2002); Rudolf Anthes' 1954 diary from Egypt, entry for 12 April 1954, Expedition Records: Egypt, Box 39, Folder 2, UMA.

31 See Carruthers, William (2014, forthcoming), 'Egyptology, Archaeology and the Construction of Revolutionary Egypt, c. 1925–1958', unpublished PhD dissertation, University of Cambridge, chs. 3 and 4.

32 For Petrie and these ideals see Gange, David (2013), *Dialogues with the Dead: Egyptology in British Culture and Religion, 1822–1922*. Oxford: Oxford University Press.

33 Anthes (1965), 6–7, makes a point of noting this work; Clarence Fisher, one of Anthes' predecessors at the University Museum, led it.

34 Alterman (2002).

35 Rudolf Anthes' 1954 diary from Egypt, entry for 11 April 1954, Expedition Records: Egypt, Box 39, Folder 2, UMA.

36 El Shakry (2007) on Tahrir Province.

37 Anthes' 1955 field diary, entry for 7 March 1955, Expedition Records: Egypt, Box 38, Folder 10, UMA.

38 Wheeler, Mortimer (1954), *Archaeology from the Earth*. Oxford: Clarendon Press, 36.

39 Anthes (1965), 2.

40 Discussion of this realization is found in Anthes (1965), 59.

41 Anthes' 1956 field diary, entry for 28 April 1956, Expedition Records: Egypt, Box 38, Folder 12, UMA.

42 Anthes (1956), 8–9.

43 For the history of the Quftis, see Quirke, Stephen (2010), *Hidden Hands: Egyptian Workforces in Petrie Excavation Archives, 1880–1924*. London: Duckworth.

44 Anthes' 1956 field diary, entry for 17 March 1956, Expedition Records: Egypt, Box 38, Folder 12, UMA.

45 Anthes' 1956 field diary, entry for 19 March 1956, Expedition Records: Egypt, Box 38, Folder 12, UMA.

46 Anthes' 1956 field diary, entry for 5 April 1956, Expedition Records: Egypt, Box 38, Folder 12, UMA.

47 Anthes' 1956 field diary, entry for 17 April 1956, Expedition Records: Egypt, Box 38, Folder 12, UMA.

48 Correspondence reveals the actual rationale for cancellation: Letter from Froelich Rainey to Percy Madeira, 15 October 1957, Expedition Records: Egypt, Box 46, Folder 1, UMA.

49 A selection of articles appeared across the Egyptian press from June 1957 onwards after Charles Muses, an American esoteric philosopher who the Egyptian government had granted permission to excavate at the site of Dahshur, attempted to remove a number of antiquities from Egypt. See Carruthers (2014 forthcoming) ch. 5.

50 Wente, Edward F. (1957), 'untitled letter', *Newsletter of the American Research Center in Egypt*, 26, 4; Wente states that the agreement was 'between Egypt and communist countries', although the date of the accord is unclear.

51 See Helen Wall to Rudolf Anthes, 4 May 1957, and Rudolf Anthes to Helen Wall, 5 June 1957, Expedition Records: Egypt, Box 38, Folder 9, UMA.

52 Muharram Kamal to Froelich Rainey, 31 October 1957, Expedition Records: Egypt, Box 46, Folder 1, UMA. For Kamal, see Bierbrier, Morris L. (2012), *Who Was Who in Egyptology*. Fourth edition. London: Egypt Exploration Society.

53 Maslihat al-Athar (1955), *Report on the Monuments of Nubia Likely to be Submerged by Sudd-el-'Ali Water*. Cairo: Government Press.

54 For one assertion of the desire to excavate at non-Nubian sites even as the Nubian work began, see John Biggs, Jr. to Froelich Rainey, 22 December 1959, Administrative Records, Director's Office, Froelich Rainey, Box 17, Folder 10.

Key texts

Alterman, Jon B. (2002). *Egypt and American Foreign Assistance, 1952–1956*. Basingstoke; New York: Palgrave.

Bier, Laura. (2011). *Revolutionary Womanhood: Feminisms, Modernity, and the State in Nasser's Egypt*. Cairo: The American University in Cairo Press.

Colla, Elliott. (2007). *Conflicted Antiquities: Egyptology, Egyptomania, Egyptian Modernity*. Durham, NC; London: Duke University Press.

Ekbladh, David. (2010). *The Great American Mission: Modernization and the Construction of an American World Order*. Princeton: Princeton University Press.

El Shakry, Omnia. (2007). *The Great Social Laboratory: Subjects of Knowledge in Colonial and Postcolonial Egypt*. Stanford: Stanford University Press.

Escobar, Arturo. (1995). *Encountering Development: The Making and Unmaking of the Third World*. Princeton: Princeton University Press.

Reid, Donald Malcolm. (1997). 'Nationalizing the Pharaonic past: Egyptology, imperialism, and Egyptian nationalism, 1922–1952', in Israel Gershoni and James P. Jankowski (eds.) *Rethinking Nationalism in the Arab Middle East*. New York: Columbia University Press, 127–149.

PART IV
(RE)CONCEIVING SOVEREIGNTY AND STATEHOOD

This part reconsiders the meaning of sovereignty and the state at the crossroads of the Cold War and decolonization. It addresses different modes of governance and various sites of conflict, as state sovereignty was redefined in an uncertain era. It emphasizes the ways in which the demarcation of borders in metropoles such as France and in decolonizing states such as the Republic of Congo became a key point of contestation, where international actors and issues met the competing claims of groups within the state. Whether through international institutions like the United Nations, supranational organizations like the British Commonwealth, the legal exception of free trade zones or national border guards, this part shows that the contingency of territorial borders in the era of decolonization necessitates reconsideration of sovereign power.

CHAPTER 9
A 'COMMONWEALTH MOMENT' IN SOUTH ASIAN DECOLONIZATION
Daniel Haines

'Sixty years ago', began the opening statement of the first programme in a BBC television series on Indian history, 'India threw off the chains of the British Empire, and became a free nation.'[1] The programme's presenter was Michael Wood, a popular historian, and his pronouncement represented a straightforward view of what decolonization meant for South Asia. Scholarship on nationalism, partition, independence and Cold War politics in South Asia has complicated the picture by questioning quite what freedom meant, and what constituted 'the nation'.[2] Historians have convincingly established that British colonial rule heavily influenced the political cultures and institutions of the states that emerged in the wake of South Asian independence in 1947.[3] This chapter argues that the making and substantial breaking of Commonwealth influence in South Asia between 1947 and 1951 revealed competing visions of national sovereignty and its relationship to international politics. In British conceptions, the Commonwealth represented an alternative to a global system of liberal, territorial nation-states. The organization of political power between Britain, India and Pakistan during these early years appeared to constitute, to paraphrase Michael Collins, a 'Commonwealth moment' in South Asia.[4] Yet Indian and Pakistani determination to make real their autonomous nation-statehood, coupled with competition for Britain's leadership in South Asia from the United States, stymied the development of this alternative model. It meant that, at least so far as South Asia was concerned, the Commonwealth moment was rather brief.

This analysis recognizes the analytical and political problems that stem from accepting nation-states as the natural organization of political power in the modern world, which are now well established in political geography and post-structuralist international relations.[5] Decolonization historiography, too, has opened ways of understanding world politics and the roles of 'national' governments, attentive to various ways that international politics can be configured. Recently, John Darwin has placed the Commonwealth within a series of developments in the British imperial system. He argues that the post-war Commonwealth represented a British world system that incorporated, rather than replaced, elements of the former empire. British Prime Minister Clement Atlee's government intended this system to regain Britain's former position as a trading centre, importing and re-exporting goods that Dominions and colonies produced. Britain's political and economic survival therefore meant the survival of a British world system as the basis of the country's own prosperity and power.[6] In other words, Britain's post-war colonial policies, particularly their emphasis on the Commonwealth, were geared towards refashioning the former empire into a new world system with its centre of gravity in London.[7]

Drawing on such work, this paper starts from the contention that decolonization in South Asia did not presage the immediate emergence of fully sovereign nation-states. European post-war imperial policies amounted to the reconfiguration of empire rather than its abolition, and no clear picture exists of how these policies played out in parts of the contemporary and former British Empire that were neither 'white Dominions' (self-governing former colonies controlled by people of European settler origin) nor formal colonies.[8] India and Pakistan, as non-white self-governing entities, fell between these two stools.

Beginning with an appreciation of British ambitions that the Commonwealth should operate as a global order, this chapter disrupts the Cold War narrative in which the USA and USSR dominated the international scene after the end of the Second World War. The first section argues that the Commonwealth provided an alternative configuration of international relations to the bipolar order, while still promoting anti-communist interests. The second section examines the effect of Commonwealth membership on sovereignty and state-formation in India and Pakistan. It highlights discussions among British, Indian and Pakistani leaders during the run-up to independence and its aftermath and underscores South Asian agency in determining the form and meaning of membership. While containing communist influence intensified British policymakers' insistence on building British-South Asian links within the Commonwealth framework, these sections together argue that the negotiated relationship between Britain, India and Pakistan had as much to do with Indian and Pakistani perspectives on sovereignty as with power-bloc strategy. The third, final section brings the Cold War back into South Asia. It argues that US policymakers tolerated, even welcomed, Britain's use of the Commonwealth to represent Western interests in South Asia during the late 1940s. But, as a detailed reading of British and American diplomatic archives reveals, US State Department officials quickly lost patience with the Commonwealth's practical failure to manage conflict between India and Pakistan at the beginning of the 1950s.

The Commonwealth as a global order

During the Cold War era, almost all of Britain's former colonies transitioned into the Commonwealth. India and Pakistan constituted an early test case for how the Commonwealth could evolve. India and Pakistan's initial experience of the Commonwealth took place in the context of a reconfiguration of global politics after the Second World War. Between the seventeenth and twentieth centuries, while organizing themselves into supposedly coherent nation-states, Europeans annexed and colonized vast swathes of territory in Asia, Africa, the Americas and Australasia. By halting the development of indigenous forms of state formation, they ensured that nation-statehood remained the preserve of Europeans and their New World descendants. During this time, the European colonial empires played a fundamental role in structuring global politics. They produced diverse forms of political organization in which commercial activity, strategy, prestige and local conditions drew imperial powers into more formal modes of rule.[9] Empires were far from a purely European phenomenon: China and Tsarist Russia also had formed vast Eurasian and Asian land empires. Between the 1910s and the 1930s, Japan's expanding empire in East and Southeast Asia had added to global imperialism's portfolio.[10] Concurrently, the League of Nations' award of mandates, such as Palestine to Britain and Syria to France, created 'halfway houses' between imperial possession and independent entity.[11]

The standard narrative of Cold War international relations leaves only a limited role for empires and post-imperial forms of international organization. Following the defeat of the Axis powers in 1945, the new superpowers, the US and USSR, promoted rival world systems that reduced the room for empire. They pushed forward alternative versions of modernity, based respectively on capitalist and communist models of development, competing for influence in the 'Third World'. Specifically, the American development model began with the idea of independent territorial nation states, constructing a world system in which national governments encouraged cross-border trade and investment. Institutions and regimes such as the International Bank for Reconstruction and Development, the International Monetary Fund and the Bretton Woods Agreement were designed to promote and maintain this world system.[12] American rhetoric, and to a lesser extent American actions, sought to dissociate the United States from European imperialism, keeping a wary eye on the growing strength of anti-colonial movements. The latter were potentially open to communist influence. The two superpowers dominated the political space in which the old colonial powers, their nationalist opponents and postcolonial successors operated.[13]

Imperial reconfiguration and decolonization played a larger role in shaping the emerging world system than a focus on nation states might suggest. In many cases, the effect of these policies was not to promote nation-states as the primary configuration of either local power or international personality. Wm. Roger Louis has pointed to British efforts to construct regional groupings of colonies within the Empire during the 1950s and the 1960s as a (failed) alternative to today's international system of discrete nation-states.[14] In another example, the short-lived Central African Federation brought together Northern Rhodesia, Southern Rhodesia and Nyasaland between 1953 and 1963.[15] Further federal experiments took place in Malaya, Nigeria and the West Indies.[16]

The Commonwealth was the largest and most pervasive post-imperial organization. During the 1950s and the 1960s, the Commonwealth expanded as the British Empire shrank. When the Second World War began, the Commonwealth already included Australia, New Zealand, Canada, South Africa and Eire (which left in 1949). After the war ended, India and Pakistan were the first colonies to become independent without large white settler populations. Consequently, they were the first Commonwealth members where indigenous leaders, not the descendants of European settlers, took control of the government. Ceylon (now Sri Lanka) followed in 1948. Ghana led a wave of West

African decolonization in 1957 and took a place in the Commonwealth. During the 1960s, several Caribbean states transitioned from colony to Dominion status.[17] By this time the African, Asian and Caribbean members far outnumbered the 'white Dominions'. These states all chose a post-imperial network over full separation. Burma, on becoming independent in 1948, was unusual in refusing membership. The Commonwealth became a large and diverse association.

In understanding the competing pressures that shaped the world order after 1945, political geographer John Agnew provides a helpful point of departure. Building on his earlier critiques of traditional notions of territorial sovereignty within states, Agnew presents 'sovereignty regimes' as a model of how the openness of states to pressures from other states, or even non-state actors, translates into global politics and economics. Agnew's prime concern is to show that the traditional notion that sovereignty resides in territorially bounded nation-states (that is, discrete areas in which one central government holds supreme authority, including the power to represent the interests or inhabitants of that area to powers outside the nation-state's boundaries) is false, and in fact states have never held unchallenged authority over the spaces they occupy. He uses the example of international currency systems after the Second World War to illustrate the extent to which nations are dependent on, and their actions limited by, other states and international systems. In his depiction, such practices constitute sovereignty regimes, which allow us to understand sovereignty as always partially devolved and networked among states and international institutions.[18]

The analytical advantage of Agnew's model is to move scholarship away from reductionist, 'classical' international relations theory, which posits sovereign nation-states as the basic unit of the global order, both a container for political action within a given 'national' territory and an agent that interacts with other nation-states on the world stage. Thinking about sovereignty regimes offers a way to understand international organizations such as the Commonwealth as something more than a collection of separate nation states. Rather, it represented an alternative configuration of political and economic power.

Contemporary Commonwealth leaders would not necessarily have agreed with this interpretation. Indeed the organization was far less cohesive than the federal schemes in Africa, Southeast Asia and the West Indies. The 1926 Balfour Report and 1931 Statute of Westminster had declared Commonwealth Dominions to be autonomous and equal with Britain. British and Commonwealth leaders portrayed it as a family or community of nations based on shared heritage and mutual accommodation.[19] The longer history of the Commonwealth was, therefore, one of the evolution of political authority-sharing and economic cooperation across the white parts of the Empire. As Collins has shown, for the self-governing Dominions, the Commonwealth won out over alternative late nineteenth- and early twentieth-century proposals for imperial federations, with a united supreme government for the metropole and the colonies.[20] The Commonwealth that emerged out of the Second World War was, in 1945, still an exclusively white organization in which mutual understanding among peoples of British heritage was considered more important than a clearly defined relationship.[21]

The mid-twentieth-century Commonwealth served more as a consensus-building tool than a platform for the projection of British authority. In 1946, the Labour government moved towards reducing discrimination against women in British nationality legislation, in order to bring it into line with a new norm set by Australia and Canada.[22] British policymakers took seriously the views of other Commonwealth countries on South Asian affairs, from how to approach the transfer of power in 1946, to possible action in 1951 to intervene into India and Pakistan's dispute over Kashmir's 1947 accession to India, which Pakistan contested.[23] Contemporary writing on the Commonwealth recognized that it depended on common interests rather than the centralization of control in London.[24] As an international order, then, the Commonwealth allowed imperial governance to devolve while maintaining a set of relationships that would enable members to present a reasonably united front to the outside world. That outside world was, first and foremost, the communist bloc. But it could well include Britain's Cold War partner, the United States: London sought to promote Australia as the Commonwealth's representative in the southern Pacific as a counterweight to the United States' building-up of Japan. British policymakers thought that their colleagues in Washington underestimated Japan's potential for future aggression against Western interests – in distinct contrast to American faith in Japan as a bulwark against communist China's influence in Asia.[25] Indeed, Britain's Ministry of Defence went so far as to suggest that a united, properly coordinated Commonwealth could, with its great geographical reach, be better placed defensively than either the US or USSR.[26]

In British post-war policy, then, the loss of British India as a major colony heightened the Commonwealth's importance as an alternative to formal empire by maintaining Britain's place in world affairs. As one British diplomat later wrote, 'India and Pakistan were the show-pieces of the post-war Commonwealth.'[27] Keeping India and Pakistan in the Commonwealth was important for British prestige, defence strategy and commercial relations.[28] British strategists saw a stable, cooperative South Asia as the key to protecting Western access to Middle Eastern oil and communications with the Pacific.[29] Ensuring that India and Pakistan would maintain constitutional links with Britain through membership of the Commonwealth preoccupied Rear-Admiral Louis Mountbatten, India's last Viceroy, during the negotiations with South Asian leaders that led to partition.[30] Indeed, Attlee had given Mountbatten specific instructions to maintain British influence in India while delivering independence.[31]

The entry of India and Pakistan into the Commonwealth was possible because of the constitutional, rather than revolutionary, form that South Asian independence took. Mountbatten played a key role in organizing the systems of government in the succeeding states. This was characteristic of British decolonization. Tony Smith has contrasted the British gradualist approach to colonial autonomy, and ultimately decolonization, with the lack of political mechanisms in the French Empire to form a bridge between colonial subjugation and full independence.[32] One optimistic historian has declared that the evolution of responsible government in India, as across the empire, was an 'escalator towards Independence'.[33] More recent, detailed analyses of constitutional development in colonial India have instead emphasized the consistency with which British representatives in New Delhi and London attempted to find formulae that would satisfy nationalist energies while leaving control of India's finances, trade policy and military power in British hands.[34]

Yet Indian and Pakistani leaders had their own reasons for agreeing to membership, derived largely from the manner in which independence came to South Asia. The decolonization of India and Pakistan was a fraught, contested and hurried process, not at all the culmination of a logical progression from colony to nation-state. During independence negotiations in 1947, the colonial Government of India and the leading nationalist parties, the Indian National Congress and the All-India Muslim League, all contributed to the form that independence would take. Mohammed Ali Jinnah, the Muslim League leader and architect of Pakistan, was agreeable to Commonwealth membership, partly with a view to securing third-party intervention against India in case of bilateral disputes. After Jinnah's death in 1948, Pakistani leaders and press continued to portray the Commonwealth as a potential source of support in Pakistan's dispute with India over Kashmir. They expressed repeated, vocal disappointment at that support's failure to materialize.[35]

The Congress leadership, while less enamoured of a continuing formal connection with Britain, accepted it as the price for assurances that only two states, India and Pakistan, would attain Dominion status. This agreement precluded other possible units, such as a conglomeration of the princely states or an independent Bengal, from seceding from India under the Commonwealth banner.[36] Accepting Dominion status under the Commonwealth meant that Congress could take over government from the British quickly.[37] The Commonwealth also offered Jawaharlal Nehru, India's first Prime Minister, an opportunity to influence decolonization in the wider British Empire.[38] Consequently, India and Pakistan became independent as Dominions, with symbolic and constitutional links to the Crown, but both the Indian and Pakistani leaderships were far more concerned with securing their governments' authority at home and abroad than with supporting Britain's global ambitions.

The Commonwealth, then, was not inherently a Cold War animal. Its establishment in the white Dominions of Australia, South Africa, Canada and New Zealand – before the First World War – long predated Western-Soviet tensions. While India and Pakistan attained independence just as the Cold War began to dominate world politics, British policymakers' desire to maintain a stake in their affairs can be read as maintaining their accustomed influence in the subcontinent. Indeed, the Cold War perhaps gave London a further justification for asserting leadership in the region. By analogy, Michael Cox has argued that superpower bipolarity during the 1950s gave both the US and USSR justifications for promoting their own national interests in the name of a supposedly international cause.[39] Britain's Cold War role, in other words, coexisted comfortably with an attempt to preserve some of the power that the country had acquired through empire-building. As the next section will show, the practical working of the Commonwealth in South Asia after independence had even less to do with the Cold War and everything to do with India and Pakistan's mutual antagonism.

Statehood and sovereignty in South Asia's Commonwealth nations

Quite what the practical working of the Commonwealth comprised proved difficult to pin down. As D.K. Fieldhouse wrote in 1966, 'the Commonwealth did nothing as a whole, and performed no necessary function'.[40] The Commonwealth had no implications for the formal, or *de jure*, sovereignty of any member. It gave nobody in Britain any formal control over the policies or actions of anyone in other member states. The Commonwealth had no system of defence, diplomacy, law or currency. Its economic links, such as the Sterling Area and tariff preferences, were formed out of bilateral arrangements and were available to non-members as well.

An important ambiguity in India and Pakistan's postcolonial relationship with Britain, as mediated through the Commonwealth, related to sovereignty. The transfer of power in 1947 lodged the highest decision-making authority with the constituent assemblies of India and Pakistan. But British officials who retained prominent positions under South Asian governments, ranging from police officers to provincial governors, continued aspects of the colonial relationship. Their continued loyalty to Britain meant that the governments of India and Pakistan continued to share a measure of *de facto* sovereignty with Britain. Agnew stresses that 'de facto [sic] sovereignty is all there is'.[41] In Agnew's reading, actors with loyalty to one state can, through practical interventions into affairs in the territory nominally belonging to another state, expose the complexity of sovereignty arrangements. The Commonwealth formed a kind of sovereignty regime, but one in which the structure of relations was far from apparent. Rather than try to define the Commonwealth as a type of sovereignty regime (Agnew offers four archetypes), this following section suggests an understanding of British intervention into specific aspects of Indian and Pakistani autonomy through what I will call 'sovereignty stakes'.

Two major issues demonstrated the tension between British policymakers' desire to maintain South Asia in a subordinate relationship and South Asian leaders' converse determination to capture full control of their states. First, the question of who would serve as Governor General in each state arose during the transfer of power negotiations. Second, India's intention to become a republic caused friction among Commonwealth members shortly after independence. These issues showed that Indian and Pakistani leaders were able to change and reinterpret the nature of the Commonwealth through their dealings with it. The new members, following the earlier example of the white Dominions, became part of a process of defining how far the Commonwealth would serve as a supra-state location of power.[42] Both Nehru and Jinnah pushed for greater autonomy and fuller sovereignty, pulling away from Britain's vision of the Commonwealth as a strong international system.

The tussle over who would replace the viceroy as the Crown's representative in the new Dominions demonstrated the tensions between state-building and Britain's retention of partial sovereignty in South Asia. Mountbatten made a bid for the post of Governor General in both states, on the basis that he could facilitate cooperation and induce restraint in each government's dealings with the other.[43] Nehru accepted Mountbatten as Governor General of India. In this role, Mountbatten claimed to have used his influence with Nehru to advocate a cool head in relation to the Kashmir conflict.[44] Mountbatten also influentially advised Nehru on cabinet reconstruction, economic policy and appointments of ambassadors and governors, often informally.[45] As the head of state, if not the head of government, Mountbatten's Governor Generalship was an important symbol of India's continuing association with Britain.

Jinnah, by contrast, was suspicious of the wide-ranging powers that a common Governor General would have. In particular, he feared the possibility that such an official might favour one Dominion over the other. He was also concerned with establishing a strong central government, and perceived the value of a Governor General wholly committed to Pakistan.[46] Jinnah therefore took the position himself. As Ayesha Jalal has argued, Jinnah's actions in the context of 'a fluid sovereignty' enabled him to stem the flow of power into outside hands.[47] Holding office only in India, Mountbatten's attempt to maintain a British stake across South Asia was only partly successful.

Nehru's administration, in a separate matter, also showed itself determined to set its own constitutional path. Congress also had a long-standing pledge to slough off India's constitutional subordination to the British Crown, dating from January 1947 (before independence).[48] But a Dominion that rejected the British monarch as its sovereign automatically left the Commonwealth, as had Burma in 1948. This meant that if the Indian parliament declared India to be a republic, in which sovereignty was vested in the people and not in King George VI, the country's Commonwealth membership would lapse. In London, Prime Minister Clement Attlee and Foreign Secretary Ernest Bevin were concerned that if India left the Commonwealth, Pakistan, Ceylon and Britain's other Asian colonies might follow. The white Dominions were split: New Zealand and Canada prioritized the association's cohesion over the extent of its membership, and opposed allowing a republic to be a member.[49] On the other hand the Australian Prime Minister, J.B. Chiefly, favoured retaining India as a member, since the latter was a valuable trading partner and sometime ally in Southeast Asian affairs.[50]

Pakistan and Ceylon had a rather different take on India's republicanism. They were mainly interested in the Commonwealth as a counterweight to India's regional dominance. Pakistan, with leaders especially hostile to India, posed a particular problem. Liaquat Ali Khan, Pakistan's Prime Minister, suggested that Pakistan would follow India into republicanism if that course turned out not to diminish the advantages available to member states. On the other hand, Sir Mohammed Zafrullah Khan, Pakistan's Foreign Minister, favoured retaining the Crown allegiance as a condition of membership, meaning that India ought to be ejected if it became a republic. The Prime Minister of Ceylon, D.S. Senanayake, also recommended that the Commonwealth insist on Crown allegiance.[51]

Eventually, the Commonwealth Prime Ministers agreed in April 1949 to compromise. India became a republic but continued to recognize the King as 'the symbol of the free association' of Commonwealth members. At the meeting, Nehru even convinced his fellow Prime Ministers to leave aside the issue of Cold War power-blocs – specifically, his refusal to form any strategic pacts or alliances geared towards containing communism – and secured room for an explicitly non-aligned India in the new Commonwealth. This occurred even before Nehru had helped crystallize a more formal non-aligned movement at the 1955 Bandung Conference, alongside Gamal Abdel Nasser of Egypt and Sukarno of Indonesia. The Commonwealth Prime Ministers' Conference in 1949 also agreed to refer, in future, to the 'Commonwealth of Nations' rather than the 'British Commonwealth'. Several leading British newspapers, namely the *Times*, *Guardian*, *Telegraph* and *Economist*, applauded the compromise formula.[52]

It went down less well in Pakistan. The Chiefs of the Imperial General Staff toured South and Southeast Asia in 1949 and reported that:

> In Pakistan ... the feeling is very strong indeed that we are at great pains to avoid doing anything which might hurt India's feelings, but that we are indifferent to the needs or the fate of Pakistan. This attitude, which is almost an obsession was brought to the fore by the decision at the Commonwealth Conference to allow India to remain in the Commonwealth as a Republic.[53]

They noted that the republic issue inflamed longer-running jealousies over Kashmir, which 'Prevent[ed] either country from looking further afield or giving any serious thought to defence planning on a worldwide basis'.[54] The Chiefs of Staff were primarily concerned with forming India and Pakistan into the cooperative bedrocks of a Middle East defence pact, geared towards preventing Soviet expansion into the oilfields of Iraq, Iran and the Gulf.[55] India–Pakistan tensions, in other words, scuppered London's plans for regional military coordination favouring Western interests. Individual nation-statehood therefore looked increasingly like the basis of political organization in South Asia. As nation states waxed, the Commonwealth waned. American policymakers, who had been banking on the Commonwealth as a bulwark against communism in South Asia, looked on with consternation. The following paragraphs outline the shift in American thinking that led to greater US intervention in the region.

The Commonwealth vs. the Cold War

The Commonwealth provided Britain with an intermediary relationship with South Asia between total independence and colonialism, and the United States was therefore willing for Britain to take the key role in the West's relationship with South Asia so long as the Commonwealth helped maintain Western interests, as defined by American policymakers. But once the Commonwealth proved unable to improve relations within South Asia, American officials were more willing to step in as a result of Cold War concerns. In so doing they responded to assertions of autonomy by South Asian leaders along the lines of those discussed in the previous section. At the same time, US voices provide an alternative perspective on the Commonwealth's continuing relationship with imperialism. Wm. Roger Louis and Ronald Robinson have highlighted tensions in 1950s Washington between the conflicting imperatives of supporting European imperial adventures, in the name of anti-communism, and seizing opportunities to incorporate decolonizing territories into a US-centred world system.[56] Under the pressures of Cold

War politics, hostility between India and Pakistan, coupled with American impatience with British leadership in the region, had the most damning implications for the Commonwealth's integrity as a power-bloc.

The Commonwealth's failure to intervene effectively in India–Pakistan hostilities over Kashmir first led American policymakers to become embroiled in subcontinental politics. Other South Asian conflagrations, such as Pakistan and Afghanistan's clash over sovereignty in Pakistan's northwestern tribal zone, exacerbated matters.[57] Existing scholarship has examined the intricacies of British and American policy towards South Asia during the late 1940s and the 1950s in relation to Cold War strategy. The role of the India–Pakistan territorial dispute over Kashmir has received particular attention.[58] Suffice to say, US policymakers feared that instability in Kashmir would drive either India or Pakistan, or both, to seek a closer relationship with the USSR in order to gain financial and military aid. The rest of this chapter will focus on Britain's loss of initiative to the US State Department in the West's South Asia relations. By effectively muscling Britain out of its historical position of paramount regional influence, the United States asserted its brand of bilateral alliances and treaty organizations at the expense of the Commonwealth's alternative model of affective relations and informal alignment.

It was not always thus. After the Second World War, European empires were still an important force in world politics. For the most part, the United States coexisted with them. Vigorous disagreements between British and American planners for the post-war world, lasting until 1945, had helped provoke British promises of progressive self-government in the colonies.[59] Britain's willingness to transfer power in India in 1947 satisfied Americans that the dissolution of the empire and the creation of a multiracial Commonwealth would, to quote Louis, 'provide the basis of a new order of stability and progress'.[60] As Indian and Pakistani independence began, then, the United States seemed poised to accept the Commonwealth as a peer. Citing limited resources and lack of South Asia expertise, the State Department left Britain to represent American ideological interests there.[61] In other geopolitical arenas, notably the Pacific, the United States was also content to let the Commonwealth combat communism.[62] The Marshall Plan era instead focused American attention on Western Europe, which not only was strategically important against the Soviet bloc, but also provided a valuable trading partner as American aid rebuilt the European economies. American policymakers were not concerned with upholding the Commonwealth *per se*, let alone protecting continued European imperial control over colonial possessions. But the spectre of Soviet influence throughout the Third World, and the reality of Soviet control over Eastern Europe, prompted an American reconsideration. The United States came to the aid of Britain and France in Southeast Asia once the Cold War intensified in 1947, helping prop up their empires.[63] By leaving South Asia as a British and Commonwealth sphere of influence, the United States accorded the Commonwealth tacit peer recognition, from one power to another.

State Department officials inaccurately viewed British influence and Commonwealth relations as virtually synonymous. A note addressed to the US Secretary of State in 1950, for example, suggested in the context of an upcoming Commonwealth conference in Colombo that 'the UK together with Canada may be able to provide the impetus to keep negotiations open and pave the way for some agreement' between India and Pakistan.[64] Accordingly, State Department officials consulted closely with their British counterparts on South Asian affairs between 1947 and 1951.[65] Reluctant US involvement in the Kashmir question resulted from its leading role in the UN Security Council, not strong American interest in the dispute.[66] The State Department still relied on Britain and the Commonwealth to take the leading role in Security Council debates and other UN efforts to bring about a Kashmir settlement.[67]

But the Commonwealth's prime position in South Asia slipped quickly at the beginning of the 1950s. The outbreak of the Korean War in late 1950 undermined US interests in East Asia. Involvement in the neighbouring South Asian region also became more attractive to American policymakers concerned with containing the Soviet Union and the People's Republic of China.[68] Before these events, the State Department had been reluctant to favour either India or Pakistan for fear of damaging relations with the other. Afterwards, US Cold War planners emphasized Pakistan's strategic geographical proximity to the Soviet Union.[69] Pakistani leaders' apparent willingness to join in with Western defence initiatives also contrasted with Nehru's insistence on non-alignment. Meanwhile, the Commonwealth Relations Office's attempt to walk the line between India and Pakistan over Kashmir appeared to yield little benefit. In a shifting geopolitical situation, US policymakers came to doubt the value of a partnership with Britain in the region. Most officials in the State Department considered the *Pax Britannica* to be spent as a real force, especially after the damage that Britain's disputes with Egypt and Iran did to its Middle Eastern prestige.[70] Indeed, Britain's performance in Middle East policy was, if anything, even more disastrous than its South Asia agenda.[71]

If Britain and the Commonwealth were not effective in managing South Asian affairs, Americans saw no reason to bow to them. A State Department assessment of the Commonwealth in relation to India–Pakistan problems in November 1950 was scathing. The report condemned the Commonwealth's role in managing regional relations. Writing about the Kashmir issue, the report claimed that:

> The dispute is in a very real sense a Commonwealth problem, but efforts at mediation by the Commonwealth have been unavailing and future efforts would seem to be undesirable. … It has been evident that the UK is unwilling to adopt any position which would in its opinion adversely affect its relations with India or Pakistan.[72]

Britain's efforts to maintain the middle ground in India–Pakistan disputes brought little thanks from Indian and Pakistani commentators, as the State Department well knew.[73] One American official wrote in January 1951 that 'UK leadership in South Asia has been so weak that the premises on which we based our agreement to UK leadership may now be open to some question'.[74]

State Department criticisms of Britain and the Commonwealth in South Asia also embodied a different vision than that of the Commonwealth of how the 'free world' ought to function. In early 1951, Donald Kennedy of the Office of South Asian Affairs was slated to visit London for talks with British officials. The visit provoked reflection within the State Department on the nature of American cooperation with Britain. Internal briefing notes emphasized the rivalry between a system based on American influence over a collection of mutually autonomous states and the Commonwealth's attempt to project British power, with its continuing colonial connotations. At least one paper emphasized the need to divorce American interventions from 'existing traces of colonialism' attached to the 'so-called Commonwealth mechanism'. At the same time, the writer concluded with some insight, the United States should think of Britain as an equal partner in the Commonwealth 'rather than as an imperial nation whose word is law among the other Commonwealth countries'.[75] Other briefing papers emphasized the desirability of a world where friendship and commerce between the 'the US and like-minded countries' who opposed communism transcended the relics of an imperial past.[76]

These briefing papers only represented one strain of thinking in the State Department. The overall trend in American policy circles remained deferential to British expertise on South Asia, and in practice, Kennedy took a softer line in London. A senior Foreign Office official reported that the talks confirmed that American and British approaches and objectives were similar.[77] British and American policymakers continued to liaise over India–Pakistan disputes throughout the 1950s.[78] Yet the frustration that American policymakers expressed with Commonwealth management of South Asian affairs, and the pressure that they themselves increasingly brought to bear on the problems, highlighted the weakness of the Commonwealth in dealing with violent disputes between members. From 1953, President Dwight D. Eisenhower's administration launched an intensified fight against worldwide communism, pushing the United States into a closer relationship with Pakistan, a key member of the Baghdad Pact.[79] The United States–Pakistan military alliance in 1954 marked American ascendency in the West's relationship with South Asia. It meant that any possibility that the Commonwealth could serve as an interstate alternative to Westphalian statehood in the region died alongside British regional influence.

Conclusion

In 1965, another war between India and Pakistan brought the Commonwealth's apparent influence in South Asia to a new low. Afterwards, Indian parliamentarians, disgruntled that Britain had failed to support the country's cause against Pakistan, debated leaving the Commonwealth. Diplomatic circles reverberated. The Indian High Commissioner in Colombo, K.C. Nair, talked with his fellow High Commissioners from Australia and Canada about strained Commonwealth relations. The Australian and Canadian emissaries objected to the way that Indian politicians were framing the nature of Commonwealth membership, Nair wrote. Why, they asked, did the debates in the Indian parliament portray Commonwealth membership as pertaining first and foremost to India's relationship with Britain? In their view, all members of the association were free and equal. A breach in India's diplomatic relationship with Britain should, on that basis, be irrelevant to India's participation in the Commonwealth. One of the High Commissioners suggested that instead of India leaving, the other members should expel Britain. The High Commissioner, Nair thought, was only half-joking.[80] In the end, India stayed in.

This snapshot from the mid-1960s offers a tantalizing glimpse of a possible world in which the Commonwealth lived up to its rhetoric of freedom and equality among peers – to the logical conclusion that Britain was not an essential part of the association. But, as the events discussed in this chapter demonstrate, the Commonwealth's relationship with decolonizing South Asia revolved around Britain's interactions with India and Pakistan. These interactions quickly turned sour. By 1951, just four years after independence came to South Asia, Britain had lost a considerable degree of goodwill from India, Pakistan and the United States due to its mismanagement of South Asian affairs within a Commonwealth framework. Without such goodwill, Britain struggled to take a leading role in the region, despite the continued presence of British personnel in South Asian military and administrative forces.[81]

Challenges to the Commonwealth also came from the United States. In Washington, thinking in the State Department already was moving towards a degree of intervention in the subcontinent that would displace the Commonwealth as a major influence. The Truman administration increasingly leaned towards a strategic rationale for a military relationship between the United States and Pakistan between 1951 and 1953. On the other side of the partition boundary, the arrival of Chester Bowles as the US Ambassador to India in October 1951 helped thaw the icy relationship that had developed between the American and Indian governments.[82] American disillusionment with the British agenda for the Commonwealth, especially what American officials perceived as Britain's preference for ineffectively appeasing Indian and Pakistani demands, rather than taking assertive action to quash potential communist influence, spurred them to a more direct approach.

Even earlier, political pressures in India and Pakistan had been building towards greater autonomy and state-building along Westphalian lines. Such pressures arose in great part from nationalist ambitions that pre-dated independence. Jinnah's assumption of Pakistan's Governor Generalship and India's choice of a republican constitution demonstrated determination in Karachi and New Delhi to uphold the logic of anti-colonial freedom movements. While Jinnah used his positive disposition towards the Commonwealth to try to tempt concessions from Mountbatten during the independence negotiations, he had no intention of encouraging the British government to retain any more power in Pakistan than the lack of personnel in the central government and armed forces made necessary. Nehru, for his part, was equally determined that India should move towards a regional leadership role with a president, not the British monarch, as the symbol of the Indian nation. At the same time, both countries were disappointed by the Commonwealth's failure to back their position comprehensively in bilateral disputes. That nothing in the Commonwealth's make-up gave it any power to compel India and Pakistan to resolve their differences showed that the strengths of Britain's relations with the white Dominions (mutual understanding without formal rules) were the association's undoing in terms of gaining real influence in South Asia.

This chapter has, however, emphasized that India's and Pakistan's status as fully independent nation-states was far from settled during the early days of decolonization. To overlook this would fail to do justice to Britain's attempt to retain influence in South Asia. Despite close collaboration at times, Britain and the United States competed to incorporate India and Pakistan into rival models of cooperation between distinct political-territorial-administrative units. From an American point of view, these units were nation-states. From the point of view of Britain, which was still an imperial power in Africa and the Middle East, Dominion status and the Commonwealth offered an alternative middle ground to the hard distinction between colony and nation. It was Indian and Pakistani decision-making that substantially erased that middle ground and privileged territorial state sovereignty.

The late 1940s and the early 1950s were thus a moment in which the seemingly irresistible rise of the singular nation state as the chief actor in global history, which classical international relations theory posits as natural, was anything but. Like imperial reconfigurations in Africa, the Middle East and Southeast Asia, the Commonwealth in India and Pakistan constituted an alternative mode of international politics. Understanding the early years of South Asian independence within this framework allows us to place it in the longer historical perspective of changes in the global political system throughout the twentieth century. Dominion status for India and Pakistan followed on from self-government for the white colonies around the turn of the century. Briefly, it interposed before Cold War power-bloc politicking ensured that the separation between individual nation-states in the developing world would form the framework for American hegemony. This chapter's contribution has been to confirm the dislodging of the ahistorical narrative of the rise of nation-statehood in international relations, even in the seemingly straightforward field of constitutional arrangements, international disputes and Cold War strategy. Instead, as its conclusions suggest, scholars must be open to perceiving the varied forms that political authority has taken in different parts of the world, and at different moments in history.

Notes

1 (2007), 'Beginnings', *The Story of India*, BBC Two.

2 Chatterjee, Partha (1993), *The Nation and its Fragments: Colonial and Postcolonial Histories.* Princeton: Princeton University Press; Khan, Yasmin (2007), *The Great Partition: The Making of India and Pakistan.* New Haven: Yale University Press. On the impact of Cold War politics on India and Pakistan, see McMahon, Robert (1994), *The Cold War on the Periphery: The United States, India, and Pakistan.* New York: Colombia University Press.

3 Jalal, Ayesha (1985a). *The Sole Spokesman: Jinnah, the Muslim League and the Demand for Pakistan.* Cambridge: Cambridge University Press; Chatterjee, Partha (1986), *Nationalist Thought and the Colonial World: A Derivative Discourse?* London: Zed for the United Nations University.

4 Collins, Michael (2013), 'Decolonisation and the "federal moment"', *Diplomacy & Statecraft*, 24(1), 21–40.

5 See especially Agnew, John (1994), 'The territorial trap: The geographical assumptions of international relations theory', *Review of International Political Economy*, 1(1), 53–80; Ruggie, J.G. (1993), 'Territoriality and beyond: Problematizing modernity in international relations', *International Organization*, 47(1), 139–174.

6 Darwin, John (2011), *The Empire Project: The Rise and Fall of the British World-System, 1830–1970*. Cambridge: Cambridge University Press.

7 Louis, Wm. Roger and Robinson, Ronald (1994), 'The Imperialism of Decolonization', *The Journal of Imperial and Commonwealth History*, 22(3), 462–511.

8 Louis and Robinson (1994); Hopkins, Anthony (2008), 'Rethinking decolonization', *Past & Present*, 200, 211–247; Connelly, Matthew (2002), *A Diplomatic Revolution: Algeria's Fight For Independence and the Origins of the Post-Cold War Era*. Oxford: Oxford University Press.

9 Gallagher, John and Robinson, Ronald (1953), 'The imperialism of free trade', *The Economic History Review*, New Series, 6(1), 1–15.

10 Louis, Wm. Roger (1971), *British Strategy in the Far East 1919–1939*. Oxford: Clarendon Press, 19–49.

11 Pedersen, Susan (2007), 'Back to the League of Nations', *American Historical Review*, 114(4), 1091–1117, p. 1099.

12 Agnew, John and Corbridge, Stuart (1995), *Mastering Space: Hegemony, Territory and International Political Economy*. London: Routledge, 20–39.

13 Westad, Odd Arne (2007), *The Global Cold War: Third World Interventions and the Making of Our Times*. Cambridge: Cambridge University Press.

14 Louis, Wm. Roger (2006), 'Suez and decolonization: Scrambling out of Africa and Asia', in *Ends of British Imperialism: The Scramble for Empire, Suez and Decolonization: Collected Essays*. London: IB Tauris, 27.

15 Murphy, Philip (2006), ' "Government by Blackmail": The origins of the Central African Federation reconsidered', in Martin Lynn (ed.) (2006), *The British Empire in the 1950s: Retreat or Revival?* Basingstoke: Palgrave MacMillan; Collins (2013).

16 Louis (1986), 267.

17 Nadis, M. (1970), *The Second British Empire 1783–1965: A Short History*. Reading, Mass.: Addison-Wesley, 214.

18 Agnew, J. (2005), 'Sovereignty regimes: Territoriality and state authority in contemporary world politics', *Annals of the Association of American Geographers*, 95(2), 437–461.

19 Singh, Anita Inder (1985), 'Keeping India in the Commonwealth: British political and military aims, 1947–49', *Journal of Contemporary History*, 20(3), 469–481, p. 470.

20 Collins (2013), 23–24.

21 Moore, R.J. (1987), *Making the New Commonwealth*. Oxford: Clarendon Press, ch. 1.

22 British women marrying 'alien' men lost their British nationality, while non-British women marrying British men automatically acquired it. Paul, Kathleen (1995), ' "British subjects" and "British stock": Labour's postwar imperialism', *Journal of British Studies* 34(2), 233–276, pp. 237–242.

23 US Embassy London to Secretary of State, 30 July 1951, 'India-Pakistan, May-July 1951', Box 230, A2600, RG 84, US National Archives II, College Park (NARA).

24 Wade, William W. (1949), 'India and the Commonwealth', *Foreign Policy Reports*, 25(7), 88.

25 McLean, David (2001), 'Australia in the Cold War: A historiographical review', *The International History Review*, 23(2), 299–321, p. 306.

26 Devereux, David R. (1989), 'Britain, the Commonwealth and the defence of the Middle East 1948–56', *Journal of Contemporary History*, 24(2), 327–345, p. 331.

27 Lord Saint Brides (1986), 'Britain, the United States, and South Asia', in Wm. Roger Louis and Hedley Bull (eds.) (1986), *The 'Special Relationship': Anglo-American Relations Since 1945*. Oxford: Clarendon Press, 295. Saint Brides was British High Commissioner in Pakistan 1961–1966 and in India 1968–1971.

28 'Draft brief on Item VI of Agenda for US-UK talks', 1 February 1951, DO 35/3055, no. 12, United Kingdom National Archives, Kew (TNA). On the Middle East in British imperial policy after the Second World War, see Louis (2006).

29 Singh, Anita Inder (1992), 'Divergent world-views, divergent strategies: How America took Britain's place in Pakistan, 1947–54', *Contemporary Record*, 6(3), 474–496, p. 478.

30 'Minutes of Viceroy's Twenty Fourth Staff Meeting', 1 May 1947, in Nicholas Mansergh and Penderel Moon (eds.) (1981), *The Transfer of Power Documents: Volume X: The Mountbatten Viceroyalty: Formulation of a plan 22 March – 30 May 1947*. London: HM Stationery Office, no. 272.

31 Kumarasingham, Harshan (2013), 'The "Tropical Dominions": The appeal of Dominion status in the decolonisation of India, Pakistan and Ceylon', *Transactions of the Royal Historical Society*, 23, 223–245, pp. 232–233.

32 Smith, Tony (1978), 'A comparative study of French and British decolonization', *Comparative Studies in Society and History*, 20(1), 70–102, pp. 74–76.

33 Grierson, E. (1972), *The Imperial Dream: The British Commonwealth and Empire 1775–1969*. London: Collins, 252.

34 Bridge, Carl (1986), *Holding India to the Empire: The British Conservative Party and the 1935 Constitution*. London: Oriental University Press; Muldoon, Andrew (2009), *Empire, Politics and the Creation of the 1935 India Act: Last Act of the Raj*. Farnham: Ashgate.

35 UK High Commissioner in Pakistan to CRO, Opdom 2, 25 January 1950, FO 371/84198, TNA; 'Brief for talks with Mr McGhee', 1 February 1951, DO 35/3055, no. 14, TNA; Report of the High Commissioner for India in Pakistan for the second half of November 1952, 3 December 1952, File 45/R&I/52, Ministry of External Affairs, Historical Division (R&I Section), National Archives of India, New Delhi (NAI).

36 Moore (1987), 7–17.

37 Kumarasingham (2013), 233.

38 Ahmed, Y. Rafeek (1991), 'India's membership of the Commonwealth – Nehru's role', *Indian Journal of Political Science*, 52(1), 43–53.

39 Cox, Michael (1990), 'From the Truman Doctrine to the second superpower détente: The rise and fall of the Cold War', *Journal of Peace Research*, 27(1), 25–41, pp. 30–31.

40 Fieldhouse, D.K. (1966), *The Colonial Empires*. Cited in Grierson (1972), 296.

41 Agnew (2005), 437.

42 Thornton, A.P. (1986), 'The Transformation of the Commonwealth and the "Special Relationship"', in Louis and Bull (1986), 367.

43 Jalal, Ayesha (1985b), 'Inheriting the Raj: Jinnah and the governor-generalship issue', *Modern Asian Studies* 19(1), 29–53, p. 29.

44 'The Governor General's personal report no. 3 [sic: in fact it's no. 8]', 3 February 1948, Mss Eur D714/86, India Office Library, London (IOL).

45 Kumarasingham, Harshan (2010), 'The Indian version of first among equals – executive power during the first decade of independence', *Modern Asian Studies* 44(4), 709–751, pp. 728–732.

46 Jalal (1985b), 48–50.

47 Jalal (1985b), 53.

48 Kumarasingham (2013), 232.

49 Darwin (2011), 550–554.

50 Moore (1987), 172–177.

51 Moore (1987), 180–181.

52 Moore (1987), 190–195.

53 Chiefs of Imperial General Staff tour notes on South East Asia with special reference to Malaya, November 1949, File 'Note on tour of South East Asia, October 1949: India/Pakistan', part I, FO 371/76053, TNA.

54 Chiefs of Imperial General Staff tour notes on South East Asia with special reference to Malaya, November 1949, File 'Note on tour of South East Asia, October 1949: India/Pakistan', part I, FO 371/76053, TNA.

55 Singh (1992).

56 Louis and Robinson (1994), 21.

57 Leake, Elisabeth (2013), 'The Great Game anew: US Cold-War policy and Pakistan's North-West Frontier, 1947–65', *The International History Review*, 35(4), 783–806.

58 McMahon (1994); Panigrahi, D.N. (2009), *Jammu and Kashmir, the Cold War and the West*. New Delhi: Routledge.

59 Louis, Wm. (1977 edn.), *Imperialism at Bay: The United States and the Decolonization of the British Empire, 1941–1945*. Oxford: Clarendon, 496–547.

60 Louis, Wm. Roger (1986), 'American anti-colonialism and the dissolution of the British Empire', in Louis and Bull (1986), 267.

61 Hagerty, Devin T. (2003), 'US Policy and the Kashmir dispute: Prospects for resolution', in Sumit Ganguly (ed.), *The Kashmir Question: Retrospect and Prospect*. London: Frank Cass, 95; Dasgupta, C. (2002), *War and Diplomacy in Kashmir 1947–48*. New Delhi: Sage, 10.

62 Miller, J.D.B. (1986), 'The "Special Relationship" in the Pacific', in Louis and Bull (1986), 383–384.

63 Louis and Robinson (1994), 468.

64 George McGhee and Mr. Hickerson to Secretary of State, 6 January 1950, CDF 690D.91/1–650, RG 59, NARA.

65 US Embassy London to Loy Henderson, 10 March 1948, CDF 745.45F/3–1048, RG 59, NARA; US Embassy London to Secretary of State, 18 March 1948, CDF 745.45F/3–1848, RG 59, NARA; US Embassy London to Secretary of State, 12 May 1948, CDF 745.45F/5–1248, RG 59, NARA.

66 Acting Secretary of State to Embassy in India, 31 December 1947, in Office of the Historian (1972), *Foreign Relations of the United States, 1947*. Vol. 3. Washington: US Government Printing Office, 192–193.

67 Williams, W.S.L., SOA Office Memorandum, 11 October 1950, CDF 690D.91/10–1150, RG 59, NARA.

68 Leake (2013).

69 McMahon (1994), 123.

70 Louis (1986), 281; McMahon, (1994), 152.

71 Louis, Wm. Roger (1984), *The British Empire in the Middle East 1945–1951: Arab Nationalism, the United States, and Postwar Imperialism*. Oxford: Clarendon Press, 738.

72 'Examination of the Frictions and Tensions of the Region', notes for the South Asian Regional Conference, February–March 1951, 'SOA Regional Conference Documents, Set 1, Folder 1', Box 4, 57D462, RG 59, NARA.

73 UK High Commissioner in Pakistan to CRO, Opdom 1, part II, 24 December 1949 to 6 January 1950, FO 371/84198, TNA; State Department Memorandum of Conversation, 'Reported Pak withdrawal from British Commonwealth', 8 November 1956, 'UK & Commonwealth, Relations', Box 11, NND 1305, RG 59, NARA.

74 'Possible US and/or UK Action to Bring About Ind-Pak Rapprochement', 30 January 1951, 'Mr Kennedy London Talks, February 1951', Box 3, 57D373, RG 59, NARA.

75 'International Position of South Asian Countries', February 1951, 'Mr Kennedy London Talks, February 1951', Box 3, 57D373, RG 59, NARA.

76 'Review of US and UK Objectives with Respect to South Asia', February 1951, 'Mr Kennedy London Talks, February 1951', Box 3, 57D373, RG 59, NARA.

77 S.J.L. Olver, Foreign Office, to UK Ambassador in Washington, DC, 21 February 1951, no. 15, DO 35/3055, TNA.

78 State Department to US Embassies, London and New Delhi, 18 July 1951, CDF 690D.91/7–1851, RG 59, NARA; Assistant Secretary Allen, NEA, to Under Secretary, State Department, CDF 690D.91322/3–23856, RG 59, NARA.

79 Panigrahi (2009), 122.

80 K.C. Nair, Indian High Commissioner in Ceylon, to K.M. Kannampilly, Joint Secretary, Indian Ministry of External Affairs, 29 November 1965, File 125(39)-S II, 1964, Ministry of External Affairs, Southern Division, no. 24, NAI.

81 Ansari, Sarah (2014), ' "The curious case of Sir Gilbert Grace": Police, corruption and provincial loyalties in 1950s Karachi'. *South Asian History and Culture* 5(1), 54–74.

82 McMahon (1994), 112.

Key texts

Agnew, John. (1994). 'The territorial trap: The geographical assumptions of international relations theory', *Review of International Political Economy*, 1(1), 53–80.

Agnew, John and Corbridge, Stuart. (1995). *Mastering Space: Hegemony, Territory and International Political Economy*. London: Routledge.

Darwin, John. (2011). *The Empire Project: The Rise and Fall of the British World-System, 1830–1970*. Cambridge: Cambridge University Press.

Hopkins, Anthony. (2008). 'Rethinking decolonization', *Past & Present*, 200, 211–247.

Moore, R.J. (1987). *Making the New Commonwealth*. Oxford: Clarendon Press.

Singh, Anita Inder. (1993). *The Limits of British Influence: South Asia and the Anglo-American Relationship*. London: Pinter.

CHAPTER 10
SOVEREIGNTY IN THE CONGO CRISIS
Ryan M. Irwin

On 5 July 1960, only five days after the Congo's independence, the commanding general of the newly formed Congolese national army, Emile Janssens, called a meeting with his non-commissioned officers in Leopoldville to discuss signs of indiscipline he had detected among his African soldiers. Born in Belgium in 1902, Janssens was a blunt and outspoken man, unaccustomed to diluting his words with tact or diplomacy, and he seemed to possess an iron-clad hold on the Congo's emerging military establishment. The general strode into the room, with nearly 200 non-coms standing stiffly at attention, walked to the blackboard and wrote AFTER INDEPENDENCE = BEFORE INDEPENDENCE. That afternoon, the first instance of outright disobedience against European officers began, and by the evening a full-scale mutiny was on. In the subsequent weeks, the Congo spiralled out of control, reaching a nadir at the end of the year with the arrest and then murder of the country's first African prime minister, Patrice Lumumba.[1]

Making sense of the Congo's independence is difficult. A dizzying number of individuals, organizations and states came together in central Africa during the early 1960s, each with a distinct perspective and strategy. The Congo was simultaneously a hotbed of inter-African intrigue, a playground for the superpowers and a turning point in the decolonization process. This chapter does not try to tackle the full complexity of Congolese independence.[2] It looks instead at a fork in the road in 1960, when the situation was at its most fluid, and it raises a question that strikes to the heart of the negotiated nature of postcolonial independence in Africa: How should historians think about the Katanga province's failed secession from the Congo?

The move inaugurated an ambiguous period in global history. Initiated under the leadership of Moïse Tshombe just days after the mutiny of Congo's national army, the secession triggered the so-called 'Congo crisis', shorthand for the six-year power struggle that preceded Joseph Mobutu's rise to power in 1966. Tshombe's declaration of independence not only prompted the largest UN intervention to that date – surpassed only in the 1990s – but also triggered a wider debate about the meaning of sovereignty after decolonization. This chapter explores a trio of questions: what was the case for Katangan statehood? How did the Cold War affect Congolese sovereignty? And finally, how did the ensuing crisis change the international community? An array of core concepts, sovereignty included, carried unsettled, negotiated, definitions in the years that surrounded African decolonization. Tshombe and Lumumba articulated their claims in ways that revealed some of the origins and implications of these underlying ambiguities. Looking at the Congo story highlights useful tensions, as well as the unusual role – intellectually and politically – played by the superpowers as each fought to consolidate and extend its influence at the Cold War's midpoint.

Irreconcilable differences?

So, first: Was there ever a legitimate case for Katangan statehood? Conventional wisdom says no: that Tshombe was merely a stooge of Belgian mining interests whose power stemmed from his willingness to pass along Katanga's riches to neocolonial overseers. Any argument to the contrary faces a daunting set of macroeconomic statistics. For instance, the Katanga region was always the richest province of the Belgian Congo; it provided 65 per cent of the colony's exports on the eve of independence. Katanga's principal mining company, Union Minière du Haut-Katanga, was the world's foremost supplier of cobalt and uranium and a major force on the copper and tin markets, and taxes on the company's profits covered one-third of the colony's budget in the mid-1950s.[3] This sort of operation, which required foreign expertise, led to European settlement, and about a third of all non-Africans in the Congo could be found in Katanga. The province's African population, estimated to be 1.5 million in the mid-1950s, was the smallest of any Belgian province, meaning that the ratio of Europeans to Africans was about one to fifty, a sharp contrast to the situation elsewhere in the Congo, where that ratio was closer to one to 140.[4] Looking back on Katanga's secession in 1962, journalist Collin Gonze wrote, 'Company directors ... might have adjusted to [Congolese independence] and continued business as usual', but 'they chose, instead, to think of Leopoldville control as a threat to their existence', hence the Katanga secession.[5] Unthinkable, in the face of this much money and these many Europeans, was that Tshombe might act independently of Union Minière.

Up-close, the situation was less straightforward. Like many corporations that relied on native labour, Union Minière had undercut African activism by importing its workforce from different parts of the continent, which made exploitation easier by ensuring that the individuals in Union Minière's mineshafts rarely shared the same language or self-understanding.[6] 'Indirect rule' was the name Frederick Lugard gave to this style of governance in British colonial Africa, and it arguably worked for a time in Belgian Congo as well.[7] However, after a series of strikes in the 1940s, Union Minière had moved to 'stabilize' the situation by encouraging its migrant workers to settle down and establish roots in local communities, amongst the Lunda, Luba or Sanga peoples.[8] The result was more bureaucracy and more unrest. Discontent rarely centred on abstractions such as colonialism: Katangan politics was about immigration and power. In Elisabethville, for instance, the Sanga, who saw themselves as the area's original inhabitants, insisted on exclusive control of Belgium's local administrative offices on the grounds that their new neighbours – the Kasai and Chokwe, hailing from central Congo and Angola, respectively – should acknowledge Sanga suzerainty. Convinced that migrant communities made infinitely better colonial surrogates, the Belgians went in the opposite direction, effectively putting Kasai and Chokwe évolués at the helm of urban management and land reform in 1957. Debate in Katanga on the eve of decolonization focused not on Union Minière's existence, but on the distribution of patronage among the growing number of people who now claimed the province as their home.[9]

Tshombe emerged from this milieu. His rapid rise stemmed, in part, from his argument that Katanga's original inhabitants were being disenfranchised by Belgium's newly 'stabilized' approach to government. It was a simple take on a complex issue, but he was not entirely incorrect. Tshombe's political party, the Confederation de Associations Tribales du Katanga (CONAKAT), was formed in 1958, the same year as Lumumba's Mouvement National Congolais (MNC), and it cultivated an alternative to Congolese nationalism that was grounded in regional politics and ethnic consciousness. The organization was more than a puppet of Union Minière; CONAKAT first and foremost was an alliance of the Lunda, Luba and Sanga against the Chokwe, Kasai and their perceived supporters, especially in the local Balubas community.[10] For Tshombe, the issue at hand was not the existence of Belgians in central Africa; it was the nature of representative government in an age of rapid demographic and political change. His understanding of Katangan sovereignty, and Belgium's future in the Congo basin more broadly, was linked to infighting about who controlled the province's newly created administrative offices. From the very beginning, Belgian decolonization was not an end in itself, but a way to put local administrative jobs in the hands of CONAKAT's supporters.[11]

At the heart of the secession crisis, then, was a quintessentially postcolonial problem: the relationship of borders to people. In the Congo, as in many communities across Africa during the mid-twentieth century, the line that separated the colonizer from the colonized was somewhat clearer at the level of officialdom than on the ground, where Europeans often projected their authority through surrogates, and Africans experienced colonialism through land reform, gender norms and migrant labour policies.[12] As momentum grew in 1959 for Congolese independence, debate erupted about the contours of Congo's postcolonial national state. Educated by Methodist missionaries from the American south, Tshombe couched his viewpoint in early American history and began to advocate for a federal government of autonomous, sovereign states, not unlike America's Articles of Confederation.[13] Territorial boundaries, he argued, were best determined by shared language, history and kinship. While Tshombe accepted aspects of pan-Africanism, especially its rejection of white paternalism and celebration of blackness, he was always sceptical of the MNC's unity plan and hostile towards the claim that the peoples within Belgium's Congo colony constituted a coherent African nation. His protests grew louder during mid-1960, when Lumumba, who hailed from the Kasai region and likely knew migrant workers who had travelled to work in Katanga's mines, sidelined him (and others) during the final negotiations over the Congo's new government. Going into the Roundtable Conference of early 1960, where Belgians officially accepted Congolese decolonization, Tshombe wrongly had assumed that his political support within Katanga would give him leverage at the negotiating table. Katanga, in theory, would emerge as the Virginia of a Congolese federation: strong, independent and influential. However, as the Belgians accelerated their timetable for withdrawal that summer, MNC officials quietly emptied the provincial government's bank account in Katanga, centralizing control of the region's resources in Leopoldville, while curtailing CONAKAT's influence in Lumumba's emerging governing coalition.[14] Decolonization, when it came that June, did the exact opposite of what Tshombe hoped. Rather than enhancing the prestige of the Lunda, Luba and Sanga, independence eroded CONAKAT's influence and placed 'foreign' Africans, or Lumumba's supporters, at the helm of Katanga's economy and government.

Tshombe's subsequent argument – that incorporation into the Congo was a greater threat to CONAKAT's supporters than collaboration with Belgium – raised deeper questions about the nature and meaning of decolonization. Did ethnic groups have the right to control their perceived homelands, or had Union Minière's labour policies muddled such a supposition? More pointedly, was it possible for a leader of African descent to credibly demand freedom *from* an African nationalist like Lumumba?[15] Tshombe's answers put him at odds with other Congolese leaders and highlighted tensions that quietly undergirded the international rhetoric about decolonization in 1960. Consider the Afro-Asian bloc's famous 'decolonization declaration' at the United Nations that year, which lambasted discrimination and framed colonialism as an obstacle to economic cooperation, celebrating the premise that local people could attain freedom only if they controlled their natural resources.[16] Katanga's secession challenged this formula by upending the implicit binary between freedom and colonialism. Here was an articulate and politicized movement, led by a well-connected, charismatic politician, which claimed that anti-colonialism, as deployed by Lumumba, was preventing the Katangan people, as defined by CONAKAT, from enjoying the fruits of their sovereignty. For Tshombe, everything turned on the meaning of self-rule, which he equated with control of the administrative posts created in the late 1950s and, by extension, the tax revenue that came from economic activity on land 'belonging' to the Lunda, Luba and Sanga. By defining peoplehood and territory so narrowly, Tshombe was implicitly challenging the idea that colonialism was the principle threat to African freedom. Centralization, regardless of its justification, was the problem, making the question of who owned Katanga's mines irrelevant; what mattered was who benefited from their operation.[17]

This claim was not articulated in a vacuum. While Tshombe reached out to Western capitalists, going so far as to create a public relations firm in Geneva to highlight Katanga's potential as a trade partner (at a price), Lumumba blamed the Congolese mutiny and ensuing deaths on European imperialists. For Lumumba, Tshombe's understanding of sovereignty, tethered so closely to local issues and modelled on early American history, failed to grasp migrant labour's political purpose within Belgium's imperial system and the way Europeans had exploited African ethnic identity. 'I don't know how the United States is organized', Lumumba lamented in early 1960. What mattered was that the 'riches of the Congo [were] a common patrimony' to be distributed by a unitary, centralized government.[18] The common experience of Belgian rule, not language or kinship, defined Congolese peoplehood, according to Lumumba, and any revision of the Congo colony's borders would erode the territory's influence in the postcolonial era.

Since political power required centralization, it followed that 'the time-honored weapon' of 'divide and rule' constituted the main barrier to 'genuine liberation' in central Africa, which, in turn, was tacitly measured by the MNC's control of the bureaucracies that managed affairs within the Congo.[19] Katanga's bid for self-rule, in Lumumba's mind, was more than just a blow to the idea of a singular Congolese national economy; it marked the opening gambit in the recolonization of his country. 'The gist of the matter is that the imperialists want to lay their hands on our country's riches and to continue exploiting our people', he argued in July 1960. 'Tshombe, in particular, is an agent of the Belgian imperialists. Everything he says and writes is not his own. He merely mouths the words of the Belgian colonialists.'[20] Tshombe had few qualms about using Belgians to advance CONAKAT's goals.[21] Yet, by dismissing his rival as an imperialist puppet, warning of a monolithic colonialism while downplaying the localized nature of Tshombe's message, Lumumba distracted attention from the harder questions that CONAKAT was asking: Who constituted 'our people', and why did the MNC have sole authority over Katanga and its projected tax revenue?

To outside observers, these were tough, familiar questions. Nationalists across the African continent were grappling with the fact that people came to decolonization with different expectations and goals in the late 1950s, and with so many African leaders struggling to come to terms with their own postcolonial borders (and the restless populations therein), it is not difficult to see why Lumumba had wide support among African leaders who expressed pan-African sympathies. His was a view that resonated with anyone struggling with the challenges of establishing a governing coalition that overcame regionalism.[22] This general sympathy was enhanced by Lumumba's relationships with Kwame Nkrumah and Ahmed Sékou Touré, leaders of Ghana and Guinea, respectively. Lumumba had attended Nkrumah's 1958 All-African People's Conference in Accra, and both Nkrumah and Touré saw him as the key to ensuring that Africa's largest country embraced their plan for continental unity after independence. In 1960 Lumumba went so far as to sign a secret protocol with Nkrumah that outlined the contours of a Congo-Ghana union, which would establish an embryonic United States of Africa.[23] The Congo's prime minister may have had little sense of American history, but his Ghanaian counterpart had been educated at Lincoln University and drew explicit analogies between the Congo's future and the United States' past. Unlike Tshombe, however, Nkrumah saw American history through the prism of his alma mater's namesake. Although it had taken time, US leaders had moved 'beyond the petty wranglings of the separate states and created a Union', Nkrumah extolled in late 1960. In an age of rapid industrialism, Africa needed a similarly 'strong political union' that could 'bring about full and effective development' of the continent's resources.[24]

Looking glass

The United States' place in this debate segues to a second question: How did the Cold War affect Congolese sovereignty? The Soviet Union's motivations were fairly straightforward.

In the three years before the Congo's independence, Nikita Khrushchev's government had successfully established contact with Ghana, Guinea and Mali as part of a wider outreach initiative – stretching from South Asia to the Caribbean – and the Congo was an obvious target for Soviet patronage: it was large, strategically located and replete with mineral riches. We know now that Moscow established backchannel relations with Lumumba in mid-1959, and while Lumumba was neither communist nor Marxist, he never waivered in his support of import-substituting industrialization, on the premise that widespread industrialization could come through planning and centralization, and loudly promised that the destruction of 'foreign monopolies' would enhance postcolonial Congo's control over trade, thereby providing the Congolese people with real independence.[25] This was music to any Marxist's ears, and as Katanga slipped from the prime minister's grasp in July 1960, Khrushchev indulged his opportunistic side, announcing that summer that Moscow would give direct support to Lumumba if the international community failed to stop the 'imperialist aggression against the Republic of Congo'.[26] For Moscow, the Congo's problems had nothing to do with local politics in Katanga; everything turned on Leopoldville's control of the national economy.

We also know now that the Soviet Union was not as powerful as it seemed to some observers in the early 1960s. Moscow's nuclear arsenal made it a de facto superpower, but stripped of these weapons, the country was essentially a middle-income power directing an unsustainable portion of its natural and economic resources to compete with a rival that was always richer, more influential and more technologically vibrant. Diplomatically, the 1956 Hungary uprising had spoiled Khrushchev's fleeting détente with the United States, and by 1960 Mao Zedong was openly challenging the Soviet Union's legitimacy and leadership within the communist world. Moreover, India, Indonesia, Egypt and Iraq, despite their willingness to drain Moscow's coffers, had proved unpredictable allies, leaving Khrushchev desperate to score some sort of diplomatic victory as African decolonization accelerated.[27] Historians rightly observe that unlike the United States, where the CIA seemed to plot against any foreign official who defied US power, the Soviet Union never contemplated killing Tshombe or any other leader of a pro-Western developing country.[28] However, this lack of initiative had as much to do with Moscow's paltry capacities abroad as the moral rectitude of its leaders. The Soviet Union arguably lacked the military instruments to end Tshombe's secession, leaving Khrushchev's bellicosity as Moscow's principal diplomatic weapon.

American officials approached the Congo crisis from a wholly different vantage point. President Dwight D. Eisenhower's first response to the secession was to underscore that while Washington would 'do its duty through the UN', any sort of 'unilateral action' was out of the question.[29] The wiser course was to replicate the 1956 Suez mission, when a multi-country UN coalition had successfully restored order and pushed the Israelis out of Egypt. Washington's primary aim was to get the Belgians out and the United Nations in. The Cold War undoubtedly animated the president's thinking, especially at the tactical level. If the 'Soviets tried to send in combat forces *without* a UN request', he explained in 1960, the United States would simply have the Secretariat 'say that no troops other than those requested by the United Nations [are] allowed to come in'.[30] This was the essence of containment: the United States would remain on the sidelines, but so too would the Soviet Union. Yet, strategically, Eisenhower's invocation of the United Nations hinted at a deeper set of objectives. Questions about the Congo's national economy, and about the issues that pitted Lumumba against Tshombe, barely registered behind closed doors in Washington in 1960. If Tshombe approached sovereignty through the prism of local governance and Lumumba sought freedom through centralization, US policymakers tended to nudge both sides in a different direction. For Washington, sovereignty – in the Congo and beyond – conferred not freedom from the international community but the right to obey international law and disagree at the General Assembly. From the very beginning, American officials were more focused on the location of the Congo crisis than the ideas that separated the antagonists.[31]

US leaders saw the Congo crisis through the prism of liberal internationalism. In an era of growing 'mutual involvement', where Washington determined land and budget reforms in other countries and leaders abroad lamented US racial policies, the United Nations served as 'a school for political responsibility', a State Department official explained in a paper that year. The United Nation's 'monopoly channel of involvement' kept Soviet and American soldiers on the sidelines together, but there was little doubt, in Washington at least, that the organization was an instrument of US soft power. 'The words, the concepts and the principles that we are heir to are natural to mankind', the paper explained. 'It is therefore natural that when broad, internationally-agreed concepts are developed' – concepts like sovereignty – 'they tend to be congenial to us and to our traditions'.[32] John Foster Dulles was more direct in a speech before his death in 1959, when he argued explicitly that international law – as defined by the International Court and applied to UN members – was the best response to decolonization. Once sovereign states took a seat at the United Nations, this law would theoretically promulgate a form of independence that was wholly compatible with free trade, collective security and economic development. Sovereignty, in other words, conferred the freedom to participate in an interdependent community anchored by American ideas and money. Against this backdrop, the Congo crisis was an opportunity for Americans to extend the authority of 'informed' world opinion into Africa.[33] 'If the Congo operation can be maintained long enough', Assistant Secretary of State Harlan Cleveland wrote in late 1960, there would invariably 'be other vacuums to fill with pacifying troops and administrative know-how and economic aid'. For Cleveland, the antecedent was more obvious than the irony, as he celebrated this project as 'the most formidable task that organized society has faced since the time of Rome'.[34]

The United Nation's ensuing Congo operation put the conflicting expectations of the various protagonists in sharp relief. At the Security Council's request, UN Secretary-General Dag Hammarskjöld assembled a large, multinational peacekeeping force in June, the Opération des Nations Unies au Congo (ONUC), but its arrival in Leopoldville merely underscored the fact that if the analogy to American history held, Lumumba was essentially pursuing a Lincolnian path – freedom through centralization – with neither a military nor an established base of support. The mutiny effectively deprived the Congo of its armed forces, and the MNC, while prominent, held just forty-one of the 137 parliament seats after the country's 1960 election.[35] It was a tenuous position at best. As ONUC forces streamed into the Congo, Lumumba announced that they would be fighting in Katanga, which was both unlikely, since the Security Council's instructions were strictly limited to the withdrawal of Belgian soldiers, and contradictory, in the sense that Lumumba's fight against a supposedly monolithic colonialism now rested on a military force organized from New York.[36] Like a good diplomat, Hammarskjöld threw words at this problem, but it was an unbridgeable divide. 'Would [the] United Nations … submit [Katanga] to the immediate control and authority of the central government against [the province's] wishes?' the secretary-general asked that summer. His answer limited Lumumba's options. ONUC, Hammarskjöld wrote, was not a rental army to be deployed at the behest of local officials, and a 'nonunitary' solution, involving a federated Congo, might still resolve the impasse between Lumumba and Tshombe.[37]

Ralph Bunche had the unenviable job of breaking this news to Lumumba. An African American political scientist who had moved from the State Department to the UN Secretariat after the Second World War, Bunche had distinguished himself by the late 1950s as a Nobel Prize-winning peacemaker and Hammarskjöld's closest advisor.[38] Like those in Eisenhower's inner circle, Bunche saw the 1956 Suez crisis as a blueprint for the Congo operation. The United Nations 'is a peace force', he explained in a private memorandum to his senior officers in July 1960, 'just as the United Nations Emergency Force (UNEF) has been a peace force for four-and-a-half years along the line between Egypt and Israel'.[39] While Lumumba called on ONUC to invade Katanga, Bunche prepared the United Nations for a long stay in central Africa. These efforts were not entirely unsuccessful; ONUC steadily removed Belgian personnel from the Congo on Bunche's watch and stabilized aspects of the political situation.[40] Yet, among Lumumba's supporters, the UN operation was dismissed as indecisive. Ghana's Henry Alexander, who commanded his country's contingent within ONUC, lamented Bunche as an American proxy, while Guinea's military leaders loudly called on the United Nations to enter Katanga and drive white settlers 'into the sea'.[41] Bunche visited Katanga in early August, and Hammarskjöld sought Security Council approval to expand ONUC's mission into the Congo's breakaway province, but Lumumba's patience had evaporated by month's end. Increasingly suspicious of the United Nation's delays, he began to harass Bunche's entourage in Leopoldville. 'Lumumba gets worse and worse', Bunche wrote to his wife. 'He is the *lowest* man I have ever encountered.'[42]

Lumumba did not record his reflections about Bunche, but he did not have to. His request for a Soviet intervention spoke volumes. (And it triggered CIA station chief Lawrence Devlin's infamous cable that the Congo was now 'experiencing [a] classic communist effort [to] take over [the] government', which presaged the secret machinations that culminated in Lumumba's death.)[43] The hitch, of course, was that Moscow did not actually have the ability to intervene in the Congo; Khrushchev's flare for dramatic prose elided the fundamental asymmetry of the superpower game in the early 1960s. While ONUC could land coalition forces in the Congo just forty-eight hours after the Security Council authorized its mission there, largely because of American money and planning,

Moscow's outdated IL-18 aircraft could not even reach Leopoldville without stopping first in Rome, Rabat and Accra. Each leg of the journey was fifteen hours, and Soviet aid, when it finally reached Lumumba in the early autumn, consisted mostly of food provisions and defunct weapons, neither of which addressed the underlying problem that the prime minister was an unskilled military leader who had no way to distribute these resources to his supporters.[44] Lumumba's instinctive desire to internationalize the Congo crisis – even as he lambasted Tshombe for reaching out to Western capitalists – merely underscored the contingent nature of Congolese sovereignty in 1960. The Congo was an unsettled idea being pitched to a uniquely international audience, and without UN action, the underlying fissure between Tshombe and Lumumba would remain unsettled.

Resolutions and martyrs

This raises a final question: How did the Congolese imbroglio change the international community? On the ground, the disagreement between Tshombe and Lumumba reached an appropriately ambiguous turning point in September. The prime minister lost control of his government that month, partly because of CIA meddling, but mostly because he had failed to establish a viable political coalition to support his ambitions. Joseph Mobutu, who had been appointed head of the Congo's nascent military forces, placed the prime minister under house arrest that month, prompting further secessions in the northwest, where Lumumba's support was the strongest, which, in turn, culminated in Mobutu's decision to send the prime minister to Elisabethville where he was tortured and eventually murdered in January. By early 1961, there were essentially four Congos – governed from Leopoldville, Elisabethville, Stanleyville and South Kasai, respectively – all vying for the recognition of anyone who would listen. Ghana and Guinea interpreted this turn of events as an assault on the premise of pan-Africanism. 'The central issue is that of unity', Ghana's *The Spark* explained. 'Not unity for the sake of unity ... but anti-imperialist unity, unity for world peace, unity for liberation and for economic independence and advance – *with a single direction*'.[45] Other African leaders countered that the issue was not pan-Africanism, but federalism. The continent needed to strive not for 'the political integration of sovereign African states', but for 'unity of aspirations' from 'the point of view of African social solidarity and political identity'.[46] The original issues behind the Katanga debate were not only intact; they now served as a prism to think about the larger, more ambitious project of African unity. These two sides could agree only that Tshombe's days were numbered. Lumumba's killing effectively sealed his fate. Although the contours of postcolonial Congo continued to be unsettled and contested, most observers agreed that some sort of unity government was preferable to four separate Congos, especially if the leaders of these countries were now killing each other. The alternative seemed too chaotic.

In this respect, the secession enlarged ongoing disagreements about the nature and meaning of postcolonial sovereignty. Within Africa, the crisis led to the creation of the so-called Casablanca group – Ghana, Guinea, Mali, Morocco and the United Arab Republic (which included an alliance between Egypt and the Middle Eastern state of Syria) – and the first collectively agreed-upon definition of neocolonialism, which would become a key element of African revolutionary discourse during the mid-1960s. In framing neocolonialism as 'the survival of the colonial system in spite of formal recognition of political independence in emerging countries', the group further demonized Tshombe and drew a sharp contrast between the Congo and Algeria, where an anti-colonial revolution was ostensibly providing a truer path through the thicket of decolonization.[47] A rival Monrovia bloc, comprising countries from French West Africa and British East Africa, immediately took issue with this definition and comparison. With so many leaders still reliant on European money and advice, especially across French West Africa, neocolonialism seemed to imply that some postcolonial governments were freer than others. This debate never truly ended, but the Casablanca and Monrovia movements forged an uneasy compromise during the negotiations for the Organization of African Unity (OAU) by shifting attention to the threat of white rule in southern Africa and acknowledging that sovereignty could not be revoked in the name of pan-Africanism. According to the OAU, if a country had a seat at the UN General Assembly, its neighbours had an obligation to respect its borders.[48]

Ironically, this pact codified the importance of the United Nations to African independence, just as the Soviet Union moved to denounce the organization. Embarrassed by Moscow's paltry intervention and angered by Lumumba's death, the Congo crisis left Khrushchev convinced that the UN Secretariat belonged to the United States. 'I spit on the UN', he said in late 1960. 'It's not our organization'. Convinced that the 'good-for-nothing' Hammarskjöld was 'sticking his nose in important affairs which are none of his business', the Soviet premier led his country's 1960 UN delegation in an unprecedented effort to replace the secretary-general with a troika that spread power evenly among the Western bloc, the Soviet Union's satellites and the 'Third World'.[49] Despite heavy lobbying of Africa's Casablanca group, Khrushchev's plan failed to gain traction in New York, prompting histrionics that left many observers deeply rattled. In the subsequent months, Khrushchev not only withdrew financial support from the United Nation's Congo mission – plunging the organization into a budget crisis that lasted into the 1970s – but also announced that disarmament talks would move forward only if the United States changed the United Nation's structure, inaugurating the tensions that presaged 1962's Cuban Missile Crisis.[50] The lesson of the Congo was that rhetoric was not enough; parity with the United States required bolder action.

For Washington, the Congo crisis revealed the outlines of a serious problem. 'The fact is that in 1960 there were seventeen new countries admitted to the United Nations, and in that period between 1955 and 1963 or 1964 the United Nations grew tremendously', Assistant Secretary of State for International Organization Affairs Francis Wilcox reflected in an interview after his retirement. 'Our position began to change because as these new countries were admitted we lost the kind of control we had over the General Assembly, the kind of support we'd been able to muster through the years.' Between the 'Latin countries' and the 'NATO countries', the United States could shape the 'vote for our position on almost any important issue' – until the Congo crisis of 1960. The breakdown did not come for another few years – 1965–1970, according to Wilcox – but ONUC's mission was the harbinger of things to come.[51] The idea that Americans could cultivate a predictable crop of leaders in the Congo and then manage their expectations at the General Assembly began to falter because of the events of 1960. Although US policymakers faced other intractable problems in these years, the secession underscored the fact the United Nation's newest members wanted the organization to be something more than a school to teach political responsibility. The Congo crisis raised deeper questions about the durability of American soft power, even as it hinted at the tension between US history – the lessons of which were being appropriated in deeply contradictory ways – and US foreign policy, which was increasingly remaking itself to match the ambitions of *Pax Romana*.

Hammarskjöld saw the Congo in comparable terms. Tshombe's gambit, he wrote, inaugurated the 'fourth great turn in modern history', comparable in importance to the French, Soviet and Nazi revolutions.[52] Each of these previous upheavals had forced the international community to confront profound questions about sovereignty and interdependence and had culminated in destructive bursts of nationalism that left tens of millions dead. Like many mid-century internationalists, Hammarskjöld saw the United Nations not as a post-national utopia so much as an instrument to police against the 'pan-'isms that had succeeded Napoleon's conquests, the Bolshevik revolution and the Second World War. By design, the organization protected and respected the political independence of small states, like Hammarskjöld's own Sweden, which had fought to navigate Europe's revolutions, even as it bound these governments into a superstructure based on Western notions of international law, collective security and economic interdependence. Hammarskjöld, in other words, was predisposed to see the worst in Lumumba's pan-Africanism; the premise that true freedom turned on government centralization and racial unity had a familiar, unsettling ring.[53] For the UN secretary-general, the exact form of the Congo's postcolonial government never mattered as much as the Congo's commitment to the authority and values of the United Nations. In this regard, the Congo tested not just the relationship of anti-imperialism and ethnic identity to modern statehood, which remained the central conceptual issue on the ground going into 1961, but whether the United Nations could successfully *manage* the combustible cauldron of sovereignty and nationhood in the postcolonial era.

Conclusion

This hints then at this paper's conclusion. The meaning of management changed dramatically as 1960 turned to 1961. Having declared that ONUC was not for rent in 1960, Hammarskjöld spent 1961 implementing Operations Rum Punch and Morthor, which saw ONUC disarm Katanga's armed forces.[54] On the surface, this about-face resulted from the confluence of a dynamic new cohort at the UN General Assembly and Moscow's unrelenting support for Congolese unity at the UN Security Council. Under the surface, however, as Wilcox observed, the United Nations was changing fundamentally. If the organization began 1960 as an instrument of American influence and hegemony, eager to prevent recrudescence of 1787, 1917 or 1933, the Congo transformed that sentiment. By 1961, running the United Nations, Hammarskjöld wrote, had 'become a bit like fighting an avalanche':

> You know the rules – get rid of the skis, don't try to resist but swim on the surface and hope for a rescuer. (Next morning historians will dig up the whole rotten mess and see how many were buried.) A consolation is that avalanches... always come to a stop and that thereafter you can start behaving like an intelligent being again – provided you have managed to keep afloat.[55]

Hammarskjöld became the Congo's second martyr. His plane mysteriously crashed that September, as he was trying to negotiate Katanga's reincorporation into the Congolese state. His death prompts two final thoughts. First, the Congo's birth proved that the United Nations could *not* manage the problems revealed by African decolonization. Unlike in Korea and the Middle East, where the organization seemed to enhance regional stability, things fell apart in central Africa, leading the United States, at least, eventually to abandon multilateralism in favour of Mobutu's iron-fist. As the task of paying for ONUC plunged the United Nations into financial disrepair, key powerbrokers, especially in Washington, started the process of rethinking global governance.[56] Second, the crisis exposed contradictions behind the wordplay of independence. Lumumba's fate foreshadowed the limits of anti-imperialism as decolonization's guidebook – people came to the decolonization project with a diverse set of expectations and grievances – just as Moscow's intervention illuminated the surprising gap between the rhetoric and reality of the Cold War. Ironically, the lesson for many Third World diplomats was not that postcolonial sovereignty was inherently performative, reliant on an attentive audience and an institutional stage; it was that the UN agenda still belonged to the West. The Congo crisis, in this respect, became the opening act in a drama that saw the UN architects scale back their expectations for the organization, just as Third World diplomats came to see those architects as the cause of their weakness. The result was more politics and less clarity, with the question underlying the Katangan secession – what is decolonization? – subsumed by a polycentric international environment.

Notes

1 For anecdote, see Young, Crawford (1966), 'Post-independence politics in the Congo', *Transition*, 26, 34–41, p. 34.

2 For a useful starting points, see Gerard-Libois, Jules and Verhaegen, Benoit (1961), *Congo, 1960*. 2 vols. Brussels: Centre de Recherche et d'Information Socio-Politiques; Willame, Jean-Claude (1990), *Patrice Lumumba: La Crise Congolaise Revisitée*. Paris: Karthala; Kalb, Madeleine G. (1982), *The Congo Cables. The Cold War in Africa: From Eisenhower to Kennedy*.

New York: Macmillan; Kent, John (2010), *America, the UN and Decolonisation: Cold War Conflict in the Congo*. London: Routledge.

3   Gérard-Libois, Jules (1966), *Katanga Secession*. Madison: University of Wisconsin Press, Chapter 1.

4   Crowley, Daniel (1963), 'Politics and tribalism in the Katanga', *Western Political Quarterly*, 16(1), 68–78, p. 68.

5   Gonze, Collin (1962), 'Katanga secession: The new colonialism', *Africa Today*, 9(1), 4–6, 12, 16, p. 5.

6   (1947), 'Social policy of Union Minière du Haut Katanga', *African Affairs*, 46(183), 87–89. This policy, widespread, has been studied in many different ways. One useful primer is Cooper, Frederick (2005), *Colonialism in Question: Theory, Knowledge, History*. Berkeley: University of California Press, especially Chapter 3.

7   Dummett, Raymond (1985), 'Africa's strategic minerals during the Second World War', *Journal of African History*, 26(4), 381–408, pp. 402–403.

8   Higginson, John (1988), 'Bringing the workers back in: Worker protest and popular intervention in Katanga, 1931–1941', *Canadian Journal of African Studies*, 22(2), 199–223, pp. 210–217.

9   Crowley (1963), 71–72.

10   The Balubas people, who also saw Katanga as their historic homeland, were by far the most important allies of the Chokwe and Kasai. Each group had migrated from western Africa sometime after the thirteenth century, but anthropologists and historians tend to accept that Katanga was divided politically between the Lunda and the Balubas kingdoms after the fourteenth century. The Balubas kingdom reached its apogee sometime in the late fifteenth century, while the Lunda kingdom dominated the region until the arrival of Portuguese and Arab traders in the late seventeenth century. For useful background, see Bustin, Edouard (1975), *The Lunda Under Belgian Rule*. Cambridge, MA: Harvard University Press. For some of Tshombe's speeches, see Congo Collection, box 1, folder 13, Yale University Manuscripts and Archives, New Haven.

11   Crowley (1963), 72–76. Also, see Young, Crawford (1965), *Politics in the Congo: Decolonization and Independence*. Princeton: Princeton University Press, 34–41; Slade, Ruth (1963), *The Belgian Congo*. Oxford: Oxford University Press; Gerard-Libois and Verhaegen (1961), 240–299; Hoskyns, Catherine (1965), *The Congo Since Independence, January 1960– December 1961*. Oxford: Oxford University Press, 58–76.

12   For relevant reflections, see Cooper, Frederick (2002), *Africa Since 1940: The Past of the Present*. Cambridge: Cambridge University Press; Cooper, Frederick. (1996), *Decolonization and African Society: The Labour Question in French and British Africa*. Cambridge: Cambridge University Press; Shipway, Martin (2008), *Decolonization and its Impact: A Comparative Approach to the End of Empires*. Oxford: Wiley-Blackwell.

13   Bouscaren, Anthony (1967), *Tshombe*. New York: Twin Circle Publishing Company, 8–9, 36–40.

14   Bouscaren (1967), 19–30; also Colvin, Ian (1968), *The Rise and Fall of Moise Tshombe*. London: Leslie Frewin, chapters 1–2. Colvin offers a particularly vivid depiction of Tshombe's reaction to the appropriation of Katangan government funds in the immediate wake of Congolese independence, pp. 20–23.

15   For complementary descriptions of Tshombe's thinking on these questions, see Tshombe, Moïse (1967), *My Fifteen Months in Government*. Plano: University of Plano Press; also Bouscaren (1967); Colvin (1968); and Nawej, Kayemb Uriel (2006), *Moïse Tshombe: Visionnaire Assassiné*. Paris: Booksurge Publishing.

16 For full text, see 'Declaration on the granting of independence to colonial countries and peoples', adopted as General Assembly resolution 1514 (XV) of 14 December 1960.

17 Bouscaren (1967), chapters 2–3; Colvin (1968), Chapter 4.

18 Lumumba, Patrice, 'From Prison to the Roundtable', in Jean Van Lierde (ed.) (1972), *Lumumba Speaks: The Speeches and Writings of Patrice Lumumba, 1958–1961*. Boston: Little, Brown, and Company, 173–175. For fuller explanations, see Lumumba, Patrice (1962), *Congo: My Country*. New York: Praeger; and Willame (1990), 121.

19 Lumumba, Patrice, 'Speech at Leopoldville', in Lierde (1972), 65–67.

20 Lumumba (1961), *The Truth about a Monstrous Crime of the Colonialists*. Moscow: Foreign Language Publishing House, 53.

21 Gérard-Libois (1966), chapters 3–4.

22 For reflections, see Cooper (2002); Young, Crawford (2012), *The Postcolonial State in Africa: Fifty Years of Independence, 1960–2010*. Madison: University of Wisconsin Press; Hyden, Goran (2005), *African Politics in Comparative Perspective*. Cambridge: Cambridge University Press.

23 Nkrumah, Kwame (1967), *Challenge of the Congo*. New York: International Publishers; also Young, Crawford (2010), 'Ralph Bunche and Patrice Lumumba: The Fatal Encounter', in Robert A. Hill and Edmond J. Keller (eds.) (2010), *Trustee for the Human Community: Ralphe J. Bunche, the United Nations, and Decolonization of Africa*. Athens: Ohio University Press, 133.

24 Nkrumah, Kwame (1961), *I Speak of Freedom: A Statement of African Ideology*. London: Heinnemann, xii.

25 For recent literature, see Mazov, Sergey (2010), *A Distant Front in the Cold War: The USSR in West Africa and the Congo, 1956–1964*. Stanford: Stanford University Press; also Iandolo, Alessandro (2012), 'The rise and fall of the "Soviet model of development" in West Africa, 1957–64', *Cold War History*, 12(4), 683–704.

26 Fursenko, Aleksandr and Naftali, Timothy (2007), *Khrushchev's Cold War: The Inside Story of an American Adversary*. New York: W.W. Norton and Company, Chapter 10.

27 For a synthesis of recent literature on this topic, see Zubok, Vladislav (2007), *A Failed Empire: The Soviet Union in the Cold War from Stalin to Gorbachev*. Chapel Hill: University of North Carolina Press, especially Chapters 4–5.

28 Fursenko and Naftali (2007), 314.

29 Memorandum of telephone conversation between President Eisenhower and Secretary of State Herter, 12 July 1960, in Office of the Historian (1992), *Foreign Relations of the United States (FRUS), 1958–1960*, 14. Washington: US Government Printing Office, no. 117.

30 Memorandum of Conference with President Eisenhower, 19 July 1960, in Office of the Historian (1992), *FRUS, 1958–1960*, 14, no. 135.

31 Kalb (1982) and Kent (1910) provide useful explanations; also Zacher, Mark (1970), *Dag Hammarskjold's United Nations*. New York: University of Columbia Press.

32 Cleveland, Harlan (1961), 'The capacities of the United Nations', in Francis O. Wilcox and H. Field Haviland, Jr. (eds.) (1961), *The United States and the United Nations*. Baltimore: John Hopkins University Press, 135–136.

33 Dulles, John Foster (1956), 'The institutionalizing of peace', *Proceedings of the American Society of International Law at Its Annual Meeting*, 50, 11–25, pp. 15–17.

34 Cleveland (1961), 142.

35 Young (2010), 134.

36 For revealing accounts, see Dayal, Rajeshwar (1976), *Mission for Hammarskjold: Congo Crisis*. Delhi: Oxford University Press; O'Brien, Conor Cruise (1966), *To Katanga and Back: A UN Case History*. London: Hutchinson; Lefever, Ernest (1967), *Uncertain Mandate: Politics of the UN Congo Operation*. Baltimore: John Hopkins University Press; Urquhart, Brian (1994), *Hammarskold*. New York: W.W. Norton and Company; Kanza, Thomas (1972), *Conflict in the Congo: Rise and Fall of Lumumba*. Harmondsworth: Penguin.

37 Quoted in Lipsey, Roger (2013), *Hammarskjöld: A Life*. Ann Arbor: University of Michigan Press, 391.

38 Henry, Charles P. (1999), *Ralph Bunche: Model Negro or American Other?* New York: New York University Press, Chapter 8.

39 Quoted in Olver, John (2010), 'An unexpected challenge: Ralph Bunche as field commander in the Congo, 1960', in Hill and Keller (2010), 122.

40 For scholarly treatments of this drama, see Gerard-Libois and Verhaegen (1961); Gérard-Libois (1966); Willame (1990); Kalb (1982), among others.

41 Urquhart, Brian (1994), *Ralph Bunche: An American Life*. New York: W.W. Norton & Company, 317.

42 Quoted in Young (2010), 141–142.

43 For full explanation, see Kalb (1982), 52–55.

44 Using this Soviet support, Lumumba had attacked Katanga in early September, but the mission was a failure and prompted the events that culminated in his ouster. For details, see Iandolo, Alessandro (forthcoming), 'Imbalance of power: The Soviet Union and the Congo Crisis', *Journal of Cold War Studies*, 16(1).

45 Quoted in Wallerstein, Immanuel (2005), *Africa: The Politics of Independence and Unity*. Lincoln: University of Nebraska Press, 53, emphasis in original.

46 Wallerstein (2005), 55.

47 Quoted in Nkrumah, Kwame (1965), *Neo-Colonialism: The Last Stage of Imperialism*. London: Thomas Nelson and Sons, Ltd. The full statement on neocolonialism appears in Appendix B. For analysis of Algeria's symbolic and political importance, see Connelly, Matthew (2002), *A Diplomatic Revolution: Algeria's Fight for Independence and the Origin of the Post-Cold War Era*. New York: Oxford University Press; and Byrne, Jeffrey (forthcoming), *A Mecca of Revolution: From the Algerian Front of the Third World's Cold War*. New York: Oxford University Press.

48 For some reflections on this theme, see Irwin, Ryan (2012), *Gordian Knot: Apartheid and the Unmaking of the Liberal World Order*. New York: Oxford University Press.

49 Quoted in Fursenko and Naftali (2007), 318.

50 Fursenko and Naftali (2007), 320.

51 Wilcox, Francis O., Chief of Staff, Senate Foreign Relations Committee, 1947–1955, Oral History Interviews. Washington, DC: Senate Historical Office.

52 Quoted in Lipsey (2013), 420.

53 Zacher, Mark W. (1970), *Dag Hammarskjold's United Nations*. New York: Columbia University Press, especially chapters 1–2.

54 The best overview remains Kalb (1982), especially parts 2–3.

55 Quoted in Lipsey (2013), 447.

56 For further reflections, Irwin (2012), chapters 5–6.

Key texts

Cooper, Frederick. (2002). *Africa since 1940: The Past of the Present*. Cambridge: Cambridge University Press.

Fursenko, Aleksandr and Naftali, Timothy. (2007). *Khrushchev's Cold War: The Inside Story of an American Adversary*. New York: W.W. Norton and Company.

Gérard-Libois, Jules. (1966). *Katanga Secession*. Madison: University of Wisconsin Press.

Kalb, Madeleine G. (1982). *The Congo Cables. The Cold War in Africa: From Eisenhower to Kennedy*. New York: Macmillan.

Kent, John. (2010). *America, the UN and Decolonisation: Cold War Conflict in the Congo*. London: Routledge.

Wallerstein, Immanuel. (2005). *Africa: The Politics of Independence and Unity*. Lincoln: University of Nebraska Press.

CHAPTER 11
MALCOLM X IN FRANCE, 1964–1965: ANTI-IMPERIALISM AND THE POLITICS OF TRAVEL CONTROL IN THE COLD WAR ERA

Moshik Temkin

On 9 February 1965 at 9:50 a.m., Air France Flight 805 from London landed at Orly airport, south of Paris. On board was Malcolm X, the African American political activist, who had just spent three days in the United Kingdom at a meeting of the Council of African Organizations and was scheduled to speak in Paris that evening. He emerged from the plane alone and promptly was met by gendarmes and immigration officers who let him know that his presence in France was 'undesirable' and took him to a small room in the *zone de transit*. There they held him incommunicado for over an hour, refusing his request to phone the US embassy or contact the people waiting for him in the arrivals hall. Once they had checked, listed and copied his passport and papers, they asked him whether he would like to continue on to the next leg of his trip, Geneva, or return to London. Not without protest, he chose the second option. They obliged: whisking him out of the room and into a car outside the terminal, making sure that he came into contact with no one, they placed him on board Air France Flight 812 to London. Only some minutes after he boarded were the other passengers allowed on the plane. At 12:10 p.m., the jet took off; an hour later, Malcolm X was back in London.[1]

Having dispatched their unwanted visitor back across the English Channel, the French authorities turned their attention to the dozen or so people who had been waiting in vain for his arrival. Two men introduced themselves as Malcolm X's hosts: Lindsay Barrett, a 23-year-old Jamaican national, and Carlos Moore, a 22-year-old Cuban national. After noting the two men's protestation at Malcolm X's expulsion, as well as copying the details of *their* documents, the officers followed the waiting party out of the terminal, where they made note of the cars in which the men and women left the airport. They sent this information, including the documents found on Malcolm X, to the police *Préfecture* in Paris.[2]

This unsuccessful visit to France occurred a mere twelve days before Malcolm X (his official name at this time, according to his passport, was Malcolm Shabazz) was murdered by gunmen as he was beginning a speech at the Audubon Ballroom in Harlem. The proximity between his expulsion from France and his death in New York is one reason why this bureaucratic event at Orly has assumed awesome significance in some accounts of the end of Malcolm X's life.[3] An array of explanations, some more sinister than others, have been floated and debated over the years as part of the effort to understand why, in fact, the French authorities would not let him into their country, and what possible connection there might be between that decision and his demise soon after. The end of his life, particularly the last few days, is shrouded in mystery, and perhaps no moment is more mystifying – and less understood – than his deportation from France.

But while the shadiness of this event has been highlighted (to some extent) in the literature, its historical significance has not. Malcolm X's two trips to France, in November–December 1964 and early February 1965, have received scant attention from scholars interested not only in Malcolm X's career, but also, more broadly, in the politics of the 1960s – European, American and transnational – as well as the conditions, dynamics and limitations of internationalist and anti-imperialist political activism in this period.[4]

Malcolm X was a public figure based in New York City but also, in the last year of his life, a self-styled ambassador-at-large for black America, a globally recognized radical intellectual and human rights campaigner, a thorn in the side of the US Department of State and one of the world's foremost frequent flyers. His trips to Europe – far briefer than his voyages to Africa and the Middle East, which have enjoyed more (but not enough) scholarly attention – occurred at a moment in which African postcolonial struggles, African American freedom struggles, Cold War proxy politics, US domestic and foreign policy towards political dissent and the black nationalist, pan-African and left-wing revolutionary identities that took root among the growing African, Afro-Caribbean and African American communities in Western Europe, particularly France and Britain, combined to form a heady context for his brand of activism. Malcolm X operated at the touchy meeting point between the aftermath of decolonization and the global effects of the Cold War.

In this sense, his expulsion from France was like the eye of a storm; for historians, the event itself is worth closer examination. It can show the meaning and implications of Malcolm X's presence, desirable to some and 'undesirable' to others, in France and Europe generally. And it reveals the key means – travel control – by which Gaullist authorities in France, worried, in the wake of decolonization, about the imminent internationalization of heretofore nationally confined and monitored socio-political problems, reacted to the globalization of politics (particularly internationalist and anti-imperialist political activism) that was rapidly growing during this period, of which Malcolm X was an emblematic representative. This chapter argues that what happened to Malcolm X at the airport in France was typical of a broader response on the part of a sovereign nation-state (in this case, France) to the promotion of international politics in the Cold War era. Specifically, Malcolm X's brand of anti-imperialist politics was most unwelcome by national authorities who were anxious to keep separate what they considered national from what they considered international.[5]

Shifting the geography of the black struggle

Even as historians have duly noted the extent of Malcolm X's travels, they have yet fully to explore the global framework of his career. To the degree that the issue is written about, it is usually done to describe Malcolm X's evolving views on race in America and the political situation in the United States. Perhaps the most typical scholarly framing of Malcolm X's place in history is, misleadingly, within or vis-à-vis the history of the American civil rights movement writ large, specifically the rise of 'black power' ideologies among African Americans in the 1960s. The European dimension of the story is bypassed.[6] But, if anything, Malcolm X's last year was about shifting the geography of his politics from the United States abroad. Rather than bringing Africa to America, as most scholars suppose, he was, in a sense, doing the opposite: bringing America to Africa and, as this chapter aims to show, to Europe.[7]

Malcolm X's life and career before 1964 are largely beyond the scope of this chapter.[8] After breaking (acrimoniously) with the Nation of Islam (NOI) and its leader, Elijah Muhammad, early in 1964, Malcolm X founded two new organizations: Muslim Mosque, Inc. (MMI) and the Organization for Afro-American Unity (OAAU). These organizations rivalled not only the NOI itself, but also each other. The first was primarily religious, conservative and local, staffed mostly by men who had followed Malcolm out of the NOI; the second was secular, radical and international. Perhaps most notably, Malcolm also completed the shift in substance and tone that his activism had undergone in recent years, which had led to his split from the NOI. From the generally parochial, misogynist, American-oriented black separatism/nationalism of the NOI, he turned towards an explicitly internationalist platform that connected the condition of blacks in the United States to a broader global struggle against imperialism and capitalism and insisted that the problem facing American blacks was not a lack of civil rights, but of human rights.

Malcolm's celebrated first trip to Mecca, in April 1964, brought about a drastic change in the way he saw white people: previously 'blond-haired, blue-eyed devils', now potential allies in the struggle for black liberation.[9] But perhaps even more significant, on a political level, were the five months in 1964 he spent in Africa, visiting fourteen countries. Over the course of the year he was able to meet with several heads of state, including Kwame Nkrumah of Ghana, Gamal Abdel-Nasser of Egypt, Jomo Kenyatta of Kenya, Julius Nyerere of Tanzania, Ahmed Sékou Touré of Guinea and Ahmed Ben Bella of Algeria. These men were all charismatic postcolonial leaders whose Cold War 'non-alignment' strategies and varying fusions of African-style socialism and pan-Africanism (or pan-Arabism, in the case of Nasser and Ben Bella), as well as their pasts as anti-colonial leaders, appealed to Malcolm's evolving conception of power politics. His main African role model – and a man to whom he was frequently compared by his international supporters, before and especially after his death – was Patrice Lumumba, the first Prime Minister of the independent Republic of the Congo. Lumumba had been murdered in 1961 by internal enemies, reputedly with the support of the United States and Belgium and the complicity of the United Nations, and thus became an iconic victim of the Global Cold War.[10]

In the course of his African sojourn, Malcolm X put in motion an idea that had occurred to him, as he later recalled, during his pilgrimage to Mecca: to make the case to the international community that the United States was guilty of violating the human rights of its twenty-two million black citizens. The rationale for this strategy was simple: on the world stage, he reasoned, non-whites were in the majority, and presenting the plight of blacks in the United States as a human rights issue would be an embarrassment to the American government. In July 1964, he attended a summit meeting in Cairo of the Organization of African Unity (OAU), the namesake of Malcolm's own OAAU. Malcolm was admitted to Cairo as an observer, where he circulated among the attending leaders of thirty-four African nations a memorandum calling for support in bringing the issue of US human rights violations towards blacks before the United Nations.[11] The effort was not quite successful; many of the African leaders, while generally not shy about voicing their criticism of US domestic and foreign policy, were also hopeful applicants for US aid and would not go so far as to support such steps against the United States at the United Nations, fearing, apparently, American reprisals. (In an era in which any anti-American policy in Africa was perceived and treated by the US government as a step towards the Soviet Union, these fears were quite justified.)[12] Still, Malcolm X was able to get through the Cairo meeting a separate resolution that stated that the OAU was 'deeply disturbed ... by continuing manifestations of racial bigotry and racial oppression against Negro citizens of the United States.'[13]

On the whole, Malcolm X's African experience was mixed and somewhat paradoxical. It played a hugely transformative role in the development of his internationalist agenda, and he discovered the extent of his own appeal outside the United States. But it was also in Africa that Malcolm eventually began to come to grips with the limits of his global power. Although he was well received by heads of state, he also learned that any human rights struggle, or political initiative against the United States, particularly if taken to the United Nations, could only really be carried out if nation-states and their representatives chose to do so. The African states in which he had invested much hope would not.

Still, he did not drop the issue and was able at the end of the year to claim one, mostly symbolic, victory. During the debate held in December 1964 in the UN General Assembly on the fate of the Congo, which was mired, four years after the assassination of Lumumba, in a bloody civil war between the so-called Lumumbist forces and the pro-Western, Katanga-based regime of Moise Tshombe, African UN representatives accused the United States of 'being indifferent to the fate of the blacks and cited as evidence the attitude of the United States government toward the civil rights struggle in Mississippi'. No issue was more important (and blood-boiling) to Malcolm X and his supporters in Africa and Europe in late 1964 and early 1965 than the crisis in the Congo, which they saw as an ongoing battle between good and evil and the direct result of the reported American involvement in the murder of Lumumba and support for the western mercenaries recruited to fight for Tshombe. Connecting the situation in the Congo to the one in Mississippi was precisely the sort of politics Malcolm X wanted to advance in this period. It was also the sort of politics that the political authorities in Cold War America abhorred.[14]

Indeed, by transforming himself from a domestic firebrand into a global critic of the United States, Malcolm did not render himself particularly popular in Washington. As the *New York Times* put it,

[US] officials said that if Malcolm succeeded in convincing just one African government to bring up the charge at the United Nations, the United States government would be faced with a touchy problem…the issue…would be of service to critics of the United States.[15]

1964 was the year of the passage of the Civil Rights Act in the United States, and the State Department was anxious to trumpet this legislation abroad, particularly in Africa, as part of its Cold War policy of self-promotion. It therefore would not do that during his tour of Africa Malcolm X called the Act a 'propaganda stunt' (and the famed March on Washington, 'the farce on Washington'), and assured his African interlocutors that the situation of American blacks was worse than ever, Lyndon Johnson's rhetoric notwithstanding. Robert E. Lee, the State Department's Assistant Secretary for Congressional Relations, reported to his bosses that although African leaders may have been reluctant to support Malcolm X's propositions, 'the propaganda which was generated by his extreme statements may have caused some damage to the United States image'.[16]

In addition to the constant surveillance and harassment to which Malcolm X was subjected at home and abroad, some officials were willing to take concrete steps to silence him if necessary. In September 1964, the US attorney general wrote to FBI director J. Edgar Hoover, who had ordered constant surveillance on Malcolm, as on all other oppositional black figures, to verify whether Malcolm was in violation of the Logan Act, which forbids unauthorized citizens from negotiating with foreign governments. Hoover and the Department of Justice determined that Malcolm's activities abroad did indeed run afoul of the Logan Act and asked Secretary of State Dean Rusk 'to make appropriate inquiries of our embassies in the Middle East and Africa for any pertinent information' that would establish that Malcolm X was indeed in violation of US federal law.[17]

Malcolm X's European trips took place in the wake of, and against the backdrop of, this American official agitation over his global activism. It is also important to note that while his international stature was growing, Malcolm was also becoming increasingly marginalized in the United States; the two processes went hand in hand. Harangued by his former friends and followers in the Nation of Islam, vilified as an extremist by the media, abandoned by many of his supporters, suffering threats to his life, tracked by police and the FBI, Malcolm X, quite simply, preferred in this period to be abroad, where he was in his element. In addition, his rhetoric from this period, with its emphasis on anti-imperialism, transnational black solidarity and Third World revolution, probably found better reception in London or Paris or Accra than in Harlem or Detroit.[18] Malcolm X's trips abroad, then, were not necessarily about 'internationalizing' the African American struggle, as scholars have assumed. Rather, they were part of the *transfer* of the struggle from the United States abroad. His new sites of activism were Africa and Europe, where the triple messages of anti-imperialism, revolution and human rights rang louder and clearer than they did in the United States.[19]

'Troubling the public order'

Based on his first visit to France at the end of November 1964, the authorities did not appear, on the face of it, to have convincing reasons for refusing Malcolm X entry again. On his way back to the United States from his African trip, he first stopped for a week in Paris, officially as a guest of the *Fédération des étudiants d'Afrique noire en France* (FEANF), the so-called Afro-American Committee (which Malcolm X and his host Carlos Moore apparently wanted to set up as the Paris branch of the OAAU) and the literary journal *Présence Africaine*.

On the night of 23 November, Malcolm X gave a talk to a packed house in one of Paris's largest public halls, the *Maison de la Mutualité* in the fifth arrondissement. His speech was entitled 'The Afro-American in Face of the African Revolution', with Moore and the Haitian writer and diplomat Emile Saint-Lô serving as impromptu translators. Those in attendance included the Senegalese intellectual Alioune Diop, as well as the Martinican-French author Aimé Césaire (a leader of the *negritude* cultural movement).

Malcolm described the 'new black consciousness on the American continent' and recounted that his recent meetings with the postcolonial heads of state and the leaders of various African national liberation movements '[have] opened up to me a new vision of the struggle of black Americans and the one which the African people are waging for their genuine emancipation'. At the upcoming session of the UN General Assembly, he promised, 'we're going to try [to] charge the United States with violating the United Nations Declaration of Human Rights and also violating the United Nations Charter itself, for its refusal to bring a halt to the continued mistreatment of the 22 million black people in that country'. He ended by suggesting, provocatively, that 'since France is one of the few countries that has been able to keep from becoming a satellite of the United States, we hope that she'll help us when we bring the case up in the United Nations'.[20]

Between speech- and film-making sessions, Moore took Malcolm X for walks around the city and introduced him to various men and women from Africa and Latin America (some of whom, as it turned out, carried pictures of him in their wallets), as well as American blacks, particularly artists and writers, living out a long-standing African American cultural tradition: Parisian self-exile.[21] The atmosphere was charged; although Malcolm may not have noticed it immediately, his visit took place against the backdrop of increasing dissatisfaction with the way France treated its growing African communities, both Saharan and Sub-Saharan, in the aftermath of decolonization. This new politics clashed with the idealized perception of France as a haven for blacks and other minorities who could find there, so the story went, the sort of acceptance, respect and success that was denied to them in America.[22]

Malcolm himself certainly contributed to the electricity, both by his charisma and by the fact that he never failed to highlight the danger to his life.[23] Convinced that he was the survivor of a poisoning attempt in Cairo earlier that year, Malcolm declined to eat in restaurants and took his meals at the home of Richard Wright's widow, Ellen Wright.[24] He also spent hours at the home of the radical political cartoonist Siné, where, as Bethune filmed him, he presented his views on pan-Africanism and US politics.

Filming continued into the night after his *Mutualité* speech. As if what he usually had to say was not unnerving enough for American authorities, on this occasion he also stated, in response to a question about Red China's successful detonation of a nuclear bomb earlier that year (knowing full well that this was a particularly touchy topic for the US government):

> it's one of the greatest things that ever happened ... I do hope they will be able to build bigger and better ones every day ... the only language the European powers understand is the language of power and a dark nation has to be in a position to talk or speak the language that these imperialists understand.[25]

The next morning, reportedly not having slept for over forty-eight hours, Malcolm departed for New York; he had not seen his family in six months. But only a week later he was back in Europe for his first visit to Britain, where his main destination was the Oxford Union, the venerable debating society.[26]

Malcolm X's trip to Britain at the end of 1964 was a raucous tour de force. At the Oxford Union, where he spoke in favour of the motion 'extremism in the defense of liberty is no vice, moderation in the pursuit of justice is no virtue' (ironically, a statement originally made by Republican candidate Barry Goldwater in the 1964 US presidential election), he gave one of his most celebrated performances. In London he was welcomed and feted by an enthusiastic network of activists, artists, intellectuals, African, Afro-Caribbean and British.[27] He returned to the United Kingdom in the first week of February for another series of talks and interviews, and apparently to try to set up a London branch of the OAAU, another step towards turning his fledgling organization into a truly transatlantic body. From there, on 9 February, he flew to Paris, which brings us to the scene at the airport.

Why, then, did the French authorities not let Malcolm X into France on 9 February? This question has helped feed the flames of the man's mystique. The French official bureaucracy, it would appear, left no paper trail of the *order* to keep him out of France, only of *how* that order was followed. (Even this information is not publicly archived, nor readily made available to scholars.) What could have possibly changed in the ten weeks since late November 1964, when Malcolm *had* been let into France? Supposedly, the French, British and American press reported, the French government was now concerned that Malcolm X's presence would 'provoke demonstrations that would disturb the public order'.[28] Taken literally, as an expression of fear of physical violence, this made no sense: his previous visit to Paris had passed without incident, and the authorities would have been hard pressed to point to a single occurrence anywhere in which violence, let alone demonstrations, had accompanied his public appearances. Besides, there was nothing unusual about what he was scheduled to do: return to the *Maison de la Mutualité* to deliver a speech. Some of the evening newspapers added that the authorities found his November speech in Paris 'too violent'.[29] This was a frivolous claim: it was one of the most moderate speeches he had given in his career, an advocacy of human rights that did not include a word of criticism of France.

Understood more broadly and figuratively, however, the French officials' fear of Malcolm X troubling the 'public order' was quite reasonable, even if demonstrations were not quite what the authorities had in mind. In the same vein, it was perfectly sensible for the authorities to deem his November speech 'too violent'. The archives of the French Ministry of the Interior and the Ministry of Foreign Affairs, and of the Paris police, teem with the documentary product – most of it still classified – of the surveillance in this period of France's growing African communities, as well as of foreign (in particular American) activists.[30] These documents can tell us plenty about what the French state apparatus thought it was doing when it barred Malcolm X. They reveal what 'disturbing the public order', taken seriously, might have actually meant, how foreign anti-imperialist activists fit into this context and what we can learn from this episode about travel control politics in the Cold War years.

From human right to economic rights

Malcolm X was humiliated and furious at the expulsion. His reaction, to a large degree, dictated subsequent interpretations of the event. His rage began to take shape in the *zone de transit*, when the authorities let him know that his presence in France was 'undesirable'. On the phone with Moore and Bethune later that day from London, he spoke of what happened: 'They would not even let me contact the American embassy ... I thought I was in South Africa.' What made it even worse, from his perspective, was that this had happened in France, of all places:

> I thought if there was any country ... that was liberal in its approach to things, France was it, so I was shocked when I got there and couldn't land ... I've been all over the world – and I've been in Alabama and Mississippi – and it's the first time in my life that I was ever stopped outright.

And in a slight fit of hyperbole, he added that the expulsion, when compared with the admittance to France of the 'cold-blooded murderer' Tshombe and 'every other lowdown type of person' led him to believe that 'the French government is probably the worst racist government there is ... worse than South Africa, worse [than] the one Hitler had in Nazi Germany'. Still, he hit on something important when he reasoned that 'there's a reason [for the expulsion]. I don't blame [the French authorities]. There's a large and increasing number of dark-skinned people swelling the dark population of France and Britain, and it's giving [these countries] a great deal of cause for worry'.[31]

Like many others, Malcolm X had been, and in a way, still was, captivated by France's resilient reputation as a land of political tolerance and colour-blindness in which talented American blacks could live and thrive in equality.[32] The experience of black expatriates in the preceding decade actually suggested that France's famous tolerance had clear limits. In the 1950s and the 1960s, foreigners were expected to withhold criticism of the French state, and during the Algerian War any violation of this rule could be grounds for deportation.[33] But among many African Americans, the French reputation for tolerance lived on, perhaps due to the juxtaposition with the violent images coming out of America's racial struggles of the same period.

This naïveté about French realities was perhaps one reason why Malcolm X believed (or had suggested that he believed) that France would support his UN initiative against the United States. Another may have been de Gaulle's insistence on French independence from American foreign policy, which led Malcolm X and others to consider France one of the few countries 'not beholden' to the United States.

On this point Malcolm was both right and wrong. This period was indeed famously marked by political tensions between the United States and France. De Gaulle did not at all see French Cold War interests as aligned with the Americans', much to the frustration of Washington. At the same time, unbeknownst to Malcolm X, the French–American relationship was quite robust when it came to intelligence gathering and sharing. Both sides of that otherwise difficult relationship shared a hostility to radical politics, particularly of the sort espoused by global activists.[34] The fact that Malcolm was a thorn in the side of the American establishment would do nothing to endear him to the French.

Still, notwithstanding his anger at the French authorities, Malcolm X could not conceive of an autonomous French decision to bar him. He blamed the US government for the expulsion: he was convinced that the State Department, in league with the CIA, was determined not to let him embarrass the US abroad, and had put in a request to that effect with the French government, which had complied. According to a handwritten transcript of a phone message to Secretary of State Dean Rusk, made from Harlem three days before his death, Malcolm X demanded to know how it could be that 'while in possession of an American passport, I was denied entry to France with no explanation. I would like to lodge an official protest and insist upon an investigation ... to determine why this incident took place with no intervention from the United States Embassy'.[35] Even when heaping stinging criticism on the US abroad, Malcolm X had come to take for granted the protection bestowed on him via his American passport, and his abandonment by the American state at a moment of extreme vulnerability, sitting in the *zone de transit*, only added to his deepening sense of isolation and paranoia. There was also the irony of discovering the hard way that any effective global internationalist activism depended almost entirely on the whim of the state – grantor of passports and visas, and always in charge of border controls – whose interests were diametrically opposed to his.

In an odd little story that would later enter Malcolm X lore and bolster his reputation as a speaker of anti-imperialist truth to imperial power, he told Moore in their phone conversation that while waiting in the *zone de transit*, after having told the officers watching over him what he thought of what was being done to him, 'I gave the security forces there a penny, an English penny, and told them to give this to de Gaulle because, from my point of view, his government and country were worth less than one penny'.[36] In other, more colourful versions of this story, which took on a life of its own, the events change slightly: according to one version, Malcolm offered the penny to one of the French officers, who refused to accept it, whereupon Malcolm flung the penny to the floor.[37] The official police reports, it should be noted, make no mention of any such act on Malcolm X's part, noting that he merely 'expressed some criticism of his treatment in France, which he had considered a free country and not a satellite of Washington', and that he then boarded the flight to London 'without causing an incident'. The gesture, in any case, can be read as an act of strength on Malcolm's part but also as a symbol of his ultimate impotence: penny or no penny, flung or not flung, he could not get into the country.[38]

Although the authorities had banned the star speaker, they did not ban the rally itself, and Moore and Bethune, encouraged by Malcolm, decided to go ahead with the event at the *Maison de la Mutualité*. The turnout was far from what it would have been had Malcolm X been present, but about 350 people, according to a French agent present, turned up anyway. (In lieu of Malcolm X's speech, Moore and Bethune tried to play their recorded phone conversations with him over the speaker system; when that did not work, they simply reiterated what he had said.) The event was transformed into an angry rally against the French state and its 'racist' decision to keep Malcolm X out of the country, an act that was linked by some of the speakers to the involvement of white mercenaries from South Africa in the Congolese civil war and to the American escalation of war in Vietnam. Supporters took the stage to denounce what Moore called 'a criminal action against us all'. For activists like Moore, the supposed difference between the United States and France was exposed with this one act as a mere patina:

> when we black people ride in the metro, we see slogans written on the walls which are offensive to us. We are constantly insulted. This happens to us here in France, in the United States, where blacks are kicked and beaten ... in fact, everywhere in the western world.[39]

Others gave early supporting voice to suspicions, which would later proliferate, about US involvement in the expulsion. Eddie Barnett, an African American activist in Paris who had been waiting for Malcolm X in the arrivals hall, reported that 'there were agents of the United States government, as well as the French government, all over the airport'.[40] But perhaps the most dominant theme for the speakers was their disappointment that this had occurred in 'liberal', 'open' France. Echoing Malcolm's comments, Moore stated that

> we want the French government to hear this denunciation tonight because France has always been considered a sanctuary, a liberal country of little racism – many blacks in the United States think that France is a better place to live and they come here because they hear that there is no racism in France like there is in the United States. But it would appear that this is changing, or perhaps changed some time ago.[41]

From the phone conversations with Moore and Bethune we can glean some of what Malcolm was planning to talk about in his visit (and thus also what he might have focused on publicly had he lived). He would soon reprise some of the substance of the talk at the London School of Economics' Old Theatre, where he spoke on 11 February. In 1964 he had focused on human rights; 1965 would be the year of economic rights. Taking as a model the European Common Market, which 'looks out for the common interests of Europeans and the European economy', as he saw it, Malcolm now wanted to propose an equivalent institution that would unite 'the black people in the western hemisphere and those of the African continent ... for a positive program of mutual benefit'.[42] His rhetoric was to be less 'violent', if anything, than it had ever been, and it is hard to imagine talk of an African-oriented economic programme 'provoking demonstrations' or 'disturbing the public order'. What mattered was not so much what Malcolm X was saying, not even who he was, but what kind of political activism he represented.

From the point of view of the French officials keeping close watch on all this, the Malcolm X-less meeting looked quite different. On the day of the deportation, agents filed a flurry of reports indicating that Malcolm X's hosts planned to hold a press conference and to turn the meeting into an angry protest rally. One agent who had been at Orly reported that 'Malcom [sic] Little's deportation ... provoked angry reactions among the dozen people who were there to welcome him'.[43] But in the absence of Malcolm X, the meeting itself was, for the authorities, an unremarkable event. While the organizers boomed their denunciations of the authorities from the stage, the government agent in presence was nonchalant.

The police report about the meeting estimated that of the 350 people present, 150 were 'people of color', most of them Caribbean, and a dozen were Francophone Africans. Only thirty-five to forty of the attendees were 'French speaking', by which the agent also meant white. The report further gave a laconic summary of the fiery speeches, noting simply that most of them were in English (and thus, the implication followed, of little to no public significance). The agent woke up slightly at the sight and sound of the 'very virulent' Carlos Moore, who spoke in French. But ultimately, the report concluded, the meeting constituted a 'failure' for the organizers and a victory for the authorities. After all, as the report pointed out, French students did not turn out en masse; most of the 'French-speaking Africans' showed up mostly as a 'gesture of good will' towards the 'Afro American Committee'; the 'almost exclusive use of the English language' showed that the entire event was of limited appeal, primarily to an 'Anglophone public'.[44]

Explaining the expulsion

It is practically impossible to separate Malcolm X's politics and career, especially towards the end of his life, from the atmosphere of fear and paranoia within which he and his followers functioned. He was convinced, particularly after the expulsion, that there was an international plot to kill him; this too was part of his 'global' outlook and also part of the transnational context within which his anti-imperialist activism needs to be understood. Whereas at home he feared primarily the Nation of Islam, abroad, as he told his hosts, he feared the long reach of the US government. 'The more I think about what happened to me in France', he told his collaborator on the *Autobiography*, Alex Haley, shortly before he was killed, 'the more I think I'm going to quit saying it's the [Black] Muslims [who wanted to kill Malcolm X]'.[45] This perception was directly linked to the politics he espoused: Western imperialism's determination to keep blacks oppressed was the broader context for the American determination to destroy him personally. For many of his supporters, his murder, though attributed to the NOI, was a vindication of Malcolm X's all-encompassing anxiety, and the killers merely patsies for broader, hidden, more nefarious forces.[46]

Somewhat more plausible explanations for the expulsion have since appeared, but they have not been supported by much more evidence than the idea that the US government applied pressure on the French authorities or the theory that French intelligence wanted to prevent Malcolm X from being assassinated in Paris. One thorough and fair-minded biographer, the former *Newsweek* editor Peter Goldman, suggested that the 'real' French motive for banning Malcolm X, as opposed to their evasive official one, stemmed from opposition to Malcolm X's activities on the part of two of their recently liberated colonies, Senegal and the Ivory Coast, whose France- and West-friendly leaders (respectively, Léopold Sédar Senghor and Félix Houphouët-Boigny) worried in early 1965 that Malcolm X, 'aided and abetted' by Nasser and Nkrumah, 'might try to incite African students to overthrow moderate, pro-Western governments like their own. They naturally preferred that he not be allowed in Paris', where the African community included many students from their countries. According to this theory, Malcolm X's expulsion had less to do with the specific designs of US or French intelligence and more to do with African power politics and relations between the French government and its former colonies.[47]

Despite the lack of evidence, this is, in my view, partly the right track to take in terms of understanding the expulsion, but it is not enough. Houphouët-Boigny was an anti-communist, to be sure, but Sédar Senghor was a socialist and a co-founder with Césaire of the *negritude* movement, thus hardly hostile to the black intellectual left. In any case there is no particular reason to believe that either man would go out of his way to prevent Malcolm X from visiting Paris. One thing that *does* need to be taken into account, however, is the sort of political situation in France into which Malcolm X was perhaps unwittingly stepping.

To begin with, his hosts were revolutionaries, and thus had revolutionary ideas (or at least it would appear that way in retrospect). Some of them may have been willing to translate his speeches into action, or at least make plans to that effect. A clue to this can be found in Moore's introduction to his collection of papers, now housed at the University of California, Los Angeles. According to his own website, Moore ran a 'front' organization in Paris called 'the Afro-American Committee', at the behest of Malcolm X, to support the 'Lumumbist' cause in the Congo. 'Under the guise of planning discussion meetings', Moore states, 'this organization intended to raise funds and recruit militants to fight in the Congo, and planned a rally where Malcolm X was to be the keynote speaker'. (In his memoir, Moore goes further, calling the plan 'Malcolm's daring project' and adding that 'I began recruiting volunteers with military and medical expertise to assist the Lumumbist insurrection'.)[48]

If we take these boasts at face value, Malcolm X's planned speech for 9 February was not, then, merely a rally in favour of pan-African economic independence, but part of a plan for a concrete intervention in Africa's hottest spot at the time. However, according to Moore, 'when the time for the rally came, Malcolm X was denied entry to France'.[49] There are other sources that can corroborate, if not Malcolm X's actual intent, at least his supporters' threats: in a November 1964 letter to Nasser, for example, the American Muslim Student Association (AMSA), a group in Cairo hoping to affiliate with the Muslim Mosque, Inc., let the Egyptian President know that 'we join our brother … Malcolm X … in assuring you that there are many US military trained young Afro-Americans that, if equipped and supplied, are ready to volunteer today to take up arms beside our Congolese brothers in their just struggle'.[50] We cannot know with any certainty what Malcolm X thought of these half-baked plans, or if they were indeed part of his 'project' for the Congo, but in a letter to an American friend in Cairo, he expressed his satisfaction at having received 'a copy of the wire sent by the AMSA, fully supporting the struggle of our Congolese brothers against the puppet regime of Tshombe'. In a press release issued by the OAAU's Accra branch, he promised that 'thousands of Afro Americans' were willing to fight alongside their 'Lumumbist brothers'.[51]

There is probably no way to verify Moore's claims. But, in conjunction with other sources, they can be fruitful in helping to shift our focus away from Malcolm X and towards internal conditions in France, in particular the people with whom he associated and their place within the French state at the time. Malcolm X's November 1964 trip to Paris coincided almost exactly with Tshombe's official state visit, which was met with violent demonstrations and protest in the left-wing press, objecting to de Gaulle's hosting of a man seen as responsible (and thus reviled) for the murder of Lumumba and the ensuing Congolese bloodbath.[52] A highly publicized effort on the part of Malcolm X and his local supporters to bring attention to the Congo crisis, in which the French government had (at least temporarily) supported the side opposite to Malcolm X's, may have been the very last thing the Gaullist authorities wanted to see in early 1965.

This is the context within which the expulsion most plausibly belongs. The French state archives – police, the Ministry of Foreign Affairs, the Ministry of the Interior and the Ministry of Immigration – provide a clear picture of the growth and subsequent politicization of the African community (both students and work-seeking migrants from the former French colonies in Africa) in France in the years following decolonization and its relation to both the state bureaucracy and to foreign anti-imperialist activists, also monitored by the authorities.

The French police records show that new files were opened on each individual directly associated with Malcolm X's 9 February visit (in case the individual in question did not already have an existing police file). These files, which the police continued to maintain and fill after Malcolm X's death, contain the individual's full name, date of birth, French address, form of employment and, most important, political activity.[53]

Given these sources, we thus have a better idea of what the authorities believed was the real threat that Malcolm X posed. It had as much to do with the people waiting in the arrivals hall at Orly airport as with the man they were waiting for. The attention paid to Moore, Barrett and their friends by the French authorities at Orly was neither an accident nor an afterthought; just as they were monitored and questioned because of Malcolm X, Malcolm X was stopped and investigated because of them. Malcolm X, simply put, threatened to internationalize France's internal political condition. This was actually a double threat: anti-imperialism and internationalism.

Let in or kept out?

In banning Malcolm X from the country, the French authorities were reacting to a political *type*, not necessarily to an individual. But *what* exactly was this type? Tellingly, the official police reports on the event at Orly are curiously filled with errors of detail. Malcolm X's first *and* last names are misspelled in a variety of ways – most often they appear, respectively, as 'Malcom' and 'Shebazz' – and he is described as the 'leader of the so-called Afro-American Party', a meaningless (and erroneous) description, or as the leader of the 'black muslims'. These errors may have occurred partly because Malcolm X always went by a confusing variety of names, and also because these French officers most likely were not masters of the English language. But the officers who dealt with him at Orly seem genuinely not to have known exactly who he was, only that they had orders to prevent his entry.

In the end, the explanation for Malcolm X's expulsion at Orly may lie not in its supposedly awesome importance but rather in its representative banality. What mattered was not so much Malcolm X's specific intentions as much as what the authorities believed he represented. For Malcolm X and his supporters, the expulsion may have had great meaning, especially once tied to his murder; however, for the French authorities he may have been nothing more than a nuisance (whose precise politics they did not fully understand), a troublemaker best kept out of the country. By way of explanation, it is useful to contrast Malcolm X, in this one regard, with his great rival Martin Luther King, Jr., who visited Paris in October 1965 and spoke before an overflow audience at the same venue, the *Maison de la Mutualité*, from which Malcolm X was barred just eight months earlier.[54]

Malcolm X represented a danger to the state, in a way that King perhaps did not, in his brand of activism. King spoke as a religious figure and the most prominent leader of the mainstream civil rights movement in the United States. In fact, the documents in the file that the French police had on King show that his visit was seen and treated as primarily religious and not political in nature. King's main concern was events inside the United States. He had no beef with Europe, at least not then, and not in the direct way that Malcolm X did. The sources show that his hosts, in securing the invitation, even promised the relevant authorities that King would not have anything to say on France itself or its former colonies in Africa.[55] Malcolm X, by contrast, defined himself as an anti-imperialist and spoke in the name of a vaguely defined global community of 'dark-skinned people', including in Europe.

This difference between a nationally oriented and internationally oriented conception of politics was also the difference between being let into France and being kept out. The authorities in France did a thorough job keeping track of foreigners in their midst. But internationalization, or mixture, was an entirely different story, one that brought with it all sorts of headaches and hassles.[56] In the same way that the French authorities would want to keep out vegetables from other countries as a basic form of protectionism, so too would they wish to prevent the entry of an activist of Malcolm X's sort into its confined, controlled and heavily monitored national political environment, especially in the wake of decolonization and at the same time as the country's leaders were attempting to navigate the murky waters of the new postcolonial world.

In this sense, the expulsion of Malcolm X was a French reaction to the globalization of politics – of *its* politics – and to the mixture of its internal affairs with the universal language and global politics of anti-imperialism that Malcolm X put at the top of his agenda. Scholars have hitherto told us quite a bit about American Cold War fears concerning the decolonized world. Malcolm X plays a central if underexplored role in this story. But the juncture of Cold War politics and the aftermath of decolonization made him perhaps even more frightening to French authorities. Malcolm X could connect France to the world in all the ways that its government did *not* want it to be.

And in the end, this is also a story of the limitations of non-official public activism in an era still dominated by nation-states and their representatives. It was here, in Orly's *zone de transit*, that Malcolm X encountered the limits not only of France's political tolerance, but also of the international political activism that was supposed to transcend the boundaries between nations but, as it turned out, could not pass through customs.

Notes

1   Direction Générale de la Sûreté Nationale, 'Malcom–Little–19/5/1925', 10 February 1965, Service Central d'Identification, Fichier Centrale; for a first-person perspective on Malcolm X's return to London, see Carew, Jan (1994), *Ghosts in Our Blood: With Malcolm X in Africa, England, and the Caribbean*. New York: Lawrence Hill Books, 8–12.

2   Direction Générale de la Sûreté Nationale, Police de l'Air, Aeroport d'Orly, 'Objet: Mesure de refoulement prise à l'encontre de Shebazz Malcolm', 9 February 1965, Service Central d'Identification, Fichier Centrale; Renseignements Generaux (RG), Paris, 'Malcolm Little', 9 February 1965, 500261–0. The French sources consistently refer to this incident as a *refoulement*, a legalistic term that can best be translated as 'turning back' or 'pushing back'; I use 'expulsion' as a substitute term.

3   See, for example, Rickford, Russell (2003), *Betty Shabazz*. Naperville, Ill.: Source Books, 221–222.

4   This gap in the literature is all the more striking when contrasted with recent attention paid to Malcolm's concomitant trips to Britain (see note 27 below). Even Manning Marable's recent celebrated and lengthy biography of Malcolm X devotes less than one page to Malcolm's *refoulement* at Orly.

5   To my knowledge, there is no study of travel control and international politics in history. Border control has been thematized mostly in relation to immigration; see, for example, McKeown, Adam (2008), *Melancholy Order: Asian Migration and the Globalization of Borders*. New York: Columbia University Press. For studies of passports, see Torpey, John (2000), *The Invention of the Passport: Surveillance, Citizenship, and the State*. New York: Cambridge University Press; and Robertson, Craig (2010), *The Passport in America: The History of a Document*. New York: Oxford University Press. Saskia Sassen has written about the connections between the nation-state, migrations and different forms of globalization; Sassen (1999), *Guests and Aliens*. New York: New Press.

6   For studies of black power and civil rights that focus on Malcolm X, see, Joseph, Peniel (2006), *Waiting 'Til the Midnight Hour: A Narrative History of Black Power in America*. New York: Henry Holt; Cone, James H. (1991), *Martin and Malcolm and America: A Dream or a Nightmare?* Maryknoll, NY: Orbis Books; Sugrue, Thomas J. (2008), *Sweet Land of Liberty: The Forgotten Struggle for Civil Rights in the North*. New York: Random House. For the ways in which black power movements claimed Malcolm X as their 'patron saint' after his death, see Glaude, Jr., Eddie S. (ed.) (2002), 'Introduction: Black Power revisited', in (2002), *Is It Nation Time?: Contemporary Essays on Black Power and Black Nationalism*. Chicago: University of Chicago Press, 4 and passim.

7   For an attempt to connect Malcolm X's travels to his political philosophy, see Tyner, James A. (2003), 'Geography, ground-level reality, and the epistemology of Malcolm X', *Journal of Geography*, 102(1), 167–178. See also Gaines, Kevin (2010), 'Malcolm X in global perspective', in Robert E. Terrill (ed.), *The Cambridge Companion to Malcolm X*. New York: Cambridge University Press, 158–170.

8   Malcolm X's public image and historical reputation since 1965 have largely been shaped by two compelling but flawed sources: (1965), *The Autobiography of Malcolm X, As Told to Alex Haley*. New York: Grove Press; and the film derived from it, Lee, Spike (dir.) (1992), *Malcolm X*. 40 Acres & A Mule Filmworks. Horne, Gerald (1993), ' "Myth" and the making of "Malcolm X" ', *American Historical Review*, 98(2), 440–450, p. 445, argues that 'neither the dominant Martin Luther King-driven myth nor the alternative Malcolm X myth gives a proper account of the play of international forces'. For another critical assessment of the film (and of Malcolm X himself) see Painter, Nell Irvin (1993), 'Malcolm X across the genres', *American Historical Review*, 432–439. The most recent and exhaustive (but hugely controversial and flawed) biography is Marable, Marable (2011), *Malcolm X: A Life of Reinvention*. New York: Viking. For a discussion of this book, see Temkin, Moshik (2012), 'From Black revolution to "radical humanism": Malcolm X between biography and international history', *Humanity: An International Journal of Human Rights, Humanitarianism, and Development*, 3(2), 267–288.

9   On Malcolm X and Islam, see, Gomez, Michael (2005), *Black Crescent: The Experience and Legacy of African-Americans in the Americas*. New York: Cambridge University Press, 2005, ch. 8; De Caro, Louis A. Jr. (1996), *On the Side of My People: A Religious Life of Malcolm X*. New York: New York University Press; and Marable (2011), ch. 11 and passim.

10 For early accounts of Malcolm X's trips to Africa in 1964, see, Lacy, Leslie Alexander (1969), 'Malcolm X in Ghana', and Essien-Udom, Ruby M. and E.U. (1969), 'Malcolm X: An International Man', both in John Hendrik Clarke (ed.) (1969), *Malcolm X: The Man and His Times*. New York: MacMillan, 217–222, 235–267; Gaines, Kevin K., (2006), *American Africans in Ghana: Black Expatriates and the Civil Rights Era*. Chapel Hill: University of North Carolina Press, ch. 6; Joseph (2006), 102–108; Goldman, Peter (1974), *The Death and Life of Malcolm X*. Champaign: University of Illinois Press, 212–220. See also the correspondence in the Malcolm X Papers, box 15, folder 1, Schomburg Center for Black Culture, New York

Public Library (henceforth MXP). On Lumumba and his death, see De Witte, Ludo (2001), *The Assassination of Lumumba* (translated by Ann Wright and Renée Fenby). London: Verso.

11 'US Negro leader on African summit: Malcolm X hails OAU', *Egyptian Gazette*, 23 August 1964, 1–2; see also Malcolm X, 'The Negro's fight', *Egyptian Gazette*, 25 August 1964, 2–5.

12 For background, see Westad, Odd Arne (2005), *The Global Cold War: Third World Interventions and the Making of Our Times*. New York: Cambridge University Press, 131–143.

13 Breitman, G. (ed.) (1965), *Malcolm X Speaks*. New York: Pathfinder Press, 84. As the *New York Times* put it, '[US] officials said that if Malcolm succeeded in convincing just one African government to bring up the charge at the United Nations, the United States government would be faced with a touchy problem ... the issue ... would be of service to critics of the United States'. Handler, M.S. 'Malcolm X stirs concern of US: Black Muslim chief wants U.N. to take up question of Negro plight', *New York Times*, 13 August 1964, 1, 3. For studies dealing with race and US foreign relations in the Cold War era, see Dudziak, Mary L. (2000), *Cold War Civil Rights: Race and the Image of American Democracy*. Princeton: Princeton University Press; Borstelmann, Thomas (2001), *The Cold War and the Color Line: American Race Relations in the Global Arena*. Cambridge, MA: Harvard University Press; Anderson, Carol (2003), *Eyes Off the Prize: The United Nations and the African American Struggle for Human Rights, 1944–1955*. New York: Cambridge University Press; Plummer, Brenda Gayle (1996), *Rising Wind: Black Americans and U.S. Foreign Affairs, 1935–1960*. Chapel Hill: University of North Carolina Press; Gaines (2006); Layton, Azza Salama (2000), *International Politics and Civil Rights Policies in the United States, 1941–1960*. Cambridge: Cambridge University Press; and Von Eschen, Penny M. (1997), *Race Against Empire: Black Americans and Anticolonialism, 1937–1957*. Ithaca: Cornell University Press.

14 May, Ernest R. and Neustadt, Richard F., 'Malcolm X', *Harvard Kennedy School of Government Case Study*, Series C15–81–366, 27. According to May and Neustadt, 'this accusation embarrassed [US] Ambassador Adlai Stevenson; Malcolm considered it a significant victory'. For a critical assessment of US involvement in the Congo crises, see Weissman, Stephen (1974), *American Foreign Policy in the Congo, 1960–1964*. Ithaca: Cornell University Press. See also 'Malcolm X, back in the U.S., accuses Johnson on Congo', *New York Times*, 25 November 1964, 4, 10.

15 Handler, M.S., 'Malcolm X stirs concern of US: Black Muslim chief wants U.N. to take up question of Negro plight', *New York Times*, 13 August 1964, 1, 3.

16 Dudziak (2000), 222–223.

17 Carson, Clayborn (1991), *Malcolm X: The FBI File*. New York: Carroll and Graf, 338–339. At the time of Malcolm X's death, the investigation had not yielded an indictment. The FBI opened its Malcolm X surveillance file in 1953, one year after his release from prison. On one occasion Malcolm recorded a conversation with two FBI agents who tried to recruit him as an informant: see 'A Visit from the FBI, May 29, 1964', in Clarke (1969), 182–204.

18 See Kelley, Robin D.G. (2002), 'Stormy weather: reconstructing Black (inter)nationalism in the Cold War era', in Glaude, Jr. (2002), 67–90, for a discussion of the small internationalist networks of radical black American activists, notably Robert Williams and the Maoist-inspired Revolutionary Action Movement.

19 Some of the best sources on Malcolm X are the numerous collections of his speeches, letters and interviews. For an emphasis on the last year of his life, see Shabazz, Betty (ed.) (1970), *By Any Means Necessary*. New York: Pathfinder Press. See also Terrill, Robert E. (2007), *Malcolm X: Inventing Radical Judgment*. Lansing: Michigan State University Press.

20 'The Afro-American in face of the African revolution', 23 November 1964 (transcript), folder 1, box 6, Carlos Moore papers, Ralph J. Bunche Center for African American Studies,

University of California, Los Angeles (CMP). Elsewhere Malcolm X pointed out that by 'Afro-Americans', he meant all people of African descent in the entire western hemisphere. For the place of Malcolm X's 1964 activism in the recent evolution of human rights history, see Moyn, Samuel (2010), *The Last Utopia: Human Rights in History*. Cambridge, MA: Harvard University Press, 104–106. Malcolm X was not the only African American activist to bemoan the emphasis on civil rights at the expense of human rights. For the crucial shift from the latter to the former in an earlier period, see Anderson (2003). For the attempt to bring back the human rights framework after his death, see Jackson, Thomas. F. (2009), *From Civil Rights to Human Rights: Martin Luther King, Jr., and the Struggle for Economic Justice*. Philadelphia: University of Pennsylvania Press. See also Singh, Nikhil P. (2004), *Black is a Country: Race and the Unfinished Struggle for Democracy*. Cambridge, MA: Harvard University Press, passim.

21 See Stovall, Tyler (1996), *Paris Noir: African Americans in the City of Light*. Boston: Houghton Mifflin Press; and Fabre, Michel (1993), *From Harlem to Paris: Black American Writers in France, 1840–1980*. Champaign: University of Illinois Press. For the idea of the African diasporas and their political expressions, see Edwards, Brent H. (2003), *The Practice of Diaspora: Literature, Translation, and the Rise of Black Internationalism*. Cambridge, MA: Harvard University Press.

22 Moore, Carlos (1967), 'Malcolm … je me souviens', *Présence Africaine* 62(2), 84–89; Bethune, Lebert (1969), 'Malcolm X in Europe', in Clarke (1969), 226–234. For background, see Stovall (1996), passim.

23 See the remembrances in Himes, Chester (1995), *My Life of Absurdity: The Autobiography of Chester Himes*. New York: Thunders Mouth Press, 290–291.

24 Carlos Moore, telephone interview with the author, 13 September 2009.

25 'Malcolm X Speaks, film transcript of soundtrack interview', box 6, folder 1, CMP.

26 Correspondence and materials in folder 15, box 3, MXP.

27 Carew (1994), passim; 'Cheers for Malcolm X at Oxford', *Daily Telegraph and Morning Post*, 4 December 1964, 17. For background, see Street, Joe (2008), 'Malcolm X, Smethwick, and the influence of the African American freedom struggle on British race relations in the 1960s', *Journal of Black Studies* 38(6), 932–950; Abernethy, Graeme (2010), ' "Not just an American problem": Malcolm X in Britain', *Atlantic Studies: Global Currents* 7(3), 285–307; Tuck, Stephen (2013), 'Malcolm X's visit to Oxford University: U.S. Civil Rights, Black Britain, and the special relationship on race', *American Historical Review* 118(1), 76–103; Ambar, Saladin (2014), *Malcolm X at Oxford Union: Racial Politics in a Global Era*. Oxford: Oxford University Press.

28 'France bars Malcolm X to avoid "trouble" at meeting', *New York Herald Tribune*, 10 February 1965, 3; 'Malcolm X barred from France', *London Times*, 10 February 1965, 10; 'Malcolm X, ancien chef de file des "Black Muslims" refoulé à Orly', *L'Aurore*, 10 February 1965, 3.

29 'Carlos Moore Telephone Conversation With Malcolm X', 9 February 1965, box 6, CMP.

30 For earlier French legal and bureaucratic monitoring of foreigners and immigrants, and the uses of *refoulement*, see Lewis, Mary D. (2007), *The Boundaries of the Republic: Migrant Rights and the Limits of Universalism in France, 1918–1940*. Stanford: Stanford University Press. For postcolonial Francophone Africa and connections with France, see Chafer, Tony (2002), *The End of Empire in French West Africa: France's Successful Decolonization*. Oxford: Oxford University Press; and Cooper, Frederick (2002), *Africa Since 1940: The Past of the Present*. New York: Cambridge University Press. For the politics of citizenship and foreigners in France, see, Weil, Patrick (1991), *La France et Ses Étrangers: L'aventure d'une Politique D'immigration, 1938–1991*. Paris: Gallimard; and Gastaut, Yves (2000), *L'immigration et*

L'opinion en France sous la Ve Rèpublique. Paris: Seuil. For background on French state surveillance between 1958 and 1968, see Faligot, R. and Guisnel, J. (2006), *Histoire Secrète de la Ve République*. Paris: Editions La Découverte.

31 'Malcolm X telephone conversation with Lebert Bethune, London-Paris, Feb. 9, 1965, 8:30 p.m.', box 6 (unpublished transcript), folder 1, CMP.

32 For background, see the essays in Chapman, Herrick and Frader, Laura (eds.) (2004), *Race in France: Interdisciplinary Perspectives on the Politics of Difference*. New York: Berghahn Books.

33 See Stovall, Tyler (2000), 'The fire this time: Black American expatriates and the Algerian War', *Yale French Studies*, 98, 182–200.

34 See Temkin, Moshik (forthcoming), 'American internationalists and transatlantic travel control in the era of Vietnam', in Andrew Preston and Doug Rossinow (eds.) (forthcoming), *Outside In: Transnational and International Dimensions of Modern American History*. For the complex relationship between De Gaulle and American administrations see, for example, the essays in Paxton, Robert O. and Wahl, Nicholas (eds.) (1994), *De Gaulle and the United States: A Centennial Reappraisal*. Oxford: Bloomsbury Academic Press.

35 Letter to Dean Rusk, folder 4, box 3, MXP. Between 'determine' and 'why' the words 'the validity of the American …' are crossed out.

36 'Carlos Moore Telephone Conversation with Malcolm X'.

37 See, for example, Goldman (1974), 254.

38 Direction Générale de la Sûreté Nationale, Service Central d'Identification, Fichier Centrale, 'Malcom–Little–19/5/1925', 10 February 1965. Translation is mine: The security officers, having written down 'un pays de liberté', may have misunderstood Malcolm X's English when he probably said 'liberal country' or 'free country'.

39 'Transcript of the Recorded Proceedings of the Protest Rally Held at the Maubert Mutualité on 9 Feb. 1965, in Protest of Malcolm X's Banning by the French Authorities', box 6, folder 1, CMP.

40 Transcript of the Recorded Proceedings of the Protest Rally Held at the Maubert Mutualité on 9 Feb. 1965, in Protest of Malcolm X's Banning by the French Authorities. Years later, when interviewed by Tyler Stovall of the University of California Berkeley Department of History, activist Bette Woody recalled being at Orly airport and seeing 'two FBI guys–these are FBI, speaking English, looking American–came and got him … and we never saw him again'. Stovall (1996), 268. Malcolm made no mention of meeting any American officials during the process.

41 'Transcript of the Recorded Proceedings of the Protest Rally'.

42 (1965), 'Telephone Conversation with Malcolm X', *Présence Africaine*, 62(2), 68. For the activists' summary of Malcolm X's French trips, see Moore, Carlos and Bethune, Lebert (1965), 'L'Heritage de Malcolm-X', *La Vie Africaine*, 57(1), 16–18. Malcolm X apparently got a severe case of the flu the day after his return to London from Paris. For his response to the expulsion while in the United Kingdom, see Carew (1994), 17–18.

43 'Malcolm Little', GA-L7, Archives de la Préfecture de Police de Paris, Paris, France (APPP).

44 'Malcolm Little', GA-L7, Archives de la Préfecture de Police de Paris, Paris, France (APPP).

45 (1965) *Autobiography*, 438.

46 This view would gain traction, in particular, in the American underground left-wing press of the late 1960s. See for example Norden, Eric, 'The murder of Malcolm X', *The Realist*, February 1967, 1–7. Marable (2012), 418–449 and passim, deals directly (and more soberly) with the murder and its background.

47 Goldman (1974), 255: 'Malcolm had been scissored ... in the power politics of Africa and its continuing liaison with the white West ... the tact that forbade anyone's saying so at the time has nourished the conspiracy theory of Malcolm's assassination ever since, and conspiracies, in the popular culture of the Left, are the monopoly property of America and the CIA.'

48 Moore, C. (2008), *Pichón: A Memoir*. Chicago: Chicago Review Press, 279.

49 Moore, Carlos, 'Biography', <http://www.drcarlosmoore.com/pdfs/Carlos-Moore-Collection_ Finding-Aid09.pdf> [accessed 17 March 2013]. A modified version of this biographical statement appears on the Bunche Center website, <http://www.bunchecenter.ucla.edu/index. php/carlos-moore-collection-overview-2/carlos-moore-biography/> [accessed 17 January 2014].

50 The Executive Committee, American Muslim Student Association, 'Letter to His Excellency President Gamal Abdel Nasser', 28 November 1964, Cairo, folder 14, box 3, MXP.

51 Quoted in Gaines (2006), 200.

52 'Voyage a Paris de Monsieur Moise Tschombe, Premier Ministre du Congo Ex Belge', FA 99, 4520, APPP; 'Tshombe a eu la reception qu'il merite', *L'Humanite*, 1 December 1964, 1; 'Manifestation au Trocadero', *Le Figaro*, 1 December 1964, 1; 'Manifestation Lumumbiste a l'etoile: trente arrestations', *L'Aurore*, 1 December 1964, 1.

53 RG 725–331, APPP.

54 Branch, Taylor (2006), *At Canaan's Edge: America in the King Years 1965–68*. New York: Simon & Schuster, 354. The title of King's talk was 'The Church in a World in Revolution'.

55 'Martin Luther King, Jr', RG-734951, APPP.

56 For earlier French resistance to the internationalization of its major conflict of the post–Second World War period, see Connelly, Matthew (2002), *A Diplomatic Revolution: Algeria's Fight for Independence and the Origins of the Post-Cold War Era*. New York: Oxford University Press.

Key texts

(1965). *The Autobiography of Malcolm X, As Told to Alex Haley*. New York: Grove Press

Goldman, Peter. (1974). *The Death and Life of Malcolm X*. Urbana: University of Illinois Press.

Marable, Manning. (2011), *Malcolm X: A Life of Reinvention*. New York: Viking.

Shabazz, Betty (ed.). (1970). *By Any Means Necessary*. New York: Pathfinder Press.

Temkin, Moshik. (2012). 'From Black revolution to "radical humanism": Malcolm X between biography and international history', *Humanity: An International Journal of Human Rights, Humanitarianism, and Development*, 3(2), 267–288.

Terrill, Robert. E. (ed.) (2010). *The Cambridge Companion to Malcolm X*. New York: Cambridge University Press.

CHAPTER 12
FROM FOREIGN CONCESSIONS TO SPECIAL ECONOMIC ZONES: DECOLONIZATION AND FOREIGN INVESTMENT IN TWENTIETH-CENTURY ASIA

Christopher Miller

David Sassoon would have looked out of place in any of the Chinese cities whose commerce he dominated during the mid-nineteenth century. The bushy beard, tall turban and flowing Middle Eastern robes, the Arabic language he spoke or the Hebrew alphabet with which he wrote: these were not usual sights on the quays of Canton or Shanghai, where Sassoon built a mercantile empire shipping opium and textiles across the Indian Ocean and South China Sea. But in other ways, Sassoon was typical of his era. Like many of the tycoons who dominated Asia's trade during the nineteenth and early twentieth centuries, from Cheong Fatt Tze of Penang to Tan Kah Kee of Singapore, Sassoon made his fortune far from his native country. Of course, 'native country' was a concept that had little meaning for him as a Baghdad-born Jew, a British subject who could not speak English, a Bombay businessman whose familial wealth reshaped Shanghai's skyline. Instead of countries, Sassoon's world was a string of cities: Bombay, Calcutta, Rangoon, Hong Kong, Shanghai, Singapore, London.[1]

Port cities, the great trade entrepôts that funnelled goods and people from their rural hinterlands to overseas markets, were the defining feature of Asia's trade in the early twentieth century. It was through port cities that many of Asia's most important interactions with colonialism took place. Often, as in British India, port cities were part of larger territories that were governed as colonies. Sometimes they were administratively separate. For example, the British governed the 'Straights Settlements' – Singapore, Penang and Malacca – separately from the rest of the Malay Peninsula. Perhaps most controversial were the instances when imperialists carved out special privileges in port cities that officially belonged to other countries, creating 'foreign concession zones'. This happened across the world, from the Mediterranean to the Persian Gulf, but the practice was most prominent in China.[2] In these cases, imperialism was less about direct control of territory by an outside power and more about dominance of economic structures – a type of influence that declarations of sovereignty did not necessarily reverse.

Foreign concession zones were eliminated in the mid-twentieth century as European empires collapsed. But by the end of the twentieth century, special territorial and commercial privileges had reappeared, reborn as 'special economic zones' (SEZs). Like foreign concessions during the age of empire, these new zones offered foreign-owned businesses special tax, regulatory and customs incentives to set up shop. Yet the politics in this later time was decidedly different. Foreign concessions during the colonial era were evidence of the formal or informally colonized country's weakness – proof that government could not provide economic growth without compromising sovereignty. But when such zones were resurrected in the late twentieth century, this chapter shows, SEZs were embraced by countries whose geopolitical situation or domestic politics meant that fears about Western imperialism no longer played the dominant role in their outlook on foreign investment. Cold War-era geopolitical shifts meant that the West was no longer seen as the main threat to national sovereignty. As the usefulness of these zones became recognized – and as it became clear that they facilitated Western investment without a significant sacrifice of political sovereignty – even countries that had made economic independence a central facet of their ruling ideology decided to try them out.

In a sense, the spread of these zones, from only eleven in 1970 to ninety-six zones in more than two dozen countries by 1981, resurrected the world of port cities that had marked the age of empire.[3] But unlike the age of imperialism, the boom in SEZs that began in the 1970s was initiated and firmly controlled by developing-world states, not by rapacious Western imperialists. The two examples that this chapter examines, Taiwan and mainland China, were far from the only developing countries to host SEZs. But their experience, and their debates about the utility of special zones, sheds light on broader questions about imperialism, sovereignty and national identity: issues that profoundly shaped how newly independent states decided to regulate their economies.

This chapter traces the fall and rise of special zones for foreign investors in China. The concepts of these zones, the chapter will argue, are worth examining not only for their specific role in attracting investment and providing portals for foreign business to engage with developing countries. Indeed, this chapter will suggest that the history of SEZs sheds light on a series of broader questions about how states and economies interacted during the long twentieth century. Countries' decisions about whether to allow free trade or whether to seek foreign investors are usually ascribed either to different approaches to economic theory, or to domestic political struggles between winners and losers from trade.[4] The story told here, about China's attitude towards using special zones to attract foreign investment, suggests that Cold War-era geopolitical shifts were an important factor in determining attitudes towards foreign economic engagement. The People's Republic of China and Taiwan drew on similar historical experiences and intellectual roots when it came to foreign concession zones during the colonial era: they were both strongly opposed to the zones that had facilitated what they saw as Western and Japanese pillaging before 1945. Yet the two countries' distinct paths towards adopting SEZs in the era after the Second World War shed light on how their differing engagements with anti-imperialism and the Cold War shaped their foreign economic policy. Taiwan adopted SEZs (there called 'export processing zones') in the 1950s, soon after it became politically separate from mainland China, whereas the PRC remained resolutely opposed to such zones until the end of the 1970s. Ultimately, China's and Taiwan's decisions to embrace special zones were driven in large part because they found that newer geopolitical competitors were a greater threat to their security than the West.

The origins of foreign concessions in China

Portugal was the first European country to gain a foothold in China when it colonized Macau in the 1500s, but most foreign concessions in China dated from the late nineteenth and early twentieth centuries. Britain won its first right to concessions in 1842 after defeating China in the Opium War. Over the next century, twenty-five such zones were established in China by Japan, Britain, France, Germany, Italy, Belgium and Austria-Hungary. Every concession was in a port city, near either a river or the ocean.[5] Within the concession zones, foreign powers received special rights. They often stationed military forces there, ran their own postal services and other government bodies, and their citizens were subject to different judicial processes than Chinese.[6] Perhaps most importantly, from the perspective of merchants who pushed for such concessions, the treaties that created them usually demanded China offer low tariffs on imported goods, even though Chinese producers were often not provided similar access to foreign markets.[7]

Though foreign concessions were forced on China by outside powers – and though they were often strongly opposed by Chinese popular and elite opinion – they did provide a few local economic benefits. Fewer foreigners would have done business with China without guarantees of their property and personal safety. China itself was torn apart by major rebellions twice during the second half of the nineteenth century, and the concession zones, often guarded by foreign militaries, gave a sense of security to European and Japanese traders. The legal extraterritoriality that foreigners received, which provided them with separate judicial processes, increased investors' confidence in the security of their property. Yet despite the foreign concessions' ability to attract investment, they were highly unpopular among Chinese. The zones were unaccountable to the Chinese government, critics argued, and prolonged China's period of weakness and its inability to stand up to European imperialism. Even though China was still nominally independent, opponents of the zones argued that China needed to control foreign merchants' activities directly in order to be truly sovereign. As a result, opposition to the concession zones was a major rallying cry for critics of European and Japanese imperialism.

When European empires began to unravel in the 1940s, trade networks also collapsed: from Shanghai to Malacca, Calcutta to Colombo, entrepôt cities lost influence and slumped into decline. The trade flows upon which they had thrived were disrupted by new national boundaries, and the cities themselves were submerged within much larger structures – nation states – which dominated them politically. By the middle of the twentieth century, the geography of Asian economies was marked not by cities, but by the borders of new nation-states. This chapter will begin by tracing the ideologies that dominated China's decolonization and demanded that port cities, sites of complicated sovereignty and 'foreign' influence, be directly controlled by the central government, without which China could never be fully sovereign. Across Asia, and across the decolonizing world more generally, the political tide that brought in new nation states swept out foreign investors. In the process, countries such as China lost profitable opportunities for trade but gained cherished independence.

Creating 'national' economies in newly independent states

Many activists and politicians across the 'Third World' saw political sovereignty as simply the first step in the campaign for complete decolonization. They believed that political and economic sovereignty were closely intertwined, and in both contexts they defined sovereignty as state control. Thus regardless of economic ideology – communist or capitalist, developmentalist or socialist – many new national leaders sought to use their states to police economic boundaries, restrict foreign capital and reduce dependence on trade. In some countries, like the People's Republic of China (PRC), this meant expropriating most foreign property in order to move quickly towards communism. It also required, in the view of most Chinese communists, developing domestic industry so that the country was not dependent on imports from Japan and the West. Mao is today remembered for presiding over a catastrophic famine and economic collapse, but there was a certain rationality to his economic policy, particularly after his split with the Soviet Union. In the age of empires, he believed, China had relied on foreigners for industrial goods and new technology but had been repeatedly defeated in war. Self-strengthening was not really possible when the enemy was already firmly entrenched in Shanghai's port. Real independence meant cutting off China's reliance on imports and developing its own industrial base instead. As Mao himself argued, 'Without [domestic] industry, there can be no solid national defense, no people's welfare, and no national prosperity and power'.[8]

It was not only communists who wanted economic decolonization to accompany political independence. Non-communist governments also asserted their sovereignty by reducing economic dependence on, and interaction with, the West. Indeed, the notion that economic decolonization needed to follow political decolonization was widespread across the Third World in the early decades of the Cold War. At international gatherings like the Bandung conference and at meetings of the non-aligned movement, leaders of countries newly free from colonialism shared political strategies for achieving economic independence. Many prominent postcolonial leaders, from Burma's Ne Win to Indonesia's Sukarno, embraced policies designed to achieve economic sovereignty to accompany political independence. Even in the most extreme cases, anti-imperialism and 'economic independence' were not interpreted to mean a complete rejection of all foreign trade. But across much of the decolonizing world, trade and capital flows, especially from the former colonial powers in the West, were seen as potential threats that needed to be carefully managed and controlled by the state.

Taiwan's creation of the Kaohsiung export processing zone

Taiwan was an exception to this trend. Even during the heyday of decolonization and the peak of anti-imperialist sentiment in developing national politics, not all countries focused so determinedly on economic independence. These policymakers worried that extensive imports from the West would waste scarce capital, but unlike Mao, they did not fear the West or adopt import substitution to reduce their reliance on economic exchange with the West and thereby bolster their economic independence. In Taiwan, the West was not a potential threat but a crucial ally, and the political realities of the Cold War profoundly shaped how Taiwan interacted with Western capital. When the leaders of the Chinese nationalist Guomindang Party escaped to Taiwan after losing the Chinese Civil War in 1949, the island was poor and battle-scarred, and its future prospects were dismal. Throughout the 1950s, as the communists and Western-aligned nationalists in East Asia threatened to clash violently, Taiwan's survival depended on American support. The country ranked fifth in the world in foreign aid received per person.[9] Taipei's need to retain American support against their shared communist enemies meant that taking an anti-imperial position – a position that sought to reduce Western influence – would have left Taiwan defenceless against the communist government on the mainland. Since Taiwan did not embrace 'economic sovereignty' as a central platform of its political system, as it wanted not to reduce its ties to the West but to increase them, its dalliance with import substitution was neither deep nor long lived. The island began to embrace economic integration with the West soon after its separation from mainland China.

Besides defence, which was the government's primary focus during the 1950s, Taipei sought economic growth by reforming at home rather than expanding abroad. Landownership was redistributed, for example, using funds from Japanese businesses that had been expropriated after the war.[10] Since most of the population lived on farms, agricultural development was Taipei's main concern, though industry was promoted through the standard tools of import substitution, such as protective tariffs and an undervalued exchange rate. Because of political uncertainty about the country's future path and because of Taiwan's inward focus, foreign trade and investment remained at low levels throughout the 1950s.[11]

Taiwanese officials realized, however, that they needed to attract more foreign capital in order to industrialize. To do so, Taiwan's government decided to leverage private economic connections with the United States and other capitalist countries, reconstructing some of the economic networks that the end of informal empire had torn down. The government began promoting exports as a means of earning foreign exchange. In 1959, Taipei issued a nineteen-point Economic and Financial Reform Program, liberalizing trade restrictions.[12] The following year, it created incentives to attract foreign investment, 'permitting unlimited repatriation of earnings and 15% annual repatriation of capital' and offering a five-year tax holiday to foreign investors.[13]

Even before these investment measures were passed, the government had begun preliminary planning for the creation of a zone in which foreigners would receive incentives to create export-oriented businesses. When the idea first arose in 1956, it encountered immediate political problems.[14] As K.T. Li, an Economics and Finance Minister and one of the zone's strongest proponents, later explained:

> major psychological barriers and a number of minor problems had to be overcome … Chinese resentment of the extraterritoriality (freedom from local

jurisdiction) enjoyed by foreigners in prewar China created opposition to both free trade zones and [export processing zones]. There was a sincerely held concern that Taiwan was yielding sovereignty in the zones to foreign investors in the name of trade and investment.[15]

Li and other backers of the zones argued that this was untrue and unimportant. 'Although it is true that the zones allowed investors to operate under a different set of rules than those outside', Li pointed out, 'they were nonetheless [Taiwanese] rules'.[16] In addition, there was no alternative policy that would make the country more independent. Reducing ties with the West would put Taiwan at greater risk from the mainland. Taiwan ultimately saw Beijing as a greater threat to its sovereignty than Western businesses. As a tiny island in a standoff with its largest neighbour, in one of the poorest corners of the globe, Taiwan needed trade and investment for growth to take off. As more and more policymakers began to accept these arguments, Li later recounted how 'sovereignty ceased to be an issue'.[17] Political sovereignty, of course, still was valued: that is why they were fighting with the mainland, after all. But after this first battle over the zones in the 1950s, foreign investment was not seen as a threat to sovereignty, but as a source of support for Taiwan's position vis-à-vis Beijing. And investment from Western businesses, which in the age of empire had been seen as agents of imperialism, took on a very different valence in the Cold War, where they provided further guarantees of Taiwan's security from the mainland. The SEZs won widespread support once they were seen to bolster, not weaken, the island's sovereignty.

By 1960, Taiwan's Ministry of Economic Affairs began formally studying how it could create an export zone that could compete with Hong Kong – a British colony that welcomed Western capital – as a location for foreign investment.[18] The idea rapidly gained popularity among Taiwan's economic and financial elite.[19] In 1965, Taiwan introduced legislation establishing special zones at Kaohsiung, on the southern tip of the island.[20] Construction began that year, and the Kaohsiung Export Processing Zone was formally inaugurated and opened for business on 3 December 1966.[21] Businesses jumped at the opportunity to open factories in a country that was staunchly anti-communist, had exceptionally low wages and now offered investment incentives. The first company to set up shop was a clothing manufacturer from Hong Kong, and within two years, more than 128 companies had plans to build factories in the zone.[22] Demand was higher than expected, so the government quickly decided to open two additional zones, one at Nantze and the other in Taichung.[23] Foreign money rushed in, and within twenty years the zones had attracted half a billion dollars of capital, almost 10 per cent of all foreign investment in Taiwan.[24] Taiwan's neighbours began to take note. The country's investment boom led to rapid growth, in stark contrast to the economic catastrophe on the mainland. These SEZs were not solely responsible for Taiwan's take-off, of course, but across Asia they were widely seen as a crucial ingredient in the country's success.

Special economic zones in China's 'reform and opening'

The revolution that swept across the PRC in the late 1940s was as much a revolt against imperialism as it was against capitalism. To a good Marxist-Leninist, that could only be natural: Lenin himself had pointed out that imperialism marked the highest stage of capitalism.[25] The country had certainly suffered from imperialism: several European countries, as well as Japan, had controlled foreign concessions in China before the Second World War, and beginning in the 1930s, Japan had begun to seize Chinese territory outright. Economic influence had led to political control. As a result, Chinese leaders believed it was impossible to strengthen China's sovereignty if there were so many foreigners inside China's territory, especially foreigners from the capitalist West, China's Cold War enemy. In addition to nationalizing property and collectivizing agriculture after the revolution, the PRC moved to reduce its connections with foreign economic partners. As Mao explained in 1949,

> If we imagine our country to be a family house, it is very dirty inside. Firewood, trash, dust, fleas, bedbugs, and lice are everywhere ... We need to get rid of all those dirty things and put our house in order. Only when the house in cleaned up ... will we invite our guests to come in.[26]

Foreign concession zones, areas in which imperialist powers had previously received special legal privileges, were a particularly dirty corner of the Chinese house. The European, American and Japanese businesses that had exploited China via the zones represented the pinnacle of imperialism, and as a result, special zones were particularly distrusted by Chinese leaders. They insisted that economic contacts should not compromise China's political sovereignty. Even as China lurched from the Great Leap Forward to the Cultural Revolution, and even after Mao's death in 1976, Chinese officials continued to equate a high degree of economic autarky with political independence. As late as 1977, on the eve of China's decision to open its economy to foreign investment, a PRC study of SEZs in other Asian countries insisted that special preferences for foreign capitalists were present-day manifestations of imperialism.[27] From the perspective of Beijing, the Cold War made Western imperialism seem even more threatening, as the West's military presence was greater after 1945 than at any previous point.

But from Beijing's perspective, by the late 1970s, international politics had begun to look less black-and-white. The outbreak of border skirmishes with the USSR in the late 1960s suggested that Soviet 'hegemonists' were as great a threat as Western 'imperialists'. The West was no longer the main threat to Chinese sovereignty. Meanwhile, several Asian territories that were US Cold War allies, such as Taiwan, Hong Kong, Singapore and South Korea, had seen their economies grow rapidly, confounding the presumption that the presence of Western businesses drained wealth away from developing countries. As Deng Xiaoping consolidated his position in the Chinese Communist Party in the late 1970s, China's orientation slowly began to shift. Many economic reforms were pushed through on Deng's watch, including the decollectivization of agriculture, industrial streamlining and price liberalization. But Deng's proudest achievement was opening SEZs, which provided investment incentives similar to those of Taiwan.[28] That is not to say that the creation of these zones was Deng's own idea.[29] Given the success of such zones in East Asia and worldwide, Chinese officials had been examining them for years, even sending study teams to neighbouring countries to learn what worked and what did not.[30] Provincial officials also played an important role. Guangdong Province, which would eventually host three of the initial four SEZs, bordered Hong Kong and had first-hand knowledge of how integration with the capitalist economy could transform a poor economy. Because of its proximity and its Chinese-speaking population, Hong Kong offered an obvious channel for foreign capital investment into the PRC, and Guangdong's leader, Xi Zhongxun, the father of China's current president, embraced the idea of closer economic ties with Hong Kong.

As part of Deng's policy of 'reform and opening', which called for more international economic contacts, the government issued in 1979 a new law governing Chinese enterprises' joint ventures with non-Chinese companies, formally allowing foreign direct investment.[31] The first proposal came from Yuan Geng, a Hong Kong businessman looking for more space to run his ship-scrapping business. Guangdong and the central government enthusiastically embraced the idea, giving Yuan a plot of land upriver from Hong Kong on which to dismember old ships and sell them for scrap.[32] Because of the scale of attracted foreign capital, Beijing perceived this first investment as a great success. As news ricocheted through the Party, the Central Committee issued Document No. 50, giving special authority to Guangdong and Fujian Provinces to create zones to attract investment from foreign businesses.[33]

Four cities were initially designated as SEZs: Shenzhen, Zhuhai and Shantou in Guangdong, and Xiamen in Fujian.[34] These cities had clear advantages that made them attractive to foreign investors. The Guangdong SEZs were close to Hong Kong, while Xiamen was directly across the straights from Taiwan. These ties mattered. Shantou, one of the zones in Guangdong, was selected because of its historic ties with emigrants to Hong Kong and Southeast Asia; more than one million people in Hong Kong have roots in Shantou.[35] In the initial stages of foreign investment, the fact that many initial investors were ethnically Chinese assuaged China's fears about the political ramifications of foreign investment. For the PRC, investment from ethnic Chinese businesses from Hong Kong, Singapore and elsewhere in Southeast Asia was crucial. It had several advantages: they were nearby, shared a culture and language with China and had plenty of resources and experience doing business in developing economies.[36] Above all, investment by overseas Chinese avoided sticky questions about imperialist exploitation that Western capital would have immediately brought to the fore. After all, it was argued, China's sovereignty could not be threatened by members of its own nation. China's bet on its cross-border kin paid off, in political and economic terms. In 1981, two years after the SEZs were established, 91 per cent of investment in Shenzhen originated in Hong Kong.[37]

Location and shared roots were not the only attractions for foreign business. Compared with most of the PRC, the zones' tax burden on companies was lighter, and business regulations were far less intrusive. The corporate income-tax rate for joint ventures in the SEZs was half that in the rest of China, 15 per cent compared with 33 per cent outside the zones.[38] Land rents were generally cheaper than elsewhere in China, and, more importantly, materials needed for manufacturing could be imported without paying duties.[39] Labour laws also were amended in business' favour: besides gaining access to a labour market of nearly one billion people willing to work for rock-bottom wages, companies in the Guangdong SEZs were exempt from certain national labour regulations, giving businesses leeway to write contracts as they saw fit, excluding unions and allowing for unrestricted dismissal of employees.[40]

Political challenges to the special economic zones

Foreign capital rushed into the SEZs. Soon investors came not only from Hong Kong, but also from around the world. One analyst reported 'a machinery plant (Swiss), container plant (Danish), stone quarry (Australian), soft drink plant (U.S.), feedmill (U.S.-Thai), fish farm (Japanese), electronics factory (Japanese), explosive chemicals storage warehouse (U.S.), and pig farm (Philippines)'.[41] By 1984, Hong Kong and Macau constituted only 12 per cent of foreign investment in the SEZs, Southeast Asian capital accounted for 27.6 per cent and Western firms for 60.4 per cent.[42] The success of the zones led Beijing in 1984 to give fourteen additional cities the right to accept foreign investment and to create even larger zones along the Yangzi and Pearl River Deltas the following year.[43] The triumphal mood in the SEZs was summed up by the float that Shenzhen sent to Beijing's 1984 parade marking the thirty-fifth anniversary of the founding of the PRC, which prominently showcased the saying, 'Time is money and efficiency is life.'[44]

This outward confidence masked a series of tense debates within the Chinese Communist Party about the wisdom of such zones. These debates were not simply about the efficacy of the zones themselves, but about the usefulness of foreign investment, the role of the Chinese state and the meaning of concepts like sovereignty and exploitation that had been central to the formation of the PRC and its policies under Mao. Although the Party had rallied around Deng after left-wing Maoists were sidelined in the late 1970s, it was still rife with deep divides over how to interpret the current state of international politics and economics and how China should seek to interact with the outside world. Was global capitalism exploitative? Or could it be harnessed to China's advantage? Did economic exchange with the West and Japan threaten China, or was it an opportunity? Was China's position strengthened by hunkering down and keeping out foreigners, or should China work with foreigners to develop new technologies more rapidly and build wealth? These debates split on ideological as well as generational lines: with the exception of Deng, older party members tended to be more sceptical of former imperialists than younger ones, who were more interested in emulating Japan than resisting it.

This ideological contest played out in many policy arenas, but the most important manifestation of this debate was over SEZs. Some officials, including Chen Yun, the party's second most powerful figure behind Deng, opposed SEZs from the start because of the legacy of foreign concessions.[45] Knowing this, SEZ officials deliberately emphasized the differences between SEZs and foreign concession zones, underlining China's full sovereignty over the zones' territory. This involved some complicated legal gymnastics. The law stated that although enterprises in the SEZs were compelled to obey Chinese law, their main regulator was the Guangdong Administrative Committee in Charge of Special Economic Zones, suggesting that they were, in fact, under a different legal regime.[46] Since that was a politically dangerous notion – giving foreigners different laws was the mark of a foreign concession – the SEZ backers denied that different legal standards really existed. As one pro-SEZ article pointedly insisted, 'All sovereign rights within a special zone (including legislative, judicial, administrative, and economic rights) are controlled by our government. All units of enterprises and undertakings and personal activities within the special zones must abide by the laws of China.'[47] Chinese critics of SEZs feared that by giving special legal rights and tax privileges to foreign businesses, the businesses would accumulate political power and threaten the prerogatives of the Chinese state. Backers of the zones had to insist repeatedly that, unlike in the age of empires, this was not a danger.

Despite these assurances, Chen Yun sided vocally with anti-SEZ forces. He believed that China did not need foreign investment and that foreigners could not be trusted. He told other party leaders that 'foreign capitalists were not just looking for normal profits, but "surplus profits"', explaining his opposition to joint ventures between Chinese and foreign businesses.[48] Chen based his beliefs on sound Marxist-Leninist theory. He made a point of rereading Lenin's *Imperialism: The Highest Stage of Capitalism* after Deng's reforms had begun, and told another party leader 'that Lenin's characterization remained valid, and that we were still in the era of imperialism'.[49] Chen was not alone in this belief. The Portuguese had initially rented Macau for drying out fishing nets, the party's orthodox pointed out, but 400 years later they still had not left.[50]

Defenders of the zones admitted that the SEZs did allow some exploitation but argued that since it was on a small scale and carefully controlled by the state, it was worth it. 'With the socialist economic holding the dominant position', one official argued, 'the kind of exploitation involved is nothing to be afraid of'.[51] This argument came under concerted attack in 1985 by a group of top CCP officials. The charge was led by Hu Qiaomu, one of the chief ideologists in the CCP who was known to hold orthodox views on the question of reform. In an article published in an internal party journal, *Zuzhi Renshi Xinxi*,

> Hu sharply criticized the zones, evoking their similarities to the foreign enclaves in the 19th-century treaty ports. Hu recalled that 'the Qing dynasty adopted an indifferent attitude' toward the concessions, at the expense of 'China's legal rights'. He suggested that the present Chinese government had already gone too far in yielding to the 'inordinate demands' of foreigners ... Moreover, Hu charged, foreign businessmen 'show no respect' for Chinese unions and 'forget even the laws of their own countries when they come to the SEZs'.[52]

Hu's article sparked a ferocious debate among China's intellectuals and historians. Were the zones actually comparable to the foreign concessions? If so, Deng's policy of 'reform and opening' was putting at risk China's sovereignty and the gains of the revolution by surrendering territory and economic advantages to the Japanese, Americans, French, British and Germans – the very powers that had worked to emasculate China just a generation earlier; or was this time somehow different? Perhaps China's nuclear weapons meant it no longer needed to fear attack. Or perhaps the rapid growth of neighbours like Taiwan and Malaysia meant capitalism was not a zero-sum game after all. Hu's criticism sparked a cascade of articles that debated which historical analogy was most appropriate to China's contemporary situation. Critics on the party's left saw Deng as no better than the Qing Court during the 1894–1895 Sino-Japanese War, failing, as one writer put it, 'to play the slightest role in protecting state sovereignty and territorial integrity'.[53] Opponents retorted that rejecting all things foreign was an essentially conservative viewpoint not befitting of a true socialist.[54]

Deng managed temporarily to quiet opposition to SEZs in 1985, but he could not silence critics for long. Debate erupted again three years later in 1988, when Zhao Ziyang, the *de jure* head of the CCP, proposed turning all of Hainan Island into an SEZ and leasing some of the land to a Japanese company.[55] This was announced around the same time that Zhao proclaimed his 'coastal development strategy' of integrating all of China's coastal regions – more than 40 per cent of China's population – into international markets.[56] This was too much for party conservatives, who launched a renewed attack. In addition to Hu Qiaomu, even party elder Li Xiannian, who was closely involved in creating the SEZs, believed that the Hainan Island lease was 'a loss of dignity, an insult to our nation, and a betrayal of our nation's sovereignty'.[57] An office run by leading conservative politician Deng Liqun collected compromising material suggesting that the SEZs 'would degenerate into "foreign concession zones"'.[58]

In the end, Deng Xiaoping's insistence overcame the objections of party conservatives. Deng Xiaoping backed Zhao Ziyang, the General Secretary of the CCP, who argued that China had nothing to fear from foreign economic contacts. For these men, Lenin was no longer relevant: the age of imperialism had passed. Trade, Zhao insisted, was not begging, but mutual exchange: a 'form of self reliance'. Foreign concessions happened in the past because the Qing dynasty was 'corrupt and impotent', Zhao suggested, but the PRC was neither. He urged compatriots to look at investors' fears that China's government might change its preferential policies towards foreign businesses. Did that not prove Beijing was fully sovereign?[59] The world had changed since 1949, Zhao argued, and China had too. Foreign investment no longer threatened sovereignty; it strengthened it by making China wealthier and providing it with new technology. And the SEZs were not controlled by imperialists; they were deliberately created by the increasingly strong Chinese state. Under communist party rule, Beijing had cleaned up the dirty house that Mao lamented in 1949. Now, Zhao insisted, it was safe to invite guests.

China's politics lurched towards renewed orthodoxy after the party crushed protests at Tiananmen Square in 1989. But even though Zhao Ziyang was deposed and imprisoned, Deng insisted that the new climate of nationalism and ideological orthodoxy should not apply to economics. His famous 'southern tour' in 1992, in which he visited several economically dynamic cities in China's south, was intended to ensure that the country did not renew its isolation from the global economy. Two of Deng's four stops on the tour, in Shenzhen and Zhuhai, were cities with SEZs.[60] While there, he argued that China needed more foreign investment, not less.[61] Deng's tour marked the final victory of those looking to integrate China into the global economy, since it ensured that opponents of SEZs were sidelined or forcibly retired.[62] In 1992, Vice Premier Tian Jiyun gave a speech mocking the sovereignty-obsessed Leninists. 'Couldn't you establish a special economic zone for leftists?' he asked. 'Salaries would be low, you would rely on coupons, you would have to stand in line to buy everything.'[63] His remarks were recorded and spread across China via bootleg cassette tapes.[64] China had decided that the age of economic imperialism was over.

Decolonization and globalization

The origins of today's globalized economy are usually explained with reference to debates among Western economists or contests between centrally planned communism and free market capitalism. The story told here about Asia's SEZs suggests that this is incomplete. In China and Taiwan, one of the main ideological debates about how to interact with the global economy focused on political, not economic, outcomes. Rather than debating output or living standards, political rhetoric focused on imperialism and the nation-state. The central policy question was whether confronting imperialism and asserting sovereignty required some degree of economic autarky. Many of the first countries to create SEZs, like Taiwan, Malaysia and Mauritius, had politics that were uniquely immune to demands for anti-Western economic autarky, either because of geopolitical necessity or because precarious ethnic balances meant that hard-line nationalist politics garnered limited support. The Cold War played a particularly important role in this process. As the perceived communist threat spread during the early Cold War, many governments in Asia decided that Western imperialists were less of a threat than domestic insurgencies or the communist powers in China and the Soviet Union. Countries that feared communism were less likely to see the West as a threat and more likely to embrace its trade. They tended to create special economic zones as a result.

As export zones spread, critics from across the Third World alleged that the re-emergence of a string of cities across the Indian and Pacific Oceans that were specially designed to attract foreign capital amounted to the resurrection of 'colonial' models of economic exchange.[65] Indeed, arguments that special zones of foreign investment exploit labour persist to this day. But anti-imperialist opposition to SEZs quickly receded in Taiwan, then later even in communist China, as the Cold War geopolitical environment also changed. Before 1945, the main threat to Chinese sovereignty had been Western and Japanese imperialists. In this era, foreign concessions did undermine sovereignty, particularly when, as in China, foreigners stationed military forces in the zones. In

Shanghai, that meant that foreigners had troops in one of the country's biggest cities. Capitalism and informal empire went hand-in-hand. But the context of the Cold War changed this because it introduced new threats to Asian countries' sovereignty, some of which were perceived to be more dangerous than Western informal empire. In Taiwan, the perceived danger of Western and Japanese business was far overshadowed by the threat of invasion from the mainland. Because of this, Taiwan used SEZs to attract Western capital and bolster its sovereignty against the communist threat. Several decades later, Beijing came to a similar conclusion: the Soviet Union was a greater threat than the West. It, too, decided that SEZs were not only less dangerous than before, but they could actually increase China's sovereignty by giving the country more room for manoeuvre against its chief geopolitical threat, the Soviet Union. Even though SEZs looked similar to foreign concession zones, the changed geopolitical context of the Cold War meant that, for many countries, informal imperialism facilitated by Western capital was less of a threat.

Notes

1　Roland, Joan (1999), 'Baghdadi Jews in China and India in the nineteenth century', in Jonathan Goldstein (ed.), *The Jews of China*. Armonk, NY: M.E. Sharpe, 142; Roth, Cecil (1941), *The Sassoon Dynasty*. London: Robert Hale; Jackson, Stanley (1968), *The Sassoons*. New York: Dutton; 'Sassoon family', *Oxford Dictionary of National Biography*, <http://www.oxforddnb.com/view/article/58221> [accessed 12 March 2014]; Stein, Sarah Abreyeva (2011), 'Protected persons? The Baghdadi Jewish diaspora, the British state, and the persistence of empire', *American Historical Review*, 116(1), 80–108.

2　Tabak, Faruk (2009), 'Imperial rivalry and port-cities: A view from above', *Mediterranean Historical Review*, 24(2), 79–94.

3　Basile, Antoine and Germidis, Dimitri (1984), *Investing in Free Export Processing Zones*. Paris: OECD, 22.

4　See, for example, Frieden, Jeffrey (2006), *Global Capitalism: Its Fall and Rise in the Twentieth Century*. New York: Norton.

5　Gao, James Z. (2009), *Historical Dictionary of Modern China (1800–1949)*. Maryland: Scarecrow Press, 124.

6　Gao (2009).

7　Dong Wang (2005), *China's Unequal Treaties: Narrating National History*. Lanham, MD: Lexington Books, 10.

8　Nayar, Baldev Raj (1972), *The Modernization Imperative and Indian Planning*. Delhi: Vikas, 91.

9　Barrett, Richard and Whyte, Martin King Whyte (1982), 'Dependency theory and Taiwan: Analysis of a deviant case', *American Journal of Sociology*, 87(5), 1064–1089, p. 1070. Aid data is from pp. 1958–1965.

10　Barrett and Whyte (1982), 1068.

11　Riedel, James (1975), 'The nature and determinants of export-oriented direct foreign investment in a developing country: A case study of Taiwan', *Weltwirtschaftliches Archiv*, 111(3), 505–528, p. 508.

12 Kuo-ting Li (1988a), *Economic Transformation of Taiwan, ROC*. London: Shepheard-Walwyn, 28.

13 Wang (2005), 26–27. Domestic investors received similar incentives.

14 For more detail on the intellectual trajectory of such zones, see the chapter by Patrick Neveling in this volume.

15 Kuo-ting Li (1988b), *The Evolution of Policy Behind Taiwan's Development Success*. New Haven: Yale University Press, 95; Vogel, Ezra (1991), *The Four Little Dragons*. Cambridge, MA: Harvard University Press, 26.

16 Li (1988b), 95.

17 Li (1988b), 95.

18 Li (1988b), 96.

19 Li (1988b), 97.

20 Wang (2005), 28.

21 Li (1988b), 97.

22 Li (1988b), 97.

23 Li (1988b), 97.

24 Li (1988b), 98; Riedel (1975), 512.

25 Lenin, Vladimir (1917), *Imperialism: The Highest Stage of Capitalism*. Petrograd: Zhizn'i Znanie.

26 Gaddis, John (1997), *We Now Know*. Oxford: Oxford University Press, 54.

27 Crane, George (1990), *The Political Economy of China's Special Economic Zones*. London: M.E. Sharpe, ch. 2, especially p. 24.

28 Vogel, Ezra (2011), *Deng Xiaoping and the Transformation of China*. Cambridge, MA: Belknap Press, ch. 14.

29 Zhao Ziyang's memoirs attribute the idea to Deng, but this is dubious.

30 Stoltenberg, Clyde (1984), 'China's Special Economic Zones: Their development and prospects', *Asian Survey*, 24(6), 637–654, p. 638. See also Crane (1990), ch. 2, p. 24.

31 Nishitateno, Sonoko (1983), 'China's special economic zones: Experimental units for economic reform', *International and Comparative Law Quarterly*, 32(1), 175–185, p. 175.

32 Vogel (2011), 396–398; Crane (1990), 26.

33 Vogel (2011), 399.

34 Wang, Jici and Bradbury, John H. (1986), 'The changing industrial geography of the Chinese Special Economic Zones', *Economic Geography*, 62(4), 307–320, p. 307.

35 Wang and Bradbury (1986), 312.

36 Fenwick, Ann (2012), 'Evaluating China's Special Economic Zones', *Berkeley Journal of International Law*, 2(2), 376–397, p. 376.

37 Fenwick (2012), 384.

38 Nishitateno (1983), 178–179.

39 Nishitateno (1983), 179–180.

40 Pattison, Joseph E. (1981), 'Special Economic Zones in the People's Republic of China: The provincial experiment', *China Law Reporter*, 140(3), 141–166, pp. 153–154.

41 Stoltenberg (1984), 647.

42 Wang and Bradbury (1986), 312.

43 Crane, George (1994), '"Special things in special ways": National economic identity and China's Special Economic Zones', *The Australian Journal of Chinese Affairs*, 32, 71–92, p. 85.

44 Fewsmith, Joseph (1986), 'Special Economic Zones in the PRC', *Problems of Communism* 35(6), 78–85, p. 78.

45 Zhao Ziyang (2009), *Prisoner of the State*. New York: Simon & Schuster, 101; Crane (1990), 29.

46 Pattison (1981), 147–148.

47 Fenwick (2012), 381, citing Shouchun, Wang and Kanghua, Li (1981), 'A brief discussion of the role of Special Economic Zones in our country', *Guoji Maoyi Wenti*, 1.

48 Zhao (2009), 102–103.

49 Zhao (2009), 102–103.

50 Zhao (2009), 107.

51 Stoltenberg (1984), 639, citing Wang Dacheng (1981), 'Special Economic Zones', *Beijing Review*, 24(12), p. 3.

52 Fewsmith (1986), 81.

53 Fewsmith (1986), 82, citing Liao Zonglin (1985), 'On the question of patriotism and national betrayal during the Boxer Rebellion', *Guangmin Ribao*, p. 3.

54 Fewsmith (1986), 82.

55 Crane (1994), 85; Zhao (2009), 105.

56 Crane (1994), 85.

57 Zhao (2009), 106.

58 Zhao (2009), 102.

59 Zhao (2009), 107.

60 Vogel (2011), 664.

61 Vogel (2011), 673.

62 Vogel (2011), ch. 23.

63 Crane (1990), 71.

64 Crane (1990), 71.

65 See Takeo, Tsuchiya (1978), 'Free Trade Zones in Southeast Asia', *Monthly Review*, 29(9), 29–39.

Key texts

Barrett, Richard and Whyte, Martin King. (1982). 'Dependency theory and Taiwan: Analysis of a deviant case', *American Journal of Sociology*, 87(5), 1064–1089.

Crane, George. (1990). *The Political Economy of China's Special Economic Zones*. London: M.E. Sharpe.

Li, Kuo-ting. (1988). *Economic Transformation of Taiwan, ROC*. London: Shepheard-Walwyn.

Vogel, Ezra. (2011). *Deng Xiaoping and the Transformation of China*. Cambridge, MA: Belknap Press.

Wang, Wei-ming. (1981). *The Establishment and Development of Kaohsiung Export Processing Zone (KEPZ), 1965–1975: A Study of Economic Decision-Making in Taiwan, ROC*. Taipei: Asia and World Institute.

PART V
DEFENDING THE STATE: INTELLIGENCE AND VIOLENCE

The final part of this volume re-examines old evidence and gives it a new twist. It explores the legacies of colonial rule as a security state, particularly in the uses and abuses of intelligence. In the South Asian context, leaders were able to manipulate intelligence relations for their own aims, but in other contexts, colonial officials reasserted the brutal violence of empire. It considers the lingering relations between colonizer and colonized, revealing a story of coercion and co-option in the violent yet subversive ways in which the Cold War and decolonization interacted.

CHAPTER 13
ARCHIVES, INTELLIGENCE AND SECRECY: THE COLD WAR AND THE END OF THE BRITISH EMPIRE

Caroline Elkins

Governments try to press upon the historian the key to all the drawers but one, and are very anxious to spread the belief that this single one contains no secret of importance ... [I]f the historian can only find out the thing which the government does not want him to know, he will lay his hands on something that is likely to be significant.

Herbert Butterfield, 1951[1]

On the eve of decolonization from Malaya, colonial officials worked around the clock to avoid the embarrassment that their predecessors had suffered in India but a decade earlier. Then, in New Delhi, a cloud of ash hung over the independence-day ceremonies, threatening to disrupt not only the festivities of the day, but also future Anglo-Indian relations. The ash that filled the sky and littered distant paths came from Britain's colonial incinerators. The fires rendered to dust countless colonial-era files. Document destruction was a hallmark of British retreat from India, although the process, with its lingering plumes of ash covering the skyline of New Delhi, was hasty at best, and sloppy at worst.

In Malaya and Singapore, colonial officials took a much different tack. There, the colonial men-on-the-spot assured their superiors in London that 'the risk of compromise or embarrassment arising out of any paper left behind is very slight'. Discussions ensued regarding the 'top secret registry' of documents with instructions to 'remove not only certain listed papers but also any unsuitable for Malayan eyes'. 'It was further recognized', in Malaya, 'that the actual withdrawal and destruction of the material in question would have to be done with utmost security and discretion'. After much consideration, including dumping documents at sea from Port Swettenham and destroying them in the local incinerator in Kuala Lumpur, the colonial government opted to ship multiple crates of files to the 'first class incineration facilities' at the naval base in Singapore via civilian trucks to provide 'additional "cover" for the operation'. All packing was done by 'expatriate personnel and carrying by Chinese coolie labour' to avoid arousing Malaysian notice; armed escorts were also on hand. Convoys of heavily guarded lorries drove from Kuala Lumpur to Singapore under the cover of darkness where crate upon crate of documents were set alight at Britain's secure naval base.[2] By the operation's completion, the British colonial government had rendered all files into ash, although not before destruction certificates, or papers documenting the documents' eradication, were created for each document destroyed, copies of which were sent to the Colonial Office in London.[3]

For decades, the evidence for wide-scale document destruction on the eve of Britain's decolonization was sparse, at best. At Britain's National Archives in Kew, only a few fragments remained chronicling the disposal of files at the time of decolonization in India and Malaya, for example. For historians, locating these documents was a needle-in-the-haystack exercise, as not only were they sparse, but they were also circuitous to find. In the case of India and Malaya few documents remained, and they were located not in the colonies' files, but rather in the end of empire files for Nigeria.

This paucity of documentation was upended in January 2011. It was then that a young, junior desk officer for the Foreign and Commonwealth Office (FCO), Edward Inglett, discovered in Hanslope Park – the site of some of the British Government's most closely kept state secrets – some 8,800 files from thirty-seven former colonies, all spirited away at the time of decolonization. These files were those that had escaped the incinerators in New Delhi, Singapore and elsewhere, and were spirited back to London, held under lock and key for decades: that is, until they were compelled to light in the context of the now historic Mau Mau reparations case in the High Court of London.[4]

Filed in the spring of 2009, the Mau Mau case was the first of its kind. With the British Empire in the dock, five elderly Kenyans alleged that they had suffered systematic torture and abuse at the hands of British colonial agents in the detention camps, screening centres and emergency villages of Kenya during the Mau Mau Emergency. They claimed the British government was liable for their sufferings, and the FCO was the named defendant in the case. From the start, the claimants' attorneys filed multiple requests for document production; each time, the FCO claimed they held nothing that was not otherwise available at The National Archives (TNA). But a suspicious Inglett decided, after yet another claimant request in the fall of 2010, to sleuth further, and it was then that he learned that some 300 boxes of files removed from Kenya on the eve of independence, and taking up nearly 100 linear feet of storage space, were in the bowels of Hanslope Park, or 'spook central' as it is locally known because of its links to MI5, MI6 and other secretive British operations. Alongside of the Kenya files were thousands of others related to the thirty-six other former British colonies.

The 'Hanslope Disclosure', as the High Court termed the new cache of files, was an extraordinary discovery by any standard. When announced in Parliament and in the High Court, the archival revelation set off a media firestorm. The British government apologized profusely, while expressing deep embarrassment. Robert Jay, QC, acting for the FCO in the Mau Mau case, told the High Court how 'the existence of the repository [that] was discovered ... no doubt caused embarrassment to my clients understandably'.[5] Inglett sought 'to convey sincere and unreserved apologies on the FCO's behalf to both the Claimants and the Court'.[6] With its tail between its legs, however, the British government protested vigorously that the loss of the documents was nothing but the result of administrative error and cost controls. Rejecting any claims of cover-up Whitehall insisted that:

This failure to publish has a lot more to do with a sheer lack of resources ... All historical documents need to be read by reviewers ahead of their transfer to the National Archives. But there has always been the problem that other material received higher priority. As a result, the files relating to the former colonies have just been sitting in a corner and neglected.[7]

In Parliament, Lord Howell of Guildford publicly acknowledged for the first time in April 2011 the full extent of the archival find, along with Britain's historic practice of removing files from its former colonies prior to decolonization. Noting how 'the FCO holds around 8,800 files from 37 former British Administrations', he went on to state that 'It was ... general practice for the colonial Administration to transfer to the United Kingdom, in accordance with Colonial Office instructions, shortly before independence, selected documents held by the Governor which were not appropriate to hand on to successor Government.' From Aden and Cyprus to Palestine and Singapore, colonial officials – under direct orders from London – culled and then burned the majority of sensitive files while repatriating others. The contents of the repatriated files, Lord Howell promised, would be reviewed and 'those selected for permanent preservation will be transferred to the National Archives for the public to access'.[8]

Lord Howell's rather laconic pledge was scarcely enough, however. The British media, in particular, demanded transparency. Three days later, Britain's Foreign Secretary William Hague responded. Personally assuring the public that a full disclosure process was under way, Hague gestured not only to the historical significance of the Hanslope discovery, but also to its ethical meanings. 'This process of transparency is overdue, essential to upholding our moral authority as a nation, and in the long term interests of our country', the Foreign Secretary declared. He confirmed that mistakes with the Mau Mau files had been made, and that they should have been 'properly recorded and made available to the public', though he continued to reiterate that there was 'no deliberate attempt to withhold information'. Instead, Hague sought to capitalize on the moment as best he could, standing on a newfound, moral high ground of full disclosure. 'We are a government that believes in transparency and openness', and to that end, Hague stated:

> We will release every part of every paper of interest, subject to any legal exemptions. This work will be overseen by a senior and independent figure appointed by me. The willingness to shine a light on our faults and to learn from our mistakes of the past is an enduring strength of British democracy.

With deference to Britain's history of liberalism, the Foreign Secretary observed how 'for hundreds of years' the British parliamentary system had held government to account not only in Britain but also throughout its empire. 'The law', Hague noted with a hint of foreshadow, 'does not stop at our shore'.[9]

If one were to believe the media, the British government and several historians, the discovery of the Hanslope documents and their subsequent release to Britain's National Archives at Kew were watershed moments.[10] True to his word, Hague first appointed

Anthony Cary, former British High Commissioner to Canada, to undertake a thorough, internal review as to how and why the 2,000 boxes of colonial-era files were out of reach of the public for decades, in violation of the Public Records Act of 1958. According to the Cary Report, which Hague deposited in the libraries of both houses of Parliament, the British government, despite the best intentions of the FCO staff, was guilty of administrative mismanagement, as opposed to any kind of conspiratorial suppression of historical evidence. Lord Howell took the Cary Report to be nothing short of a vindication for the British government, and he 'fully endorse[d] ... [the] tribute' that Cary made towards the 'professionalism and commitment of current FCO staff', which included both Inglett and the records management staff at Hanslope Park and elsewhere.[11]

In his next act towards full transparency, Foreign Secretary Hague set his sights on releasing the long-held, colonial-era files. He appointed a Cambridge don of American history, Anthony Badger, as independent reviewer of the transference of all of the end-of-empire documents found at Hanslope Park to the National Archives at Kew. Termed the 'migrated archives', some 8,800 files of documents that had been, in the words of the Cary Report, 'irregularly held' by the FCO ran into millions of pages. Badger, who was not an expert in British or imperial history, had a monumental task in front of him. According to the Foreign Secretary, Badger would work closely with the FCO leadership to 'provide assurance to the wider public that the process is being carried out in accordance with my commitment to transparency, notably my intention to release every part of every paper of interest, subject only to legal exemptions'.[12] In other words, aside from those files exempted under the Freedom of Information Act – that is, those files posing a threat to national security or personal privacy – everything that Inglett's search uncovered in Hanslope Park would be handed over to the public.

In April 2012, the British government released the first tranche of migrated archives to a media circus of its own making. With cameras zeroing in on the archival behemoth at Kew and reporters clamouring to touch the newly released, colonial-era parchments, headlines in Britain trumpeted the 'secrets' emerging from the government's official records.[13] The FCO fed the media frenzy, issuing official news statements of its open-book approach to the document transfers; in total there would be six tranches of file releases, with the last making its way to Kew by the end of 2013.[14] Certainly there were a few nuggets from which the journalists could quote, but, overall, there was more flash than substance in the British government's debut of the migrated archives.

Throughout, Badger was a forthright servant in his capacity as official document tsar. While the Cambridge professor conceded that the discovery of the files in Hanslope Park had placed the British government in an 'embarrassing, scandalous' position, he was insistent 'that the release of the migrated archives is a very conscientious and transparent process and that the Foreign Secretary's goal of releasing every paper of interest will be met'.[15] The redactions, according to Badger, were less than 1 per cent of the material being deposited in the archives. However, as the media and some historians have heralded the discovery and release of the migrated archives as ushering in a new era of end-of-empire documents, Badger himself has been more measured. The American history professor found the bits in the newly released files that tell the story of the 'banality of bureaucracy', or the day-to-day running of empire, to be of historical value. This is no small matter, as the view from the periphery is something that only historians who have travelled to far-flung archives in places like Kuala Lumpur and Tel Aviv have been able to access. Nonetheless, when reflecting on the migrated archives as a whole, Badger wrote:

> I am not sure this is going to cast dramatic new light on the messy history of the transition to independence or provide 'smoking guns' on the nature of London's and the colonial government's responsibilities for the dirty wars fought against nationalist insurgents or nail down government complicity in torture and atrocities.[16]

In short, there is no new, large cache of archival smoking guns in Kew. While the estimated number of documents contained in the migrated archives runs into the millions of pages, the document dump is, as Badger points out, largely filled with mundane details about on-the-spot colonial administration.

There is, though, one crucial exception to Badger's observation. The migrated archives chronicle, for the first time in substantial detail, the systematized processes of document removal and destruction – processes that were carefully choreographed from the Colonial Office. Indeed, as in Malaya in 1957, similar processes would repeat themselves elsewhere over the next two decades, including in Kenya where colonial officials established an elaborate system of strongrooms, lock-boxes, special couriers and hand-selected officers for the massive document culling exercise that began in 1958 and continued apace until independence five years later.[17] Throughout, British agents in Nairobi, Kampala, Dar es Salaam and elsewhere deliberately withheld from the infernos all documents that contained 'Legacy' material. That is, all files that would not 'embarrass Her Majesty's Government' and had no 'security, political or individual personal implication' fell into the official 'Legacy' category and were thus preserved, in the words of one colonial official, for the 'historical' record. By the time the purging process was complete, massive numbers of incriminating files were torched. In Kenya, for instance, some three-and-a-half tons of documents had been put to the wind, and those that remained in Nairobi told an incomplete story, at best, of British colonial rule.[18]

Archives and empire: A new era of transparency?

The Hanslope Disclosure, and the migrated archive process that ensued, constitutes a kind of disclosure that is, in fact, only a disclosure insofar as how we, as historians, choose to read it. Indeed, based upon the Disclosure's contents, and the context of its release, in particular, there is little reason to believe that the British government, for the first time in its modern-day bureaucratic history, has parted the seas of transparency. Badger, for all of his efforts, was convinced that 'The scale of the embarrassment inflicted on the FCO – the humiliating circumstances in which the FCO had to go to court to admit that it had misled the court – is perhaps the best guarantee of full disclosure of the records.'[19] Yet it is here that the Cambridge professor, despite his best intentions, fails to place the discovery of documents at Hanslope either in their full legal and historical contexts or in the context of the paradoxes of liberalism in all of its imperial forms.

To begin, the transparency announcements were being made at the same time that the British government was in the dock over alleged crimes committed during the Mau Mau Emergency in Kenya. Even with the weight of the Court behind them, the claimants and their historical experts, myself included, only gained access to some 30 per cent of the files found at Hanslope Park. Moreover, the FCO admitted to having lost, perhaps in the 1990s, thirteen missing boxes of Top Secret Kenya files and another 160 or so Top Secret boxes from multiple other former colonies. To date, these boxes of files have not been found. And, importantly, of the new evidence found in the files the FCO did offer up scores and scores of files chronicling for the first time the scope and scale of document destruction: something that ultimately would be beneficial to the British government's defence in the case, if the Court read them in a particular way around issues of statute of limitations. Together, these contextual factors should raise question marks, at the very least, about the level of newfound transparency on the part of Foreign Secretary Hague and his Foreign and Commonwealth Office.

Issues surrounding document disclosure and secrecy, however, were scarcely new to the British government. In some ways, the Kenya case is a textbook response from Her Majesty's bureaucracy. The first clue is the internal report that Hague commissioned, and Anthony Cary executed, to investigate how the 8,800 files pertaining to the end of the British Empire had gone missing for so long. When filed publicly in May 2011, the Cary Report's findings would prove reminiscent of countless internal investigations that took place during the era of British colonial rule. Stopping short of being a full whitewash, the report expended much effort to exonerate staff members of the FCO and TNA, with repeated references to lack of funds and understaffing. This is certainly fair enough, although the collective amnesia of countless individuals who gave testimony to Cary because of their involvement with the handling and responsibility of the 'misplaced' files from the time of their arrival in Britain at the end of empire until their discovery in early 2011 is striking. Indeed, throughout the Cary Report, the bobbing and weaving of eye-witnesses, the lack of any accountability for the questionable circumstances surrounding the discovery of the records in Hanslope Park and the continued disappearance of the Top Secret boxes outside of an internal government investigation smack of similar, and successful, efforts at cover-up during the colonial era. In fact, in Kenya and elsewhere, the British government, time and again, expended strenuous effort to avoid external investigations into allegations of torture in its empire, instead offering up internal reports in the post–Second World War era that lauded British officials for their transparency and impartiality. I do not doubt that the FCO and TNA staff work under difficult conditions, being understaffed and underfunded, much like colonial officials of yesteryear's empire. Yet, the similarities in the processes of internal investigations and their whitewashing outcomes offer a window into the performative practices of British secrecy and cover-up.

So, too, does the appointment of an official, academic expert to offer gravitas to the British government's claims to truth and transparency. There is a long tradition of the

British government convening special committees to examine the roll-out of its nation's past, and with it, how best to handle historians whose sleuthing could uncover episodes that the British government preferred to remain hidden, or at best managed. One of the many arrows in the government's quiver of deception has been the co-option of academics to serve as official historians for sensitive periods of Britain's past. In his landmark study on Britain's Secret Service, Richard Aldrich dissects, among other things, the recruitment and indoctrination of official historians into the secrets of Ultra, or the code used to crack Hitler's Enigma communications. These same historians were impressed not to betray official secrets, but rather to offer up watered-down versions of wartime intelligence. Indeed, as Aldrich intones, 'The story of modern secret service offers us a clear warning. Governments are not only adept at hiding substantial secrets, they are quick to offer their own carefully packaged versions of the past.'[20]

In the case of its Secret Service cover-up, the scale of the government's efforts was enormous. It needed 'a concerted programme for the management of history equivalent to a wartime deception operation itself', which included, according to Aldrich, not only the indoctrination of official historians, but also the coordination of 'well-packaged programmes of document release'. Such processes, much like the release of the migrated archives, allowed the British government in the instance of Ultra to reach beyond a stonewalling approach and offer up a carefully choreographed document-release process that effectively set the research agenda for a new generation of historians. Information management quickly became crucial for the British government, and it embarked upon a repetitive process of occasionally making a public display of placing more sensitive Secret Service files into the public domain, with newspaper headlines proclaiming 'MI5 thrills historians with secret service archives'.[21] In reality, these document dumps were a kind of 'good faith distraction material', with enormous volumes of little real substance. The entire process, however, has been enormously effective, with Aldrich concluding:

> This problem of scale distracts us from the wider problems of selection and destruction of documents … Most historians are remarkably untroubled by this and some have come to think of the selected materials in the Public Record Office as an analogue to reality … The danger is that those who work only on this controlled material may become something close to official historians, albeit once removed. There is a potential cost involved in researching in government-managed archives where the collection of primary material is quick and convenient. Ultimately there is no historical free lunch.[22]

This free-lunch warning was issued in the historical context of Britain's Secret Service documents and the archives that house them. Yet, it is equally applicable to the ways in which historians have written about the end of the British Empire, particularly in the era of the Cold War, avoiding for decades the issue of colonial violence, and fetishizing the written documents that had been carefully tended and disclosed as part of the British government's long-standing tradition of information management, especially in the years following the Second World War. So, too, is it relevant to the nature of the Hanslope Disclosure and subsequent government assurances of transparency not only in its transference of the migrated archives to Kew, but also in its release of files through the process of legal discovery in the Mau Mau case. At stake are questions of secrecy, historians' complicity in reproducing official narratives of empire and the value of the contents of the archives as opposed to the processes that led to their creation and management.

At stake is also the question of ideology, or more specifically the recurrent paradoxes in the liberal project in empire. Historians from Oxford, Cambridge and University of London – better known as the Golden Triangle – were, for decades, contributors to the myth of British imperial triumph. From towering figures like Reginald Coupland and his outright airbrushing of colonial violence that was occurring under his nose to more measured and distanced histories, like those of John Gallagher, that took readers away from what Richard Drayton calls the 'scene of the crime', historians edged closer and closer to becoming official scribes of the British establishment.[23] It is easy to dismiss this trend as one reflecting underlying, and sometimes overt, racist notions; or as an indication of the methodological conservatism of the Golden Triangle, which saw the signs and symbols of colonial bureaucracies as embedded in written documents located in official archives; or even as a form of professional laziness, albeit shrouded in methodological concerns, that dismissed other forms of evidence, whether written or oral, as unusable because, in reality, accessing them – whether in the foothills of Kenya or in the humid archives of Penang – was both costly and physically and emotionally burdensome to excavate. In reality, all of these factors have some merit, and together they comprise just some of the paradoxes of liberal imperialism, whether playing out on the ground in empire itself, in the compilation of archives or on the pages of accounts chronicling the imperial past.

The propensity to emancipate and repress, liberate and discriminate, disclose and erase, are all hallmarks of liberalism, particularly in its imperial forms. Contradictory impulses and legitimate and illegitimate practices coexisted side-by-side, which explains why the British government, past and present, has been able to sanitize its own obfuscating archival practices under the guise of careful record-keeping. Indeed, one of the very difficult issues in assessing, for instance, the British government's information-management efforts is that some of its practices are standard of bureaucracies, and their concealments are not necessarily intentional, but rather a function of administrative blindness and occasional misadventure. This is the point of the Cary Report, which, for the most part, has been accepted as a reasonable explanation for the disappearance of 8,800 end-of-empire files, and the likely permanent loss of 170 boxes of 'Top Secret' files.

When one peels back the layers, however, and looks closely at empire, particularly its archival forms and the processes that created them, internal reports like that of Cary and histories such as those scripted in the Golden Triangle for decades become far less credible, or at least highly problematic. Indeed, like the British colonial government that they document, these reports and histories erase the complexities of the liberal project in empire. In particular, the British government, with its mutually constitutive forms of liberalism and imperialism, found itself constantly balancing the exigencies of strategic necessity with the need for legitimizing accountability. It often fell short on the latter, as the process of recent end-of-empire document disclosure reveals, and instead relied on tried and true methods of 'good faith distraction' and official secrecy.

There is an intimate connection between the deeply political nature of archives and the production of historical knowledge. This is clearly revealed when examining the intimate relationship between official British archives, the recent Hanslope Disclosure and secrecy, on the one hand, and the pernicious and deeply embedded processes of British intelligence gathering, the end of empire and the Cold War, on the other. To unpack this relationship, and to understand its lasting effects on the postcolonial world, one must examine critically the history of Britain's intelligence services, the individuals who served in these organizations and the role that the archives have played in concealing as much information on systematized violence and torture at the end of empire as they have revealed.

Archives and alibis: Intelligence and the end of the British Empire

Archives are bureaucracies, and they are also a kind of anti-politics machine. The British National Archives, like other official archives, offers a kind of double bookkeeping system, keeping states accountable on the one hand, while also providing the means for certain forms of obfuscation, often couched in terms of governance and public security, on the other. In short, the archive serves as an alibi for an accessible, objective truth: one that relates to the idea of making society and democracy. Yet, until one broadens the archive, democracy cannot be realized, whether in historical scholarship or in society at large. Indeed, the two are intimately linked. This is particularly evident when examining the role of British imperial intelligence gathering during the Cold War.[24]

The need for effective intelligence gathering was a recurring theme in Britain's empire. The three-year Anglo-Boer War, with its precedent-setting use of concentration camps and scorched-earth policies against civilians, was viewed in London as a failure, not only on an operational side – with some 45,000 British troops needed to squeeze a negotiated settlement out of the Afrikaner insurgents – but also on the intelligence side. Together with the mounting German threat, shortcomings that were laid bare during the Anglo-Boer War prompted the British government to create the first peacetime intelligence department in the fall of 1909, when the Committee on Imperial Defence took the lead in creating what was an intelligence system with decided roots in the empire. By the time of the First World War, Britain's Secret Service Bureau was split into domestic and foreign branches, with Military Intelligence 5, or MI5, overseeing domestic intelligence, including counter-espionage, counter-sabotage and counter-subversion. Military Intelligence 6, or MI6, was responsible for the foreign branch of the Secret Service Bureau. Each unit had twin designations, with MI5 also known as the Security Service, and MI6 as the Secret Intelligence Service, or SIS.

By the end of the First World War, the expansion of Britain's security state was significant by any measure. Progress was made in gathering and assessing intelligence, with card-index systems and coordination with the intelligence branches of Britain's three military units – the Royal Air Force, army and navy – all being introduced. While each branch of the military would go on to maintain its own intelligence department, MI5 and MI6 were cross-cutting departmental units that also, in the decades ahead, would find themselves collaborating in various ways with intelligence officers from various British military branches.

From the security state's inception, turf wars punctuated the relationship between MI5 and MI6, some of which centred on responsibility for the empire. It was during the First World War that MI5 created a new department, D-Branch, to oversee German-backed subversion in British territories. By the end of the conflict, MI5's D-Branch had gone a long way towards developing a network of intelligence information in the empire. By the interwar period, it was MI5 that eventually took on full responsibility for the empire and Commonwealth, whereas MI6's operations were confined to a three-mile demarcation line outside of all British territories around the globe. In some ways, this jurisdictional streamlining was as much a reflection of economy as it was organization: serious cutbacks in Britain's security state slashed the number of intelligence operatives to just thirty in 1938, leaving MI5 woefully understaffed, and scarcely the imperial intelligence service necessary to keep the spread of Nazi subterfuge, let alone the growth of communism and anti-colonial nationalism, at bay.[25]

For decades, the role of intelligence collecting was largely missing from the end-of-empire literature. This was due, in part, to the secrecy surrounding Britain's intelligence services. Indeed, it was not until the late 1980s that the British government placed its intelligence services on a statutory basis for the first time, with MI5 being recognized in 1989, and the SIS and the Government Communications Headquarters (GCHQ, later renamed post-war British SIGINT service) in 1994. During this period, Whitehall inaugurated the Waldegrave Initiative on Open Government, which brought in independent historians, in roles similar to that of Tony Badger with the Hanslope Disclosure, to review and declassify government records, including files from the intelligence services. In addition, the British government recruited two historians, Keith Jeffery and Christopher Andrew, who had privileged access to government files that were inaccessible to other historians and who wrote official histories of the first forty years of the SIS and the centenary history of MI5, respectively.[26]

More recently, Calder Walton, Andrew's research assistant with similar privileged access to MI5 files, published the first comprehensive account of British intelligence during the overlapping eras of the end of empire and the Cold War. Walton's *Empire of Secrets: British Intelligence, the Cold War and the Twilight of Empire* suggests:

> that the current state of the history of Britain's end of empire is in the same position that the history of the Second World War was in before the disclosure of the Ultra secret. By ignoring the role of intelligence, our understanding of the demise of the British empire is at best incomplete, and at worst fundamentally flawed.[27]

Looking beyond his privileged access to MI5 files, Walton makes a bold assertion about the nature of the end-of-empire intelligence files. Ignoring the intonations of Aldrich and others working on security files, Walton claims, 'the result of the government's declassification process is that there are now almost too many intelligence records relating to the British empire to study'.[28] This observation may well be valid, although the question is what kinds of files are to be found in this now-voluminous cache of documents, and what files are missing? Indeed, as the recent Hanslope Disclosure suggests, the documents chronicling violence at the end of empire – a process in which MI5 played a crucial role – were systematically destroyed at the time of decolonization, and more recently culled, as the document release in the context of the Mau Mau High Court demonstrates. Still, Walton takes his 'too many intelligence files' one step further, suggesting that the Hanslope Disclosure is a watershed moment for document releases on intelligence at the end of empire. He writes how:

> the 'rediscovered' records are said to contain some of the grimmest paperwork on the history of Britain's end of empire … Thanks to the Kenyan case … we can now see that Hanslope Park acted as a depository for records detailing the most shameful acts and crimes committed in the last days of the British empire. This is the first book to draw on that secret archive.[29]

Walton fails to understand, let alone interrogate, the overarching issue of archive as alibi, a point to which I shall return. Nonetheless, his work does offer a useful chronicling of Britain's intelligence service at the end of empire. As he points out, increasingly throughout the twentieth century, MI5 representatives were deployed throughout the empire and Commonwealth as Security Liaison Officers (SLOs). There, often under the guise of being cultural attaches or secretaries in the colonial administration, the SLO's job was to provide 'liaison, supply of external intelligence, training [and] operational advice'. In addition, one of their crucial roles was to train local special branch members of the colonial police force, as it was the special branch that was responsible for the day-to-day intelligence gathering in the empire during the Cold War. In fact, after 1945, MI5 routinely deployed its representatives out into the empire to train, en masse, local members of the special branch. By the early 1950s, MI5 had a total staff of some 840 members, with nearly thirty SLOs posted around the world; this number would peak during the end-of-empire era to forty-two SLOs working outside of Britain.[30]

From the top of its hierarchy down to its agents on the ground, MI5 was very much a product of the empire. The first director general of MI5, Vernon Kell, recruited MI5 candidates exclusively from a circle of friends and family whom he knew, with a majority of his recruits coming from posts in India and other British colonies. Kell's successors, first David Petrie and later Percy Sillitoe, also served in the empire as the head of the intelligence branch in Delhi and in the British South Africa Police Force, respectively; together, they continued the colonial, old-boy recruiting practices for Britain's secret service, as did several of the director generals that followed them. It was hardly surprising, then, that MI5 colleagues were connected not only through sensibilities and shared experiences of colonial rule and pastimes, but also through a culture of empire that reflected the contradictions of the liberal project abroad, and increasingly at home.[31]

Importantly, many MI5 representatives were not only recruited from the empire for work at home, but after the Second World War many MI5 representatives who were directly involved in wartime internment, interrogations and intelligence-gathering in sites like Camp 020 and the London Cage were, once again, redeployed into the empire to assist with intelligence gathering as the tide of nationalist insurgencies rose.[32] They included Sir John Shaw, who had barely escaped death in the King David Hotel and later went on to head Sillitoe's 'Overseas' or 'OS' section; Alex Keller, who fought against the Zionists at the end of the Mandate and was later brought into OS section, only to be redeployed to empire as the head of Security Intelligence Far East (SIFE); Alex MacDonald, who served in the India police, then in Kenya, before becoming MI5's first Security Intelligence Advisor (SIA) seconded to the Colonial Office in London; and John Prendergast, who was deployed to multiple end-of-empire hotspots, including Palestine, the Gold Coast, the Canal Zone in Egypt, Kenya, Cyprus and Aden, among many others.

During the era of the Cold War and end of empire, MI5 and its SLOs created an intelligence web across the globe that reflected, at least in part, Britain's broader economic, strategic and Cold War interests. In the aftermath of the Second World War, Britain was fiscally bankrupt and dependent upon the United States for an economic bailout, as well as loans for post-war rebuilding efforts. Britain looked to its vast empire, with its enormous potential value, as the silver bullet to its financial crisis. Prime Minister Attlee's foreign secretary, Ernest Bevin, looked to the oilfields of the Middle East, rubber plantations of Malaya and the other commodity-producing colonies scattered throughout the world as future sources of cash and a way out from under America's fiscal thumb. Ultimately, Bevin made himself clear on this point: Britain would only 'pull its weight in foreign affairs' once it had cut its financial dependence on the United States.[33] The foreign secretary had the full support of other members of the cabinet, who similarly believed the situation to be dire and that 'the colonial empire could make a major contribution towards the solution of our present economic difficulties'.[34]

The political and strategic value of Britain's empire was also not to be underestimated, particularly in a realigned post-war world of East versus West. Despite its enfeebled position after the war, Britain staked its claim as one of the Big Three great powers with the dawn of the Cold War, or at least the strongest of the world's middle powers. Ruler of an empire that still extended over swaths of Asia, Africa, the Americas and the Pacific, London legitimately remained one of the more powerful players on the post-war international scene. Moreover, as relations between East and West rapidly deteriorated after 1945, the strategic value of colonial territories such as Singapore, Aden, Kenya, Cyprus and Hong Kong grew.

The Cold War changed the rules of the game, and American policy, at least nominally anti-imperialist, was much more willing to tolerate and even support a continuing British Empire in the face of a rising communist threat. Anti-communism quickly trumped anti-imperialism, and the United States threw its weight behind bolstering its allies, including Britain and France, in defence of Western Europe. '[W]e need ... these countries to be strong', Senator Henry Cabot Lodge, Jr. declared when testifying to the Senate on the North Atlantic Treaty, 'and they cannot be strong without their colonies'.[35] Much to the chagrin of some in the State Department and Pentagon, the United States found its 'most important collaborators' in Britain and its empire and Commonwealth.[36] By June 1948, a State Department memo was unequivocal in rendering the United States' practice of bolstering Britain's empire into policy, stating:

> The United Kingdom, the Dominions, Colonies and Dependencies, form a world-wide network of strategically located territories of great military value, which have served as defensive outposts and as bridgeheads for operations. Subject to our general policy of favoring eventual self-determination of people, it is our objective that the integrity of this area be maintained.[37]

The 'special relationship' between Britain and the United States would evolve in the post-war era, with London increasingly tethered to Washington's view of the new world order. Clearly the strategic value of Britain's empire, and its real and perceived bulwark against communism, helped render the Anglo-American relationship of particular value to Britain's one-time colony. By 1947, the importance of Britain's empire to the fight against communism meant, in Wm. Roger Louis's words, 'the Americans subsidized the imperial system generously in one way or another as a measure of national defense'.[38]

Nonetheless, successive British governments in the post-war era conflated Cold War imperatives with nostalgia for British global power of yesteryear, and believed that Britain's economic burdens and dependence upon the United States were ephemeral. Consecutive governments held onto the notion that Britain was one of the Big Three, together with the United States and Soviet Union, and that in due time, Britain would emerge an independent operator on the global scene. It was a position shared by many Labour and Conservative leaders, alike, and while Bevin most succinctly captured this sentiment in his memo, 'The threat to Western civilization', one could easily imagine Churchill having penned Bevin's sentiments whereby the Foreign Secretary wrote:

> ... it should be possible to develop our own power and influence equal to that of the United States of America and the USSR. We have the material resources in the Colonial Empire, if we develop them, and by giving a spiritual lead now, we should be able to carry out our task in a way which will show clearly that we are not subservient to the Unites States of America or to the Soviet Union.[39]

Such a view of the international order and Britain's place within it created as much conflict as cooperation in Anglo-American relationships. The United States poured billions of dollars into the Marshall Plan to aid European economic recovery and to rebuild a unified system that would serve as a bastion against the spread of communism from the East. Washington was less than pleased when Labour and Conservative governments both rejected plans for a kind of United States of Western Europe. Prioritizing empire and Commonwealth above all else, Whitehall refused to support a European federalist system or participation in a European army, which Washington viewed as essential to Western security and the rearming of Germany. Such intransigence also placed the United States, not to mention Britain, in precarious ideological and political positions with regard to post-war human rights accords and their connection to self-determination. The ideological thrust behind Britain's approach to human rights accords, self-determination and its empire reflected the contradictions of the liberal imperial enterprise that had been apparent since the nineteenth century. It was, however, the particular circumstances of the post–Second World War era that threw these contradictions in relief as never before, laying bare the paradoxes in Britain's post-war position on human rights and fundamental freedoms, particularly when evaluated against the backdrop of its continued empire, if not imperial expansion.

It is this context – one of steadfast, imperial resurgence that revealed contradictions in Britain's liberal imperial project – in which the intelligence web linking various parts of the colonial landscape unfolded during the Cold War. Driving much of the work of Britain's intelligence service was the overarching concern with Soviet communism. Britain, the United States and other Western powers feared that the Cold War would usher in potential Soviet influence over various colonies throughout the world in the post-independence aftermath. Moreover, the fear of a third world war loomed large, and as Walton rightly points out:

> The British intelligence community reasoned that if such a war erupted, Britain, or more likely what remained of it, would have to rely on the empire and Commonwealth for support, as it had done in both previous world wars, and would not need to fear a Soviet 'fifth column' in those countries. This required building up local security services sufficiently robust to prevent Soviet intrusion in those states seeking independence from Britain.[40]

Yet, in the aftermath of the Second World War, local intelligence services throughout the empire were, by most accounts, understaffed, poorly trained, lacked local language knowledge and any sense of overall coordination either within the colony or between the colony and metropole. The atrophied state of MI5 would quickly be tested during the early years of the Cold War when Britain's efforts at imperial resurgence were met with one insurgency after another throughout the empire. Beginning with the Zionist uprising in Palestine and followed by insurgencies in Malaya, Kenya, Cyprus, Aden and elsewhere, Britain found itself mired in costly and protracted end-of-empire wars around the world.

In the face of the Soviet threat and recurring insurgencies, MI5 scrambled in the post–Second World War years to reform colonial security services throughout the empire. These efforts were catalysed when, in April 1955, General Sir Gerald Templer – fresh off of his turn as High Commissioner and chief architect of counter-insurgency policy in Malaya – published his famous, colonial security report. In response to Templer's recommendations, the Colonial Office established its own Internal Security Department (ISD), the existence of which was to be kept secret. With a global mandate, the ISD worked closely with all of Britain's secret service units, whilst MI5 continued to increase its number of SLOs in the empire. To this end, some MI5 representatives had already been permanently posted in the empire, such as Jack Morton, who assumed the role of Director of Intelligence in Malaya under Templer and would later move onto MI5's overseas affairs, or E-Division, eventually ending his career in Northern Ireland. Others, like John Prendergast and Alex Kellar, who eventually headed MI5's Overseas Division from 1958 to 1962, would criss-cross the empire in the decades following the Second World War, serving as troubleshooters in times of local crises.[41] Still others, like Alex MacDonald, took on multiple roles, overseeing the intelligence training initiative throughout the empire. A veteran of the Indian police and a protégé of Templer's in Malaya, MacDonald took nearly sixty trips to some thirty British colonies and dependencies between 1954 and 1957. Whilst on locale, he personally oversaw the training of, on average, 250 colonial special branch members per year, with this number climbing to nearly 400 by 1959. Back in the metropole, MacDonald was headquartered at Leconfield House in London where he took seriously Templer's warning that colonial governments had to take intelligence matters more seriously if they were to deal effectively with local insurgencies. Indeed, Templer minced no words on this point when he wrote:

> Whereas in the military world 'Intelligence' is a highly specialized field of its own, in the Colonial (and other civilian) services it naturally tends to be regarded as merely one aspect of the political 'knowledge' which permeates the whole business of administration. Nor is this aspect held to be a very important one: 'intelligence' is often considered to be a narrow, if sensational, function of the police. The administration is apt not to concern itself closely with the machinery for its collection and appreciation, nor with its relation to security in the broadest sense. As a result, security intelligence has I think come to be regarded as a kind of spicy condiment added to the Secretariat hot-pot by a supernumerary and possibly superfluous cook, instead of being an expertly planned and expertly delivered dish of its own.[42]

For his part, MacDonald established training courses for senior officials, with recruits lectured to widely on such topics as Soviet intelligence and Sino-Soviet communism, surveillance, interrogation, accurate registry-keeping, card index-filing systems, interception, defectors and agents.[43]

When examined through the lens of Soviet influence and postcolonial intelligence services, Walton sees Britain's efforts at colonial security reform as a success. He points to both the abeyance of Soviet influence in many of Britain's former colonies, together with the fact that SLOs posted in every major British colony and dependency 'without significant exception ... were asked by new national governments to remain in place after independence, and liaised closely with those new governments'.[44] In effect, MI5 and its global and indigenous intelligence networks in the empire offered a postcolonial 'bulwark against anti-Western propaganda spewed out by the Sino-Soviet Bloc'.[45] Both he and Alex Keller, the onetime head of MI5's Overseas Division, agree that without

MI5's networks, it was likely that Soviets would have been far more successful in their efforts to turn the former British Empire a different shade of red. Keller underscored this point, when he later wrote:

> In the case of the African Commonwealth countries, I have felt – profoundly so – that the contributions that we as Security Service have been making to their own security by our training facilities, by our service of information, and by the close links which we are building up in running joint agent operations, together constitute a record of which we can be legitimately proud ... We have built up in these new emergent territories cadres of indigenous officials who admire, respect and trust us and who can do much to influence their political masters in the right direction ... We shall never be able to make any African country pro-West but, by this kind of support, we can at least assist them to sit on the fence and not fall over on the wrong side.[46]

At the same time, there is no avoiding the fact that MI5 was stretched thinly across the globe and consistently misread the insurgent landscape, whether in Palestine, Malaya, Kenya or elsewhere. Indeed, time and again, counter-insurgencies throughout the empire persisted for years and were notable for their lack of effective intelligence gathering and assessments, particularly in the early years of the wars. This was due, in part, to the intelligence service's fixation on the Soviet threat. There was little understanding of nationalism outside of communism; nationalism was coded in East versus West, which in turn influenced the nature of intelligence gathering, as well as the analyses of intelligence from insurgents and their supporters. In effect, the Cold War cloud hung over counter-insurgency operations, particularly intelligence gathering, and this, in turn, influenced the ways in which counter-insurgencies were coded and understood.[47]

Related to this was MI5's under-appreciation of local circumstances. Like their brethren in the various special branches, MI5 representatives, many of whom had imperial experience prior to joining the intelligence service, internalized a particular ethos about the colonized population – an ethos that was steeped in liberalism's 'civilizing mission', Western hubris and decidedly racist outlook. There was scarcely consideration of the legitimacy of insurgent demands, or of the depth of anti-colonial sentiment felt by the grassroots, civilian populations, many of whom supported the insurgents in Palestine, Malaya, Kenya and elsewhere, as the so-called passive wing. Nor was there an appreciation of the ways in which colonial governments and MI5 representatives fuelled civil wars in the waning days of empire and left them behind as part of their legacies. Put another way, there was a significant cultural barrier to attributing an ideology of resistance to ordinary peasants and local populations. Thus, even when intelligence structures were more fully established, liberalism's failure to appreciate the situation based upon broader notions of race and British imperial endeavours precluded both useful collection and assessment of intelligence throughout the empire. In fact, many operations and methods of intelligence gathering only worsened the insurgencies and anti-colonial sentiments, broadly defined.

Colonial violence and other forms of knowing

Wilful and conscious exclusions of other forms of knowing defined the end-of-empire field for decades. Today, there is a danger – despite, or because of, the recent document discoveries at Hanslope Park – of continued over-representing of the contents of the official archive and, with it, over-fetishizing of written evidence and dismissal of oral testimonies from the former empire or evidence held in memoirs, literature and other forms of knowing from the one-time periphery. This is particularly true when considering the intersection between intelligence, end of empire and the Cold War. Walton's work, while useful in placing MI5 and intelligence fully into the Cold War and end-of-empire landscape, lamentably offers a carefully packaged version of the past: one that is, in many ways, a reflection of the British government's choreographed exercises in document releases and co-optations of official historians in writing narratives about the Anglo-intelligence services, whether in the empire or elsewhere. As Aldrich intoned in his critique of official historians working on Ultra, 'governments are not only adept at hiding substantial secrets, they are quick to offer their own carefully packaged versions of the past'. 'Official histories', or those that are one-step removed, as in the case of Walton, do not challenge the contents of the archives, and often over-represent the significance of recent disclosures, as Walton does with the end-of-empire files discovered at Hanslope Park. Walton suggests that these files contain 'the most shameful acts and crimes committed in the last days of the British empire', although he only cites some six documents from the new, migrated archives. Such evidentiary slights of hand, when coupled with an uncritical acceptance of official histories and archives, present an enormous problem when seeking to understand fully the role of intelligence at the end of empire.

This is most evident when focusing on the question of violence and MI5's role in the systematic abuses that characterized Britain's conduct during counter-insurgency operations in the era of the emerging Cold War. Certainly, Walton does not shy away from violence perpetrated against insurgents throughout the empire. At issue is who was perpetrating the violence and whether or not there was anything systematic about its nature. It is here that Walton and others take at face value such MI5 guidelines as those compiled in 1961, which read:

> Physical violence or mental torture – apart from moral and legal considerations – opposed to – short sighted – like willfully damaging engine of car wanted for long journey – under violence anyone will talk – you may get a confession to prevent torture but it will not be the truth – Intelligence gained usually is useless.[48]

In other words, Walton views MI5 and British intelligence more broadly as above the colonial underbelly of British imperial rule in the waning days of empire. In his assessment, British counterterrorism, which resulted in mass detentions, murders, such as those of sixteen-year-old Alexander Rubowitz, detainees at Hola Camp in Kenya and scores of others in Cyprus at the hands of death squads known as 'Her Majesty's

Torturers', were all indirect results of misguided and outdated military policies, as well as a handful of so-called bad apples.

It is here, however, on the question of intelligence gathering and systematized violence, where Britain's commitment to imperial resurgence and Cold War imperatives converged. They led to the creation of police states in each counter-insurgency location and the deployment of individuals and practices that embraced various uses of torture and violence as a means through which to gather intelligence, however faulty it may have been. A far more expansive, integrative and critical reading of the MI5 files, from not only the official archives but also written and oral archives from throughout the former empire, is fundamental to linking the role of Britain's intelligence service to the broader project of imperial resurgence in the context of the Cold War.

Take, for example, the role of MI5 in the establishment of Camp 020 and the London Cage during the Second World War, and Combined Services Detailed Interrogation Centres (CSDICs) in Germany and various parts of the world in the aftermath of the conflict. Camp 020 was the domain of Lieutenant-Colonial 'Tin Eye' Stephens. Styled as such because of the monocle permanently affixed to his right eye, Tin Eye was a typical MI5 recruit, having cut his teeth in the empire. Tin Eye and his MI5 compatriots, along with members of the military and other branches of Britain's intelligence services, would have crucial roles to play in establishing interrogation centres first in Britain and later in continental Europe and the empire. In time, interrogation centres would dot Britain's landscape, with two of the most notorious, the London Cage and Camp 020, located in the nation's capital where their eavesdropping systems combined with heavy-handed tactics to produce an extraordinarily effective, albeit morally and legally questionable, system of intelligence gathering. As the War Office, in a secret briefing memo in the fall of 1941, stressed:

> The Combined Services Detailed Interrogation Centre (C.S.D.I.C.) [i.e. Camp 020] is administered by the War Office (M.I.9) on behalf of all three Services and has the duty of extracting all forms of information from enemy [Prisoners of War] by special methods of interrogation. It is no exaggeration to say that the results achieved are of the greatest operational importance to all three Services and to the [Political Warfare Executive].[49]

Uses of wartime interrogation were overseen at the highest levels of British governance. At the outset of the Second World War, spy fever gripped Britain, and Churchill scarcely escaped its clutches. Convinced at the time that a Fifth Column of Nazi sympathizers and spies were poised to subvert Britain's war effort from within, the prime minister endorsed the use of detention without trial for suspected traitors and spies until, in his words, 'this malignancy in our midst has been effectively stamped out'.[50] Churchill also took particular interest in intelligence gathering, so much so that he created the secretive Whitehall committee, the Home Defence (Security) Executive, in May 1940, the same month he moved into Downing Street. Philip Cunliffe-Lister, the first Earl of Swinton, chaired the Security Executive and packed it with a who's who of future counterterrorist and secret service notables, including the young, Oxford-educated barrister, Kenneth Diplock, who was being groomed for his future legal role in defending Britain's counterterrorist methods and suspension of due process, which later resulted in the eponymous, if not infamous, Diplock Courts of Northern Ireland. For some, the Security Executive smacked of a 'Conservative Front organization' of the worst kind. In the end, Camp 020 was the direct responsibility of the Security Executive and MI5, despite the fact that on paper, the Home Office oversaw the interrogation centre, while the War Office, in theory, staffed it.[51]

Throughout the war, Tin Eye Stephens was the commandant of Camp 020. By all accounts, including Stephens', 'the camp was entirely a novel venture'.[52] This new enterprise, which evolved with much trial and error, included the recruitment of interrogators who were defined as either 'breakers' or 'investigators', with breakers responsible for establishing a detainees' guilt and an investigator fleshing out the details and relevant intelligence.[53] According to Stephens, breakers were a particular brand of individual who were 'born not made', and they had to hate the enemy, something that could be learned. Later, when writing the official history of Camp 020, Stephens did not equivocate:

Perhaps the first class breaker has yet to be born. Perhaps he has yet to be recruited from the concentration camps, where he has suffered for years, where, above all he has watched and learnt in bitterness every move in the game. First and foremost there must be certain inherent qualities. There must be an implacable hatred of the enemy. From that is derived a certain aggressive approach, a disinclination to believe without independent corroboration, and above all a relentless determination to break down the spy, however hopeless the odds, however many the difficulties, however long the process may take. Indeed, in the classic case of Ernesto HOPPE seventy-seven days of attack, frustration, sweat and disappointment at last brought their reward.[54]

Whilst dozens of interrogators were recruited, Stephens personally oversaw all of the detainees and the 'special methods of interrogation' at the MI5 centre. Ultimately, Tin Eye was accountable to Guy Liddell and Dick White, the first and second in command of MI5's B-Division, as well as Churchill's Security Executive. It was Dick White who was in the trenches of overseeing the interrogations centres: an experience that would have future bearing on Britain's secret state more broadly, as White would go on to head both MI5 and MI6, a unique achievement in the history of Britain's secret state. In fact, White's experiences with detention and interrogation went well beyond Camp 020, as this was but one of the principle wartime detention and interrogation centres. The War Office worked closely with MI5 in establishing nine 'cages', or interrogation centres, around Britain where enemy suspects would be screened to determine whether or not they would be dispatched to one of the country's POW centres or to London for further interrogation. There, in the nation's capital, were two notorious interrogation sites. The first was Stephen's Camp 020. The second was known as the London Cage and, like Camp 020, was staffed with a phalanx of interrogators and clerks, many of whom were military men who had experience in the empire, and others of whom were German and Austrian nationals working on behalf of the British Army.

It was, however, the commandant of the London Cage who had an imperial heritage that was as expansive as his propensity to write down his wartime interrogation experiences. Alexander Scotland, a one-time military intelligence officer, was brought out of retirement specifically for his interrogation services and the running of the cage. Having been awarded an Order of the British Empire for his success in interrogating German POWs, Scotland had battle scars that extended back to the turn-of-the-century empire in Africa. Having left for wartime adventure, Scotland missed out on the Anglo-Boer War and, instead, moved to neighbouring German South West Africa, where he eventually joined the German Army, changed his last name to Schottland and fought in the genocidal wars against the Herero and Namaqua populations who resisted colonial rule. The Germans also suspected him of being a British spy. Scotland was incarcerated in Windhoek, the colony's capital, for over a year, where he got his first taste of interrogation, albeit on the receiving end. German techniques left a deep impression upon Scotland, with him later recalling, 'During the long, arduous questioning I was given by the staff officer attached to the German colonial troops, I learned perhaps the most valuable lesson of my career in South Africa ... I acquired some of the techniques of interrogating an enemy subject.'[55]

Back in wartime London, Scotland's cage and Stephen's Camp 020 both became subjects of scrutiny when several prisoners alleged torture and other cruelties. In the case of Camp 020, multiple fingerprints were at the alleged crime scene, including those of Swinton and the Security Executive who, together, handpicked Harold Dearden to be the camp's chief medical officer. It was Dearden who worked alongside Stephens and the other interrogators, devising torture techniques that were conducive to plausible deniability defences and thus left few marks, including starvation tactics, sleep deprivation and threats of hanging and death by firing squads. One former prisoner recalled Dearden and how

> [i]t was not long before my memory began to deteriorate [at Camp 020]. Certain periods of my life completely disappeared from my mind ... [the resident doctor] stated to me plainly that the treatment was intended to produce a state of 'mental atrophy and unreserved loquacity'.[56]

In the case of the London Cage, allegations of mistreatment came from several former prisoners. In 1943, Otto Witt lodged a formal protest with Britain's War Secretary for his alleged tortures. A few years later, torture allegations surfaced in Hamburg where members of the Gestapo were tried for the murder of fifty RAF officers who had been shot after tunnelling their way out of Stalag Luft III – a feat so extraordinary, it was later the subject of the Hollywood movie, *The Great Escape*. Many of the defendants claimed that they were systematically beaten and tortured in the London Cage, and only then signed confessions; they each gave detailed descriptions of their ordeals under Scotland's watch. Fourteen of the fifty defendants were hung, and nothing came of their accusations of abuse in the cage. Later, Fritz Knochlein levelled a litany of allegations of systematic ill-treatment meted out to him and other prisoners, detailing how they were humiliated, starved, water tortured, worked without respite and sleep deprived, among other things.[57] At the time, Knochlein was facing the death penalty for the murder of 124 British soldiers, and hence his allegations were considered suspect; nonetheless, the British government took them seriously enough, given their lengthy and detailed nature, to consider an inquiry, although it ultimately decided to pass, as given Knochlein's crimes, 'any court of inquiry into these allegations would be futile'.[58] Knochlein was eventually executed, though not before the local London police, according to Scotland, 'called in to enquire why such a din was emanating from sedate Kensington Palace Gardens'. It turns out the neighbours heard Knochlein's screams, though Scotland attributed them to Knochlein losing his mind and 'shrieking in some half-crazed fashion'.[59] Until the end, Scotland readily admitted to various psychological techniques and acts of humiliation, though denied the use of any physical torture, despite the extensive, corroborating evidence offered by an array of former prisoners, and the fact that Scotland himself would later pen a manuscript on the London Cage in 1954, which, prior to the government's heavy censoring, contained methods of interrogation that would cause 'considerable embarrassment to HMG', according to the Foreign Office. MI5's legal adviser was clear that, if published without serious redaction, Britain would be open to legitimate charges of breaching Geneva Conventions. When finally published three years later, Scotland's *London Cage* was a watered-down version of its earlier form, though still many in the British government worried over leaks from the original manuscript.[60]

The significance of Tin Eye Stephens, Scotland, Camp 020 and the London Cage is profound when reading the landscape of intelligence during the era of imperial resurgence in the Cold War. Indeed, Tin Eye would move on to the infamous CSDIC interrogation centre in Bad Nenndorf, Germany, where he and several of his underlings would bring their interrogation methods to bear on suspected Nazi war criminals. Eventually, their methods became the subject of a full court of inquiry investigation, headed by Tom Hayward. Hayward's final report, nearly 130 pages in all, provided extensive evidence of abuse and torture at Bad Nenndorf at the hands of MI5 representatives. Nonetheless, Stephens, who denied any involvement in the torturous methods until the end, was acquitted in his courts martial, as was one of his underlings. Only one junior officer was charged with minor offences and dismissed from the army. Ultimately, no one up the chain of command was held accountable for the crimes committed in Bad Nenndorf, which included gross torture and murder. Bottom line, the techniques honed at Camp 020 and Bad Nenndorf were considered to be too good to be given up, and too dangerous politically to be revealed. In fact, all details of wrongdoing were kept from the public for decades.[61]

These files were, however, available to Walton at the time of his research. Instead of interrogating them, or reading them alongside memoirs and other private accounts, he accepts at face value Stephen's denial of the use of torture. While he found the internment without trial of nearly 30,000 foreign nationals in Britain during the Second World War 'a lamentable low point in the history of civil liberties', Walton concluded, despite overwhelming evidence:

> Contrary to what we might assume, and contrary to its ominous first appearances, Camp 020 did not permit the use of physical coercion during interrogations ... The MI5 officer who ran Camp 020, Lt. Col. Robin Stephens, enforced a strict policy of no physical violence, or 'third degree' measures, in the facility.[62]

Moreover, Walton ignores the extensive investigative reporting that Ian Cobain conducted for *The Guardian* on Camp 020 and the London Cage, which was subsequently expanded upon substantially in Cobain's work, *Cruel Britannia*.[63]

The significance of this recreation of the official narrative of wartime interrogation extends well beyond Britain, as MI5 policies and personnel were soon deployed throughout the empire. In fact, within a decade after the Second World War, multiple interrogation centres like Camp 020 and that at Bad Nenndorf mushroomed all over the empire and other spheres of British influence. In Palestine, Syria, Iraq, Greece, India and various parts of North and East Africa, among other places, CSDICs soon became the sites for Cold War and end-of-empire intelligence gathering where, according to a War Office report, the continuity of personnel and the wartime 'lessons learned have obvious value'.[64] Later, these methods, as well as the interrogation structures necessary to facilitate their implementation, would be exported to various parts of the empire, including places like Palestine, Kenya, Malaya and Cyprus, where Britain waged counter-insurgencies against indigenous populations demanding independence from colonial rule. In Malaya, for example, where Jack Morton of MI5 took the lead on streamlining intelligence gathering and introducing what were becoming widespread British interrogation practices, Walton notes how:

> Before Morton's arrival in Malaya there was no dedicated intelligence interrogation facility in the colony, only police (CID) interrogation facilities. On MI5's recommendation, in April 1949 a specialized intelligence interrogation centre was established for the Special Branch near Kuala Lumpur, modeled on MI5's successful wartime facility, Camp 020.[65]

Furthermore, MI5 troubleshooters like Prendergast passed through nearly every major counter-insurgency operation. Walton tells us little about what Prendergast and others were actually doing, in part because this information is not contained in the official archive. Instead, in the case of Prendergast, one must travel to former colonies like Cyprus, where oral testimonies and locally produced histories, published only in Greek, link Prendergast and others to the infamous Omorfita Police Station and Lefka Interrogation Centre, among various locations of interrogation, where electric shock, water torture, toe and fingernail removal and hanging until near death were part of the larger arsenal of abuse: abuse that bore striking similarities to the tortures deployed in MI5 sites elsewhere in the empire, such as the Mau Mau Investigation Centre in Embakasi, Kenya, as well as to wartime interrogation centres and post-war CSDICs.[66]

There is considerable work to be done on the history of intelligence at the end of empire. Insofar as Walton offers a valuable contribution, we can now understand better the circulatory patterns of members of MI5 in the Cold War-era British Empire, as well as the concerted efforts undertaken to train MI5 representatives in the empire, together with countless members of local Special Branches, in the tactics of intelligence gathering and interrogation. That said, the field currently falls woefully short, in any integrated way, of understanding what actually happened during intelligence gathering, and why. To do so, a vastly expanded excavation of archives in various parts of the former empire, a compilation of oral archives and a more robust methodological and theoretical toolkit are needed. So, too, are interrogations of the British state's deliberate strategy of concealment, charade investigations (past and present) and patterns of co-opting official historians. Indeed, it is through this process of examining archive as subject, and drawing analogies between processes of concealment and secrecy both in the past and in the present that we, as historians, can expand our toolkits and gain deeper understandings of the processes of intelligence gathering, interrogation and torture that unfolded during the interlocking eras of end of empire and the Cold War: processes that had profound effects on the postcolonial world, as structures and cultures of secrecy, authoritarianism, violence and the jettisoning of human rights as protected under international law were all legacies that were embedded both ideologically and legally in their bulwarks against communism, as well as in the personnel, including scores of MI5 agents, that remained behind after British decolonization to assist in the implementation of tried-and-true methods of intelligence gathering and state security.

Notes

1   Butterfield, Herbert (1951), *History and Human Relations*. London: Collins, 196.

2   A.J. Brown, Office of the UK High Commission in the Federation of Malaya, to R.W. Newsham, Commonwealth Relations Office (CRO), Secret memorandum, 17 October 1957, DO 186/17, United Kingdom National Archives, Kew (TNA).

3   A.J. Brown (1957).

4   For background details on the case, see Elkins, Caroline (2011), 'Alchemy of evidence: Mau Mau, the British Empire, and the High Court of Justice', *The Journal of Imperial and Commonwealth History*, 39(5), 731–748.

5   'Archive at "spook central" had secret Mau Mau files', *The Times*, 8 April 2011.

6   Second Witness Statement of Edward Inglett, 7 February 2011. *Ndiku Mutua and 4 Others and the Foreign and Commonwealth Office*. Case no. HQ09X02666. London: Royal Courts of Justice, 15.

7   'Mau Mau case casts light on colonial records', *Financial Times*, 6 April 2011.

8   'Public records: colonial documents', Statement by the Minister of State, Foreign and Commonwealth Office, Lord Howell of Guilford, *House of Lords Debates*, 5 April 2011.

9 'Hague lifts the lid on Britain's secret past: Foreign Secretary responds to *Times* campaign', *The Times*, 9 April 2011.

10 The range of the media spectrum was caught up in this moment of transparency frenzy, although later, *The Guardian* published more in-depth coverage questioning the British government's release of files. See, for example, the work of Ian Cobain and Richard Norton-Taylor, 'Files that may shed light on colonial crimes still kept secret by UK', *The Guardian*, 25 April 2013.

11 Cary, Anthony, 'The migrated archives: what went wrong and what lessons should we draw?' [also known as the 'Cary Report'], 24 February 2011; Hansard, *House of Lords Debates*. Public Records: Colonial Documents, the Minister of State, Foreign and Commonwealth Office (Lord Howell of Guilford), 5 May 2011.

12 Hansard, *House of Lords Debates*. Public Records: Colonial Documents, the Minister of State, Foreign and Commonwealth Office (Lord Howell of Guilford), 30 June 2011.

13 For example, Ben Macintyre's series of article for *The Times*, including 'Secret colonial files may show more blood on British hands', 7 April 2011.

14 The FCO had a separate section of its website dedicated to the migrated archives, their review and schedule of release that offered various news releases and documents, such as the Cary Report. This section of the FCO's website since has been taken down.

15 'The secrets that shamed the last days of empire', *The Guardian*, 18 April 2012; Badger, Anthony (2012), 'Historian, a legacy of suspicion and the "migrated archives"', *Small Wars & Insurgencies*, 23(4–5), 799–807, pp. 803, 806.

16 Badger (2012), 803.

17 For examples of document selection and destruction throughout the British Empire, see, for example, Secretary of State for the Colonies, 'Disposal of classified record and accountable documents', 3 May 1961, FCO 141/6957, TNA; Governor of Uganda to Secretary of State for the Colonies, 'Constitutional development and the archives', 22 March 1961, FCO 141/6957, TNA. This is further confirmed by multiple other Colonial Office telegrams in the Hanslope Disclosure addressed to governments in Uganda, Tanganyika and Zanzibar, all of which outline consistent policies for document destruction. These telegrams, sent between 1961 and 1962, reference earlier, collective telegrams, dating as far back as December 1948 for the destruction and removal of materials. Finally, in March 1963, a memorandum outlining the 'Watch' system, nearly identical to that which had been implemented in Kenya, was also circulated in Zanzibar. For Nigeria see, for example, the file of documents located in 'Disposal of Nigerian Government Archives', DO 186/17, TNA. For choreographing of document destruction in Kenya, including lock-boxes and strongrooms, see, for example, Internal Memorandum, 8 April 1963, Bates 012888–89, GO/ DS3, Hanslope Disclosure (HD); Ross to Weeks, Secret Registry, 6 December 1961, Bates 024222, 1943/17/B, HD; 'Transfer of watch files to the governor's office', 23 March 1962, Bates 024215, 1943/17/B, HD; and 'Transfer of "Watch" files to the governor's office', 16 March 1962, Bates 024216, 1943/17/B, HD.

18 Memorandum from Ellerton, 'The designation of "Watch"', 13 May 1961, Bates 024225–231, 1943/17/B, HD; Letter from the Ministry of Defence to various departmental heads, Provincial Commissioners and Permanent Secretaries, 13 May 1961, Bates 013042, I&S.137/ O2(S), HD; Secretary of State for the Colonies, 'Disposal of classified record and accountable documents', 3 May 1961, FCO 141/6957, TNA; Governor of Uganda to Secretary of State for the Colonies, 'Constitutional development and the archives'.

19 Badger (2012), 801–802.

20 Aldrich, Robert J. (2002), *The Hidden Hand: Britain, America, and Cold War Secret Intelligence*. New York: The Overlook Press, 1.

21 Aldrich (2002), 6.

22 Aldrich (2002), 7–8.

23 Drayton, Richard (2011), 'Where does the world historian write from? objectivity, moral conscience and the past and present of imperialism', *Journal of Contemporary History*, 46, 671–685, p. 678.

24 I am indebted to Jean and John Comaroff, Martha Minow, Richard Drayton, Kirsten Weld and other participants in the History, Archive, and Law Workshop held at the Radcliffe Institute in October 2013 for these concepts.

25 Simpson, A.W. Brian (1992), *In the Highest Degree Odious: Detention without Trial in Wartime Britain*. Oxford: Oxford University Press, 37–40; Bloch, Jonathan and Fitzgerald, Patrick (1982), *British Intelligence and Covert Action: Africa, Middle East and Europe since 1945*. Dingle: Brand Book Publishers, Chapter 1; and Walton, Calder (2013), *Empire of Secrets: British Intelligence, the Cold War and the Twilight of Empire*. London: Harper Press, 24–29.

26 Andrew, Christopher (2010), *The Defence of the Realm: The Authorized History of MI5*. London: Allen Lane; Jeffery, Keith (2010), *MI6: The History of the Secret Intelligence Service*. London: Bloomsbury.

27 Walton (2013), xxii.

28 Walton (2013), xxii.

29 Walton (2013), xxx–xxxi.

30 Walton (2013), xxvii–xxix, 143.

31 Hoare, Oliver (2000), 'Introduction', in Hoare (ed.) *Camp 020: MI5 and the Nazi Spies*. Richmond: Public Record Office, 8; Walton (2013), 24–29; Sillitoe, Percy (1955), *Cloak without Dagger*. London: Cassell.

32 For the fullest discussions of Camp 020 and the London Cage, see, for example, Cobain, Ian (2012). *Cruel Britannia: A Secret History of Torture*. London: Portobello Books, 7–11; Hoare (2000), 1–30; and Walton (2013).

33 Murphy, Philip (2012), 'Britain as a global power in the twentieth century', in Andrew Thompson (ed.) *Britain's Experience of Empire in the Twentieth Century*. Oxford: Oxford University Press, 54.

34 As quoted in Hyam, Ronald (2006), *Britain's Declining Empire: The Road to Decolonisation 1918-1968*. Cambridge, MA: Cambridge University Press, 131.

35 Latham, Michael E. (2011), *The Right Kind of Revolution: Modernization, Development, and U.S. Foreign Policy from the Cold War to the Present*. Ithaca: Cornell University Press, 29.

36 Louis, Wm. Roger (2006), *End of British Imperialism: The Scramble for Empire, Suez and Decolonization*. London: IB Tauris, 459–460.

37 Burk, Kathleen (2008), *Old World, New World: Great Britain and America from the Beginning*. New York: Atlantic Monthly Press, 578.

38 Louis (2006), 460.

39 Hyam (2006), 137–138.

40 Walton (2013), 126.

41 This is a point Walton and Cobain, in different ways, make in their works. See Walton (2013) and Cobain (2012).

42 Templer Report, 23 April 1955, CAB 129/76/CP(55), TNA.

43 Course for senior officers on intelligence and security subjects, CO 1035/55, TNA; Walton (2013), 145–147.

44 Walton (2013), 112.

45 Walton (2013), 339.

46 Andrew (2010), 469.

47 For a genealogy of East versus West coding of anti-colonial movements and insurgencies, see, for example, Westad, Odd Arne (2005), *The Global Cold War: Third World Interventions and the Making of Our Times*. Cambridge, MA: Cambridge University Press, Chapter 3.

48 As cited in Walton (2013), 189.

49 'Interference with the work of C.S.D.I.C. by the construction of the aerodrome at Bovingdon: Note for V.C.I.G.S', c. October 1941, WO 208/3456, TNA.

50 *House of Commons Debates*, vol. 361, cc 794–795, 4 June 1940.

51 Simpson (1992), 185–191; and Cobain, Ian (2012), 7–11.

52 Stephens, R.W.G. 'A digest of ham', in Hoare (ed.) (2000), 41.

53 Hoare, 'Introduction', in Hoare (ed.) (2000), 18; Stephens (2000), 107.

54 Stephens (2000), 107–108.

55 Scotland, Alexander Paterson (1973, new edition), *The London Cage*. London: G. Mann, 21.

56 Simpson (1992), 242.

57 Knochlein, Fritz (2005), *The London Cage: The Experiences of Fritz Knochlein*. Canterbury: Steven Book.

58 'The secrets of the London Cage', *The Guardian*, 11 November 2005.

59 Scotland (1973), 81.

60 Cobain (2012), 31–33; Streatfeild, Dominic (2007), *Brainwash: The Secret History of Mind Control*. London: Thomas Dunne Books, 365–366.

61 Plans and reports appertaining to general conditions at D.I.C., April 1947, FO 1030/274, Part II, TNA; Statement from prisoners, General, April 1947, FO 1030/274, Part III, TNA; Statements from doctors and camp commandants at hospitals and D.I.C.s, April 1947, FO 1030/275, TNA; Statements of warders, medical orderlies, etc., April 1947, FO 1030/276, Part V, Appendix A, TNA; Statements of prison control officers and interrogators at D.I.C., April 1947, FO 1030/277, TNA; Statement of Colonel Stephens, Statement of Capt. Smith, Notes of Lt. Col. Short, and Statement of Major Mallalieu, April 1947, FO 1030/278, TNA; Cobain (2012), 62–70.

62 Walton (2013), 34, 65.

63 For example, 'The secrets of the London Cage', *The Guardian*, 11 November 2005; and Cobain (2012).

64 Attachment 'D', Notes on CSDIC Mediterranean, part 1, CSDIC-Med, 'CSDIC (Mediterranean)', no date, and Appendix I, 'Use of "I" Source in Mediterranean and Middle East Theatres of War between Oct 1940 and May 1945', no date, WO 208/3248, TNA; 'The interrogation of prisoners of war', c. May 1943, WO 208/3458, TNA.

65 Walton (2013), 187.

66 For Cypriot evidence, see anonymous interview with author, Nicosia, Cyprus, August 2013; anonymous interview, Limassol, Cyprus, 2013; and Spanou, Giannis Chr. (1997), *EOKA: That's How Greeks Fight*. Domniki Georgopoulou (trans.). Nicosia: Andreas I. Spanos

Publications. For evidence of the Mau Mau Investigation Centre, see Caroline Elkins (2005). *Imperial Reckoning: The Untold Story of Britain's Gulag in Kenya*. New York: Henry Holt, 87, 100; and various historians' witness statements and claimants' skeleton arguments in *Ndiku Mutua and 4 others and the Foreign and Commonwealth Office*. Case no. HQ09X02666. London: Royal Courts of Justice.

Key texts

Aldrich, Robert J. (2002). *The Hidden Hand: Britain, America, and Cold War Secret Intelligence*. New York: The Overlook Press.

Cobain, Ian. (2012). *Cruel Britannia: A Secret History of Torture*. London: Portobello Books.

Drayton, Richard. (2011). 'Where does the world historian write from? objectivity, moral conscience and the past and present of imperialism'. *Journal of Contemporary History*, 46, 671–685.

Elkins, Caroline. (2011). 'Alchemy of evidence: Mau Mau, the British Empire, and the High Court of Justice'. *The Journal of Imperial and Commonwealth History*, 39(5), 731–748.

Walton, Calder. (2013). *Empire of Secrets: British Intelligence, the Cold War and the Twilight of Empire*. London: Harper Press.

CHAPTER 14
TINKER, TAILOR, SOLDIER, SUBVERSIVE: INDIA, PAKISTAN AND THE POLITICS OF COLD WAR INTELLIGENCE
Paul M. McGarr

It is in a bleak and suffocating Indian prison cell, in the mid-1950s, that George Smiley, the eponymous British Cold War secret intelligence officer immortalized by the novelist, John le Carré, first encounters his Soviet nemesis, Karla. 'The Indian authorities arrested him [Karla] at our request and carted him off to Delhi jail', Smiley subsequently confides to a colleague. 'As far as I remember we had promised the Indians a piece of the product. I *think* that was the deal.'[1] In fact, the close and collaborative Cold War relationship that Western intelligence agencies established with their South Asian counterparts was more complex and intriguing than le Carré's readers can possibly have imagined. Subject to oppressive surveillance by Britain's colonial security apparatus during the first half of the twentieth century, leading nationalist figures in the Indian subcontinent were left with an abiding distrust of foreign intelligence services. Nevertheless, as the process of post-war European decolonization coalesced with the onset of the Cold War, Indian and Pakistani policymakers sanctioned the establishment of clandestine intelligence partnerships with their former British colonial rulers and London's foremost ally, the United States.

South Asia's historic association with modern intelligence practice is particularly strong. Scholars of the subcontinent have documented the extensive networks of indigenous spies, political informants and propagandists that were co-opted by the East India Company during the eighteenth century to safeguard British interests in South Asia from internal revolt and external threats. In 1901, Rudyard Kipling immortalized the secret intelligence war, or 'Great Game', fought between agents of the British and Russian governments in northern India during the second half of the nineteenth century, in his novel, *Kim*.[2] Indeed, by the time the British retreated from the subcontinent in August 1947, the historic manipulation of India's deep and flexible system of social communication by the colonial security state had contributed to the emergence of a political paradigm rife with paranoia and conspiracy.[3]

Little systematic attention has been given to the broader socio-political impact of British and American intelligence activity in India and Pakistan during the Cold War. In the United Kingdom, the publication of authorized histories of Britain's Secret Intelligence Service (SIS or MI6) and Security Service (MI5) has shed some light on the establishment and operation of intelligence liaison relationships between Britain and its former South Asian empire.[4] Yet, path-breaking though they are, the state-sponsored works of Keith Jeffery and Christopher Andrew are narrowly conceived, and seldom stray far beyond the insular and parochial field of intelligence operations and into the realm of transnational politics. Moreover, existing British intelligence literature neglects arguably the most significant clandestine operation undertaken by Britain in postcolonial South Asia: that of the Foreign Office's Information Research Department (IRD). Equally, the absence of a comprehensive account of the American Central Intelligence Agency's (CIA) Cold War operations in India and Pakistan and, more precisely, that organization's impact on Washington's wider relations with South Asia, represents a lacuna in the voluminous body of scholarship on the United States' intelligence community.[5]

Paradoxically, between the early 1950s and the mid-1970s, as covert interventions by British and American intelligence services in the internal affairs of countries such as Iran, Guatemala, British Guiana, Indonesia, the Congo and Chile were derided across the developing world as unacceptable manifestations of neocolonialism, India and Pakistan quietly consolidated their intelligence links with the West. Drawing upon recently declassified official records and private papers, this chapter focuses on the pressures faced by Indian and Pakistani leaders to underpin state security while, at the same time, upholding popular conceptions of national sovereignty. Specifically, emphasis is placed upon the importance of strategies adopted by governments in India and Pakistan to co-opt the assistance of British and American intelligence agencies in containing emerging Cold War threats, whether in the guise of indigenous communist movements or external pressures from the People's Republic of China and the Soviet Union. In Pakistan's case, the institutionalization of intelligence collaboration with Britain and the United States is also shown to have had an additional, regional dimension, serving, in part, as an insurance policy against Indian irredentism.

British intelligence liaisons with India and Pakistan in the early Cold War

Prior to India's independence, Britain's imperial security service in the subcontinent played a central role in London's effort to suppress South Asian nationalism. Once South Asia had gained its independence, however, Britain's intelligence agencies switched from their traditional task of subduing nationalist politicians and took on a new role supporting the fledgling governments of independent India and Pakistan. Establishing strong intelligence links with New Delhi and Karachi, London rationalized, would help preserve British interests in the region; keep India and Pakistan ostensibly aligned with the West; act as a barrier to communist penetration of the subcontinent; and, not least, demonstrate to the United States that Britain remained an international partner worth having.[6]

In seeking to forge a new intelligence partnership with India and Pakistan, the United Kingdom's colonial legacy in South Asia presented British policymakers with challenges, as well as opportunities. Indira Gandhi, the daughter of India's first premier, Jawaharlal

Nehru, and a future national leader herself, would later attest to the deep psychological impression that had been left on nationalist politicians by Britain's imperial security agencies.[7] Echoing such sentiment, B.N. Mullik, the head of India's Intelligence Bureau throughout the 1950s, suggested that Nehru's exposure to repressive colonial security practices had left the Indian leader with a 'natural' and 'strong prejudice' against foreign intelligence organizations.[8] In short, India's political class had reason not to cooperate with Britain in the intelligence field after 1947.

In Pakistan's case, an additional factor made intelligence collaboration with Britain problematic. During the transfer of power in South Asia, Anglo-Pakistani relations were embittered by the conviction of Pakistan's politicians that London had favoured India when it came to partitioning the subcontinent and dividing the Raj's physical inheritance. Above all, Pakistan's leaders accused Britain's last Viceroy and the first Governor General of India, Lord Louis Mountbatten, of bad faith by allowing the Hindu ruler of the predominately Muslim princely state of Kashmir to sign an instrument of accession with India, rather than Pakistan.[9] In September 1947, the political impediments to Anglo-Pakistani intelligence cooperation were underscored when the *Pakistan Times* published a facsimile of a letter from a British official in Pakistan to Guy Liddell, MI5's Deputy Director. Although only hinting at the possibility of intelligence coordination between London and Karachi, the *Pakistan Times* trumpeted the letter's existence as evidence of a British plot to subvert Pakistan's government.[10] The following January, Liddell's Pakistani counterpart confirmed privately to MI5 that, for the time being, lingering anti-British sentiment in Pakistan made a formal intelligence liaison between the two countries politically impossible.[11]

However, pressing strategic concerns ultimately superseded the personal misgivings and political complications inhibiting both Indian and Pakistani policymakers from working with Britain in the intelligence arena. As nascent states subject to formidable fissiparous pressures, India and Pakistan had much to gain from tapping into British expertise in the internal security field, a good deal of which had been accumulated in South Asia. Keeping potentially subversive movements in check, whether of a religious or communal persuasion or on the left or the right of the political spectrum, represented an important consideration for Indian and Pakistani leaders. In the nominally secular Republic of India, with its significant Muslim minority, New Delhi was concerned with keeping a lid on simmering Hindu nationalism.[12] Indian government officials were also anxious to contain the subversive threat posed by a large and well-supported Communist Party of India (CPI).[13]

In Pakistan, internal security concerns surrounding the political role of the *ulama*, or arbiters of Muslim laws and customs, were magnified by the nation's physical division into two ethnically and linguistically diverse wings, separated by a thousand miles of Indian territory. Additionally, a deep, genuine fear inside Pakistan that India might seek to reunite the subcontinent by force provided an overriding *raison d'être* for intelligence collaboration with Britain and the United States. Specifically, Pakistan's Intelligence Bureau coveted access to the training, technical expertise and networks of information production and analysis available to Western intelligence agencies.[14] Put another way,

Pakistani collaboration with British and American intelligence offered a means to offset some of the nation's strategic vulnerability in relation to its much larger and more powerful Indian neighbour.

Britain's Security Service had maintained discrete links with its Pakistani counterparts after 1947, despite the political risk that this entailed.[15] In 1951, MI5's patience was rewarded when Pakistan's growing insecurity vis-à-vis India produced a breakthrough in intelligence cooperation. In February that year, Pakistan's Prime Minister, Liaquat Ali Khan, advised the British government that he would welcome an exchange of declared, or openly avowed, Security Liaison Officers (SLOs).[16] The SLO concept was not new. During the Second World War, MI5 had stationed SLOs across the British Empire. The SLO function was to provide security advice to local governments and act as conduit for the exchange of information between London and Britain's imperial outposts. It was not to engage in acts of subterfuge or espionage.[17] Shortly after formalizing its relations with MI5, Pakistan cemented its place in the British intelligence club, when Sayid Kazim Raza, the head of Pakistan's Intelligence Bureau, travelled to London to participate in a Commonwealth Security Conference.[18]

In late 1947, MI5 had persuaded India's Home Minister, Vallabhbhai Patel, to approve an exchange of SLOs with Britain.[19] Within a year, the success of the SLO experiment in India prompted Guy Liddell to crow, 'There is no doubt that Nehru [and] Patel ... are anxious to maintain the British connection. Their difficulty is to put their former policy of "driving the British out of India" into reverse without losing face'.[20] Although Liddell's characterization of Indo-British relations was certainly overblown, MI5 did enjoy notably close relations with India's intelligence service.[21] Mullik later acknowledged that the intimacy of the relationship had led Nehru to suspect that India's Intelligence Bureau (IB) was guilty of simply 'dishing out intelligence which the British continued to supply to it'.[22] The last MI5 officer was withdrawn from India in the late 1960s, not at New Delhi's behest but as a consequence of sweeping cuts forced on the Security Service by a Whitehall bureaucracy searching for overseas savings to ease the financial burden on Britain's faltering economy.[23] On being informed by Martin Furnivall Jones, MI5's then-director general, of the Security Services' decision to pull back from South Asia, S.P. Varma, head of IB, expressed regret that Britain had chosen to terminate 'the longstanding [intelligence] contact at a personal level which has proved invaluable to us'.[24]

Attempts by the British Secret Intelligence Service, MI6, to establish a covert, or undeclared, presence in South Asia proved less fruitful. In the late 1940s, Archibald Nye, Britain's High Commissioner in New Delhi, opposed proposals to set up 'an embryo' SIS station, or base of operations, in India. Nye argued that such a move would yield little useful intelligence and risk aggravating Indo-British relations. The case against SIS in India strengthened after Nehru's government took exception to the behaviour of two SIS personnel discovered to be operating in the country, both of whom were declared persona non grata.[25] In response, Britain's Prime Minister, Clement Attlee, effectively proscribed SIS activity in India.[26] Under the 'Attlee Directive', as it came to be known, the empire and Commonwealth remained under the jurisdiction of the

Security Service until well into the 1960s, and were largely shielded from SIS's 'cloak and dagger' operations.[27]

The British did maintain a covert intelligence presence in the subcontinent, however, in the guise of the Information Research Department. The IRD was established in 1948 by the Foreign Office to counter the spread of Soviet propaganda within Britain and overseas.[28] IRD personnel seconded to British diplomatic missions abroad were tasked with feeding clandestine anti-communist literature to local journalists, politicians and academics. In India, IRD counted Mullik among its best customers.[29] In 1962, IRD posted its first resident officer to the subcontinent. Peter Joy, who operated under cover provided by the British Information Service, forged relationships with India's Ministry of External Affairs, Press Information Bureau and All India Radio. In October 1962, following the outbreak of Sino-Indian hostilities, IRD began conducting two concurrent operations in the subcontinent, one 'official', the other not. The official operation, which was 'virtually requested by the Indian authorities', supplied anti-Chinese material to Indian government departments and state-sponsored agencies. The unofficial operation continued to promote broader anti-communist themes through established networks.[30] By 1967, IRD was working with more than 400 'well-placed and influential individuals throughout India', some of whom received secret payments for their services. Moreover, two publishing houses in the Indian capital and a regional newspaper article redistribution service were paid to disseminate IRD material on a non-attributable basis through a British cover organization, the International Forum.[31]

A second IRD officer, Antony Hornyold, followed Joy out to the subcontinent. Officially First Secretary in the British Chancery in Karachi, in reality Hornyold fed a steady stream of IRD anti-communist literature to Pakistan's External Affairs Ministry, which then passed it on to other government departments in the northern administrative centre of Rawalpindi. Precisely what impact, if any, such material had on Pakistan's government proved difficult to gauge. 'We have little knowledge', the British Foreign Office conceded, 'of what use is made of it [IRD product]'.[32] Nonetheless, British officials expressed satisfaction that a wide range of contacts within Pakistan's government 'were very ready to talk [with IRD officers] about the shape of the world, events in China and so on'.[33] Much like MI5, IRD proved instrumental in institutionalizing a close, durable intelligence relationship between Britain and its former South Asian colonies.

The United States and Cold War intelligence in India and Pakistan

In the late 1940s, America's diplomats were preoccupied by a looming communist threat to Western Europe and the Mediterranean littoral. In Washington, the Truman administration attached little strategic importance to India and Pakistan, and expected London to uphold Western interests in Britain's former South Asian empire. The US intelligence community, in contrast, took a more active interest in the subcontinent. In June 1949, T.G. Sanjevi, the head of India's Intelligence Bureau, was invited to the United States for talks with America's intelligence agencies. George Kennan, then Director of

Policy Planning at the State Department, attached considerable importance to Sanjevi's visit. Kennan had been instrumental in the creation of the Office of Policy Coordination, which oversaw US covert operations prior to the establishment of the CIA's Directorate of Plans in 1952. Noting that Sanjevi was 'very close' to Nehru, Kennan urged the CIA and Federal Bureau of Investigation (FBI) to foster strong relations with India's intelligence chief. Reinforcing Kennan's message, America's ambassador in New Delhi, Loy Henderson, cautioned US intelligence officials that Sanjevi's trip to the United States was likely to have 'wide ramifications in our over-all relations with India'.[34]

Unlike the FBI, whose enigmatic director, J. Edgar Hoover, ignored Kennan's counsel and snubbed Sanjevi during his stay in Washington, the CIA feted India's senior intelligence officer. Warmly welcomed and lavishly entertained by a succession of senior Agency figures, including Director of Central Intelligence, Roscoe Hillenkoetter, Sanjevi left the United States as a friend of the CIA.[35] Significantly, India's intelligence supremo embraced the Agency's offer to explore 'the possibility of establishing an official liaison on Communist matters'.[36] Sanjevi's visit to North America was to cast a long shadow over Indo-US intelligence relations and Washington's broader interaction with New Delhi. By currying Sanjevi's favour, the CIA ensured that, in a reversal of the British position, it was the United States' clandestine espionage service, rather than its security service, the FBI, that became India's American Cold War intelligence partner.[37]

The CIA went on to develop a significant operational capability in South Asia. From the early 1950s, IB 'looked the other way' as CIA aircraft violated India's airspace supporting guerrilla fighters in Chinese-controlled Tibet. Later in the decade, the Agency helped spirit the Dalai Lama out of Lhasa and into northern India, following an abortive Tibetan uprising.[38] Having initially operated from a single 'station', or base of operations, in New Delhi, the CIA extended the scope of its activities, establishing smaller outstations in erstwhile Bombay, Calcutta and Madras. One contemporary American observer in India recorded that local Agency personnel appeared active, 'more than anything else in getting inside the [ruling] Congress Party for purposes of information or influence'.[39] In 1959, the CIA worked with the Congress Party to remove a democratically elected CPI administration in the southern Indian state of Kerala. By secretly channelling funds to Congress Party functionaries and local anti-communist labour leaders, the CIA helped destabilize, and eventually dislodge, Kerala's communist government.[40]

A series of subsequent CIA 'failures', beginning with the loss of a U-2 spy-plane over the Soviet Union in May 1960 and culminating in the Bay of Pigs fiasco the following April, had little impact on Indo-US intelligence cooperation. In fact, an upsurge in American economic and political support for New Delhi in the late 1950s, occasioned by Washington's concern at burgeoning communist influence in Kerala and West Bengal, largely insulated the Agency from Indian censure.[41] Following a brief Sino-Indian border war in 1962, the CIA expanded its role in South Asia. The Agency began to assist Indian intelligence in equipping and training a clandestine warfare unit to monitor Chinese military supply routes into Tibet. In addition, the CIA oversaw the insertion of nuclear-powered surveillance equipment on two of India's Himalayan peaks, with a view to collecting data on Chinese atomic tests.[42]

By the mid-1960s, however, festering tensions between Washington and New Delhi on issues ranging from the provision of US military assistance, and the supply of American food aid, to the escalating conflict in Vietnam, weakened the CIA's position in India.[43] At the same time, damaging revelations surfaced in the Indian press that suggested the CIA had recruited assets, or informers, at the very top levels of the Indian government.[44] Moreover, to the exasperation of the US Ambassador in India, Chester Bowles, the Soviet foreign intelligence agency, the KGB, working in tandem with the Moscow-controlled Indian Communist Party, began to capitalize upon the CIA's travails in India, real and imagined.[45] 'Unfortunately', a dispirited Bowles informed Washington, in March 1967, '... [the] U.S. stance [on India] is being ... heavily fogged by widespread public and Parliamentary uneasiness regarding admitted and alleged CIA activities ... .'[46]

The previous month, CIA officials had been shocked when the American west-coast magazine, *Ramparts*, exposed the Agency's long-standing financial relationships with a number of international educational and cultural bodies. *Ramparts* documented the CIA's provision of covert funding to, among others, the National Students Association, Asia Foundation and Congress for Cultural Freedom (CCF). In India, where a general election campaign was under way, an outpouring of public indignation ensued when it was confirmed that the Indian Committee for Cultural Freedom, an offshoot of the CCF, had accepted CIA money.[47] The public relations challenge Bowles faced as a result of the *Ramparts* furore was exacerbated weeks later, when *The Washington Post* published a commentary written by his predecessor in India, John Kenneth Galbraith. The former ambassador's essay discussed the CIA's operational remit in the subcontinent, noting in the process that the Agency's 'activities were generally known to, and involved no conflict with, local [Indian government] authorities'.[48]

Groups on the left of India's political spectrum seized upon the *Post* article as proof that the CIA was actively subverting democracy in South Asia. Infuriated at Galbraith's indiscretion, CIA Director Richard Helms curtly informed the Harvard professor that he had 'raised unshirted hell in India'.[49] On 23 March, India's Foreign Minister, M.C. Chagla, announced that a 'thorough' inquiry would be conducted into CIA interference in Indian politics. 'We cannot permit foreigners or foreign governments to dictate to us what sort of a government we should have or what sort of people should be elected', Chagla asserted. 'We will unearth any activity that is objectionable, that is against the [Indian] national interest.'[50] After 1967, the spotlight cast upon the CIA in India was to have a transformative impact upon US diplomacy in the region. For the remainder of the Cold War, and beyond, elements hostile to the United States, inside and outside the subcontinent, employed the CIA as a political wedge to unhinge Washington's relations with the government of India.

Pakistan's interaction with America's intelligence agencies mirrored the tortuous relationship that developed between the Indian government and the CIA. The Communist Party of Pakistan had been ruthlessly suppressed after 1947 and did not constitute a political threat to the country's authoritarian ruling class.[51] Consequently, the interest taken by British and American intelligence in Pakistan stemmed less from a need to 'save' the country from communism and more from the country's strategic location at a crossroads between the Soviet Union, communist China and the oilfields of the Persian Gulf. In particular, the CIA and the National Security Agency, the American body responsible for collecting communications and signals intelligence, regarded Pakistan as an ideal location from which to spy on Soviet Russia and China.

America's intelligence entrée into Pakistan was assisted by the latter's strategic weakness. Pakistan's political leaders were conscious that whatever proportion of national output was directed into defence and security, it could never offset India's preponderant economic and military power.[52] Accordingly, in May 1954, Pakistan sought to underwrite its long-term security by signing a bilateral defence agreement with the United States. The country went on to join both the Southeast Asia Treaty Organisation and the Middle East Treaty Organisation, or Baghdad Pact. Both these organizations were American-sponsored collective security bodies, the ostensible purpose of which was to contain communist influence in Asia and the Middle East. By the middle of the decade, in the words of one future Pakistani prime minister, the nation had become 'America's most allied ally in Asia'.[53]

In tandem, the CIA negotiated a number of secret protocols with the government of Pakistan. Under these, the Agency operated electronic listening posts and mounted aerial reconnaissance flights from facilities in Pakistan, with a view to gathering intelligence on missile development and nuclear tests behind the Iron and Bamboo curtains.[54] Three years later, the shooting down of an American U-2 spy-plane over the Soviet Union led Pakistan to revaluate the risks inherent in its intelligence alliance with the United States. The ill-fated CIA aircraft had begun its covert flight into Soviet-controlled airspace from Peshawar, in northern Pakistan. This, in turn, led an irate Soviet premier, Nikita Khrushchev, to summon Pakistan's ambassador to the Kremlin and ask pointedly, 'Where is this place Peshawar? We have circled it in red on our maps.'[55] After the U-2 incident in May 1960, Pakistan approached its intelligence relationship with the United States with greater circumspection, and started to hedge its Cold War bets. Conspicuously, an oil exploration agreement with the Soviets helped mend broken fences with Moscow, while the normalization of Sino-Pakistani relations was advanced by the demarcation of the border between China and the northern portion of Kashmir under Pakistan's control.

Furthermore, towards the end of the decade, with the US–Pakistan alliance having become embittered following Washington's decision to suspend US military assistance to India and Pakistan after the outbreak of hostilities in the subcontinent in 1965, the CIA's position in the country became increasingly precarious. In 1967, an incident of 'suspicious' behaviour on the part of a Second Secretary attached to the American Embassy in Rawalpindi ended with the US diplomat's expulsion from Pakistan. The US official, a source in Pakistan's Ministry of Foreign Affairs confided to a British colleague, was a CIA officer who had been caught approaching government employees for secret information.[56] Less than a year later, Pakistan's government drew a symbolic line under its intelligence alliance with the United States when it decided to shut down a major CIA facility at Badaber, near Peshawar. Rejecting American entreaties to reconsider the decision, Pakistan's president, Muhammad Ayub Khan, emphasized that, much as in

India, the CIA's public profile in Pakistan had transformed the Agency into a politically noxious symbol of neo-imperialism.[57] From Pakistan's perspective, its intelligence alliance with the United States, much like broader US–Pakistan relations, had come to represent a historical anomaly of the Cold War that had outlived its usefulness.[58]

Indira Gandhi and the politics of intelligence

Back in India, the psychological writing had been on the wall for the CIA, and Indo-US relations more generally, almost from the moment that Indira Gandhi became India's Prime Minister, in January 1966. One CIA report noted that 'left-of-centre Indian officials, including Mrs. Gandhi, have long held a conspiratorial view of U.S. activities in India which has been a smouldering source of resentment against the United States'.[59] Or, as another American intelligence officer put it, 'CIA agents ... were to be found according to Madame Gandhi, beneath every charpoy and behind every neem tree.'[60] To many Western diplomats, Gandhi appeared 'vain', 'emotional', 'authoritarian' and prone to 'irrational' fits of pique when events turned against her.[61] Moreover, from Washington's perspective, an anti-American undercurrent appeared to influence many of Gandhi's actions and utterances.[62]

Equally, as one US Ambassador to India, Daniel Patrick Moynihan, has pointed out, Gandhi had few qualms about cooperating with foreign intelligence agencies, including those of the United States, when it suited her interests to do so. In his 1978 memoir, *A Dangerous Place*, Moynihan confirmed that to his knowledge, the CIA had twice intervened in Indian politics. On both occasions the Agency had funnelled money to the ruling Congress Party in a bid to head off the election of communist governments in Kerala and West Bengal. In one instance, the Ambassador charged, CIA money was passed directly to Gandhi in her capacity as Congress Party president.[63] Moreover, as Nehru's closest political confidante and, after 1964, a cabinet minister in her own right, it is hard to conceive that Gandhi was not aware of, if not complicit in, joint initiatives with the CIA, which the Indian government sanctioned in the wake of the Sino-Indian border war.

From January 1969, with Richard Nixon occupying the White House, the CIA and US government found themselves on a collision course with Gandhi and the Congress Party. On taking office, Nixon's administration quickly concluded that peace and stability in South Asia could best be maintained by furnishing Pakistan with sufficient American economic and military assistance to counterbalance New Delhi's preponderant regional power. In December 1971, to Gandhi's dismay, Nixon 'tilted' decisively towards Pakistan following a fresh outbreak of Indo-Pakistan hostilities. In turn, Gandhi infuriated the Nixon administration by frustrating American efforts to prevent East Pakistan's transformation into the independent nation-state of Bangladesh.[64] Strained Indo-US relations were further aggravated by differences over India's burgeoning ties to the Soviet Union, the ongoing war in Vietnam, a rupee debt that New Delhi had accumulated purchasing US grain and India's fledgling nuclear weapons programme. Within the confines of Nixon's testosterone-fuelled Oval Office, Indians came to be characterized as 'bastards', while Gandhi herself was derided in crude and chauvinist terms as an 'old witch' and a 'bitch'.[65]

Increasingly, whenever India's economy tanked or the Congress Party found itself in political difficulty, Gandhi found political expediency in laying blame on the malign influence of an American hand. During the autumn of 1972, confronted with mass communist-orchestrated protests against rampant inflation, food shortages and rising unemployment, Gandhi and senior Congress officials elected not to admonish the CPI, but instead to implicate the CIA and the Agency's Indian 'accomplices' with fomenting unrest. In September, the Congress president, S.D. Sharma, delivered a string of public speeches in which the CIA was accused of scheming to 'throttle the Indian economy'. On 9 October, on the eve of a national Congress convention in Gujarat, Gandhi added her own voice to the chorus of anti-CIA rhetoric by openly asserting that ' … elements in India, who had always been voicing opposition to the Government's political economic and foreign policies, were receiving encouragement from foreign sources'.[66]

Much of India's English-language press dismissed the allegations levelled at the CIA by Sharma and Gandhi as a 'barefaced political stunt'. The right-wing Indian periodical *Thought* observed sardonically that Gandhi had chosen to deliver her anti-CIA polemic in the very location where Mahatma Gandhi's autobiography, *Experiments with Truth*, had played out. In an editorial entitled 'Hitting out wildly', a Calcutta daily disparaged Gandhi's implication that India's economic difficulties were 'due to CIA "machinations"' as simply 'too infantile to be considered seriously'.[67] Casting a satirical, if equally damning, eye on the CIA rumpus, the *Indian Express* printed a cartoon on its front page which depicted Sharma advising the Indian premier that 'This week's CIA activities include four price-rise demonstrations, seven buses hijacked by students, plus one cyclone in Orissa'.[68]

Gandhi's tendency to conflate political opportunism and the CIA appeared to be similarly in evidence in June 1975, after the Allahabad High Court controversially found the Indian Prime Minister guilty of minor electoral malpractice during the 1971 general election. If upheld by India's Supreme Court, the ruling threatened to invalidate Gandhi's status as an MP and bring down her government. Later that month, with her political opponents smelling blood and protestors having taken to India's streets in almost equal numbers to both support and denounce her, Gandhi declared a State of Emergency, suspended civil liberties and jailed her political opponents. Senior Congress Party figures loyal to Gandhi began attributing the unrest that had preceded the imposition of martial law to a 'foreign hand', and declared defiantly, in reference to recent exposés of subversive CIA activities in South America, that the Indian government 'would not allow Delhi to be turned into Chile'.[69] On 15 August, as India commemorated its independence from British imperial rule, Gandhi gave an interview to a Congress Party news sheet, *Socialist Weekly*, in which she observed pointedly, 'Have these several Western countries not given full moral and material support to the most authoritarian regimes of Africa and Asia? Have we so soon forgotten what happened to Chile?'[70]

Members of India's political opposition who had avoided imprisonment openly mocked the idea that external forces had been plotting to subvert the government. One Indian MP took to wearing a badge that proclaimed, 'I am a CIA agent', and made a tidy profit in the bargain by selling copies to his parliamentary colleagues.[71] Yet, actions undertaken in the name of the US government by the CIA in the early 1970s can be seen to have played at least a part in reinforcing the negative perception of America's foreign intelligence service held by many Indians in general, and by Gandhi in particular. Circumstantial evidence linking the United States with those responsible for the assassination of Bangladesh's premier, Sheikh Mujibur Rahman, in August 1975, and exposés in *The New York Times* alleging that the CIA had run an agent inside Gandhi's cabinet during the 1971 Indo-Pakistan War, unsettled the Indian premier.[72] Above all, however, the CIA's complicity in the bloody right-wing coup that removed the government of Salvador Allende in Chile in September 1973 deeply affected Gandhi. After Allende's demise, Gandhi was genuinely concerned that she might be the next target on a Nixon administration list for regime change.[73]

American attempts to reassure Gandhi and the Congress Party that the US government wished them no harm proved to be ham-fisted and ineffectual. The American Deputy Chief of Mission in New Delhi was despatched to assure personally India's premier that 'the US had not' meddled in Chilean domestic politics.[74] Weeks later, Gandhi watched as the CIA's Director, William Colby, informed a televised session of the Senate Intelligence Committee that, between 1970 and 1973, the Agency had spent more than $8 million in an effort to destabilize Allende's government. Early in 1973, shortly after he arrived in India as US Ambassador, Moynihan had joked to Nixon's National Security Adviser, Henry Kissinger, that 'The paranoia out here is thicker than the dust.'[75] Following Colby's testimony, a disheartened Moynihan bemoaned that by handling the Chile question in such an inept manner, the US government had done a first-rate job of self-sabotage. On 10 September 1974, Moynihan griped to Kissinger that Gandhi was now certain, ' ... that we would be content to see her overthrown, as we have, to her mind, been content to see others like her overthrown'.[76]

To Moynihan's vexation, Colby later compounded Gandhi's fear that the CIA was out to get her by launching a spirited public defence of America's covert action record. On 13 September, having first acknowledged the CIA's work in 'assisting' America's friends to assume office in a number of foreign countries, Colby went on to assert, 'I can envisage situations in which the United States might well need to conduct covert action in the face of some new threat that developed in the world.'[77] In response, a bewildered Moynihan was left 'groping' for an explanation as to why Colby had deemed it expedient publicly to debate the virtues of CIA operations. On 3 December, in a message to Kissinger, Moynihan asked candidly, 'Is it out of the question that some thought might be given in Washington to the effect in India of statements such as the Director has made? Is it that nobody knows? Or is it that nobody cares?' Half the Indian government, Moynihan added, suspected that the CIA was up to no good in India, while the other half was astute enough to recognize that by demonizing the Agency, and its purportedly nefarious activities in the subcontinent, they could outflank the Congress Party's domestic critics.

Colby's outburst of candour, Moynihan underlined, had once again increased the likelihood that the CIA would be dragged into India's internal politics.[78]

Indeed, despite assurances provided to Gandhi by Moynihan and his successor as ambassador in India, Bill Saxbe, that they would resign if evidence emerged of CIA interference in Indian domestic affairs, Indian politicians and sections of the country's media continued to accuse the CIA of acts of subversion throughout the 1970s.[79] Saxbe, in particular, spent much of his time as ambassador in India, between February 1975 and late 1976, making clear to every senior Indian official that he encountered that an improvement in Indo-US relations 'just cannot take place while the Prime Minister and other high Indian leaders continue to poke away at the US'.[80] By early 1976, with Gandhi's government having disregarded numerous warnings from the State Department to desist in its open criticisms of the CIA, the Ford administration decided to punish New Delhi. In Washington, India's Ambassador T.N. Kaul was frozen out by the White House. A range of joint Indo-US scientific and educational programmes were curtailed, and plans to resume developmental assistance to India, which had been halted in 1971 during the Indo-Pakistan War, were postponed. Rationalizing the United States' punitive policy to India's Foreign Minister Y.B. Chavan, Saxbe confirmed that Washington had simply run out of patience with Gandhi and the Congress Party. '[We have] reach[ed] a point', Saxbe informed Chavan, 'at which we don't feel we can continue to cooperate if attacks [on the CIA] continue.'[81]

Conclusion

The Cold War relationship between the intelligence services of Britain and the United States and the governments of India and Pakistan was complex and often conflicted. For much of the early post-independence period, the CIA and MI5 operated in the subcontinent with the knowledge and support of local intelligence services and senior figures inside South Asia's ruling political parties. From 1967 onwards, however, public revelations implicating the CIA in illegal and morally questionable activity propelled the Agency into the centre of a political storm in India that, while varying in intensity, remained a dominant feature of wider American interaction with the region for the remainder of the Cold War. Likewise, following the U-2 incident in May 1960, disquiet inside Pakistan over the extent to which CIA operations in the north of the country threatened to compromise the country's sovereignty, both physically and symbolically, resulted in a diminution in the US-Pakistani intelligence relationship.

During the final two decades of the Cold War, the CIA was invariably characterized as a socio-political malefactor within South Asia. Well into the 1980s, Washington bridled at periodic swipes from Indian and Pakistani leaders who, while continuing to cooperate surreptitiously with the CIA, openly charged the United States with interference in the subcontinent's internal affairs.[82] Revealingly, the British intelligence presence in India and Pakistan attracted far less political opprobrium and media comment. To a degree, this doubtless reflected recognition within India and Pakistan of Britain's waning international influence and increasingly junior global role alongside an American superpower. Nonetheless, the lower public profile maintained by MI5 and IRD in the subcontinent and the absence of a significant clandestine SIS presence there are noteworthy.

Indeed, as the United States' relations with India and Pakistan came under increasing strain, the CIA served as a convenient vehicle through which South Asia's political classes vented populist anti-American sentiment. An appreciation on the part of Indian and Pakistani leaders that the Agency could function as a political lightning rod, deflecting attention away from their mismanagement of domestic problems, propelled the CIA to the forefront of US regional diplomacy. In this sense, although after 1947 India and Pakistan followed very different political trajectories and developed divergent geo-strategic outlooks, governments in both countries viewed Western intelligence services as instruments that could be used to consolidate state power and bolster postcolonial nation-building.

Initially, India and Pakistan sought assistance from the CIA and MI5 to help combat fissiparous pressures from forces inside and outside the subcontinent. Later in the Cold War, after both countries had been given cause to question the value of American security guarantees, and past CIA indiscretions came under scrutiny from the global press, Indian and Pakistani politicians modified their relations with the intelligence services of Britain and the United States. Publicly labelling their Western intelligence partners as insidious threats to the sovereignty of nations throughout the Global South, governments in India and Pakistan sought to explain away domestic travails and offer a compelling rationale for national cohesion in a time of crisis. In fact, the degree to which Indian and Pakistani policymakers were able to manipulate their relationships with MI5 and the CIA challenges the traditional view of nations within the developing world as the unwitting victims of Western intelligence. Local agency, in the Indian subcontinent at least, appears to have been particularly influential in directing the course of the intelligence Cold War.

Since 1991, the conclusion of one war, and the start of another, has transformed the Western intelligence relationship with India and Pakistan. Revealingly, in 2009, the first overseas trip made by Leon Panetta on becoming director of the Central Intelligence Agency was to New Delhi to discuss intelligence cooperation in the 'war on terror' with his Indian counterpart. During the first decade of the twenty-first century, the politics of intelligence in South Asia has been turned on its head. In Pakistan, the CIA has conducted clandestine operations on an unprecedented scale. American intelligence-led missions astride Pakistan's border with Afghanistan; the apprehension of Osama bin Laden in Abbottabad; and the use of US aerial drones to eliminate Pakistani nationals linked to al-Qaida have placed the Agency firmly in a global media spotlight. The CIA's association with controversial intelligence practices has acted as a new, especially toxic form of public diplomacy. In a reversal of the intelligence situation that pertained in India and Pakistan for much of the Cold War, it is now primarily in Islamabad, rather than New Delhi, that CIA action against perceived threats to American interests stirs political controversy and provokes popular animosity.

The resurgence in CIA activity within the South Asian subcontinent has seen familiar debates resurface in Pakistan surrounding the meaning and enforcement of state sovereignty; the extent of official collusion with foreign intelligence agencies; and the purportedly hidden neo-imperialist agenda of US foreign policymakers.[83] Meanwhile, the politics of intelligence in South Asia remains conflicted. The paradox of being seen to uphold popular conceptions of national integrity while, at the same time, preserving national security with direct assistance from foreign powers continues to trouble Pakistani leaders. In August 2008, the hackneyed response to this conundrum employed by one senior Pakistani official was encapsulated in a cable sent from Islamabad to Washington by the then-US Ambassador to Pakistan, Anne Patterson. Reflecting on a private conversation with Pakistan's Prime Minister, Yousaf Raza Gilani, Patterson reported that Gilani had dismissed domestic pressure on his government to halt US military action against militant groups operating on Pakistani soil with the comment, 'I don't care if they [the CIA] do it [drone strikes] as long as they get the right people. We'll protest in the National Assembly and then ignore it.'[84]

Notes

1 le Carré, John (1974), *Tinker, Tailor, Soldier, Spy*. London: Hodder & Stoughton, 232.

2 Kipling, Rudyard (1901), *Kim*. London: Macmillan.

3 See Bayly, C.A. (1996), *Empire and Information: Intelligence Gathering and Social Communication in India, 1780–1870*. Cambridge, MA: Cambridge University Press; Popplewell, R.J. (1995), *Intelligence and Imperial Defence*. London: Routledge; and French, Patrick (1997), *Liberty or Death: India's Journey to Independence and Division*. London: Harper Collins.

4 See Andrew, Christopher (2009), *The Defence of the Realm: The Authorized History of MI5*. London: Allen Lane; Jeffery, Keith (2010), *MI6: The History of the Secret Intelligence Service, 1909–1949*. London: Bloomsbury. Also Walton, Calder (2013), *Empire of Secrets: British Intelligence, the Cold War and the Twilight of Empire*. London: HarperPress.

5 Historical accounts of the Agency largely overlook CIA activity in India and Pakistan. See Marchetti, Victor and Marks, John D. (1974), *The CIA and the Cult of Intelligence*. London: Jonathan Cape; Ranelagh, John (1986), *The Agency: The Rise and Decline of the CIA*. London: Weidenfeld & Nicolson; and Weiner, Tim (2007), *Legacy of Ashes: The History of the CIA*. London: Allen Lane. Memoirs of Agency officials mention South Asia sparingly: Helms, Richard (2003), *A Look Over My Shoulder: A Life in the Central Intelligence Agency*. New York: Random House; and Tenet, George (2007), *At the Center of the Storm: My Years at the CIA*. London: Harper Press. Clarridge, Duane R. (1997), *A Spy for All Seasons: My Life in the CIA*. New York: Scribner provides some insight into the work of a CIA officer in Cold War India. Accounts of ambassadorial tours offer brief glimpses of CIA activity in the subcontinent. See Galbraith, John Kenneth (1981), *A Life in Our Times: Memoirs*. London: Andre Deutsch; Bowles, Chester (1971), *Promises to Keep: My Years in Public Life, 1941–1969*. New York: Harper and Row; Moynihan, Daniel P. (1978), *A Dangerous Place*. Boston: Little Brown.

6 See McGarr, Paul M. (2013), *Cold War in South Asia: Britain, the United States and the Indian Subcontinent, 1945–1965*. Cambridge, MA: Cambridge University Press, 27–28.

7   Gandhi, Indira (1975), *India: The Speeches and Reminiscences of Indira Gandhi, Prime Minister of India*. London: Hodder and Stoughton, 17.

8   Mullik, B.N. (1972), *My Years with Nehru, 1948–1964*. New Delhi: Allied Publishers, 57.

9   See Jalal, Ayesha (1985), *The Sole Spokesman: Jinnah, the Muslim League and the Demand for Pakistan*. Cambridge, MA: Cambridge University Press.

10 Guy Liddell Diaries (GLD), 8 September 1947, 44–45, KV/4/469, UK National Archives, Kew (TNA).

11 GLD, 15 January 1948, 9, KV/4/470, TNA.

12 Gundevia, Y.D. (1984), *Outside the Archives*. New Delhi: Sangam Books, 208–209.

13 'Reds hinder nation's advance, says Nehru', *Hindustan Times*, 13 January 1960.

14 GLD, 22 October 1948, 182–183, KV/4/470, TNA.

15 GLD, 20 October 1948, 180, KV/4/470, TNA.

16 Liesching to Attlee, 15 February 1951, PREM 8/1453, TNA.

17 Murphy, Philip (2002), 'Creating a Commonwealth intelligence culture: The view from Central Africa, 1945–1965', *Intelligence & National Security*, 17(3), 131–162, pp. 107–108, 136–137.

18 Attlee to Ali Khan, 25 April 1951, PREM 8/1453, TNA.

19 Andrew (2009), 137.

20 GLD, 5 May 1948, 90–92, KV/4/470, TNA.

21 'Visit of Captain Liddell to the Middle East', 9 June 1947, CAB 159/1, TNA; Hollis to Burke Trend, 13 November 1965, CO 1035/171, TNA.

22 Mullik (1972), 57.

23 Hollis to Burke Trend, 13 November 1965, CO 1035/171, TNA.

24 Andrew (2009), 481.

25 Kellar minute, 2 July 1951, KV/2/2512/4, TNA.

26 GLD, 15 and 22 October 1948, 176 and 182–183, KV/4/470, TNA.

27 Andrew (2009), 442.

28 See Defty, Andrew (2004), *Britain, America and Anti-Communist Propaganda, 1945–53: The Information Research Department*. Abingdon: Routledge.

29 Martin to Bozman, 7 October 1953, FO 1110/603, TNA.

30 Drinkall, 'I.R.D. Work in Connection with the Sino/Indian Dispute', 14 November 1962, DO/196/99, TNA.

31 Visit of Nigel Clive to India and Pakistan, 5 December 1967, FCO 95/290, TNA.

32 Jackson to Rivett-Carnac, 12 June 1964, PR/1011/3, FO 1110/1741, TNA.

33 Spence to Stephenson, 5 October 1967, FCO 95/205, TNA.

34 Satterthwaite to Webb, 15 June 1949, Folder Memorandum to the Secretary 1949, Box 2, 57D373, RG 59, US National Archives II, College Park (NARA).

35 Sparks to Henderson, 8 July 1949, Folder Official Informal July 1949, Box 2, 57D373, RG 59, NARA.

36 Henderson to Sparks, 17 April 1950, and Klise to Henderson, 18 April 1950, Folder Official informal Jan-May 1950, Box 2, 57D373, RG 59, NARA.

37 Satterthwaite to Webb, 15 June 1949, Folder Memorandum to the Secretary 1949, Box 2, 57D373, RG 59, NARA.

38 See, Conboy, Kenneth and Morrison, James (2002), *The CIA's Secret War in Tibet*. Lawrence: University of Kansas Press; Knaus, John Kenneth (1999), *Orphans of Cold War: America and the Tibetan Struggle for Survival*. New York: Public Affairs.

39 Rosenthal to Salisbury, undated, Box 159, CIA Series 1965–1966, Harrison Salisbury Papers, Butler Library, Columbia University, New York City.

40 Ellsworth Bunker, Oral History, 18 June and 17 July 1979, Butler Library, Columbia University, 67–68.

41 See McGarr (2013); and Dauer, Richard P. (2005), *A North-South Mind in an East-West World: Chester Bowles and the Making of United States Cold War Foreign Policy, 1951–1969*. Westport: Praeger Publishers.

42 See Komer to McGeorge Bundy, 14 October 1965, Box 13, Folder 6, Robert W. Komer Papers, Lyndon John Library, Austin, Texas (LBJL); and Rostow to Johnson, 30 April 1966, Intelligence File, Box 2, Folder India's Unconventional Warfare Force, National Security File (NSF), LBJL.

43 'Not so quiet Americans', *Guardian*, 28 October 1972.

44 Gopal, Sarvepalli (1984), *Jawaharlal Nehru: A Biography, Vol. 3, 1956–1964*. London: Jonathan Cape, 122.

45 Bowles to Rusk, 27 April 1967, Folder Political Affairs & Relations India 1967 Chester Bowles, Box 4, 71D385, RG 59, NARA.

46 Bowles to Johnson, no. 13991, 29 March 1967, India, Folder 4, Box 131 [2 of 2], NSF Country File, LBJL.

47 Bowles (1971), 544.

48 'CIA needs a tug on its purse strings', *Washington Post*, 12 March 1967.

49 Helms to Johnson, 28 March 1967, Folder CIA Vol. 3 [1 of 2], Box 9, NSF, LBJL.

50 'India to conduct inquiry on C.I.A.', *New York Times*, 24 March 1967.

51 Murray to CRO, 25 November 1954, DO 201/5, TNA.

52 Meeting between Nehru and Mikoyan, 26 March 1956, New Delhi, Subject File no. 19, 1956, Subimal Dutt Papers, Nehru Museum and Memorial Library, New Delhi.

53 Ayub Khan, Muhammad (1967), *Friends Not Masters: A Political Autobiography*. Oxford: Oxford University Press, 130.

54 'Statement of US Policy Toward South Asia', 21 August 1959, NSC 5909 Series, 63D351, RG 59, NARA; and Adams to Rountree, 5 May 1959, 790D.5-MSP/5-559, Central Files (CF), RG 59, NARA. Also Cohen, Stephen (1976), 'U.S. weapons and South Asia: A policy analysis', *Pacific Affairs*, (49), 49–69.

55 'The U-2 incident and Soviet pressures on Pakistan', 2 June 1960, 033.90D11/6-260, CF, RG 59, NARA.

56 Stratton to Duff, 13 September 1967, POL/F/65, FCO 37/200, TNA.

57 Hunt to Duff, 29 April 1968, FCO 37/200, TNA; Baxter, Craig (ed.) (2007), *Diaries of Field Marshal Mohammad Ayub Khan, 1966–1972*. Karachi: Oxford University Press, 242.

58 Thornton to Spain, 19 June 1968, Folder Pakistan 1968, Box 5, 72D5, RG 59, NARA.

59 'National Intelligence Survey: India September 1973', CIA-RDP01-00707000200070032-3, CIA Records Search Tool, NARA.

60 Smith, Russell Jack (1992), *The Unknown CIA: My Three Decades with the Agency*. New York: Berkley Books, 13.

61 'Mrs. Indira Gandhi', 15 January 1964, Prime Minister Nehru Jan-May 1964, Box 5, 68D207, RG 59, NARA.

62 Moynihan to Kissinger, No. 3458, 27 March 1973, Electronic Telegrams, 1/1/1973-21/31/1973, Central Foreign Policy Files (CFP), RG 59, NARA.

63 Moynihan (1978), 41.

64 Nixon, Richard M. (1978), *RN: The Memoirs of Richard Nixon*. New York: Simon & Schuster, 526–531.

65 See conversation between Nixon and Kissinger, Washington, 26 May 1971, and Conversation between Nixon and Kissinger, Washington, 5 November 1971, Office of the Historian (2005), *Foreign Relations of the United States, 1969–1976*, Volume E–7, Documents on South Asia, 1969–1972, Nos. 135 and 150, <http://history.state.gov/historicaldocuments/frus1969-76ve07> [accessed 7 March 2013].

66 Roberts to Martin, 19 October 1972, FCO 95/1347, TNA.

67 'Hitting out wildly', *Statesman*, 12 October 1972; *Thought*, XXIV(42), 14 October 1972.

68 USIS Media Reaction Report, New Delhi, 26 September 1972, FCO 95/1388, TNA.

69 Schneider to Secretary of State, No. 07903, 16 June 1975, Electronic Telegrams, 1/1/1975-21/31/1975, CFP, RG 59, NARA.

70 *Socialist Weekly*, 15 August 1975.

71 Schneider to Secretary of State, No. 08067, 19 June 1975, Electronic Telegrams, 1/1/1975-21/31/1975, CFP, RG 59, NARA; and Moynihan (1978), 150.

72 Kissinger to Moynihan, No. 242175, 10 December 1973, Electronic Telegrams, 1/1/1973-21/31/1973, CFP, RG 59, NARA.

73 See Frank, Katherine (2002), *Indira: The Life of Indira Nehru Gandhi*. London: Harper Collins, 373–374; and Malhotra, Inder (1989), *Indira Gandhi: A Personal and Political Biography*. London: Hodder & Stoughton, 291–292.

74 Moynihan to Secretary of State, No. 12063, 10 September 1974, Electronic Telegrams, 1/1/1974-21/31/1974, CFP, RG 59, NARA.

75 Moynihan to Kissinger, 11 March 1973, I-377, India: White House 1973, Daniel P. Moynihan Papers, Manuscript Division, Library of Congress, Washington, D.C. (DMP).

76 Moynihan to Secretary of State, No. 12063, 10 September 1974, Electronic Telegrams, 1/1/1974-21/31/1974, CFP, RG 59, NARA.

77 William Colby, 'The view from Langley', 13 September 1974, I-371, India: Central Intelligence Agency Folder, DMP.

78 Moynihan to Kissinger, No. 16066, 3 December 1974, I-371, India: Central Intelligence Agency Folder, DMP.

79 Saxbe to Secretary of State, No. 09951, 24 July 1975, Electronic Telegrams, 1/1/1975-21/31/1975, CFP, RG 59, NARA.

80 Saxbe to State Department, No. 1767, 5 February 1976, India, Box 12, Presidential Country Files for Middle East and South Asia, Gerald Ford Presidential Library, Ann Arbor, Michigan (GFPL).

81 Saxbe to State Department, No. 787, 15 January 1976, India, Box 12, Presidential Country Files Middle East and South Asia, GPFL.

82 'US Congressional Perspectives of India', Country File India 1985 [3] [OA-ID 19797], George W. Bush Library, College Station, Texas.

83 See, for example, 'CIA drone strikes violate Pakistan's sovereignty, says senior diplomat', *Guardian*, 3 August 2012.

84 Patterson, Anne W., 'Immunity for Musharraf likely after Zardari's election as President', ref. 08ISLAMABAD2802_a, 23 August 2008, <https://www.wikileaks.org/plusd/cables/08ISLAMABAD2802_a.html> [accessed 10 December 2013].

Key texts

Andrew, Christopher. (2009). *The Defence of the Realm: The Authorized History of MI5*. London: Allen Lane.

Galbraith, John Kenneth. (1981). *A Life in Our Times: Memoirs*. London: Andre Deutsch.

McGarr, Paul M. (2013). *Cold War in South Asia: Britain, the United States and the Indian Subcontinent, 1945–1965*. Cambridge, MA: Cambridge University Press.

INDEX

Note: Locators followed by the letter 'n' refer to notes.

All-African People's Conference 207
All-India Muslim League 24, 190
Alliance for Progress 64, 70, 72, 77
Amer, Mustafa 170–171
Anthes, Rudolf 171–177
Arab-Israeli War of 1948 112–113
Arab-Israeli War of 1967 167
Arthur D. Little (ADL) 67, 70–73, 75–76, 81n. 34
Aryanism 145, 147–152, 156–160

Baghdad Pact 108, 196, 292
Bandung conference 4, 8, 73, 138, 167, 193, 242.
    See also non-aligned movement
    and human rights 109
Ben Bella, Ahmed 221
Bevin, Ernest 192
    attitude towards America of 268–269
Black Power 221
Bowles, Chester 28, 35–36, 197, 291
Brezhnev, Leonid 156
Bulganin, Nikolai 30

Camp 020 268, 274–278
'Central Asian Civilization' project 158–160
Central Intelligence Agency (United States) (CIA)
    in the Congo 208, 210–211
    and Malcolm X 227
    in Middle East 109, 172
    in South Asia 286, 290–298
Chinese Communist Party (CCP)
    in Malaya 125–126, 128–138
    and special economic zones 245–249
Chinese Nationalist Party. *See* Guomindang
civil rights 4, 7, 96, 220, 232
    and Communist Party 89
    Malcolm X's position on 221–223, 235n. 20
collectivization
    in India 22, 24, 28–33, 35
    in Vietnam 43–45, 50, 54–55
Comintern. *See* Communist International
Commonwealth 2, 8, 183, 185–198
Communist International (Comintern)
    and anti-colonialism xi, 5
    in Malaya 125–126, 128–134, 136–138
    and nationalism 94, 147

Communist Party
    of China (CCP). *See* Chinese Communist
        Party
    of India (CPI) 24, 27, 287, 291
    of Indonesia (PKI) 129
    of Malaya (MCP). *See* Malayan Communist
        Party
    of the United States (CPUSA) 10, 87, 89, 97
    of Vietnam 45
Congress Party. *See* Indian National Congress
Césaire, Aimé 224, 230

Daily Worker 92–93, 96, 98
de Gaulle, Charles
    hosting Moise Tshombe 231
    policy toward America of 227
de-Stalinization 153
Deng Xiaoping 245–250
Department of Egyptian Antiquities 170
Du Bois, W.E.B.
    anti-imperialism of 88–90
    and communism 92–93
Dulles, John Foster 109, 209

Eisenhower Doctrine 107–108, 112, 118
Eisenhower, Dwight D. 34–35, 196, 208–210.
    See also Eisenhower Doctrine
export-oriented development 64, 69–77

Federal Bureau of Investigation (United States)
    (FBI) 223, 237n. 40, 290
Five-Year Plans
    Chinese 31–33
    Indian 28–33
    Vietnamese 50–51
Foreign and Commonwealth Office (FCO)
    258–262, 280n. 14
Foreign Office's Information Research Department
    (IRD) 286, 289, 297

Gafurov, Bobodzhan Gafurovich 11, 145–147,
    149–160
Gandhi, Indira
    relationship to America and CIA of 286,
        293–296

Index

gender 5–6, 89–90, 94, 96–99, 205
Geneva Agreement 45
Great Depression 65, 127, 134
Guomindang (Chinese Nationalist Party) 125, 128, 243

Hammarskjöld, Dag 209–210, 212–214
Hanslope Disclosure 12, 258–267, 273, 280n. 17
High-Yielding Rice Varieties 44–45
Ho Chi Minh 130, 132
Hu Qiaomu 248–249
human rights 85, 107, 115–117
 and Malcolm X 220–225, 229
 post-war British policy towards 270, 279
 Universal Declaration of 109, 175

import-substitution 66, 69, 73
Indian Intelligence Bureau (IB) 287–289, 290
Indian National Congress
 and CIA 290, 293–296
 and collectivization 31–33
 criticisms of 27, 29
 and decolonization 190, 192
 relationship to Soviets of 23–24
Institute for Oriental Studies (IVAN) 145, 154–159
International Monetary Fund (IMF) 187
International Rice Research Institute 47
Israel 114–115, 118–119, 208, 210
 and cooperative farming 32

James, Cyril Lionel Robert 5, 91
Jinnah, Mohammed Ali 190–192, 197
Johnson, Lyndon 46–47, 223
Jones, Claudia 92, 94–99, 103n. 43

Kashmir 189–190, 192–195, 287, 292
Kenyatta, Jomo 221
Khan, Liaquat Ali 192, 288
Khan, Muhammad Ayub 292
Khrushchev, Nikita 153–157
 conflict with Mao of 155
 and the Congo 208, 210, 212
 outreach to India of 29–30, 35–36
 and Pakistan 292
Kissinger, Henry 47, 53, 295
Kuomindang. See Guomindang

Li Lisan 129, 133
Li Xiannian 249
London Cage 268, 274–278
Lumumba, Patrice 3, 8, 203, 205–214, 221–222, 231

Malaya 3, 10, 123, 125–139
Malayan Chinese Association (MCA) 10, 125–127, 131, 133–138
Malayan Communist Party (MCP) 125–139
Malayan Emergency 3, 125–128, 133–135
Malik, Charles 10, 107–119
Mao Zedong 155–156, 208, 242, 245, 247, 249
Marshall Plan 97, 194, 269
Mau Mau
 Emergency 3, 258, 262
 reparations case 258–259, 264, 267
McCarthy era 65, 96, 99. See also McCarthyism
McCarthyism 10, 88, 90–91
Menon, Vengalil Krishnan Krishna 24
Military Intelligence 5 (MI5) 265–268, 270–275, 277–279. See also Hanslope Disclosure
 archival records of 258, 263
 authorized history of 285
 in South Asia 287–289, 296–297
Military Intelligence 6 (MI6) 265–266, 275
 See also Hanslope Disclosure
 archival records of 258
 authorized history of 285
 in South Asia 288
minzu 130–132, 137–138
Mit Rahina 167, 170–178
Mobutu, Joseph 203, 211, 214
modernization theory 9, 43–44, 46
Molotov, Vyacheslav Mikhailovich 24
Moscoso, Teodoro 68–70, 72, 74
Mountbatten, Lord Louis 189, 191–192, 197, 287
Muñoz-Marín, Luis 63, 66, 70–71
Muslim League. See All-India Muslim League

Nasser, Gamal Abdel 108, 167, 193, 221, 230–231
Nation of Islam (NOI) 221, 223, 229–230
nation-building 1, 9
 and the CIA 297
 in Malaya 128
 and Soviet Oriental Studies 146–147, 149–150, 160
Nehru, Jawaharlal
 and agriculture 28–35
 and communism 23–25
 criticism of Khrushchev of 154
 and decolonization 1, 190–192
 and foreign intelligence 287–288, 290, 293
 and non-alignment 195
 and state-building 197
neocolonialism 212, 286
Ngo Dinh Diem 45–46
Nguyen Van Thieu 47, 50, 53–54
Nixon, Richard M. 47, 53, 293–295

Nkrumah, Kwame 207, 221, 230
non-aligned movement 4, 64, 73–78, 242
Nyerere, Julius 221

O'Dell, Jack 89
Operation Bootstrap 63, 69–70
Organization for Afro-American Unity (OAAU) 221–222, 224–225, 231
Organization of African Unity (OAU) 212, 222

pan-Africanism 205, 211–213, 221, 224
pan-Arabism 108, 110, 114, 118–119, 221
pan-Asianism 132–133, 138
peasantry 31–32, 43–56, 174, 272. *See also* collectivization
    and class 43, 45, 55
    and tenancy 50
periodization 4, 8–10, 99
Point Four Program 27, 64, 70–72, 77, 171
Popular Front 88–92
Prebisch, Raúl 73
Puerto Rico Industrial Development Company (PRIDCO) 66–72, 74, 81n. 41

race 3, 5, 12, 272. *See also* Aryanism
    in America 87–99, 221
    and category of 'Aryan' 145, 152, 156
    in context of Malayan Emergency 131–132, 135–136
racism 87–99, 157, 228
Red Cross 25, 27
Robeson, Paul 89, 91–92
Rostow, Walt 43, 46

Security Liaison Officers (SLOs) 267–268, 271, 288
self-determination 1, 8, 85, 128, 269–270
    in connection to African American freedom movement 87, 89, 102n. 29, 107, 110–119
    Soviet attitude toward 145, 160
    Wilsonian ideology of 65
Sham'un, Kamil 107–109, 117–118
Singapore 127, 138, 239, 245–246, 257–259, 268
Sino-Indian relations 31–35
Sino-Soviet split 156–160
sovereignty 3, 8, 11–12, 183
    and the Commonwealth 185–198
    and the Congo Crisis 203–214

Lebanese 112–119
    and special economic zones 240–251
    Western intelligence as threat to 296–298
Soviet Academy of Sciences 24, 154–157
stagflation 69, 73
Stalin, Josef 21, 28, 94, 148–153. *See also* de-Stalinization
    and purges 89, 151
Subramaniam, Chidambaram 33, 35
Suez Crisis 108, 117, 167–168, 176–178
    as model for American response to the Congo Crisis 208–210

Taiwan 1
    communism in 129
    and export processing zones 70, 74–78, 81n. 34, 240, 242–246, 249–251
Tan Cheng Lock 127, 131, 133
Tet Offensive 45–47, 49, 56
Touré, Ahmed Sékou 207, 221
Truman Doctrine 97
Truman, Harry S. 27. *See also* Point Four; Truman Doctrine
    and Point Four 171
    and Puerto Rico 63, 70
    South Asia policy of 197, 289
Tshombe, Moise 203–213, 222, 226, 231

UNCTAD (United Nations Commission on Trade and Development) 73
UNIDO (United Nations Industrial Development Organisation) 64, 73–79
United Arab Republic (UAR) 109, 117–118, 167–168, 212
United Nations (UN) 3, 7–8, 183, 195. *See also* UNCTAD; UNIDO
    Charles Malik and 107–109, 112, 115–119
    and the Congo Crisis 203, 206, 208–214
    and development 64, 73–75
    and human rights violations 221–224, 235n. 13
USAID 48–49, 51–52, 74, 171

Vietnamization 47

World Agriculture Fair 34
World Bank 64, 76–77, 79

Zhao Ziyang 249
Zionism 112–113, 116, 118–119

9